The
Classic 1000
Calorie-counted
Recipes

The Classic 1000 Calorie-counted Recipes

by
Carolyn Humphries

foulsham
LONDON • NEW YORK • TORONTO • SYDNEY

foulsham

The Publishing House, Bennetts Close,
Cippenham, Slough, Berkshire SL1 5AP

ISBN 978-0-572-03057-5

Cover photographs © Anthony Blake Picture Library (main picture)
and Powerstock (inset)

Photographs by Phil Wilkins

Printed in Great Britain by St Edmundsbury Press Ltd, Bury St Edmunds, Suffolk

Contents

Introduction

Many of us feel we need to lose weight but following a strict diet sheet can be daunting to say the least. With the best will in the world, after a few days the diet seems to go out the window, leaving you hungry and disappointed. Boring meals, not enough of them or being deprived of your favourite foods are the most common reasons for failure.

Now you can eat gourmet meals, enjoy every mouthful *and* lose weight. Each day, choose a breakfast, lunch and dinner from the recipes provided, plus you can enjoy a mid-morning and afternoon snack from the mouth-watering selection given. You can even have the odd tipple. You'll find you're eating better than you've ever done in your life and feel fit, healthy and slim into the bargain!

My *Classic 1000 Calorie-counted Recipes* will help only if you use them for every meal. It's no good kidding yourself that you've had a 'slimming' lunch from the book so it's OK to go out and binge on a cream tea in the afternoon.

Losing weight means reducing your calorie intake on a daily basis. But I assure you that there are so many quick and easy recipes that you won't have to slave over a hot stove all day. I've included loads of ideas using convenience foods and lots suitable for packed lunches too. In many cases you can just throw a few ingredients together with fabulous results. It's a book crammed with delicious combinations of flavour, texture and colour that will blow your mind – but not your waistline!

A Healthy Balance

Crank dieting is stupid. Your body needs the proper balance of nutrients to keep you fit and healthy. By cutting out a particular food group, you may lose weight, but you'll also become unfit and probably ill. So every day you must have:

- Proteins for body growth and repair. The best sources are fish, lean meat, poultry, dairy products and eggs. Eat 2–3 small portions a day.
- Carbohydrates for energy. Contrary to popular belief they are not fattening; it's the fat or sugar you mix with them that piles on the calories. Best sources are bread (all types), pasta, rice, cereals (including breakfast cereals but choose wholegrain varieties not sugar-coated ones) and potatoes. Eat plenty.
- Vitamins and minerals for general well-being. Best sources are fruit and vegetables, preferably fresh but frozen or canned in water or natural juice with no added sugar or salt are fine. Eat at least 5 portions a day.
- Fat (the dieter's enemy). The fat your body needs occurs naturally in other foods so keep added fat to a minimum and eat very sparingly (see Good Diet Tips right).
- Fibre for healthy body functioning. Eat plenty of fruit and vegetables, wholegrain cereals, skins on potatoes.

Good Diet Tips

- Choose low-fat diet yoghurts, cheeses, cream etc.
- Drink skimmed milk.
- Eat as many vegetables or salad stuffs as you like – but not laced with gallons of oil or melted butter!
- Remove all fat or skin from meat and poultry before eating.
- Grill (broil) rather than fry (sauté).
- Have only a scraping of low-fat spread on bread and don't add extra to vegetables before serving.
- Use only the minimum of fat for cooking.
- When browning meat for a made-up dish, dry-fry (sauté) rather than adding fat.
- Don't add sugar to fruits, cereals or drinks.
- Choose low-calorie brands of soft drinks, dressings etc.
- Drink plenty of water.
- Choose canned fruits in natural juice only, not syrup, and drink unsweetened pure juices (beware the cartons of fruit juice drinks that contain sugar and other additives).
- Don't fill up on shop-bought biscuits, cakes or sweets. Choose healthier alternatives like fruit, salads or raw vegetables. However, you'll find wonderful snack recipes in this book, some of which seem positively sinful!
- Check labels for reduced-fat cheeses and cream. But beware of cream substitutes which often have more calories than the real thing!
- Don't weigh yourself more often than once a week.

Sneaky Eating Tips

You shouldn't be hungry at all if you cook from this book. But if you are normally used to very large portions, try any of the following:

- Use a smaller plate for meals.
- Use thin-sliced bread, then you can have two slices if you want which makes you feel you've had more.
- A glass of naturally sparkling mineral water with your meal will help fill you up (and between meals zip it up with a slice of lemon or lime).
- Use a strong-flavoured cheese in cooking, then you won't need so much to give it a good flavour.
- Cut foods into smaller pieces or thinner slices. Have the same number as normal – you'll think you've had the same but you'll actually have had less.
- Chew slowly and eat small forkfuls. Your meal will last longer.
- Never go shopping on an empty stomach – it's too tempting.
- Try to time meals for before you're ravenously hungry.
- If you feel really peckish, eat some raw carrots – or any salad vegetables, a bunch of grapes or slices of apple – to keep you going and take the edge off your appetite.
- A drink of meat or yeast extract – a teaspoon in a mug of boiling water – is another good way to take the edge off your appetite or fill up between meals.
- Keep a packet of sugar-free chewing gum handy and chew between meals. Alternatively, clean your teeth instead of grabbing a biscuit – it really works!
- Always take the trouble to make your meal look appetising. A sprinkling of parsley or vegetables attractively arranged can help you enjoy what you're eating rather than just eating for the sake of it.

Using this Book

As I said before, this book can help only if you use it for all your meals. Dipping in for the odd low-calorie recipe won't make any difference to your weight: you have to eat sensibly long-term for it to have a lasting effect. But this doesn't mean you have to eat anything different from the rest of your family. The food is good and nourishing for everyone and there are recipes for every occasion too so you can still entertain with confidence, knowing that you're not going to have gained several pounds by the following morning! Simply choose a breakfast, lunch and dinner with a snack mid-morning and afternoon every day and you can't go wrong.

To lose weight your energy (calorie) intake from food and drink needs to be less than your energy output (the number of calories you burn up). An average man burns up about 2500 calories a day, a woman about 1900. If you've only got a few pounds to lose, you may want to have a fairly low calorie intake – say 1500 calories for a man, 1000 for a woman. But if you are planning a long-term massive weight reduction, you need to take it more slowly – 1900 for a man and 1500 calories for a woman would be a good starting point.

If you choose a day's meals and find it contains fewer calories than you intended – great! Alternatively you can always have an extra slice or two of bread (at about 75 calories a slice), extra plain-cooked potatoes, pasta or rice, or choose that day to treat yourself to a tipple or two! If you have a higher than planned calorie intake one day, then make sure you have a lower one the next. Let yourself be flexible as all these recipes really will help you to lose weight and you don't want to be a slave to a diet.

No-effort Calorie Counting

You'll see all the recipes are calorie-counted into groups. Each recipe has been rounded up to the nearest 50 calories so you won't have to spend hours with a calculator and you'll know you are always 'in credit' because many recipes in the section may be quite a few calories fewer than the maximum! So set your target of how many calories you want to eat in a day and choose recipes that will make up to that. But don't give yourself a headache – you can mix and match from any of the recipes and you'll still lose weight, but it will be a much more gradual process. Once you've reached your target, start eating the number of calories you will automatically use up in a day (approximately 1900 for a woman, 2500 for a man) and you should maintain the weight loss.

Drinks

Make sure you drink plenty of water – from the tap, filtered or mineral according to your preference. If you're really not keen on it, flavour it with a low-calorie squash.

Pure fruit juices are good for you but should be classed as part of a meal. I've included them in the breakfast counts because that's when I like a glass (and the vitamin C in them helps you absorb iron in foods like fortified breakfast cereals). If you drink a small glass at other times of the day, add on 50 calories a glass).

Tea and coffee are fine in moderation but drink them preferably after meals or in between as the tannin in these beverages impairs the absorption of some essential nutrients. Use skimmed milk or drink them black (tea with lemon is good). But NO sugar. If you have a sweet tooth, you'll have to use artificial sweeteners, but ideally you should wean yourself off the sweetness as it will help your diet as a whole.

Try to consume at least 300 ml/½ pt/1¼ cups of skimmed milk during the day but that includes what you put on cereal or use in cooking.

Alcohol is not a dieter's friend since it contains lots of empty calories. However, far be it from me to say you must abstain completely. Have it as a treat with a meal or as an occasional evening tipple to sip and enjoy. But never drink alcohol to quench your thirst. Allow yourself a drink only if you are under the limit of calories for the day, don't drink in place of good nutritious food and, if you must drink spirits, make sure you have low-calorie mixers

As a guide, count 100 calories per single measure of alcohol, that is a half-pint of beer or lager, a wineglass of wine, a small sherry or a single measure of spirits. This is actually an overestimation but it means you'll be 'in credit' rather than the other way round! But beware because if you've decided on 1000 calories a day, and you treat yourself to two glasses of wine or a double G&T, it's a fifth of your daily calories!

A Typical 1000-calorie Day

Breakfast:
A small glass of pure orange juice
Mixed Mushrooms on Toast
Tea or coffee

Mid-morning snack:
An apple

Lunch:
Roast Lemon Chicken with Vegetable Platter
Fresh Fruit Salad

Mid-afternoon snack:
Jumbo Digestive Biscuit

Dinner:
Tropical Club Sandwich
Speedy Chocolate Mousse

Notes on the Recipes

- **All calorie counts are per serving.**
- All spoon measures are level: 1 tsp = 5 ml; 1 tbsp = 15 ml.
- Ingredients are given in metric, imperial and American measures. Use only one set per recipe, never a combination.
- Eggs are medium unless otherwise stated.
- Choose a low-fat spread suitable for baking (it doesn't have to be suitable for frying [sautéing] for these recipes) and for spreading – read the label.
- All herbs are fresh unless dried are specifically called for. If you wish you can substitute dried for fresh, using only half the quantity or less as they are very pungent, but chopped frozen varieties are much better than dried. There is no substitute for fresh parsley and coriander.
- Always wash, dry and peel, if necessary, fresh produce before use.
- All preparation and cooking times are approximate and are intended as a guide only.
- Always preheat the oven and cook on the shelf just above the centre unless otherwise stated.
- For baking, check that you use artificial sweetener granules that are suitable for cooking; some are only for use at the table. I use a brand that is ten times lighter than sugar, so where I would normally have used 15 ml/1 tbsp sugar I have used 1.5 ml/¼ tsp sweetener.
- If cooking for serious vegetarians, make sure the cheese you use is suitable for vegetarians as well as being low in fat – read the labels. Also, use a vegetarian form of Worcestershire sauce – the original contains anchovies!
- Where I have called for very low-fat dairy produce like yoghurt or quark, you may be able to find virtually fat-free varieties – choose these every time!
- Use low-fat cheeses whenever possible. Some hard cheeses may be called 'reduced-fat' – these are fine.
- Non-stick cookware needs very little greasing. Use it whenever possible.

Big Breakfasts

Breakfast is perhaps the most important meal of the day. You must give your body fuel to keep it going through the morning whether you're on a diet or not. If you start off the day hungry, you'll be far more tempted to have biscuits with your morning coffee or pig out at lunchtime. Try to get up a little earlier so you can enjoy the meal rather than grabbing a piece of toast as you rush out of the door. The serving suggestions are included in the calorie count.

CALORIES OR LESS

Mixed Mushrooms on Toast

SERVES 2

100 g/4 oz mixed oyster, button or chestnut mushrooms, sliced
5 ml/1 tsp low-fat spread
15 ml/1 tbsp water
15 ml/1 tbsp chopped parsley
A pinch of paprika
Salt and freshly ground black pepper
2 slices toast (any type), with a scraping of low-fat spread

Put the mushrooms in a pan with the low-fat spread and water. Cook, stirring, for 2 minutes. Add the parsley, paprika and a little salt and pepper, then cover and cook for 3 minutes or until the mushrooms are tender. Remove the lid and cook rapidly until all the liquid has evaporated, stirring all the time. Pile on to the toast and serve immediately.

Serving suggestions: a glass of pure fruit juice; coffee or tea.

Devilled Mushrooms on Toast

SERVES 2

10 ml/2 tsp low-fat spread
100 g/4 oz button mushrooms
15 ml/1 tbsp water
30 ml/2 tbsp snipped chives
2 tomatoes, skinned, if liked, and chopped
10 ml/2 tsp tomato ketchup (catsup)
10 ml/2 tsp Worcestershire sauce
A few drops of Tabasco sauce
2 slices bread

Melt the low-fat spread in a saucepan. Add the mushrooms and water and cook, stirring, for 2 minutes. Add half the chives and the remaining ingredients and simmer for about 5 minutes until the mushrooms are cooked and bathed in sauce, stirring occasionally. Boil rapidly for a minute or so, if necessary, to reduce the liquid. Meanwhile, toast the bread and place on warm plates. Spoon the mushrooms on top and sprinkle with the remaining chives.

Serving suggestions: a fresh peach; coffee or tea.

Italian Tomatoes

SERVES 2

2 slices bread
4 tomatoes, halved
A few drops of olive oil
Freshly ground black pepper
25 g/1 oz/¼ cup Italian Mozzarella
   cheese, grated
8 basil leaves, shredded

Toast the bread on one side. Turn over and top with the tomatoes, cut sides down. Add literally one drop of oil over each tomato half and add a good grinding of black pepper. Grill (broil) for about 3 minutes until the tomatoes are softening. Add the Mozzarella and shredded basil and flash briefly under the grill (broiler) until the cheese begins to melt. Serve straight away.
Serving suggestions: a glass of pure fruit juice; coffee or tea.

American Hash Browns

SERVES 2

2 large potatoes, diced
1 onion, finely chopped
15 g/½ oz/2 tbsp low-fat spread
2.5 ml/½ tsp paprika
Salt and freshly ground black pepper
Brown table sauce

Cook the potatoes in boiling, salted water for about 5 minutes or until just tender. Drain. Meanwhile, fry (sauté) the onion in the low-fat spread in a frying pan (skillet) for 2 minutes, stirring. Add the potatoes, paprika and a little salt and pepper. Fry, pressing and tossing with a fish slice, over a high heat until golden brown and the potato is becoming mushy. Serve on two warmed plates with a little brown sauce.
Serving suggestions: ½ grapefruit; coffee or tea.

Baked Egg

SERVES 1

1.5 ml/¼ tsp low-fat spread
1 egg
10 ml/2 tsp low-fat single (light)
   cream
Salt and freshly ground black pepper

Use the low-fat spread to very lightly grease a ramekin dish (custard cup). Break in the egg, then spoon the cream over. Sprinkle with salt and pepper and bake in a preheated oven at 200°C/400°F/gas mark 6 for 8–10 minutes or until cooked to your liking. Serve hot.
Serving suggestions: ½ grapefruit; 1 wholegrain crispbread with a scraping of low-fat spread; coffee or tea.

Baked Egg with Mushrooms

SERVES 1

5 button mushrooms, sliced
15 ml/1 tbsp water
1.5 ml/¼ tsp low-fat spread
1 egg
10 ml/2 tsp low-fat single (light)
   cream
Salt and freshly ground black
   pepper

Cook the mushrooms in the water for 2 minutes, stirring. Lightly grease a ramekin dish (custard cup) with the low-fat spread. Add the mushrooms. Break in the egg, then spoon the cream over. Season lightly. Bake in a preheated oven at 200°C/400°F/gas mark 6 for about 8–10 minutes or until cooked to your liking.
Serving suggestions: ½ grapefruit; 1 puffed wheat crispbread with a scraping of low-fat spread; coffee or tea.

Baked Egg with Tomatoes

SERVES 1

**1.5 ml/¼ tsp low-fat spread
1 or 2 tomatoes, chopped
1.5 ml/¼ tsp Worcestershire sauce
1 egg
10 ml/2 tsp low-fat single (light)
cream
Salt and freshly ground black
pepper**

Grease a ramekin dish (custard cup) with the low-fat spread. Add the chopped tomato and sprinkle with the Worcestershire sauce. Carefully break in the egg and spoon over the cream. Season with a little salt and pepper. Bake in a preheated oven at 200°C/400°F/gas mark 6 for 8–10 minutes or until cooked to your liking. Serve straight away.
Serving suggestions: 1 small slice of melon; 1 puffed wheat crispbread with a scraping of low-fat spread; coffee or tea.

Berlin Bite

SERVES 1

**1 slice pumpernickel
5 ml/1 tsp very low-fat soft cheese
1 thin slice Westphalian ham (lean
only)
1 tomato, sliced
A parsley sprig**

Spread the pumpernickel with the cheese and top with the ham, then the tomato slices. Garnish with the parsley sprig before serving.
Serving suggestions: ½ grapefruit; coffee or tea.

Honey Nut Slices

SERVES 1

**10 ml/2 tsp low-fat spread
5 ml/1 tsp chopped mixed nuts
5 ml/1 tsp clear honey
A pinch of grated nutmeg
(optional)
3 slices French stick, just over
5 mm/¼ in thick**

Mash the low-fat spread with the nuts, honey and nutmeg, if using. Toast one side of the bread under the grill (broiler). Spread the honey nut mixture over the untoasted sides of the bread and return to the grill until golden and bubbling. Serve warm.
Serving suggestions: a small glass of tomato juice; coffee or tea.

Cheesy French Toast

SERVES 1

**5 ml/1 tsp grated low-fat strong
Cheddar cheese
10 ml/2 tsp low-fat spread
5 ml/1 tsp chopped parsley
A pinch of cayenne
3 slices French stick, just over
5 mm/¼ in thick**

Mash the cheese with the low-fat spread, parsley and cayenne. Toast one side of the bread under the grill (broiler). Spread the cheese mixture over the untoasted side and return to the grill until golden and bubbling.
Serving suggestions: a glass of pure orange juice; coffee or tea.

Fruity Breakfast Muffins

MAKES 12

**300 ml/½ pt/1¼ cups hot black tea
100 g/4 oz/⅔ cup mixed dried fruit
(fruit cake mix)
50 g/2 oz/¼ cup low-fat spread
7.5 ml/1½ tsp artificial sweetener
granules
175 g/6 oz/1½ cups self-raising
(self-rising) wholemeal flour
5 ml/1 tsp baking powder
1 egg, beaten**

Mix the tea with the fruit and low-fat spread until melted. Stir in the sweetener. Leave to soak until the mixture is just lukewarm. Stir in the remaining ingredients. Spoon into 12 sections of a greased bun tin (muffin pan) and bake in a preheated oven at 180°C/350°F/gas mark 4 for about 40 minutes until risen and the centres spring back when pressed. Remove from the tin and leave to cool on a wire rack. Serve 1 muffin per portion.
Serving suggestions: a glass of pure fruit juice; coffee or tea.

Fresh Strawberry Yoghurt

SERVES 1

**50 g/2 oz hulled strawberries
A pinch of artificial sweetener
granules
75 ml/5 tbsp very low-fat plain
yoghurt
Grated rind of ½ orange**

Mash the strawberries with the sweetener to taste. Fold in the yoghurt and orange rind and chill, if time, to allow the flavours to develop.
Serving suggestions: 2 Crisp Oatcakes (see right) with a scraping of low-fat spread and reduced-sugar marmalade; coffee or tea.

Crisp Oatcakes

MAKES 8

**75 g/3 oz/¾ cup medium oatmeal,
plus extra for dusting
A pinch of salt
1.5 ml/¼ tsp bicarbonate of soda
(baking soda)
15 g/½ oz/1 tbsp low-fat spread,
melted
60 ml/4 tbsp hot water
Extra low-fat spread, for greasing
Low-fat spread and reduced-sugar
jam (conserve) or marmalade,
to serve**

Put all the ingredients except the extra low-fat spread in a bowl and mix well to form a dough. Turn out on to a surface lightly dusted with oatmeal and roll out thinly to about a 25 cm/10 in round. Cut into eight wedges. Heat a heavy-based frying pan (skillet) and brush very lightly with a little extra low-fat spread. Add the oatcakes and cook a few at a time until firm. Turn them over carefully so they don't break and cook the other side for 2–3 minutes. Cool on a wire rack, then store in an airtight tin. Serve 2 per portion with a scraping of low-fat spread and reduced-sugar jam or marmalade.
Serving suggestions: see Fresh Strawberry Yoghurt (left).

Florida Cocktail

SERVES 2

1 orange
1 grapefruit
15 ml/1 tbsp apple juice
Artificial sweetener granules
 (optional)

Peel all the rind and pith from the orange over a bowl to catch any juice. Cut the fruit between the membranes into segments. Squeeze any juice from the rind and discard. Repeat with the grapefruit. Add the apple juice and sweeten, if liked, with artificial sweetener. Spoon into two glass dishes and serve.
Serving suggestions: 1 slice of toast with a scraping of low-fat spread and reduced-sugar jam (conserve); coffee or tea.

Fresh Fruit Platter with Yoghurt

SERVES 2

1 kiwi fruit, sliced
1 nectarine or peach, halved,
 stoned (pitted) and sliced
1 apple, unpeeled but halved,
 cored and sliced
100 g/4 oz hulled strawberries or
 1 pear, sliced
1 small carton very low-fat diet
 apricot yoghurt
Grated nutmeg

Arrange the fruits around two serving plates and place a small serving dish of yoghurt in the centre. Sprinkle the yoghurt with a little grated nutmeg and serve. To eat, dip each piece of fruit in the yoghurt and enjoy.
Serving suggestion: coffee or tea.

Greek-style Figs

SERVES 2

4 dried figs
1 small piece cinnamon stick
30 ml/2 tbsp very low-fat yoghurt

Quarter the figs and place in a small saucepan with the cinnamon stick. Just cover with boiling water and leave to soak for 2 hours. Bring to the boil, reduce the heat, cover and simmer gently until the figs are tender. Leave to cool, then chill. Discard the cinnamon stick and spoon the fruit and juice into two small dishes. Top each with a spoonful of the yoghurt and serve.
Serving suggestions: 1 slice of pumpernickel with a scraping of low-fat spread, coffee or tea.

Fruit Cocktail

SERVES 2

150 ml/¼ pt/⅔ cup apple juice
1 eating (dessert) apple, unpeeled
 and diced
1 clementine, segmented
1 pear, diced
Grated rind of ½ lemon

Place all the ingredients in a bowl. Leave to stand for 30 minutes, if time, to allow the flavours to develop.
Serving suggestions: 1 small slice of toast with a scraping of low-fat spread and reduced-sugar marmalade or jam (conserve); coffee or tea.

Fruit and Nut Yoghurt

SERVES 1

100 ml/3½ fl oz/6½ tbsp very low-fat plain yoghurt
15 ml/1 tbsp raisins
2 glacé (candied) cherries, chopped
15 ml/1 tbsp chopped hazelnuts

Mix together all the ingredients and chill before serving.
Serving suggestions: 1 small bridge roll with a scraping of low-fat spread; coffee or tea.

Tomato Pick-me-up

SERVES 1

2 ripe tomatoes
45 ml/3 tbsp pure orange juice
A good pinch of chilli powder
A dash of soy sauce
Freshly ground black pepper
Ice

Purée the tomatoes in a blender or food processor with the remaining ingredients except the ice. Taste and add more soy sauce if liked. Pour over ice and serve.
Serving suggestions: Weetabix Toast (see below); coffee or tea.

Weetabix Toast

SERVES 1

1 Weetabix
10 ml/2 tsp low-fat spread
5 ml/1 tsp reduced-sugar orange marmalade

Spread the Weetabix with the low-fat spread, then the marmalade and eat over a plate to catch the crumbs!
Serving suggestions: see Tomato Pick-Me-Up (right).

Tropical Breakfast in a Glass

SERVES 2

1 banana, roughly chopped
1 ripe mango
150 ml/¼ pt/⅔ cup coconut milk
150 ml/¼ pt/⅔ cup skimmed milk
15 ml/1 tbsp wheatgerm

Put the banana in a blender or food processor. Cut all the mango flesh off the stone (pit) and add to the machine. Purée until smooth. Add the remaining ingredients and blend until smooth and frothy. Pour into glasses and serve.

Banana Breakfast in a Glass

SERVES 1

1 ripe banana, roughly chopped
15 ml/1 tbsp wheatgerm
75 ml/5 tbsp very low-fat plain yoghurt
100 ml/3½ fl oz/6½ tbsp skimmed milk
5 ml/1 tsp clear honey

Purée the banana in a blender or food processor. Add the remaining ingredients and run the machine until the mixture is smooth and frothy. Pour into a glass and serve.

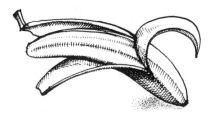

Peach or Nectarine Breakfast in a Glass

SERVES 1

1 large very ripe nectarine or
peach
15 ml/1 tbsp wheatgerm
75 ml/5 tbsp very low-fat diet
peach yoghurt
75 ml/5 tbsp skimmed milk

Put the peach or nectarine in a bowl and just cover with boiling water. Leave for 30 seconds, then rinse with cold water and peel off the skin. Cut in quarters, removing the stone (pit). Purée in a blender or food processor. Add the remaining ingredients and run the machine until smooth and frothy. Pour into a glass and serve.

Blushing Breakfast in a Glass

SERVES 1

2 small cooked beetroot (red
beets), quartered
1 small spring onion (scallion),
roughly chopped
75 ml/5 tbsp buttermilk
75 ml/5 tbsp skimmed milk
Freshly ground black pepper
15 ml/1 tbsp wheatgerm

Purée the beetroot with the spring onion in a blender or food processor. Add the remaining ingredients and run the machine until smooth and frothy. Pour into a glass and serve.

Melon and Ham Boats

SERVES 2

1 cantaloupe melon
2 thin slices lean honey-roast ham
(from a packet)
Freshly ground black pepper
2 slices cucumber

Halve the melon and scoop out and discard the seeds. Place in two shallow serving bowls. Cut the slices of ham into strips, roll up and use to fill the cavities in the melon. Add a good grinding of pepper. Thread each cucumber slice on to a cocktail stick (toothpick), pressing the stick through one side then out through the other to form a 'sail'. Secure in the centre of the 'boats' and serve.
Serving suggestions: 1 slice of toast with a scraping of low-fat spread and reduced-sugar marmalade or jam (conserve); coffee or tea.

Prunes with Yoghurt

SERVES 2

12 dried prunes
200 ml/7 fl oz/scant 1 cup hot
black tea
A piece of lemon rind
60 ml/4 tbsp very low-fat plain
yoghurt

Put the prunes in a saucepan with the tea and lemon rind and leave to soak for 2 hours. Bring to the boil, cover and simmer for 20 minutes or until the fruit is really tender. Leave to cool, then chill. Remove the lemon rind. Serve in glass dishes topped with the yoghurt.
Serving suggestions: 1 puffed wheat crispbread with a scraping of low-fat spread and yeast extract; coffee or tea.

Apricot Wheat

SERVES 1

1 Shredded Wheat biscuit
3 ready-to-eat dried apricots,
  chopped
Artificial sweetener granules
  (optional)
75 ml/5 tbsp skimmed milk, warm
  or cold

Put the Shredded Wheat in a bowl. Sprinkle the apricots over and dust with artificial sweetener, if liked. Pour over the milk and serve immediately.
Serving suggestions: see Melon with Ginger (below).

English Muffins

MAKES 6

100 g/4 oz/1 cup strong white
  (bread) flour
75 g/3 oz/¾ cup plain (all-purpose)
  flour
2.5 ml/½ tsp salt
10 ml/2 tsp easy-blend dried yeast
7.5 ml/½ tbsp low-fat spread, plus
  extra for greasing
75 ml/5 tbsp skimmed milk
About 100 ml/3½ fl oz/6½ tbsp
  hand-hot water
Cornflour (cornstarch) or rice
  flour, for dusting
Low-fat spread and reduced-sugar
  jam (conserve) or marmalade

Mix the flours in a warm bowl with the salt and yeast. Melt the low-fat spread and add the milk. Heat until hand-hot. Add to the flour mixture with enough of the hand-hot water to form a very soft dough. Use a wooden spoon, then the hands, to beat until smooth and elastic (it should be too wet to knead). Cover lightly with greased clingfilm (plastic wrap) and leave in a warm place for about 1 hour until doubled in size. Briefly knead the dough to knock it back to its original size, then divide into six equal pieces. Using hands dusted with cornflour or rice flour, shape the pieces into balls. Place on a baking sheet well-dusted with cornflour or rice flour and flatten each slightly with the palm of the hand. Cover again with clingfilm and leave to rise in a warm place for 45 minutes. Heat a very lightly greased heavy frying pan (skillet). Carefully transfer three of the muffins and cook over a gentle heat for 8–10 minutes on each side until a light golden colour. Repeat with the remaining muffins. Serve one per portion warm with a scraping of low-fat spread and reduced-sugar marmalade or jam.
Serving suggestions: ½ grapefruit; coffee or tea.

Melon with Ginger

SERVES 3

½ honeydew melon
15 ml/1 tbsp ground ginger

Cut the melon into three wedges and scoop out the seeds. Carefully cut through between the flesh and the skin but leave the flesh in place. Cut down through the centre of the flesh lengthways, then across at intervals to make small chunks. Loosen every other chunk on each side, easing them slightly away from the centre. Dust with ginger and serve.
Serving suggestions: Apricot Wheat (see left); coffee or tea.

Everyday Breakfasts under 150 Calories

1 small glass of pure fruit juice and a coffee or tea plus any of the following:

- 1 Weetabix and skimmed milk

- 1 Shredded Wheat biscuit and skimmed milk

- 25 g/1 oz/½ cup All Bran and skimmed milk

- 25 g/1 oz/½ cup Raisin Wheats and skimmed milk

- 1 boiled egg and ½ slice toast with a scraping of low-fat spread

- 2 baby bridge rolls with a scraping of low-fat spread and yeast extract

- 1 crumpet with a scraping of low-fat spread and reduced-sugar jam (conserve) or marmalade

- 1 slice of toast with a scraping of low-fat spread and reduced-sugar jam (conserve) or marmalade

- 1 slice of currant bread with a scraping of low-fat spread

- 1 thick slice of French bread (about 2.5 cm/1 in) with a scraping of low-fat spread and reduced-sugar marmalade or jam (conserve)

- 3 wholegrain crispbreads with a scraping of low-fat spread and yeast extract

- 2 wholegrain crispbreads with a scraping of peanut butter on each

·················· **BREAKFASTS** ··················

CALORIES OR LESS

Cinnamon Toast

SERVES 2

1 egg
30 ml/2 tbsp skimmed milk
3 slices bread, crusts removed
15 g/1 oz/2 tbsp low-fat spread
5 ml/1 tsp artificial sweetener
granules
5 ml/1 tsp ground cinnamon

Beat the egg and milk together in a shallow dish. Dip in the bread until coated on both sides. Heat the low-fat spread in a frying pan (skillet) and fry (sauté) the bread on both sides over a moderate heat until golden brown. Mix together the sweetener and cinnamon and dust over both sides of the bread. Cut into triangles and serve hot.
Serving suggestions: ½ grapefruit; coffee or tea.

Grilled Grapefruit

SERVES 2

1 grapefruit
5 ml/1 tsp artificial sweetener
granules

Halve the grapefruit, then cut round between the flesh and the white pith. Separate each segment each side of the membranes. Remove the central white core. Place in two flameproof dishes and sprinkle with artificial sweetener. Place under a hot grill (broiler) until the tops are bubbling and turning golden. Serve immediately.
Serving suggestions: Poached Egg on Toast (see right); coffee or tea.

Boiled Eggs with Savoury Soldiers

SERVES 1

2 eggs
1 slice bread, toasted
2.5 ml/½ tsp low-fat spread
5 ml/1 tsp yeast extract
Paprika

Put the eggs in a small pan and just cover with cold water. Cover and bring to the boil. When the water boils, time the eggs for exactly 4 minutes. Remove and place in egg cups and tap the tops with a teaspoon immediately to prevent further cooking. Meanwhile, spread the toast with the low-fat spread and then the yeast extract. Sprinkle with paprika, then cut into strips to make 'soldiers'. Cut the tops off the eggs and serve with the soldiers to dip in.
Serving suggestions: a small glass of pure fruit juice; coffee or tea.

Old English Mumbled Eggs

SERVES 2

2 slices bread
2 thin slices lean ham
2 eggs
2.5 ml/½ tsp English made mustard
Salt and freshly ground black pepper
5 ml/1 tsp skimmed milk
10 ml/2 tsp low-fat spread
25 g/1 oz mushrooms, finely chopped
25 g/1 oz/2 tbsp very low-fat soft cheese

Toast the bread under the grill (broiler) on one side only. Place the ham on the untoasted side and grill (broil) until sizzling. Meanwhile, beat the eggs with the mustard, a little salt and pepper and the milk. Melt the low-fat spread in a saucepan. Add the mushrooms and cheese and stir for 30 seconds. Add the egg mixture and cook over a low heat until just set but still creamy. Do not boil. Spoon on to the toast and serve straight away.
Serving suggestions: a small glass of tomato juice; coffee or tea.

Poached Egg on Toast

SERVES 2

2 slices toast
A scraping of low-fat spread
10 ml/2 tsp vinegar
2 eggs

Spread the toast with the low-fat spread and keep warm. Meanwhile, fill a frying pan (skillet) with water and add the vinegar. Bring to the boil and reduce to a gentle simmer. Break one of the eggs into a cup and gently slide into the water. Repeat with the remaining egg. Cook gently for about 3 minutes for a soft-cooked egg, or up to 5 minutes for a hard one. Remove from the pan with a fish slice and slide on to the toast. Serve straight away.
Serving suggestions: see Grilled Grapefruit (left).

Poached Eggs with Herbs

SERVES 2

2 slices toast
15 ml/1 tbsp low-fat spread
5 ml/1 tsp chopped parsley
5 ml/1 tsp chopped thyme
5 ml/1 tsp snipped chives
Freshly ground black pepper
15 ml/1 tbsp vinegar
2 eggs

Spread the toast with 5 ml/1 tsp of the low-fat spread. Place on two warm plates. Melt the remaining low-fat spread with the herbs and a little pepper. Fill a frying pan (skillet) with water and add the vinegar. Bring to the boil, then reduce to a gentle simmer. Break the eggs one at a time into a cup, then slide into the simmering water. Cook for 3–5 minutes to your liking. Carefully lift out of the pan with a fish slice and place on the toast. Pour the herb 'butter' over and serve.
Serving suggestions: a small glass of pure orange juice; coffee or tea.

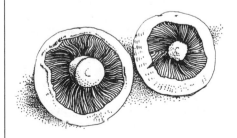

27

Scrambled Eggs on Toast

SERVES 2

3 eggs
45 ml/3 tbsp skimmed milk
10 ml/2 tsp low-fat spread
Salt and freshly ground black
**   pepper**
2 slices bread

Beat the eggs in a saucepan with the milk. Add half the low-fat spread, a little salt and a good grinding of pepper. Cook over a gentle heat, stirring all the time, until scrambled but creamy. Do not allow to boil. Meanwhile, toast the bread and spread with the remaining low-fat spread. Place on two warmed plates. Spoon on the egg and serve.

Serving suggestions: a small glass of pure fruit juice; coffee or tea.

Scrambled Eggs with Mushrooms

SERVES 2

75 g/3 oz button mushrooms,
**   sliced**
15 ml/1 tbsp water
10 ml/2 tsp low-fat spread
3 eggs
45 ml/3 tbsp milk
Salt and freshly ground black
**   pepper**
2 slices bread
15 ml/1 tbsp chopped parsley

Put the mushrooms in a saucepan with the water and half the low-fat spread. Cook, stirring, until all the liquid has evaporated. Beat together the eggs and milk with a little salt and pepper and add to the mushrooms. Cook over a gentle heat, stirring all the time, until scrambled. Do not allow to boil. Meanwhile, toast the bread and spread with the remaining low-fat spread. Place on two warmed plates. Spoon on the egg and mushroom mixture and sprinkle with the parsley before serving.

Serving suggestions: a small glass of pure fruit juice; coffee or tea.

Poached Eggs with Mushrooms

SERVES 2

50 g/2 oz button mushrooms,
**   sliced**
45 ml/3 tbsp water
Salt and freshly ground black
**   pepper**
2 slices bread
A scraping of low-fat spread
15 ml/1 tbsp vinegar
2 eggs

Put the mushrooms in a pan with the water and a little salt and pepper. Bring to the boil, cover, reduce the heat and simmer for 3 minutes or until the mushrooms are cooked. Remove the lid and boil rapidly until all the liquid has evaporated, stirring occasionally. Meanwhile, toast the bread and spread with the low-fat spread. Place on two warm plates. Fill a frying pan (skillet) with water and add the vinegar. Bring to the boil, then reduce to a gentle simmer. Break the eggs, one at a time, into a cup, then slide into the simmering water. Cook for 3–5 minutes to your liking. Spread the hot mushrooms on the toast and carefully lift out the eggs with a fish slice and slide on top of the mushrooms. Serve straight away.

Serving suggestions: a small glass of pure fruit juice; coffee or tea.

No-grease English Breakfast

SERVES 1

50 g/2 oz button mushrooms
15 ml/1 tbsp water
Salt and freshly ground black
  pepper
1 lean rasher (slice) streaky
  bacon, rinded
1 tomato, halved
1 egg
5 ml/1 tsp vinegar

Put the mushrooms in a pan with the water and a little salt and pepper. Cover and cook for about 5 minutes, shaking the pan occasionally, until tender and the liquid has evaporated. Meanwhile, grill (broil) the bacon and tomato until the bacon is crisp and golden and the tomato is just soft. Fill a frying pan (skillet) with water and add the vinegar. Bring to the boil and reduce the heat to a gentle simmer. Break the egg in a cup and slide into the water. Cook gently for 3–5 minutes until the egg is set to your liking. Remove from the pan with a fish slice and slide on a warm plate. Add the bacon, tomato and mushrooms and serve.

Serving suggestions: 1 slice of toast with a scraping of low-fat spread and reduced-sugar marmalade; coffee or tea.

Bacon and Apricot Rolls

SERVES 1

2 lean rashers (slices) streaky
  bacon, rinded
4 ready-to-eat dried apricots
1 slice toast with a scraping of
  low-fat spread

Stretch the bacon rashers by scraping them gently with the back of a knife. Cut into halves. Roll each half round an apricot. Secure each roll with a cocktail stick (toothpick), if necessary. Place on the grill (broiler) rack and grill (broil) until the bacon is crisp and brown. Transfer to a warm plate and serve with the toast.

Serving suggestion: coffee or tea.

Bacon and Banana Rolls

SERVES 1

2 lean rashers (slices) streaky
  bacon, rinded
1 small banana, cut into 4 equal
  chunks
1 slice toast and a scraping of
  low-fat spread

Stretch the bacon rashers with the back of a knife and cut each in half. Roll a piece of bacon round each piece of banana. Place on a grill (broiler) rack and grill (broil), turning occasionally, until the bacon is crisp and brown. Transfer to a warm plate and serve with the toast.

Serving suggestion: coffee or tea.

Bacon and Tomato Rolls with Mushrooms

SERVES 1

4 large, flat mushrooms
60 ml/4 tbsp water
Salt and freshly ground black
 pepper
2 lean rashers (slices) streaky
 bacon, rinded
4 cherry tomatoes
1 slice toast and a scraping of
 low-fat spread

Peel the mushrooms and remove any stalks. Place in a frying pan (skillet), gill sides up, with the water and a little salt and pepper. Cover and cook gently for 5 minutes or until the mushrooms are tender. Remove the lid and boil rapidly until the liquid has evaporated. Stretch the bacon with the back of a knife. Cut into halves and roll each piece around a cherry tomato. Secure with a cocktail stick (toothpick) if necessary. Place on the grill (broiler) rack and grill (broil) until the bacon is crisp and brown. Transfer the mushrooms to warmed serving plates, gill sides up, and lay the bacon rolls on top. Serve with the toast.

Serving suggestion: coffee or tea.

Bacon Sandwich

SERVES 1

1 slice bread with a scraping of
 low-fat spread
5 ml/1 tsp tomato ketchup
 (catsup) or brown table sauce
2 lean rashers (slices) streaky
 bacon, rinded

Halve the slice of bread. Spread one half with the ketchup or brown sauce. Grill (broil) the bacon until really crisp and golden. Place on the sauce, top with the remaining bread and eat straight away.

Serving suggestions: a glass of pure fruit juice; coffee or tea.

Egg and Bacon Sarni

SERVES 1

1 slice bread with a scraping of
 low-fat spread
1 lean rasher (slice) streaky
 bacon, rinded
2.5 ml/½ tsp low-fat spread
1 egg
Worcestershire sauce

Halve the slice of bread. Heat a non-stick frying pan (skillet) and dry-fry (sauté) the bacon until crisp. Keep warm. Wipe the pan with kitchen paper. Add the low-fat spread and brush over the base of the pan. Break in the egg and fry until set. Lift out of the pan with a fish slice and place with the bacon on one half of the bread. Add a few drops of Worcestershire sauce. Top with the remaining half slice of bread and serve.

Serving suggestions: ½ grapefruit; coffee or tea.

Breakfast Sausage Roll

SERVES 1

1 large pork sausage
1 slice bread, crusts removed
10 ml/2 tsp tomato ketchup
(catsup)

Grill (broil) the sausage on all sides until a deep golden brown and cooked through. Drain on kitchen paper. Meanwhile, spread one side of the bread with the ketchup. Put the sausage along one edge of the bread and gently roll up. Secure with a cocktail stick (toothpick). Grill, turning, until the bread is golden brown. Serve straight away.

Serving suggestions: ½ grapefruit; coffee or tea.

Sausage Kebabs

SERVES 1

2 chipolata sausages, quartered
8 button mushrooms
4 cherry tomatoes, halved
5 ml/1 tsp Worcestershire sauce
5 ml/1 tsp water

Thread the sausage pieces, mushrooms and tomatoes alternately on two skewers. Lay on a grill (broiler) rack. Mix together the Worcestershire sauce and water and brush over the kebabs. Grill (broil), turning several times, until the sausages are golden brown, brushing with the Worcestershire sauce as you turn them. Serve hot.

Serving suggestions: 1 slice of watermelon; 1 small slice of toast with a scraping of low-fat spread and reduced-sugar jam (conserve) or marmalade; coffee or tea.

Bacon and Mushroom Kebabs

SERVES 1

2 lean rashers (slices) streaky
bacon, rinded
6 button mushrooms
3 cherry tomatoes, halved
5 ml/1 tsp light soy sauce
5 ml/1 tsp water

Stretch the bacon rashers with the back of a knife, then cut each into three pieces. Roll each piece round a mushroom. Thread alternately with halved tomatoes on two skewers. Lay on the grill (broiler) rack. Mix together the soy sauce and water and brush over the kebabs. Grill (broil) until the bacon is crisp and golden, turning occasionally and brushing with the soy mixture when you turn them. Serve hot.

Serving suggestions: a glass of pure fruit juice; 1 slice of currant bread with a scraping of low-fat spread; coffee or tea.

Eggy Bread

SERVES 1

1 small egg
A dash of skimmed milk
Salt and freshly ground pepper
1 slice bread, crusts removed
15 g/½ oz/1 tbsp low-fat spread
Tomato ketchup (catsup)

Beat the egg with the milk and a little salt and pepper in a shallow dish. Add the bread and leave to soak for a few minutes. Carefully turn over and allow the other side to soak up as much of the egg mixture as possible. Heat half the low-fat spread in a small non-stick frying pan (skillet) and fry (sauté) the bread until golden brown underneath. Lift up with a fish slice. Add the remaining low-fat spread, turn the bread over and cook the other side until golden. Cut into triangles and serve straight away with tomato ketchup.
Serving suggestions: ½ grapefruit; 1 low-fat diet fruit yoghurt; coffee or tea.

Jugged Kippers

SERVES 2

2 small kipper fillets
Lemon wedges
2 thin slices brown bread with a
    scraping of low-fat spread

Put the kipper fillets in a jug, tail ends up. Pour on boiling water to cover the fish completely and leave to stand for 5 minutes. Drain, slide on to warmed plates and serve with lemon wedges and a slice of brown bread each.
Serving suggestion: a small glass of tomato juice.

Ham 'n' Egg Muffin

SERVES 1

1 English Muffin (see page 24 or
    use bought), halved
1 thin slice lean honey-roast ham
    (from a packet)
5 ml/1 tsp vinegar
1 egg

Toast the muffin halves on the grill (broiler) rack on the cut sides only. Lay the ham (folded if necessary) on one half and grill (broil) briefly. Meanwhile, fill a small frying pan (skillet) with water and add the vinegar. Bring to the boil and reduce the heat to a simmer. Break the egg into a cup, then slide into the water. Cook for 3–5 minutes to your liking. Remove from the pan with a fish slice and slide on top of the ham. Top with the other muffin half and serve.
Serving suggestions: ½ grapefruit; coffee or tea.

Egg and Tomato Muffin

SERVES 1

1 egg
1 tomato, sliced
1 English Muffin (see page 24 or
    use bought)
Freshly ground black pepper

Place the egg in a small saucepan of cold water. Bring to the boil and boil for 5 minutes. Plunge quickly in cold water, then shell as soon as it's cool enough to handle and slice. Meanwhile, warm the muffin, unless freshly made, in the oven or microwave. Split in half. Fill with the slices of tomato and egg. Add a good grinding of pepper and serve warm.
Serving suggestions: ½ grapefruit; coffee or tea.

Grilled Halloumi Cheese with Bacon

SERVES 1

*1 lean rasher (slice) streaky
bacon, rinded
50 g/2 oz Halloumi cheese, cut
into 2 slices
2.5 ml/½ tsp sunflower or olive oil*

Stretch the bacon rasher with the back of a knife. Cut in half and wrap each half around a slice of cheese. Place on a grill (broiler) rack and brush with the oil. Grill (broil) until the bacon is crisp and the cheese is turning golden. Serve straight away.
Serving suggestions: 1 slice of melon; 1 slice of crispbread with a scraping of low-fat spread and reduced-sugar marmalade or jam (conserve); coffee or tea.

Grilled Halloumi Cheese with Mushrooms

SERVES 1

*2 large, flat mushrooms
5 ml/1 tsp low-fat spread
10 ml/2 tsp water
50 g/2 oz Halloumi cheese, cut
into 2 slices
Freshly ground black pepper*

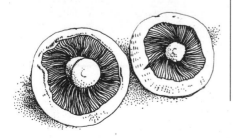

Peel the mushrooms and remove the stalks. Place on foil on a grill (broiler) rack, gill sides up. Dot with half the low-fat spread and add a teaspoon of water to each. Grill (broil) for 3–4 minutes until the mushrooms are almost cooked through. Top each with a slice of cheese, spread the remaining low-fat spread over, season with pepper and return to the grill until the cheese begins to brown. Serve straight away.
Serving suggestions: ½ grapefruit; 1 slice of wholegrain crispbread with a scraping of low-fat spread and honey.

Grilled Herring with Tomatoes

SERVES 2

*2 small herrings, cleaned
5 ml/1 tsp low-fat spread
Freshly ground black pepper
2 tomatoes, halved
2 slices wholegrain crispbread
with a scraping of low-fat
spread*

Open out the fish and lay skin side up on a board. Run the thumb firmly down the backbone a few times, then turn the fish over and lift away the backbone and as many adjacent bones as you can. Place skin sides down on a grill (broiler) rack. Dot the fish with tiny flakes of low-fat spread and dust with pepper. Grill (broil) for 4 minutes, then add the tomatoes to the rack and continue grilling until the fish is crisp and golden and the tomatoes are just soft. Serve hot with a crispbread each.
Serving suggestion: coffee or tea.

Smoked Haddock and Poached Egg

SERVES 2

**2 x 100 g/4 oz pieces smoked
  haddock fillet (preferably
  undyed)
2 eggs
2 slices puffed wheat crispbread**

Put the haddock fillets in a large
frying pan (skillet) with a lid and
cover with water. Bring to the boil,
cover, reduce the heat and poach for 3
minutes. Gently push to one side of
the pan. Break the eggs one at a time
into a cup and gently slide into the pan
beside the fish. Simmer for 3 minutes
until the eggs are just set and the fish
is cooked through. Transfer to warmed
plates with a fish slice and serve with
a crispbread each.
Serving suggestions: ½ grapefruit;
coffee or tea.

Devilled Kidneys

SERVES 2

**4 lambs' kidneys
20 ml/4 tsp low-fat spread
2.5 ml/½ tsp curry powder
1.5 ml/¼ tsp English made
  mustard
5 ml/1 tsp Worcestershire sauce
15 ml/1 tbsp tomato ketchup
  (catsup)
Salt and freshly ground black
  pepper
2 slices bread
Chopped parsley**

Cut the kidneys into bite-sized
pieces, snipping away the central
core with scissors. Melt the low-fat
spread in a frying pan (skillet) and fry
(sauté) the kidneys over a moderate
heat for 3 minutes, stirring until

browned. Stir in the remaining ingredients except the bread and parsley
and simmer gently for a further 4–5
minutes until the kidneys are tender
and bathed in sauce. Meanwhile, toast
the bread and place on two warmed
plates. Spoon the kidneys on top and
garnish with parsley before serving.
Serving suggestions: a small glass of
grapefruit juice; coffee or tea.

Summer Porridge

SERVES 2

**15 ml/1 tbsp chopped nuts
25 g/1 oz/¼ cup rolled oats
15 ml/1 tbsp clear honey
75 ml/5 tbsp very low-fat plain
  yoghurt
1 orange
75 g/5 tbsp very low-fat fromage
  frais
A few toasted flaked (slivered)
  almonds**

Mix together the chopped nuts and
oats and spread out in a shallow
baking tin (pan). Place under a moderate grill (broiler), stirring occasionally
until golden brown (be careful not to
let them burn). Leave to cool. Mix
together the honey and yoghurt. Slice
half the orange, then grate the rind
and squeeze the juice from the other
half. Mix the rind and juice into the
yoghurt mixture and fold in the fromage frais. Add the toasted oats and
nuts and mix well. Chill. Serve garnished with toasted flaked almonds.
Serving suggestion: coffee or tea.

Winter Porridge

SERVES 2

40 g/1½ oz/⅓ cup porridge oats
200 ml/7 fl oz/scant 1 cup water
A pinch of salt
Artificial sweetener granules
(optional)
Skimmed milk (optional)

Mix the oats and water in a saucepan with the salt. Bring to the boil and cook for 4–5 minutes, stirring all the time. Spoon into bowls and add sweetener to taste and a little skimmed milk, if liked.
Serving suggestions: a small glass of orange juice; coffee or tea.

Fruity Winter Porridge

SERVES 2

40 g/1½ oz/⅓ cup porridge oats
200 ml/7 fl oz/scant 1 cup water
50 g/2 oz/⅓ cup mixed dried fruit
(fruit cake mix)
Artificial sweetener granules
(optional)
Skimmed milk (optional)

Mix the oats with the water and fruit in a saucepan. Bring to the boil, reduce the heat and simmer for 5 minutes, stirring all the time. Spoon into bowls and add artificial sweetener and a little skimmed milk, if liked.
Serving suggestions: a small glass of tomato juice; coffee or tea.

Golden Porridge

SERVES 2

40 g/1½ oz/⅓ cup porridge oats
200 ml/7 fl oz/scant 1 cup water
4 ready-to-eat dried apricots,
chopped
Artificial sweetener granules
(optional)
Skimmed milk (optional)

Mix the oats and water in a saucepan. Bring to the boil, reduce the heat and cook for 3 minutes, stirring. Add the apricots and continue cooking for a further 2 minutes. Spoon into serving bowls and add sweetener and skimmed milk, if liked.
Serving suggestions: a small glass of grapefruit juice; coffee or tea.

Greek Porridge

SERVES 2

200 ml/7 fl oz/scant 1 cup water
3 dried figs, chopped
40 g/1½ oz/⅓ cup porridge oats
Artificial sweetener granules
(optional)
45 ml/3 tbsp very low-fat plain
yoghurt

Put the water and figs in a saucepan and leave to soak overnight. Stir in the oats, bring to the boil, reduce the heat and simmer, stirring, for 5 minutes. Sweeten to taste with artificial sweetener granules, if necessary. Spoon into bowls and top with a good spoonful of the yoghurt.
Serving suggestions: a small glass of grapefruit juice; coffee or tea.

Muesli

MAKES 6 SERVINGS

225 g/8 oz/2 cups porridge oats
50 g/2 oz/⅓ cup raisins
50 g/2 oz/⅓ cup sultanas (golden raisins)
50 g/2 oz/½ cup chopped hazelnuts
60 ml/4 tbsp bran
30 ml/2 tbsp artificial sweetener granules
Skimmed milk or very low-fat plain yoghurt, to serve

Mix together all the ingredients and store in an airtight container. Serve in bowls with a little skimmed milk or plain yoghurt.
Serving suggestions: 1 slice of melon; coffee or tea.

Spiced Muesli

MAKES 6 SERVINGS

Prepare as for Muesli but add 5 ml/ 1 tsp ground cinnamon and 5 ml/ 1 tsp grated nutmeg to the mixture.
Serving suggestions: a small glass of grapefruit juice; coffee or tea.

Apple Muesli

SERVES 1

1 serving Muesli (above)
1 green eating (dessert) apple, peeled and finely chopped
30 ml/2 tbsp low-fat fromage frais

Put the Muesli in a bowl. Add the chopped apple and top with the fromage frais.
Serving suggestion: coffee or tea.

Crunchy Muesli

MAKES 6 SERVINGS

175 g/6 oz/1½ cups porridge oats
50 g/2 oz/2 cups bran flakes
50 g/2 oz/½ cup toasted chopped mixed nuts
25 g/1 oz/⅙ cup currants
25 g/1 oz/⅙ cup raisins
50 g/2 oz/⅓ cup sultanas (golden raisins)
30 ml/2 tbsp artificial sweetener granules
Skimmed milk, to serve

Mix together all the ingredients and store in an airtight container. Spoon into serving bowls and add enough skimmed milk to moisten.
Serving suggestions: a small glass of tomato juice; coffee or tea.

Tropical Muesli

MAKES 6 SERVINGS

175 g/6 oz/1½ cups porridge oats
50 g/2 oz/1 cup All Bran
60 ml/4 tbsp desiccated (shredded) coconut
3 ready-to-eat dried peach halves, chopped
25 g/1 oz/¼ cup dried banana slices
50 g/2 oz/½ cup chopped mixed nuts
30 ml/2 tbsp artificial sweetener granules
Skimmed milk, to serve

Mix together all the ingredients and store in an airtight container. Spoon into serving bowls and add enough skimmed milk to moisten.
Serving suggestion: coffee or tea.

Chocolate Chip Muesli

SERVES 6

225 g/8 oz/2 cups porridge oats
50 g/2 oz/2 cups wheat flakes
25 g/1 oz/¼ cup plain (semi-sweet)
chocolate chips
50 g/2 oz/⅓ cup raisins
20 ml/4 tsp artificial sweetener
granules
Skimmed milk, to serve

Mix together all the ingredients and store in an airtight container. Spoon into serving bowls and add enough skimmed milk to moisten.
Serving suggestions: 1 slice of melon; coffee or tea.

Wholewheat Tropicana

SERVES 6

175 g/6 oz/6 cups unsweetened
wheatflakes
45 ml/3 tbsp coconut flakes
45 ml/3 tbsp chopped dates
45 ml/3 tbsp raisins
Skimmed milk, to serve

Mix together all the ingredients and store in an airtight container. Spoon into serving bowls and add skimmed milk to taste.
Serving suggestions: a small glass of pineapple juice; coffee or tea.

Chocolate and Orange Morning Rolls

MAKES 12

450 g/1 lb/4 cups strong white
(bread) flour
5 ml/1 tsp salt
Finely grated rind of 1 orange
15 g/½ oz/1 tbsp low-fat spread
10 ml/2 tsp easy-blend dried yeast
10 ml/2 tsp clear honey
1 egg, beaten
300 ml/½ pt/1¼ cups skimmed
milk, hand-hot
50 g/2 oz/½ cup chocolate chips
Low-fat spread, to serve

Mix together the flour, salt and orange rind in a bowl. Rub in the low fat spread. Stir in the yeast. Add the honey, most of the egg (reserve a little for glazing) and enough of the milk to form a firm dough. Knead gently on a lightly floured surface until smooth and elastic. Alternatively, prepare the mixture in a food processor. Return to the bowl, cover with a damp cloth and leave in a warm place for about 45 minutes or until doubled in size. Knock back and quickly knead in the chocolate chips. Shape into 12 balls and place well apart on a greased baking sheet. Leave in a warm place for 15 minutes to rise. Brush with the reserved egg and bake in a preheated oven at 220°C/425°F/gas mark 7 for 12–15 minutes or until golden and the bases sound hollow when tapped. Cool on a wire rack. Serve one roll per portion with a scraping of low-fat spread.
Serving suggestion: a glass of pure fruit juice; coffee or tea.

Irish Potato Cakes

MAKES 12

450 g/1 lb/2 cups well-mashed cooked potato
50 g/2 oz/¼ cup low-fat spread, plus extra for spreading
50 g/2 oz/½ cup wholemeal flour
A pinch of salt

Beat the potato well, then beat in the low-fat spread, flour and salt. Turn out on to a lightly floured surface and pat out to a round about 1 cm/½ in thick. Cut into rounds with a plain 7.5 cm/3 in biscuit (cookie) cutter. Re-knead the trimmings and cut again. Cook in a non-stick frying pan (skillet) for about 3 minutes on each side until golden brown. Serve two hot cakes per portion with a scraping of low-fat spread.
Serving suggestions: ½ grapefruit; 1 very low-fat diet fruit yoghurt; coffee or tea.

Cheesy Beano

SERVES 2

2 small slices bread
10 ml/2 tsp brown table sauce
400 g/14 oz/1 large can no-added-sugar baked beans
30 ml/2 tbsp grated low-fat Cheddar cheese

Toast the bread on both sides and spread one side with the sauce. Place on warmed flameproof plates. Meanwhile, heat the beans in a saucepan. Spoon over the toast, sprinkle with the cheese and flash under a hot grill (broiler) until the cheese melts. Serve straight away.
Serving suggestions: ½ grapefruit; coffee or tea.

Bean Scramble

SERVES 2

2 eggs
15 ml/1 tbsp skimmed milk
5 ml/1 tsp low-fat spread
220 g/7 oz/1 small can no-added-sugar baked beans
Salt and freshly ground black pepper
2 slices bread
Chopped parsley

Beat together the eggs and milk. Melt the low-fat spread in a small non-stick saucepan. Add the egg mixture, the beans and a little salt and pepper. Cook over a gentle heat, stirring all the time, until scrambled but still creamy. Do not allow to boil. Meanwhile, toast the bread and place on warmed plates. Spoon the bean scramble over and sprinkle with chopped parsley before serving.
Serving suggestions: ½ grapefruit; coffee or tea.

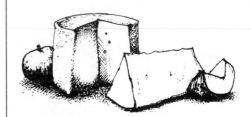

Ranch Breakfast

SERVES 2

2 chipolata sausages, chopped
6 mushrooms, quartered
30 ml/2 tbsp water
220 g/7 oz/1 small can no-added-
sugar baked beans
A good dash of Worcestershire
sauce
2 small hunks of French bread
(about 2.5 cm/1 in)

Dry-fry (sauté) the sausages in a
saucepan until a rich golden
brown and cooked through, stirring all
the time. Remove from the pan with a
draining spoon. Pour away the fat and
wipe out the pan with a piece of
kitchen paper. Add the mushrooms
and water to the pan and cook, stirring, until the mushrooms are softened and the liquid has evaporated.
Add the beans, sausages and
Worcestershire sauce. Bring to the
boil, stirring all the time. Spoon into
two bowls and serve each with a hunk
of bread.
Serving suggestions: a small glass of
pure fruit juice; coffee or tea.

Baked Potato Cakes with Caraway

MAKES 12

450 g/1 lb/2 cups well-mashed
cooked potato
50 g/2 oz/¼ cup low-fat spread,
plus extra for spreading
50 g/2 oz/½ cup wholemeal flour
A pinch of salt
30 ml/2 tbsp caraway seeds

Beat the potato well, then beat in
the low-fat spread, flour and salt.
Turn out on to a lightly floured surface
and pat out to about 1 cm/½ in thick.
Cut into rounds using a 7.5 cm/3 in
biscuit (cookie) cutter. Re-knead the
trimmings and cut again. Place on a
baking sheet and sprinkle with the
caraway seeds, pressing them lightly
into the surfaces. Bake in a preheated
oven at 200°C/400°F/gas mark 6 for
about 20 minutes until lightly golden.
Serve two hot cakes per portion with a
scraping of low-fat spread.
Serving suggestions: 1 very low-fat
plain yoghurt with 5 ml/1 tsp clear
honey; coffee or tea.

Everyday Breakfasts under 250 Calories

½ grapefruit, a cup of tea or coffee and any of the following:

- 25 g/1 oz/3 tbsp fruit and fibre cereal and skimmed milk
- 25 g/1 oz/1 cup cornflakes and skimmed milk
- 25 g/1 oz/1 cup bran flakes and skimmed milk
- 1 Weetabix and skimmed milk and 1 slice of toast with a scraping of low-fat spread and reduced-sugar jam (conserve) or marmalade
- 1 Weetabix and skimmed milk and 1 boiled egg
- 1 Shredded Wheat and skimmed milk and 1 boiled egg
- 220 g/7 oz/1 small can no-added-sugar baked beans on 1 small slice of toast with a scraping of low-fat spread
- 1 Shredded Wheat and skimmed milk and 1 slice of toast with a scraping of low-fat spread and reduced-sugar jam (conserve) or marmalade
- 25 g/1 oz/½ cup All Bran and skimmed milk and 1 slice of toast with a scraping of low-fat spread and reduced-sugar jam (conserve) or marmalade
- 2 boiled eggs and 1 small slice of toast with a scraping of low-fat spread
- 1 small croissant with a scraping of low-fat spread and reduced-sugar jam (conserve) or marmalade
- 1 muffin with a scraping of low-fat spread and reduced-sugar jam (conserve) or marmalade
- 1 crusty roll with a scraping of low-fat spread and honey
- 1 low-fat diet fruit yoghurt, 1 boiled egg and 1 small slice of toast with a scraping of low-fat spread

Stunning Soups and Starters

You can, of course, enjoy any of these as a light lunch or supper but they are ideal to serve as a first course when you're entertaining to impress your friends or family. If you want to serve bread with them, add on an extra 70 calories per average piece.

·· **SOUPS** ·································

CALORIES OR LESS

French Onion Soup

SERVES 6

1 kg/2¼ lb onions, thinly sliced
40 g/1½ oz/3 tbsp low-fat spread
900 ml/1½ pts/3¾ cups beef or vegetable stock, made with 2 stock cubes
Salt and freshly ground black pepper
6 very thin slices French bread
45 ml/3 tbsp grated Emmental (Swiss) cheese

Fry (sauté) the onions very gently in the low-fat spread in a covered saucepan for 15 minutes until soft. Remove the lid, turn up the heat and fry, stirring, for about 20 minutes, until the onions are a rich golden brown. Add the stock and bring to the boil. Reduce the heat, part-cover and simmer for 15 minutes. Season to taste. Meanwhile, toast the bread on one side only. Top with the cheese on the untoasted side. Grill (broil) until melted and bubbling. Ladle the soup into bowls and float a piece of toasted bread and cheese on top.

Tomato and Carrot Soup

SERVES 4

400 g/14 oz/1 large can chopped tomatoes
2 large carrots, grated
1 small onion, finely chopped
300 ml/½ pt/1¼ cups chicken or vegetable stock, made with 1 stock cube
5 ml/1 tsp dried oregano
A pinch of grated nutmeg
A pinch each of salt and freshly ground black pepper
1 bay leaf
A small pinch of artificial sweetener granules
15 ml/1 tbsp chopped parsley

Put all the ingredients except the parsley in a saucepan and bring to the boil, stirring. Reduce the heat, part-cover and simmer for 30 minutes. Discard the bay leaf, ladle into bowls and serve garnished with the parsley.

Tangy Tomato Soup

SERVES 4

1 onion, chopped
15 g/½ oz/1 tbsp low-fat spread
500 ml/17 fl oz/2¼ cups passata
    (sieved tomatoes)
Coarsely grated rind and juice of
    1 orange
Finely grated rind and juice of
    ½ lemon
250 ml/8 fl oz/1 cup water
Salt and freshly ground black
    pepper
A few grains of artificial sweetener
1.5 ml/¼ tsp Worcestershire sauce

Fry (sauté) the onion in the low-fat spread for 2 minutes, stirring. Add the passata, orange juice (reserve the rind for garnish), lemon rind and juice and the water. Bring to the boil, reduce the heat and simmer for 15 minutes. Season to taste with a little salt and pepper and the artificial sweetener. Stir in the Worcestershire sauce. Ladle into bowls and serve garnished with the orange rind.

Fragrant Courgette and Tomato Soup

SERVES 4

25 g/1 oz/2 tbsp low-fat spread
1 onion, finely chopped
4 courgettes (zucchini), grated
1 garlic clove, crushed
600 ml/1 pt/2½ cups vegetable
    stock, made with 2 stock cubes
400 g/14 oz/1 large can chopped
    tomatoes
15 ml/1 tbsp tomato purée (paste)
Salt and freshly ground black
    pepper
30 ml/2 tbsp chopped basil leaves
20 ml/4 tsp very low-fat fromage
    frais
4 small basil sprigs

Melt the low-fat spread in a large saucepan. Add the onion and cook, stirring, for 2 minutes. Add the courgettes and garlic and cook, stirring, for a further 4 minutes. Add the stock, the tomatoes and the purée. Bring to the boil, stirring. Part-cover, reduce the heat and simmer for 15 minutes. Season to taste and add the chopped basil. Ladle into warm bowls and top each with 5 ml/1 tsp of fromage frais and a small basil sprig.

Middle-Eastern Carrot Soup

SERVES 4

1 small onion, chopped
1 garlic clove, crushed
450 g/1 lb carrots, chopped
25 g/1 oz/2 tbsp low-fat spread
10 ml/2 tsp coriander (cilantro)
  seeds, crushed
900 ml/1½ pts/3¾ cups vegetable
  stock, made with 2 stock cubes
50 g/2 oz/⅓ cup sultanas (golden
  raisins)
Salt and freshly ground black
  pepper
20 ml/4 tsp very low-fat plain
  yoghurt
15 ml/1 tbsp chopped coriander
  leaves

Fry (sauté) the onion, garlic and carrots in the low-fat spread in a large saucepan for 5 minutes, stirring. Stir in the coriander seeds and cook for 1 minute. Stir in the stock, bring to the boil, reduce the heat, cover and simmer for 15 minutes or until the carrots are tender. Purée in a blender or food processor. Return to the pan and stir in the sultanas and salt and pepper to taste. Simmer for 5 minutes. Ladle into warmed soup bowls and garnish each bowl with a swirl of yoghurt and a little chopped coriander.

Watercress Soup Mimosa

SERVES 6

1 onion, chopped
15 g/½ oz/1 tbsp low-fat spread
350 g/12 oz watercress
15 ml/1 tbsp plain (all-purpose)
  flour
1 litre/1¾ pts/4¼ cups chicken or
  vegetable stock, made with
  2 stock cubes
Salt and freshly ground black
  pepper
1.5 ml/¼ tsp grated nutmeg
60 ml/4 tbsp low-fat single (light)
  cream
2 hard-boiled (hard-cooked) eggs,
  finely chopped

Fry (sauté) the onion in the low-fat spread for 2 minutes. Roughly chop the watercress, reserving six small sprigs for garnish. Add the chopped watercress to the onion and cook, stirring, for 2 minutes. Stir in the flour. Remove from the heat and gradually blend in the stock. Return to the heat and bring to the boil, stirring. Season with salt, pepper and the nutmeg. Reduce the heat and simmer for 20 minutes. Purée in a blender or food processor and return to the heat. Stir in the cream and reheat. Ladle into soup bowls and sprinkle the chopped egg on top. Garnish with the reserved watercress sprigs and serve straight away.

Scandinavian Cucumber Soup

SERVES 4

1 cucumber
Salt
10 ml/2 tsp dried dill (dill weed)
30 ml/2 tbsp cider vinegar
Freshly ground black pepper
300 ml/½ pt/1¼ cups very low-fat
 plain yoghurt
300 ml/½ pt/1¼ cups skimmed milk

Cut four thin slices off the cucumber and reserve for garnish. Grate the remainder into a large bowl and sprinkle with salt. Leave to stand for 10 minutes. Squeeze out all the moisture and drain off. Stir in the dill, vinegar, a little pepper and the yoghurt. Chill, if time. Just before serving, stir in the milk, ladle into bowls and garnish each with a reserved slice of cucumber.

Straciatella

SERVES 4

2 eggs
25 g/1 oz/¼ cup Parmesan cheese,
 grated
15 ml/1 tbsp chopped parsley
15 ml/1 tbsp chopped basil
A pinch of grated nutmeg
Salt and freshly ground black
 pepper
1.2 litres/2 pts/5 cups chicken
 stock, made with 3 stock cubes

Whisk the eggs, cheese, herbs and nutmeg together with a little salt and pepper. Bring the stock to the boil. Whisk a ladleful of the stock into the egg mixture. Pour back into the remaining stock. Whisk and serve straight away.

Gazpacho

SERVES 4

1 slice bread
15 ml/1 tbsp olive oil
15 ml/1 tbsp lemon juice
30 ml/2 tbsp water
1 red onion, finely chopped
1 small garlic clove, chopped
1 red (bell) pepper, roughly
 chopped
½ cucumber finely chopped
400 g/14 oz/1 large can tomatoes
15 ml/1 tbsp tomato purée (paste)
150 ml/¼ pt/⅔ cup iced water
Salt and freshly ground black
 pepper
A small pinch of artificial
 sweetener granules
2 tomatoes, finely chopped
Chopped parsley

Break up the bread and place in a bowl with the oil, lemon juice and the 30 ml/2 tbsp water. Leave to soak for 5 minutes. Place in a blender or food processor with a quarter of the chopped onion, the garlic, the pepper, half the cucumber, the canned tomatoes and the purée. Put the remaining onion and cucumber in two small serving bowls. Run the machine until the soup is fairly smooth. Chill until ready to serve. Just before serving, stir in the iced water and season with salt, pepper and a few grains of sweetener. Put the chopped tomatoes in a small serving bowl. Ladle the soup into bowls and sprinkle with chopped parsley. Serve with the chopped onion, cucumber and tomato handed separately.

Minted Pea Velvet

SERVES 6

450 g/1 lb/4 cups frozen peas
900 ml/1½ pts/3¾ cups chicken or
vegetable stock, made with
2 stock cubes
A pinch of artificial sweetener
granules
1 large mint sprig
Salt and freshly ground black
pepper
1 egg yolk
60 ml/4 tbsp low-fat single (light)
cream

Put the peas in a large pan with the stock, sweetener, mint and a little salt and pepper. Bring to the boil, reduce the heat, cover and simmer for 15 minutes. Discard the mint, then purée the mixture in a blender or food processor. Return to the heat. Blend the egg yolk with half the cream and stir into the soup. Reheat but on no account let it boil. Alternatively, cool and chill. Taste and re-season if necessary. Ladle into soup bowls and garnish with a swirl of the remaining cream.

Minestra

SERVES 4

1 small onion, grated
15 g/½ oz/1 tbsp low-fat spread
1 carrot, grated
1 turnip, grated
¼ small green cabbage, shredded
50 g/2 oz/½ cup frozen peas
25 g/1 oz quick-cook macaroni
400 g/14 oz/1 large can chopped
tomatoes
1 vegetable stock cube
Salt and freshly ground black
pepper
2.5 ml/½ tsp dried basil
2.5 ml/½ tsp dried oregano
20 ml/4 tsp grated Parmesan
cheese

Fry (sauté) the onion in the low-fat spread, stirring, for 1 minute. Add all the remaining ingredients except the Parmesan cheese. Bring to the boil, reduce the heat, stir, then part-cover and simmer for 10 minutes or until the vegetables and pasta are soft. Taste and re-season if necessary. Ladle into warmed bowls and serve with the cheese sprinkled on top.

Chinese Egg Flower Soup

SERVES 4

**900 ml/1½ pts/3¾ cups chicken
stock, made with 2 stock cubes
15 ml/1 tbsp soy sauce
30 ml/2 tbsp dry sherry
A pinch of ground ginger
25 g/1 oz/¼ cup frozen peas
½ red (bell) pepper, cut into tiny
diamond shapes
1 egg, beaten**

Put all the ingredients except the egg
in a saucepan and bring to the boil.
Simmer for 5 minutes until the peas
and pepper pieces are tender. Remove
from the heat and pour the egg in a
thin stream through the prongs of a
fork so it solidifies in 'flowers'. Let the
soup stand for 20 seconds to allow the
egg to set, then ladle into soup bowls.

Bortsch

SERVES 6

**2 celery sticks
2 carrots
1 onion
4 beetroot (red beets)
900 ml/1½ pts/3¾ cups vegetable
stock, made with 2 stock cubes
15 ml/1 tbsp vinegar
Salt and freshly ground black pepper
A small pinch of artificial
sweetener granules
30 ml/2 tbsp very low-fat fromage
frais**

Grate the vegetables straight into a
large saucepan. Add the remaining
ingredients except the fromage frais.
Bring to the boil, reduce the heat, part-
cover and simmer gently for 20 minutes
or until the vegetables are really tender.
Taste and re-season if necessary. Ladle
into soup bowls and garnish each with
a teaspoonful of fromage frais.

Beetroot and Orange Cooler

SERVES 6

**4 small cooked beetroot (red
beets), grated
600 ml/1 pt/2½ cups cold vegetable
stock, made with 2 stock cubes
15 ml/1 tbsp lemon juice
2 small oranges
300 ml/½ pt/1¼ cups very low-fat
crème fraîche
Freshly ground black pepper
Snipped chives**

Mix the beetroot with the stock and
lemon juice in a bowl. Finely
grate the rind and squeeze the juice
from one orange and add to the beetroot mixture. Remove all the rind and
pith from the second orange and cut
into six slices to use as garnish. Stir
the crème fraîche into the beetroot
mixture. Season to taste with pepper.
Chill well. Ladle into soup bowls and
serve garnished with the orange slices
and a sprinkling of snipped chives.

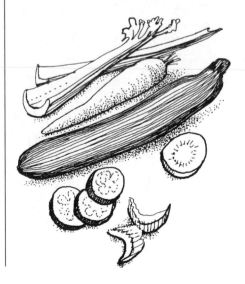

Iced Mango Mulligatawny

SERVES 6

1 small ripe mango
25 g/1 oz/2 tbsp low-fat spread
1 onion, finely chopped
1 carrot, finely chopped
30 ml/2 tbsp plain (all-purpose)
  flour
15 ml/1 tbsp Madras curry powder
1.2 litres/2 pts/5 cups beef stock,
  made with 2 stock cubes
6 coriander (cilantro) leaves

Peel the mango and cut all the flesh off the stone (pit). Heat the low-fat spread in a saucepan and cook the onion and carrot for 5 minutes until soft and lightly golden. Stir in the flour and curry powder and cook for 3 minutes, stirring, until a rich brown colour. Remove from the heat and gradually blend in the stock. Bring to the boil, stirring until thickened. Add the mango flesh. Reduce the heat, part-cover and simmer gently for 20 minutes. Purée in a blender or food processor, then leave to cool. Chill until ready to serve. Ladle into chilled soup bowls and garnish each bowl with a coriander leaf.

Winter Vegetable Soup

SERVES 6

2 onions, finely chopped
25 g/1 oz/2 tbsp low-fat spread
2 large carrots, finely diced
1 small swede (rutabaga), finely
  diced
1 potato, finely diced
1 leek, thinly sliced
600 ml/1 pt/2½ cups vegetable
  stock, made with 2 stock cubes
1 bay leaf
Salt and freshly ground black
  pepper
100 g/4 oz/1 cup frozen peas
300 ml/½ pt/1¼ cups skimmed
  milk
15 ml/1 tbsp cornflour
  (cornstarch)

Fry (sauté) the onions in the low-fat spread for 2 minutes until soft but not brown. Add the remaining prepared vegetables and toss for 1 minute. Add the stock, bay leaf and a little salt and pepper. Bring to the boil, reduce the heat, part-cover and simmer gently for 15 minutes. Add the peas and cook for a further 3 minutes. Blend a little of the milk with the cornflour until smooth. Stir in the remaining milk. Add to the pan and bring to the boil, stirring, until thickened slightly. Simmer for 2 minutes. Discard the bay leaf. Taste and re-season if necessary. Ladle into warm bowls and serve.

Cream of Mushroom Soup

SERVES 6

225 g/8 oz button mushrooms,
  chopped
1 small onion, finely chopped
25 g/1 oz/2 tbsp low-fat spread
25 g/1 oz/¼ cup plain (all-purpose)
  flour
900 ml/1½ pts/3¾ cups chicken
  stock, made with 2 stock cubes
30 ml/2 tbsp chopped parsley
150 ml/¼ pt/⅔ cup low-fat single
  (light) cream
Salt and freshly ground black
  pepper

Cook the mushrooms and onion gently in the low-fat spread for 5 minutes, stirring, until soft but not brown. Stir in the flour and cook for 1 minute, stirring. Remove from the heat and gradually blend in the stock. Return to the heat and bring to the boil, stirring. Reduce the heat and simmer gently for 10 minutes. Add the parsley and cream, reheat and season to taste. Ladle into warm bowls and serve.

Danish Consommé

SERVES 6

2 x 295 g/2 x 10½ oz/2 small cans
  beef consommé, chilled
60 ml/4 tbsp very low-fat crème
  fraîche
50 g/2 oz/1 small jar Danish
  lumpfish roe

Spoon the consommé into six cold soup bowls. Top each with a spoonful of crème fraîche, then the lumpfish roe and serve immediately.

Tyrolean Pepper Soup

SERVES 4

2 onions, thinly sliced
2 red (bell) peppers, thinly sliced
25 g/1 oz/2 tbsp low-fat spread
400 g/14 oz/1 large can chopped
  tomatoes
100 g/4 oz/1 cup sauerkraut,
  drained
450 ml/¾ pt/2 cups vegetable
  stock, made with 1 stock cube
10 ml/2 tsp paprika
Salt and freshly ground black
  pepper
20 ml/4 tsp very low-fat plain
  yoghurt
Snipped chives

Fry (sauté) the onions and peppers in the low-fat spread for 3 minutes, stirring. Add the remaining ingredients except the yoghurt and chives. Bring to the boil, reduce the heat and simmer gently for about 15 minutes until the vegetables are tender. Taste and re-season if necessary. Ladle into warm bowls and garnish each with 5 ml/ 1 tsp yoghurt and a few snipped chives.

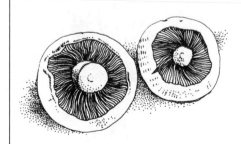

Oriental Vegetable Soup

SERVES 4

15 ml/1 tbsp sunflower oil
2 spring onions (scallions),
diagonally sliced
50 g/2 oz French (green) beans,
cut into short lengths
4 baby corn cobs, quartered
50 g/2 oz button mushrooms, sliced
1 carrot, cut into tiny matchsticks
1 small green chilli, seeded and
chopped (optional)
50 g/2 oz bean sprouts
750 ml/1¼ pts/3 cups vegetable
stock, made with 2 stock cubes
15 ml/1 tbsp soy sauce
10 ml/2 tsp sherry

Heat the oil in a wok or large saucepan. Add the prepared vegetables and stir-fry for 3 minutes. Add the remaining ingredients and simmer for 5 minutes until the vegetables are just tender but still with some bite.

Warming Pumpkin Soup

SERVES 4

25 g/1 oz/2 tbsp low-fat spread
750 g/1½ lb pumpkin, diced
600 ml/1 pt/2½ cups vegetable
stock, made with 2 stock cubes
600 ml/1 pt/2½ cups skimmed
milk
Salt and freshly ground black
pepper
Artificial sweetener granules
Grated nutmeg
15 ml/1 tbsp chopped parsley

Melt the low-fat spread in a saucepan. Add the pumpkin and cook gently, stirring, for 2 minutes. Add the stock, bring to the boil, reduce the heat and simmer for 15–20 minutes until the pumpkin is really tender. Purée in a blender or food processor. Return to the saucepan. Stir in the milk, a little salt and pepper, and artificial sweetener and nutmeg to taste. Reheat but do not boil. Ladle into warmed soup bowls and serve garnished with the chopped parsley.

Venetian White Fish Soup

SERVES 8

5 ml/1 tsp extra virgin olive oil
50 g/2 oz/¼ cup low-fat spread
1 large onion, finely chopped
1 garlic clove, crushed
1 carrot, finely chopped
400 g/14 oz/1 large can chopped tomatoes
15 ml/1 tbsp tomato purée (paste)
30 ml/2 tbsp chopped parsley
900 ml/1½ pts/3¾ cups fish stock, made with 2 stock cubes
150 ml/¼ pt/⅔ cup dry white wine
1 bay leaf
Salt and freshly ground black pepper
1 lemon
100 g/4 oz plaice fillet, cut into thick strips
100 g/4 oz cod fillet, cut into large chunks
100 g/4 oz whiting fillet, cut into thick strips
1 canned pimiento cap, finely chopped
150 ml/¼ pt/⅔ cup low-fat double (heavy) cream
8 whole unpeeled prawns (shrimp), to garnish

Heat the oil and low-fat spread in a large saucepan. Add the onion, garlic and carrot and fry (sauté) for 2 minutes, stirring, until soft but not brown. Add the contents of the can of tomatoes, the tomato purée, half the parsley, the stock, wine, bay leaf and a little salt and pepper. Bring to the boil. Cut the ends off the lemon and add the ends to the pan. Cut the rest of the lemon into eight slices and reserve for garnish. Add the fish to the pan, return to the boil, reduce the heat, part-cover and simmer gently for 20 minutes. Discard the bay leaf and lemon ends.

Season to taste. Using a draining spoon, divide the fish between eight serving dishes. Stir the pimiento and cream into the soup and reheat but do not boil. Taste and re-season if necessary. Ladle over the fish, sprinkle with the remaining parsley and garnish each bowl with a slice of lemon and a whole prawn over the rim of the dish.

Medieval Apple Soup

SERVES 6

2 large cooking (tart) apples, cored and chopped
1 litre/1¾ pts/4¼ cups lamb stock, made with 2 stock cubes
A piece of cinnamon stick
2.5 ml/½ tsp grated fresh root ginger
Salt and freshly ground black pepper
50 g/2 oz/¼ cup long-grain rice, cooked

Place the apple in a pan with the stock, cinnamon and ginger. Bring to the boil, reduce the heat, part-cover and simmer gently for 20 minutes until the apples are pulpy. Remove the cinnamon stick. Purée the soup in a blender or food processor and return to the pan. Season to taste and add the rice. Heat through, then ladle into soup bowls and serve.

Summer Fruit Soup

SERVES 4

450 g/1 lb mixed strawberries and raspberries
Artificial sweetener granules
900 ml/1½ pts/3¾ cups skimmed milk

Cut one of the strawberries into four slices lengthways and reserve for garnish. Put the remaining fruit in a saucepan and heat gently, stirring until the juices run. Turn up the heat slightly, cover and stew until soft. Stir in the sweetener to taste. Pass the fruit through a sieve (strainer) to remove the seeds. Meanwhile, bring the milk slowly to the boil, then allow to cool. Gradually stir into the fruit and chill until ready to serve. Ladle into cold bowls and float a slice of strawberry on each.

Cream of Lettuce Soup

SERVES 6

600 ml/1 pt/2½ cups chicken stock, made with 2 stock cubes
1 round lettuce, shredded
1 small onion, chopped
25 g/1 oz/2 tbsp low-fat spread
2.5 ml/½ tsp grated nutmeg
Salt and freshly ground black pepper
300 ml/½ pt/1¼ cups skimmed milk
1 egg yolk
30 ml/2 tbsp low-fat single (light) cream

Bring the stock to the boil, add the lettuce and boil for 5 minutes. Take out about 30 ml/2 tbsp of the lettuce shreds with a draining spoon and reserve. In a separate pan, fry (sauté) the onion in the low-fat spread for 3 minutes until soft but not brown. Add the lettuce and stock and season to taste with the nutmeg, salt and pepper. Simmer for 5 minutes until the onion is very soft. Purée in a blender or food processor and return to the saucepan. Stir in the milk. Whisk the egg yolk and cream together. Whisk in a little of the hot soup. Pour back into the remaining soup and heat through, stirring. Do not allow to boil. Add the reserved lettuce shreds and ladle into warm soup bowls. Alternatively cool, then chill and serve very cold.

Jellied Consommé with Mushrooms

SERVES 4

100 g/4 oz button mushrooms, sliced
300 ml/½ pt/1¼ cups water
5 ml/1 tsp lemon juice
15 ml/1 tbsp powdered gelatine
295 g/10½ oz/1 small can condensed beef consommé
45 ml/3 tbsp sherry
A dash of soy sauce
20 ml/4 tsp very low-fat fromage frais

Simmer the mushrooms in the water and lemon juice until tender. Turn into a large bowl. Blend 30 ml/2 tbsp of the hot mushroom liquid with the gelatine in a cup. Place the cup in a pan of hot water and heat gently, stirring, until the gelatine dissolves. Stir into the mushrooms and liquid with the consommé, sherry and soy sauce. Leave to cool, then chill until just set. Stir to break up, spoon into soup bowls and garnish each with 5 ml/1 tsp fromage frais.

STARTERS

CALORIES OR LESS

Melon with Parma Ham

SERVES 6

1 honeydew melon, cut into 6
slices
6 wafer-thin slices lean Parma ham
6 cherry tomatoes
6 parsley sprigs

Remove the rind from the melon and cut each wedge into two thin wedges. Halve the ham slices widthways. Wrap a piece of ham round the centre of each piece of melon and arrange on serving plates. Garnish each plate with a cherry tomato and a parsley sprig.

Manor House Grapefruit

SERVES 6

3 grapefruit
30 ml/6 tsp port
A pinch of artificial sweetener
granules
75 g/3 oz/¾ cup Stilton cheese,
crumbled

Halve the grapefruit. Cut all round the fruit between the flesh and the pith, then loosen each segment each side of the membrane with a serrated-edged knife. Place in fireproof dishes on the grill (broiler) tray. Mix the port with a pinch of artificial sweetener granules and spoon over each fruit. Scatter the crumbled cheese over. Grill (broil) for about 4 minutes until the cheese melts and bubbles. Serve straight away.

Spiced Melon and Clementine Cocktail

SERVES 6

1 honeydew melon
3 clementines
2 pieces stem ginger in syrup,
chopped
45 ml/3 tbsp apple juice
6 mint sprigs

Halve the melon and discard the seeds. Scoop out the flesh with a melon baller or spoon and place in a bowl. Peel and segment the clementines and add with the ginger and apple juice. Chill for at least 1 hour to allow the flavours to develop. Spoon into glass dishes and garnish each with a mint sprig.

Apple Crunch

SERVES 4

1 red-skinned eating (dessert) apple
¼ cucumber, diced
1 celery stick, sliced
30 ml/2 tbsp dry white wine
100 g/4 oz/1 cup cooked peas
5 ml/1 tsp dried summer savory
Freshly ground black pepper

Core and dice the apple but do not peel. Mix with the remaining ingredients. Spoon into individual glass dishes and serve straight away.

Florida Cocktail

SERVES 6

3 grapefruit
300 g/11 oz/1 small can mandarin
  orange segments in natural
  juice
6 maraschino cherries

Halve the grapefruit. Cut all round the fruit between the pith and the flesh, then remove the flesh in segments, cutting either side of each membrane. Place in a bowl with any juice. Scoop out the membranes and central core and discard, reserving the grapefruit shells. Add the contents of the can of mandarins to the grapefruit and mix well. Chill. Just before serving, place the grapefruit shells in glass serving dishes. Spoon in the grapefruit and mandarin oranges with the juice and top each with a maraschino cherry.

Pineapple Boats

SERVES 6

1 ripe fresh pineapple
225 g/8 oz/1 cup very low-fat
  cottage cheese
1 red (bell) pepper, chopped
1 green chilli, seeded and chopped
Salt and freshly ground black
  pepper

Cut the pineapple into six wedges, leaving the green leaves on. Cut most of the flesh off the skin and roughly chop, discarding any tough central core. Place in a bowl with the cheese, red pepper and chilli Mix well and season to taste. Place the pineapple skins on serving plates. Spoon the cheese and fruit mixture on to the skins and chill, if time, before serving.

Pears with Tarragon Dressing

SERVES 6

6 ripe pears
Lettuce leaves
150 ml/¼ pt/⅔ cup very low-fat
  crème fraîche
5 ml/1 tsp lemon juice
30 ml/2 tbsp low-calorie
  mayonnaise
30 ml/2 tbsp chopped tarragon
A few grains of artificial sweetener
  granules
Salt and freshly ground black
  pepper
Cayenne
Small tarragon sprigs

Peel, halve and core the pears. Place rounded sides up on a bed of lettuce leaves on six individual plates. Whisk the crème fraîche with the lemon juice, mayonnaise and chopped tarragon. Season to taste very sparingly with sweetener (literally just a few grains) and salt and pepper. Spoon over the pears, dust with cayenne and garnish with small tarragon sprigs.

Strawberry and Cucumber Platter

SERVES 6

225 g/8 oz strawberries, sliced
1 large cucumber, peeled and
 thinly sliced
Salt and freshly ground black
 pepper
45 ml/3 tbsp olive oil
15 ml/1 tbsp lemon juice
15 ml/1 tbsp chopped mint
A very few grains of artificial
 sweetener
Mint sprigs

Arrange the strawberry and cucumber slices in decreasing circles on six individual serving plates, starting with cucumber. Add a good grinding of pepper. Whisk the remaining ingredients except the mint sprigs with a little salt and pepper and drizzle over. Garnish each with a small mint sprig.

Red and Gold Salad

SERVES 4

1 head radicchio
1 head chicory (Belgian endive)
2 oranges
75 g/3 oz raspberries
Freshly ground black pepper
15 ml/1 tbsp raspberry vinegar
15 ml/1 tbsp pure orange juice

Separate the radicchio into leaves and tear into small pieces. Cut a cone-shaped core out of the base of the chicory, cut the head into chunks, then separate the layers. Cut off all the rind and pith from the oranges. Cut the fruit into thin rounds, then slice each round into quarters. Mix together the salad leaves and oranges with any juice. Spoon on to four serving plates. Dot the raspberries around, then add a good grinding of pepper. Whisk together the vinegar and orange juice and drizzle over just before serving.

Ratatouille

SERVES 6

1 aubergine (eggplant), thinly
 sliced
Salt and freshly ground black
 pepper
30 ml/2 tbsp low-fat spread
1 onion, thinly sliced
1 garlic clove, crushed
2 courgettes (zucchini), sliced
1 red (bell) pepper, cut into thin
 strips
1 green (bell) pepper, cut into thin
 strips
400 g/14 oz/1 large can chopped
 tomatoes
15 ml/1 tbsp tomato purée (paste)
5 ml/1 tsp dried mixed herbs
45 ml/3 tbsp grated Parmesan
 cheese

Put the aubergine slices in a colander. Sprinkle with salt and leave to stand for 30 minutes. Rinse thoroughly. Melt the low-fat spread in a large saucepan. Add the onion and fry (sauté), stirring, for 1 minute. Add all the remaining fresh vegetables and cook gently, stirring, for 2 minutes. Add the tomatoes, tomato purée, herbs and a little salt and pepper. Cover and simmer for 20 minutes, stirring occasionally, until the vegetables are just tender but still with some 'bite'. Spoon into individual serving bowls and sprinkle each with a little of the Parmesan cheese.

Greek-style Tomato Platter

SERVES 6

8 ripe tomatoes, sliced
100 g/4 oz/1 cup Feta cheese,
crumbled
8 black olives, stoned (pitted) and
sliced
15 ml/1 tbsp chopped oregano or
parsley
15 ml/1 tbsp white wine vinegar
15 ml/1 tbsp olive oil
Freshly ground black pepper

Arrange the tomato slices on six small serving plates. Scatter the cheese, olives and herbs over. Whisk together the vinegar and oil and drizzle over. Add a good grinding of black pepper and serve.

Artichokes with Tarragon Vinaigrette

SERVES 6

6 artichokes
60 ml/4 tbsp olive oil
30 ml/2 tbsp white wine vinegar
15 ml/1 tbsp warm water
Salt and freshly ground black
pepper
15 ml/1 tbsp chopped tarragon

Prepare and cook the artichokes as for Artichokes with Lemon 'Butter' (see right). Drain and leave to cool. Whisk together the remaining ingredients and spoon into six small bowls. Serve the cold artichokes with the dressing to dip the leaves and base in.

Artichokes with Lemon 'Butter'

SERVES 6

6 globe artichokes
15 ml/1 tbsp vinegar
90 ml/6 tbsp low-fat spread
Grated rind and juice of 1 lemon
15 ml/1 tbsp chopped parsley
Salt and freshly ground black
pepper
A pinch of cayenne
A few grains of artificial sweetener
(optional)

Twist off the stalks from the artichokes. Trim the points off the leaves, if liked. Boil in plenty of lightly salted water to which the vinegar has been added for about 20 minutes or until a leaf can be pulled off easily. Drain upside-down on kitchen paper. Meanwhile, melt the low-fat spread with the lemon rind and juice and the parsley. Season with salt, pepper and the cayenne. Add a very few grains of artificial sweetener to take off the sharpness, if liked. Pour into six small individual bowls and serve with the artichokes. To eat, pull off the leaves, dip in the lemon 'butter' and draw the fleshy part through the teeth, then discard. When all the leaves are eaten, cut off the hairy 'choke', then eat the base with a knife and fork, dipping it in any remaining 'butter'.

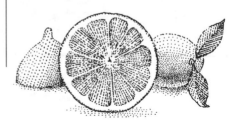

Moules Marinières

SERVES 6

2 kg/4½ lb fresh mussels in their
 shells
40 g/1½ oz/3 tbsp low-fat spread
1 large onion, finely chopped
2 wineglasses dry white wine
1 wineglass water
Freshly ground black pepper
30 ml/2 tbsp chopped parsley

Scrub the mussels, pull off the beards and scrape off any barnacles. Discard any that are open, broken or don't close when tapped sharply. Rinse well in cold running water. Heat the low-fat spread in a large saucepan. Add the onion and cook for 2 minutes, stirring, until soft but not brown. Add the mussels, wine, water and a good grinding of pepper. Bring to the boil, cover the pan and cook for 5 minutes, shaking the pan occasionally. Discard any mussels that have not opened. Ladle into large soup bowls and sprinkle with the chopped parsley before serving.

Tuna Pâté

SERVES 6

185 g/6½ oz/1 small can tuna in
 brine, drained
200 g/7 oz/scant 1 cup very low-
 fat soft cheese
15 ml/1 tbsp lemon juice
1.5 ml/¼ tsp cayenne
15 ml/1 tbsp chopped parsley
Salt and freshly ground black
 pepper
Mixed salad garnish
Paprika
6 lemon wedges
To serve:
Puffed wheat crispbread

Mash the tuna with the cheese in a bowl. Beat in the lemon juice, cayenne and parsley, seasoning to taste with salt and pepper. Spoon on to a sheet of greaseproof (waxed) paper in a sausage shape, then roll up and chill for at least 30 minutes. Unwrap and cut into 12 slices. Arrange on six serving plates with a colourful mixed salad garnish. Dust the tuna pâté with paprika and add a lemon wedge to each plate. Serve with puffed wheat crispbread

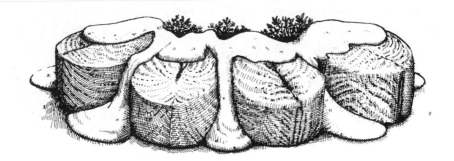

Tuna Dip with Vegetable Dippers

SERVES 6

185 g/6½ oz/1 small can tuna in
  brine, drained
60 ml/4 tbsp low-calorie
  mayonnaise
45 ml/3 tbsp very low-fat plain
  yoghurt
15 ml/1 tbsp tomato ketchup
  (catsup)
5 ml/1 tsp lemon juice
1.5 ml/¼ tsp chilli powder
Freshly ground black pepper
Snipped chives, to garnish
For the dippers:
Small cauliflower florets
Carrots, cut into matchsticks
Celery sticks, cut into matchsticks
Cucumber, cut into matchsticks
Radishes

Empty the tuna into a bowl and break it up with a wooden spoon. Beat in the remaining ingredients. Spoon into six individual small pots, garnish each pot with snipped chives and place on six serving plates. Surround with vegetable 'dippers' and serve.

Asparagus with Herb 'Butter'

SERVES 4

750 g/1½ lb asparagus
60 ml/4 tbsp low-fat spread
15 ml/1 tbsp chopped parsley
5 ml/1 tsp chopped thyme or
  oregano
15 ml/1 tbsp snipped chives
5 ml/1 tsp lemon juice
Freshly ground black pepper

Wash the asparagus. Trim off about 5 cm/2 in from the base of the stems. Tie the asparagus in a bundle. Stand the bundle in a pan of lightly salted water. Cover with a lid (or foil if the stalks are too tall). Bring to the boil, reduce the heat and cook gently for 10 minutes. Turn off the heat and leave undisturbed for 5 minutes. Lift out of the pan, untie and arrange on four warmed serving plates. Meanwhile, heat the low-fat spread in a saucepan with the herbs, lemon juice and a good grinding of pepper. Spoon over the asparagus and serve straight away.

Baked Garlicky Mushrooms

SERVES 4

8 large, flat mushrooms
25 g/1 oz/2 tbsp low-fat spread
2 garlic cloves, finely chopped
Salt and freshly ground black
    pepper
150 ml/¼ pt/⅔ cup dry white wine
150 ml/¼ pt/⅔ cup low-fat single
    (light) cream
Chopped parsley

Peel the mushrooms and remove and discard the stalks. Use the spread to grease a large, shallow ovenproof dish. Place the mushrooms in the dish, gill sides up. Sprinkle with the garlic and a little salt and pepper. Mix the wine with the cream and pour over. Cover with foil and bake in a pre-heated oven at 190°C/375°F/gas mark 5 for about 20 minutes or until the mushrooms are tender. Transfer to serving plates and spoon the garlicky juices over. Sprinkle with chopped parsley and serve.

Mighty Mushrooms

SERVES 6

450 g/1 lb button mushrooms
1 onion, finely chopped
1 garlic clove, crushed
45 ml/3 tbsp olive oil
400 g/14 oz/1 large can chopped
    tomatoes
A few grains of artificial sweetener
150 ml/¼ pt/⅔ cup red wine
Salt and freshly ground black
    pepper
Chopped parsley

Put the mushrooms in a large pan with the onion, garlic and oil. Cook, stirring, for 3 minutes until the mushrooms are softening. Add the remaining ingredients except the parsley, bring to the boil, reduce the heat and simmer for about 15 minutes until the mushrooms are cooked and bathed in a rich sauce. Stir from time to time during cooking. Serve hot or chilled, sprinkled with chopped parsley.

Mushroom Pâté with Celery

SERVES 4

25 g/1 oz/2 tbsp low-fat spread
1 small onion, finely chopped
350 g/12 oz button mushrooms,
**   finely chopped**
15 ml/1 tbsp lemon juice
200 g/7 oz/scant 1 cup very low-
**   fat soft cheese**
30 ml/2 tbsp chopped parsley
To serve:
Celery sticks

Melt the low-fat spread in a saucepan. Add the onion and fry (sauté) for 3 minutes until lightly golden. Add the mushrooms and cook, stirring, until no liquid remains. Stir in the lemon juice, turn into a bowl and leave to cool. Beat in the cheese and parsley and chill. Spoon into small pots and serve with plenty of celery sticks. To eat, either use as a dip or spread the pâté in the celery.

Oriental Green Beans

SERVES 6

750 g/1½ lb French (green) beans,
**   topped and tailed but left whole**
6 lean streaky bacon rashers
**   (slices), rinded and diced**
100 g/4 oz button mushrooms,
**   sliced**
30 ml/2 tbsp water
30 ml/2 tbsp Worcestershire sauce
30 ml/2 tbsp soy sauce
A pinch of artificial sweetener
**   granules**
30 ml/2 tbsp red wine vinegar

Cook the beans in boiling, lightly salted water until just tender. Drain. In the same saucepan, dry-fry (sauté) the bacon until crisp. Remove from the pan with a draining spoon and drain on kitchen paper. Wipe out the pan with kitchen paper to remove the bacon fat. Add the mushrooms to the pan with the water and cook, stirring, until the mushrooms are soft. Add the remaining ingredients and bring to the boil. Add the beans and bacon and toss over a gentle heat until hot through. Spoon into warm bowls and serve straight away.

Chinese Prawn Salad

SERVES 6

175 g/6 oz bean sprouts
1 small red (bell) pepper, chopped
100 g/4 oz/1 cup peeled prawns
**   (shrimp)**
10 ml/2 tsp soy sauce
10 ml/2 tsp white wine vinegar
A few grains artificial sweetener
20 ml/2 tbsp sesame oil
Salt and freshly ground black
**   pepper**
6 large lettuce leaves
1 spring onion (scallion), chopped

Put the bean sprouts in a bowl with the pepper and prawns. Mix together the remaining ingredients except the lettuce and spring onion and pour over. Toss well. Spoon on to the lettuce leaves on six individual serving plates and sprinkle each portion with a little of the spring onion.

Spanish Peppers

SERVES 6

2 green (bell) peppers, quartered
2 red (bell) peppers, quartered
2 yellow (bell) peppers, quartered
45 ml/3 tbsp olive oil
Coarse sea salt
12 black olives, halved and stoned
** (pitted)**

Fry (sauté) the peppers in the oil in a large frying pan (skillet) or wok for about 6 minutes or until tender and turning golden. Spoon on to plates with the oil and sprinkle with sea salt and the olives before serving.

Smoked Salmon Slices

SERVES 6

6 slices pumpernickel
30 ml/2 tbsp very low-fat soft
** cheese**
6 thin slices smoked salmon
6 lemon slices
6 small parsley sprigs

Spread the pumpernickel with the cheese. Top each with a slice of salmon. Make a slit in each lemon slice from the centre to the edge. Twist either side of the slit in opposite directions and place the lemon 'twist' on top of the salmon. Garnish with a tiny parsley sprig and serve.

Smoked Salmon with Scrambled Egg

SERVES 6

15 g/½ oz/1 tbsp low-fat spread
4 eggs
30 ml/2 tbsp skimmed milk
75 g/3 oz smoked salmon pieces
Salt and freshly ground black
** pepper**
3 thin slices bread
Parsley sprigs

Melt the low-fat spread in a saucepan. Beat together the eggs and milk and add to the pan. Cook over a gentle heat, stirring, until just set but still creamy. Remove from the heat and stir in the salmon. Season to taste. Spoon into six warmed ramekin dishes (custard cups). Meanwhile, toast the bread and cut into small triangles. Arrange the toast round the ramekins and garnish each with a parsley sprig.

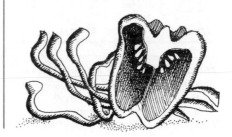

SOUPS

150

CALORIES OR LESS

Tuscan Spinach and White Bean Soup

SERVES 6

1 onion, chopped
1 garlic clove, crushed
25 g/1 oz/2 tbsp low-fat spread
900 ml/1½ pts/3¾ cups chicken
stock, made with 2 stock cubes
1 bay leaf
425 g/15 oz/1 large can cannellini
or haricot (navy) beans
450 g/1 lb spinach
Salt and freshly ground black
pepper
30 ml/2 tbsp grated Parmesan
cheese

Fry (sauté) the onion and garlic in the low-fat spread in a heavy-based saucepan, stirring, for 5 minutes until softened and lightly browned. Add the stock and bay leaf. Bring to the boil, reduce the heat and simmer for 10 minutes. Discard the bay leaf. Add the contents of the can of beans, including the liquid. Wash the spinach in several changes of cold water, then discard any tough stalks and finely shred. Add to the pan and continue cooking for 5 minutes. Season to taste. Ladle into warmed bowls and garnish each with a sprinkling of Parmesan cheese.

White Onion Soup with Croûtons

SERVES 6

4 large onions, thinly sliced
50 g/2 oz/¼ cup low-fat spread
Salt and freshly ground white
pepper
450 ml/¾ pt/2 cups vegetable
stock, made with 2 stock cubes
450 ml/¾ pt/2 cups skimmed milk
2 egg yolks
2.5 ml/½ tsp lemon juice
2 slices bread, cubed

Cook the onions gently in the low-fat spread in a covered saucepan for 10 minutes, stirring from time to time, until soft but not brown. Add a little salt and pepper and the stock. Bring to the boil, reduce the heat and simmer gently for 30 minutes until the onions are very soft and the stock is richly flavoured. Stir in the milk and heat through. Whisk the egg yolks with the lemon juice. Add two ladlefuls of the hot soup and whisk well. Return to the pan and heat through gently until slightly thickened but do not allow to boil. Taste and re-season if necessary. Meanwhile, spread out the diced bread on a baking sheet and bake in a pre-heated oven at 200°C/400°C/gas mark 6 for about 10 minutes until a deep golden brown. Ladle the soup into warmed bowls and sprinkle with the croûtons just before serving.

Chilled Prawn and Cucumber Soup

SERVES 6

1 large cucumber
450 ml/¾ pt/2 cups buttermilk
450 ml/¾ pt/2 cups skimmed milk
*225 g/8 oz/2 cups peeled prawns
    (shrimp)*
*1 large green (bell) pepper,
    chopped*
5 ml/1 tsp dried dill (dill weed)
*Salt and freshly ground black
    pepper*

Cut six slices off the cucumber and reserve for garnish, wrapped in clingfilm (plastic wrap). Peel and finely chop the remainder. Place in a large bowl with a lid. Add the remaining ingredients, seasoning to taste. Chill for several hours or overnight. Ladle into chilled bowls and float a slice of cucumber on each to garnish.

Summer Magic Soup

SERVES 6

1.2 litres/2 pts/5 cups tomato juice
*250 ml/8 fl oz/1 cup very low-fat
    plain yoghurt*
½ small onion, grated
Grated rind of ½ lemon
Lemon juice
*Salt and freshly ground white
    pepper*
*100 g/4 oz/1 cup peeled prawns
    (shrimp)*
*1 cantaloupe melon, cut into balls
    or diced*
30 ml/2 tbsp chopped basil

Whisk the tomato juice with the yoghurt, onion and lemon rind. Spike to taste with lemon juice and season lightly. Stir in the prawns. Chill for at least 2 hours. Sprinkle the melon with the basil and chill at the same time. Spoon the soup into chilled bowls and float the herb-coated melon balls on top. Serve straight away.

Creamy Cauliflower Soup

SERVES 6

1 onion, chopped
25 g/1 oz/2 tbsp low-fat spread
*1 small cauliflower, cut into small
    florets*
1 large potato, diced
*750 ml/1¼ pts/3 cups vegetable
    stock, made with 2 stock cubes*
*Salt and freshly ground black
    pepper*
150 ml/¼ pt/⅔ cup skimmed milk
*60 ml/4 tbsp low-fat double
    (heavy) cream*
Chopped parsley

Fry (sauté) the onion in the low-fat spread for 2 minutes. Add the remaining prepared vegetables and cook, stirring, for 1 minute. Add the stock, bring to the boil, reduce the heat and simmer gently for 10 minutes or until the vegetables are tender. Purée in a blender or food processor. Season to taste and stir in the milk and half the cream. Reheat. Ladle into warm bowls and garnish each with a swirl of the remaining cream and a little chopped parsley.

Curried Parsnip Soup

SERVES 6

1 onion, chopped
25 g/1 oz/2 tbsp low-fat spread
15 ml/1 tbsp curry powder
450 g/1 lb parsnips, sliced
600 ml/1 pt/2½ cups vegetable
   stock, made with 2 stock cubes
300 ml/½ pt/1¼ cups skimmed
   milk
Salt and freshly ground black
   pepper
15 ml/1 tbsp chopped parsley

Fry (sauté) the onion in the low-fat spread for 2 minutes. Add the curry powder and cook, stirring, for 1 minute. Add the parsnips and cook for a further 1 minute. Add the stock, bring to the boil, reduce the heat, part-cover and simmer for about 15 minutes until the parsnips are tender. Purée in a blender or food processor and return to the pan. Add the milk and season to taste. Heat through and serve garnished with chopped parsley.

Extra Spiced Curried Sweet Potato Soup

SERVES 6

Prepare as for Curried Parsnip Soup but use sweet potatoes instead of parsnips and add 1 fresh green chilli, seeded and chopped, with the stock.

Sweetcorn Chowder

SERVES 4

1 bunch of spring onions
   (scallions), finely chopped
1 large potato, diced
25 g/1 oz/2 tbsp low-fat spread
30 ml/2 tbsp plain (all-purpose)
   flour
300 ml/½ pt/1¼ cups chicken or
   vegetable stock, made with
   1 stock cube
300 ml/½ pt/1¼ cups skimmed
   milk
200 g/7 oz/1 small can sweetcorn
   (corn)
Salt and freshly ground black
   pepper
50 g/2 oz/½ cup strong-flavoured
   low-fat Cheddar cheese, grated
Chopped parsley

Gently fry (sauté) the spring onions and potato in the low-fat spread in a saucepan for 5 minutes. Add the flour and cook for 1 minute, stirring. Remove from the heat and gradually blend in the stock, then add the milk and sweetcorn. Return to the heat, bring to the boil, stirring, then reduce the heat and simmer very gently for 15 minutes. Season to taste. Stir in the cheese. Ladle into warmed bowls and garnish each with a sprinkling of chopped parsley before serving.

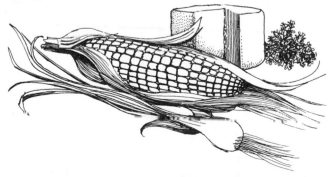

Smooth Cheese Soup

SERVES 4

1 large potato, diced
1 large carrot, diced
1 small onion, diced
1 celery stick, diced
600 ml/1 pt/2½ cups vegetable
* stock, made with 2 stock cubes*
2.5 ml/½ tsp dried mixed herbs
100 g/4 oz/1 cup low-fat Cheddar
* cheese, grated*
150 ml/¼ pt/⅔ cup skimmed milk
Snipped chives

Put the vegetables in a saucepan with the stock and herbs. Bring to the boil, reduce the heat, part-cover and simmer gently for 15 minutes until the vegetables are soft. Purée in a blender or food processor and return to the pan. Add the cheese and milk and heat until the cheese melts. Ladle into bowls and sprinkle with snipped chives before serving.

American Chowder

SERVES 6

15 g/½ oz/1 tbsp low-fat spread
1 large onion, chopped
2 lean rashers (slices) streaky
* bacon, rinded and chopped*
1 celery stick, finely chopped
1 potato, finely diced
1 large carrot, finely diced
1 small green (bell) pepper, finely
* diced*
¼ small green cabbage, finely
* shredded*
2 large tomatoes, skinned and
* chopped*
600 ml/1 pt/2½ cups vegetable
* stock, made with 2 stock cubes*
Salt and freshly ground black
* pepper*
1 bouquet garni sachet
300 ml/½ pt/1¼ cups skimmed
* milk*
30 ml/2 tbsp cornflour
* (cornstarch)*

Melt the low-fat spread in a large saucepan. Add the onion and bacon and fry (sauté) for 2 minutes, stirring. Add all the prepared vegetables and toss for 1 minute. Add the stock, a little salt and pepper and the bouquet garni sachet. Bring to the boil, reduce the heat, part-cover and simmer for 20 minutes until all the vegetables are tender, stirring from time to time. Remove the bouquet garni sachet. Blend a little of the milk with the cornflour, then stir in the remaining milk. Stir into the soup and bring to the boil, stirring. Simmer for 1 minute. Taste and re-season if necessary. Ladle into warmed soup bowls and serve.

Mediterranean Fish Soup

SERVES 6

15 ml/1 tbsp extra virgin olive oil
25 g/1 oz/2 tbsp low-fat spread
1 small onion, finely chopped
1 leek, thinly sliced
2 garlic cloves, crushed
3 ripe tomatoes, skinned and
  chopped
1 bay leaf
1 large potato, finely diced
1.2 litres/2 pts/5 cups fish stock,
  made with 2 stock cubes
15 ml/1 tbsp tomato purée (paste)
450 g/1 lb cod fillet, cut into
  chunks
15 ml/1 tbsp chopped basil
12 black olives, halved and stoned
  (pitted)
Salt and freshly ground black
  pepper
Lemon juice (optional)

Heat the oil and low-fat spread in a large saucepan. Add the onion, leek and garlic and fry gently, stirring, for 5 minutes until soft but not brown. Add the tomatoes and cook for 5 minutes. Add the bay leaf, potato, stock and tomato purée. Bring to the boil, reduce the heat and simmer gently for 15 minutes. Add the fish and continue cooking for a further 5 minutes. Stir in the basil and olives and season to taste. Spike with lemon juice, if liked, and serve ladled into warmed soup bowls.

Mushroom and Corn Chowder

SERVES 4

100 g/4 oz button mushrooms,
  sliced
1 onion, finely chopped
25 g/1 oz/2 tbsp low-fat spread
25 g/1 oz/¼ cup plain (all-purpose)
  flour
300 ml/½ pt/1¼ cups chicken or
  vegetable stock, made with
  1 stock cube
300 ml/½ pt/1¼ cups skimmed milk
320 g/12 oz/1 large can sweetcorn
  (corn)
Salt and freshly ground black
  pepper
20 ml/4 tsp low-fat single (light)
  cream
Snipped chives

Fry (sauté) the mushrooms and onion in the low-fat spread, stirring, for 3 minutes. Add the flour and cook, stirring, for 1 minute. Remove from the heat and gradually blend in the stock, then the milk and sweetcorn. Return to the heat, bring to the boil, reduce the heat and simmer gently for 10 minutes, stirring occasionally. Season to taste. Ladle into warmed bowls and garnish each with a swirl of cream and a sprinkling of snipped chives.

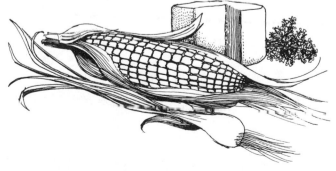

Crab Bisque

SERVES 6

1 onion, finely chopped
15 g/½ oz/1 tbsp low-fat spread
45 g/1¾ oz/1 small can dressed
   crab
45 ml/3 tbsp plain (all-purpose)
   flour
900 ml/1½ pts/3¾ cups fish stock,
   made with 2 stock cubes
5 ml/1 tsp celery salt
30 ml/2 tbsp dry sherry
150 ml/¼ pt/⅔ cup skimmed milk
150 ml/¼ pt/⅔ cup low-fat single
   (light) cream
170 g/6 oz/1 small can white
   crabmeat
Cress

Fry (sauté) the onion in the low-fat spread for 2 minutes, stirring. Stir in the dressed crab and the flour and cook for 1 minute, stirring. Remove from the heat and blend in the stock and celery salt. Return to the heat, bring to the boil, stirring all the time, then reduce the heat, part-cover and simmer gently for 15 minutes. Stir in the remaining ingredients except the cress, reheat but do not boil. Serve ladled into soup bowls and garnish with cress.

Peasant Pottage

SERVES 6

2 onions, finely chopped
2 carrots, finely chopped
1 small red (bell) pepper, finely
   chopped
25 g/1 oz/2 tbsp low-fat spread
100 g/4 oz French (green) beans,
   cut into quarters
2 tomatoes, skinned and chopped
¼ green cabbage, finely shredded
400 g/14 oz/1 large can chick peas
   (garbanzos), drained
1 litre/1¾ pts/4¼ cups vegetable
   stock, made with 2 stock cubes
Salt and freshly ground black
   pepper
1 bay leaf
45 ml/3 tbsp grated low-fat
   Cheddar cheese

Fry (sauté) the onions, carrots and pepper in the low-fat spread for 2 minutes, stirring. Add all the remaining ingredients except the cheese, bring to the boil, reduce the heat, part-cover and simmer gently for 30 minutes. Remove the bay leaf. Taste and re-season if necessary. Ladle into warmed bowls and sprinkle a little of the Cheddar cheese over each serving.

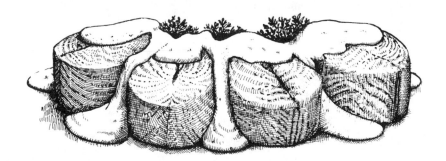

Greek Egg and Lemon Soup

SERVES 6

1.2 litres/2 pts/5 cups lamb stock, made with 2 stock cubes
50 g/2 oz/¼ cup long-grain rice
1 lemon
2 eggs
Salt and freshly ground black pepper

Put the stock in a saucepan and bring to the boil. Add the rice and simmer for 10 minutes or until the rice is tender. Thinly pare the rind from the lemon and cut into thin strips. Plunge the rind in boiling water and leave to stand for 5 minutes. Drain and reserve for garnish. Squeeze the juice from the lemon into a bowl. Add the eggs and whisk thoroughly. Add 2 ladlefuls of the hot stock to the eggs and whisk again. Remove the soup from the heat. Stir in the egg mixture and season with salt and pepper. Do not reheat. Ladle into warmed bowls and garnish each with a few strips of lemon rind.

Rich Kidney Soup

SERVES 4

225 g/8 oz lambs' kidneys, finely chopped
1 small onion, finely chopped
25 g/1 oz/2 tbsp low-fat spread
25 g/1 oz/¼ cup plain (all-purpose) flour
750 ml/1¼ pts/3 cups lamb stock, made with 2 stock cubes
1 small bay leaf
Salt and freshly ground black pepper
30 ml/2 tbsp port
Chopped parsley

Fry (sauté) the kidneys and onion in the low-fat spread for 1 minute, stirring over a fairly gentle heat so the kidney does not toughen. Add the flour and cook for 1 minute. Remove from the heat and blend in the stock. Add the bay leaf and a little salt and pepper. Return to the heat and bring to the boil, stirring, until thickened. Reduce the heat, part-cover and simmer gently for 30 minutes. Remove the bay leaf. Purée in a blender or food processor, if liked, and return to the saucepan. Stir in the port. Taste and re-season if necessary. Ladle into warmed bowls and serve, garnished with chopped parsley.

Spinach and Broad Bean Bonanza

SERVES 6

1 onion, sliced and separated into
    rings
25 g/1 oz/2 tbsp low-fat spread
1 bunch of spring onions
    (scallions), chopped
450 g/1 lb spinach
175 g/6 oz/1½ cups shelled broad
    (lima) beans
1.5 ml/¼ tsp grated nutmeg
600 ml/1 pt/2½ cups vegetable
    stock, made with 2 stock cubes
Salt and freshly ground pepper
300 ml/½ pt/1¼ cups skimmed
    milk

Fry (sauté) the onion rings in the
low-fat spread in a large saucepan
until a rich golden brown. Remove
from the pan with a draining spoon
and drain on kitchen paper. Reserve
for garnish. Add the spring onions to
the pan and fry for 2 minutes, stirring.
Wash the spinach thoroughly and discard any tough stalks. Tear the leaves
into pieces and add to the pan. Cook
until the spinach begins to soften, stirring. Add the remaining ingredients
except the milk. Bring to the boil,
reduce the heat, part-cover and simmer gently for 20 minutes. Purée in a
blender or food processor and return
to the pan. Stir in the milk. Taste and
re-season if necessary. Ladle into
warmed bowls and garnish each with
a few onion rings.

Hearty Lentil Soup

SERVES 6

1 large potato, diced
2 carrots, sliced
1 large onion, chopped
2 celery sticks, chopped
25 g/1 oz/2 tbsp low-fat spread
100 g/4 oz/⅔ cup split red lentils
1 litre/1¾ pts/4¼ cups ham stock,
    made with 2 stock cubes
1 bouquet garni sachet
10 ml/2 tsp curry powder
Salt and freshly ground black
    pepper
150 ml/¼ pt/⅔ cup skimmed milk
A few grains of artificial sweetener
    (optional)
Chopped coriander (cilantro)
    leaves

Fry (sauté) the potato, carrots, onion
and celery in the low-fat spread in
a large saucepan for 2 minutes, stirring. Add the remaining ingredients
except the milk, sweetener and coriander leaves. Bring to the boil, reduce
the heat, part-cover and simmer for
35–40 minutes or until the lentils and
vegetables are completely soft. Discard the bouquet garni. Purée the soup
in a blender or food processor and
return to the pan. Stir in the milk.
Taste and re-season if necessary,
adding a few grains of sweetener, if
liked. Ladle into warmed bowls and
serve garnished with chopped coriander.

Vichyssoise

SERVES 6

750 g/1½ lb leeks, sliced
1 large potato, chopped
25 g/1 oz/2 tbsp low-fat spread
600 ml/1 pt/2½ cups vegetable
    stock, made with 1 stock cube
150 ml/¼ pt/⅔ cup dry white wine
Salt and freshly ground black
    pepper
30 ml/2 tbsp chopped parsley
450 ml/¾ pt/2 cups skimmed milk
30 ml/2 tbsp low-fat double
    (heavy) cream
Snipped chives

Fry (sauté) the leeks and potato in the low-fat spread in a large saucepan for 2 minutes, stirring. Add the stock, wine, a little salt and pepper and the parsley. Bring to the boil, reduce the heat, part-cover and simmer gently for 20 minutes. Purée in a blender or food processor. Return to the pan. Stir in the milk, taste and re-season if necessary. Reheat but do not boil, or cool, then chill. Serve in soup bowls, garnished with 5 ml/1 tsp cream swirled on top of each and a sprinkling of snipped chives.

Almost Scotch Broth

SERVES 4

1 onion, finely chopped
2 carrots, finely chopped
1 turnip, finely chopped
1 potato, finely chopped
25 g/1 oz/2 tbsp low-fat spread
900 ml/1½ pts/3¾ cups lamb stock,
    made with 2 stock cubes
50 g/2 oz/generous ¼ cup pearl
    barley
Salt and freshly ground black
    pepper
5 ml/1 tsp dried thyme
Chopped parsley

Fry (sauté) the prepared vegetables in the low-fat spread for 2 minutes, stirring. Add the stock, barley, a little salt and pepper and the thyme. Bring to the boil, reduce the heat, part-cover and simmer gently for 1 hour or until the barley is tender. Taste and re-season if necessary. Ladle into warmed bowls and serve garnished with chopped parsley.

Pea and Ham Soup in a Hurry

SERVES 4

1.2 litres/2 pts/5 cups ham stock,
    made with 2 stock cubes
225 g/8 oz/2 cups frozen peas
50 g/2 oz/½ cup cooked ham,
    chopped
60 ml/4 tbsp skimmed milk
Salt and freshly ground black pepper
A good pinch of grated nutmeg

Simmer the peas in the stock in a saucepan for 3 minutes. Purée in a blender or food processor and return to the pan. Add the chopped ham and milk and heat through. Season to taste with salt, pepper and nutmeg and serve hot.

Chicken, Mushroom and Noodle Soup

SERVES 6

900 ml/1½ pts/4¼ cups chicken stock, made with 2 stock cubes
1 bay leaf
1 leek, thinly sliced
1 small skinless chicken breast, about 100 g/4 oz
100 g/4 oz button mushrooms, sliced
50 g/2 oz vermicelli, broken into small pieces
150 ml/¼ pt/⅔ cup dry white wine
Salt and freshly ground black pepper
15 ml/1 tbsp chopped parsley

Place the stock in a saucepan with the bay leaf, leek and chicken breast. Bring to the boil, reduce the heat, part-cover and simmer gently for 10 minutes until the chicken is really tender. Lift out of the pan with a draining spoon and cut into small pieces. Add the mushrooms and pasta to the pan with the wine. Bring to the boil and simmer for 6 minutes until the pasta is tender. Return the chicken to the pan. Discard the bay leaf and season to taste with salt and pepper. Ladle into warmed soup bowls and sprinkle with chopped parsley before serving.

Oriental Noodle Soup

SERVES 6

1.75 litres/3 pts/7½ cups beef stock, made with 3 stock cubes
5 ml/1 tsp finely chopped lemon grass
10 ml/2 tsp soy sauce
175 g/6 oz vermicelli, broken into small pieces

Bring the stock to the boil with the lemon grass and soy sauce. Add the vermicelli and simmer for 6 minutes until the noodles are tender. Taste and re-season if necessary.

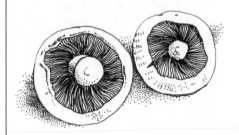

Creamy Carrot and Coriander Soup

SERVES 6

25 g/1 oz/2 tbsp low-fat spread
1 bunch of spring onions
(scallions), finely chopped
1 large potato, diced
450 g/1 lb carrots, diced
10 ml/2 tsp ground coriander
(cilantro)
900 ml/1½ pts/4¼ cups vegetable
stock, made with 2 stock cubes
20 ml/4 tsp chopped coriander
leaves
150 ml/¼ pt/⅔ cup skimmed milk
150 ml/¼ pt/⅔ cup soured (dairy
sour) cream
Salt and freshly ground black
pepper
6 coriander leaves

Melt the low-fat spread in a large saucepan. Add the prepared vegetables and ground coriander and fry (sauté), stirring for 3 minutes. Add the stock, bring to the boil, reduce the heat, part-cover and simmer for 20 minutes or until the vegetables are tender. Purée in a blender or food processor with the chopped coriander. Return to the pan and stir in the milk and cream. Season to taste and re-heat. Ladle into warmed bowls and garnish each with a coriander leaf.

Convenient Salmon and Prawn Bisque

SERVES 6

300 g/11 oz/1 small can creamed-
style sweetcorn (corn)
450 ml/¾ pt/2 cups chicken stock,
made with 1 stock cube
150 ml/¼ pt/⅔ cup skimmed milk
200 g/7 oz/1 small can pink
salmon, drained, skin and
bones removed
50 g/2 oz/½ cup peeled prawns
(shrimp)
15 ml/1 tbsp brandy
30 ml/2 tbsp low-fat double
(heavy) cream
Salt and freshly ground black
pepper
30 ml/2 tbsp chopped parsley

Mix together all the ingredients except half the parsley in a saucepan. Heat gently, stirring occasionally, until piping hot. Ladle into warmed bowls and sprinkle with the remaining parsley.

STARTERS

CALORIES OR LESS

Simple Dolmas

SERVES 6

6 large outer cabbage leaves
175 g/6 oz/1½ cups frozen diced
  mixed vegetables
2.5 ml/½ tsp dried oregano
Salt and freshly ground black
  pepper
1 egg, beaten
250 ml/8 fl oz/1 cup passata
  (sieved tomatoes)
60 ml/4 tbsp grated low-fat
  Cheddar cheese

Cut out any thick central stalk from the leaves. Blanch in boiling water for 5 minutes. Drain and rinse with cold water. Meanwhile, cook the vegetables according to the packet directions. Drain and mix with the oregano, a little salt and pepper and the beaten egg. Lay the cabbage leaves on a board and divide the vegetable mixture between them. Fold in the two sides and roll up to form parcels. Place rolled sides down in a single layer in an ovenproof dish. Spoon the passata over, sprinkle with the cheese and bake in a preheated oven at 190ºC/375ºF/gas mark 5 for 15–20 minutes until tender and the cheese has melted and is turning golden. Serve on warmed plates.

Poor Man's Caviare

SERVES 6

3 aubergines (eggplants)
½ small onion, finely chopped
1 garlic clove, crushed
3 tomatoes, skinned and chopped
60 ml/4 tbsp olive oil
Lemon juice
Salt and freshly ground black
  pepper
18 breadsticks

Grill (broil) the aubergines, turning occasionally, until the skin is blackened and the insides feel soft when squeezed. Cool slightly, then cut open and scoop out the flesh. Chop finely and place in a bowl. Add the onion, garlic and tomatoes and mix well. Beat in the oil a little at a time, then add lemon juice and seasoning to taste. Spoon into six individual serving dishes and serve with three crisp breadsticks each to dip in.

Greek Stuffed Aubergine

SERVES 6

3 aubergines (eggplants)
40 g/1½ oz/3 tbsp long-grain rice
175 g/6 oz/1½ cups minced
  (ground) lamb
1 onion, finely chopped
1 garlic clove, crushed
30 ml/2 tbsp tomato purée (paste)
5 ml/1 tsp ground cinnamon
90 ml/6 tbsp water
2.5 ml/½ tsp dried oregano
Salt and freshly ground black
  pepper
40 g/1½ oz/⅓ cup low-fat Cheddar
  cheese, grated

Halve the aubergines lengthways. Boil in a large flameproof casserole (Dutch oven) in lightly salted water until just tender. Drain, rinse with cold water and drain again. Using a spoon, carefully scoop out the flesh, leaving a wall about 5 mm/¼ in thick. Chop the scooped-out flesh. Cook the rice in boiling salted water until tender. Drain. Dry-fry (sauté) the minced lamb in a saucepan until the fat runs. Pour off the fat. Add the onion and continue frying for 2–3 minutes until all the grains of meat are separate and the onion is soft. Add the chopped aubergine, rice and the remaining ingredients except the cheese, seasoning to taste with salt and pepper. Return the aubergine shells to the casserole in a single layer. Spoon the filling into the shells. Sprinkle the cheese on top. Add enough boiling water to come half-way up the aubergine shells. Cover and simmer gently for 15 minutes. Transfer to warmed plates and serve.

Avocado Cream

SERVES 4

15 ml/1 tbsp powdered gelatine
45 ml/3 tbsp cold water
150 ml/¼ pt/⅔ cup vegetable stock,
  made with ½ stock cube
1 large ripe avocado
10 ml/2 tsp lemon juice
60 ml/4 tbsp low-calorie
  mayonnaise
A dash of Worcestershire sauce
A dash of Tabasco sauce
30 ml/2 tbsp snipped chives
5 cm/2 in piece cucumber, very
  thinly sliced

Mix the gelatine with the cold water in a small bowl and leave to soften for a few minutes. Stand the bowl in a pan of gently simmering water and stir until the gelatine completely dissolves (or place in the microwave briefly). Stir into the stock and leave to cool. Halve the avocado, remove the stone (pit) and scoop the flesh into a bowl. Mash well with the lemon juice. Beat in the mayonnaise and flavour to taste with the Worcestershire and Tabasco sauces. Stir in the chives. Stir the cool but not set stock into the avocado mixture. Divide between four individual small dishes and chill until set. Cover the top of each with overlapping slices of cucumber and serve cold.

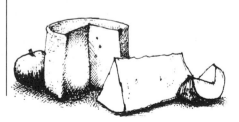

Asparagus with Sun-dried Tomato Hollandaise

SERVES 4

750 g/1½ lb asparagus
2 egg yolks
30 ml/2 tbsp lemon juice
Salt and freshly ground black pepper
5 ml/1 tsp paprika
100 g/4 oz/½ cup low-fat spread
2 sun-dried tomatoes, finely chopped
30 ml/2 tbsp chopped parsley

Trim off about 5 cm/2 in from the base of the asparagus stems. Tie the spears in a bundle. Stand the bundle in a saucepan of salted water. Cover with a lid or foil. Bring to the boil, reduce the heat and cook over a moderate heat for 10 minutes. Turn off the heat and leave undisturbed for 5 minutes. Meanwhile, put the egg yolks and lemon juice in a small bowl over a pan of hot water. Add a little salt and pepper and the paprika. Whisk gently until the sauce starts to thicken. Whisk in the low-fat spread a little at a time, whisking until thick and creamy. Stir in the sun-dried tomatoes and parsley. Lay the asparagus on warmed plates and spoon the sauce over, just below the tips.

Asparagus with Watercress Hollandaise

SERVES 4

Prepare as for Asparagus with Sun-dried Tomato Hollandaise but substitute 1 bunch of watercress, finely chopped, for the sun-dried tomatoes and omit the paprika.

Spinach Mousse with Prawns

SERVES 6

A few drops of sunflower oil
450 g/1 lb spinach
25 g/1 oz/2 tbsp low-fat spread
1 onion, finely chopped
15 ml/1 tbsp powdered gelatine
15 ml/1 tbsp Worcestershire sauce
Salt and freshly ground black pepper
300 ml/½ pt/1¼ cups low-fat whipping cream
175 g/6 oz/1½ cups peeled prawns (shrimp)
1 lemon, cut into 6 wedges

Very lightly oil a 1.5 litre/2½ pt/6 cup ring mould. Wash the spinach well, discard any tough stalks and tear the leaves into pieces. Melt the low-fat spread in a large saucepan. Add the onion and cook gently for 2 minutes. Add the spinach. Cover and cook gently for 10 minutes, stirring occasionally. Tilt the pan to allow the juices to run out. Stir the gelatine into the juices until dissolved. Purée in a blender or food processor and flavour with the Worcestershire sauce and a little salt and pepper. Whip the cream until peaking. Fold in the purée with a metal spoon. Turn into the prepared mould and chill until set. Turn out on to a serving dish and fill the centre with the prawns. Garnish with lemon wedges and serve.

Artichoke and Prawn Cocktail

SERVES 6

2 x 425 g/2 x 15 oz/2 large cans
   artichoke hearts, drained and
   quartered
225 g/8 oz/2 cups peeled prawns
   (shrimp)
45 ml/3 tbsp olive oil
30 ml/2 tbsp lemon juice
Salt and freshly ground black
   pepper
150 ml/¼ pt/⅔ cup soured (dairy
   sour) cream
50 g/2 oz/1 small jar Danish
   lumpfish roe
6 whole unpeeled prawns

Put the artichokes in a bowl and add
the peeled prawns. Drizzle the oil
and lemon juice over and season with
a little salt and lots of pepper. Toss
gently and chill until ready to serve.
Just before serving, spoon into six
wine goblets. Top each with a spoonful
of soured cream, then lumpfish roe.
Hang a whole unpeeled prawn over
the side of each glass and serve.

Scandinavian Starter

SERVES 6

350 g/12 oz new potatoes, scrubbed
90 ml/6 tbsp very low-fat plain
   yoghurt
45 ml/3 tbsp low-calorie
   mayonnaise
5 ml/1 tsp dried dill (dill weed)
4 roll-mop herrings, sliced
Salt and freshly ground black
   pepper
6 crisp lettuce leaves
1 small onion, sliced and
   separated into rings
15 ml/1 tbsp chopped parsley

Cut the potatoes into bite-sized
pieces. Boil in lightly salted water
until just tender. Drain and place in a
bowl. While still warm, add the yoghurt
and mayonnaise and toss gently. Add
the dill, herrings and a little salt and
pepper and mix together gently. Put the
lettuce leaves on six serving plates.
Spoon the potato and fish mixture on
top. Garnish each with a few onion
rings and a sprinkling of chopped parsley and serve at room temperature.

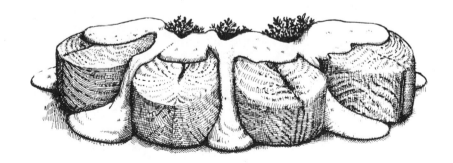

Crab and Cucumber Savoury

SERVES 6

1 large cucumber, diced
40 g/1½ oz/3 tbsp low-fat spread
225 g/8 oz button mushrooms,
  sliced
10 ml/2 tsp plain (all-purpose) flour
150 ml/¼ pt/⅔ cup fish stock, made
  with ½ stock cube
15 ml/1 tbsp dry sherry
90 ml/6 tbsp low-fat single (light)
  cream
170 g/6 oz/1 small can white
  crabmeat
Salt and freshly ground black
  pepper
Cress

Boil the cucumber in lightly salted water for 3 minutes. Drain. In the same pan, melt the low-fat spread and cook the mushrooms, stirring, for 2 minutes. Add the cucumber, cover and cook over a gentle heat for 2 minutes. Stir in the flour, remove from the heat and blend in the stock, sherry and cream. Return to the heat, bring to the boil and cook for 2 minutes, stirring. Add the crabmeat and season to taste. Heat through. Spoon into six individual serving dishes and garnish each with a little cress.

Seafood Cocktail

SERVES 6

350 g/12 oz/3 cups frozen seafood
  cocktail, thawed
Lettuce, shredded
90 ml/6 tbsp low-calorie
  mayonnaise
60 ml/4 tbsp very low-fat plain
  yoghurt
45 ml/3 tbsp tomato ketchup
  (catsup)
15 ml/1 tbsp Worcestershire sauce
10 ml/2 tsp horseradish sauce
A few drops of Tabasco sauce
Freshly ground black pepper
Lemon juice
Cayenne
6 cucumber slices
6 lemon slices

Drain and dry the seafood cocktail on kitchen paper. Put some shredded lettuce in six individual glass dishes and divide the seafood between them. Mix the mayonnaise with the yoghurt, ketchup, Worcestershire and horseradish sauces. Add a few drops of Tabasco, some pepper and lemon juice to taste. Spoon over the seafood. Dust with cayenne. Make a slit from the centre to the edge of each cucumber and lemon slice. Push one of each on the rim of each dish. Chill until ready to serve.

Jellied Eggs and Bacon

SERVES 4

4 eggs
4 lean streaky bacon rashers
(slices), rinded
295 g/10½ oz/1 small can
condensed beef consommé,
chilled
Chopped parsley

Put the eggs in a pan of cold water. Bring to the boil and cook for 4 minutes for a soft yolk and firm white. Plunge immediately into cold water to prevent further cooking. Meanwhile, grill (broil) the bacon until really crisp and brown. Cut into bite-sized pieces. Carefully shell the cold eggs and place in four ramekin dishes (custard cups). Sprinkle the bacon over. Spoon the jellied consommé on top and sprinkle with chopped parsley. Chill again until ready to serve.

Carrot and Orange Pâté

SERVES 6

15 ml/1 tbsp walnut oil
1 onion, chopped
450 g/1 lb carrots, thinly sliced
30 ml/2 tbsp clear honey
200 ml/7 fl oz/scant 1 cup very
low-fat plain yoghurt
Salt and freshly ground black
pepper
Grated rind and juice of 1 orange
6 large iceberg lettuce leaves
2 oranges, segmented
6 walnut halves

Heat the oil in a large saucepan and fry (sauté) the onion for 2 minutes, stirring. Add the carrots and toss for 1 minute. Add the honey and just enough water to cover the carrots. Bring to the boil, cover and cook gently for about 8 minutes or until the carrots are really tender. Drain and mash thoroughly with a potato masher. Leave to cool. When cold, mix with the yoghurt. Stir in a little salt and pepper, the orange rind and enough orange juice to flavour without the mixture becoming too wet. Taste and re-season if necessary. Spoon the mixture on to lettuce leaves and garnish with orange segments and a walnut half on each.

Watercress Roulade

SERVES 6

1 bunch of watercress
1 onion, finely chopped
15 g/½ oz/1 tbsp low-fat spread
4 ripe tomatoes, chopped
15 ml/1 tbsp tomato purée (paste)
A few grains of artificial sweetener
Salt and freshly ground black
    pepper
30 ml/2 tbsp snipped chives
45 ml/3 tbsp grated Parmesan
    cheese
4 eggs, separated
2 cherry tomatoes, quartered

Reserve one watercress sprig for garnish and finely chop the remainder. Dampen an 18 x 28 cm/ 7 x 11 in Swiss roll tin (jelly roll pan) and line with non-stick baking parchment so it comes about 5 cm/2 in above the rim all round. Fry (sauté) the onion in the low-fat spread for 2 minutes to soften. Add the chopped tomato, cover and cook gently for 5 minutes until pulpy. Stir in the tomato purée, sweeten slightly with just a few grains of artificial sweetener and season to taste. Keep warm. Meanwhile, put the chopped watercress, chives, 30 ml/2 tsp of the Parmesan and a little salt and pepper in a bowl. Add the egg yolks and beat well. Whisk the egg whites until stiff and fold in with a metal spoon. Turn into the prepared tin and level the surface. Bake in a preheated oven at 200°C/400°F/gas mark 6 for 10 minutes or until golden and just firm to the touch. Lay a clean sheet of baking parchment on the work surface. Dust with the remaining Parmesan. Turn the roulade out on to the cheese-covered paper. Carefully remove the baking paper with the help of a palette knife. Spread with the warm tomato filling. Roll up using the clean paper as a guide. Transfer to a warmed dish, garnish with the reserved watercress and the cherry tomato wedges and serve cut into slices.

Quail's Eggs in Nests

SERVES 6

15 ml/1 tbsp chicken Bovril
300 ml/½ pt/1¼ cups boiling water
10 ml/2 tsp powdered gelatine
10 ml/2 tsp brandy (optional)
6 quail's eggs
100 g/4 oz smooth liver sausage
50 g/2 oz/¼ cup very low-fat soft
    cheese
15 ml/1 tbsp chopped parsley
Freshly ground black pepper
12 green olives, stoned (pitted)
12 black olives, stoned (pitted)
Small parsley sprigs

Dissolve the chicken Bovril in the boiling water and stir in the gelatine until completely dissolved. Add the brandy, if using, and leave to cool. Put the eggs in a pan of cold water. Bring to the boil and boil for 4 minutes. Drain and plunge immediately into cold water. Remove the shells. Meanwhile, beat the liver sausage with the cheese and parsley and season with pepper. Divide between six ramekin dishes (custard cups) and spread over the bases and sides to form 'nests'. Put a cooked quail's egg in the centre of each, surrounded by two green and two black olives. When the chicken mixture is the consistency of egg white, spoon into the ramekins. Chill until set. Garnish each with a small parsley sprig before serving.

Sweet and Sour Tofu Salad

SERVES 6

250 g/9 oz/1 block firm tofu
For the marinade:
30 ml/2 tbsp sunflower oil
150 ml/¼ pt/⅔ cup soy sauce
30 ml/2 tbsp red wine vinegar
A good pinch of artificial sweetener granules
1.5 ml/¼ tsp English made mustard
15 ml/1 tbsp grated fresh root ginger
2 garlic cloves, crushed
30 ml/2 tbsp tomato juice
To serve:
175 g/6 oz bean sprouts
1 red (bell) pepper, cut into thin strips
2 spring onions (scallions), chopped

Cut the tofu into cubes and place in a shallow dish. Mix together the marinade ingredients and pour over the tofu. Cover and chill for 24 hours, turning occasionally. When ready to serve, mix the bean sprouts with the red pepper and shape into nests on six serving plates. Pile the marinated tofu in the centre, drizzle any remaining marinade over and sprinkle with chopped spring onion.

Cheese and Pineapple Mould

SERVES 6

A few drops of sunflower oil
1 packet sugar-free lemon jelly (jello)
228 g/8 oz/1 small can pineapple pieces in natural juice, drained, reserving the juice
3 spring onions (scallions), finely chopped
225 g/8 oz/1 cup very low-fat cottage cheese
Salt and freshly ground black pepper
6 large lettuce leaves
6 thin slices ham

Very lightly oil six individual moulds or ramekin dishes (custard cups). Make up the jelly using the pineapple juice and water. Spoon about 5 mm/¼ in in the base of each mould and chill until set. Arrange the pineapple pieces and chopped spring onion attractively on top of the jelly. Mix the cottage cheese with the remaining jelly, season to taste and spoon into the moulds. Chill until set. When ready to serve, lay the lettuce leaves on six serving plates and top each with a thin slice of ham. Loosen the edges of the moulds, stand very briefly in hot water, then turn out on to the ham.

Tonnatina

SERVES 6

4 hard-boiled (hard-cooked) eggs, sliced
4 tomatoes, sliced
85 g/3½ oz/1 small can tuna in brine, drained
Juice of ½ lemon
75 ml/5 tbsp low-calorie mayonnaise
75 ml/5 tbsp very low-fat plain yoghurt
Freshly ground black pepper
6 anchovy fillets
A few basil leaves

Arrange the egg and tomato slices attractively on six small serving plates. Blend together the remaining ingredients except the anchovies and basil, seasoning to taste with pepper. Chop three of the anchovy fillets and add to the tuna mixture. Spoon over the centre of the egg and tomato. Halve the remaining anchovies and halve again widthways. Lay two crossways on the tuna mayonnaise and garnish each portion with a few basil leaves scattered over.

Baked Mozzarella with Tomatoes

SERVES 6

6 beefsteak tomatoes, sliced
100 g/4 oz/1 cup Mozzarella cheese, grated
6 black olives, stoned (pitted) and sliced
12 basil leaves, torn
Freshly ground black pepper
15 ml/1 tbsp extra virgin olive oil
A squeeze of lemon juice
2 slices bread, diced
Garlic salt

Lay the tomato slices overlapping in six individual shallow ovenproof dishes. Sprinkle the cheese, olives and basil over. Add a good grinding of pepper and a few drops of olive oil to each, then a small squeeze of lemon juice. Place the diced bread on a baking sheet and sprinkle with garlic salt. Place the bread on the top shelf of the oven and the tomato dishes on the next shelf. Bake in a preheated oven at 200°C/400°F/gas mark 6 for about 8–10 minutes or until the bread is crisp and golden and the cheese has just melted. Remove from the oven. Sprinkle the croûtons over the cheese and tomato and serve.

Turkish Rice-stuffed Tomatoes

SERVES 4

8 tomatoes
1 small onion, finely chopped
25 g/1 oz/2 tbsp low-fat spread
50 g/2 oz/¼ cup brown rice
150 ml/¼ pt/⅔ cup chicken or vegetable stock, made with ½ stock cube
10 ml/2 tsp chopped mint
15 ml/1 tbsp pine nuts, chopped
25 g/1 oz/⅙ cup currants
Salt and freshly ground black pepper
Mint sprigs

Cut a slice off the rounded end of each tomato and scoop out the seeds in to a bowl. Reserve the slices for 'lids'. Fry (sauté) the onion in half the low-fat spread for 2 minutes until soft but not brown. Stir in the rice and stock and simmer gently for 30 minutes. Add the chopped mint, pine nuts, currants and seasoning, cover and cook gently for a further 15 minutes. taste and re-season if necessary. Stir in the tomato pulp. Spoon into the tomato shells and stand in a shallow baking tin (pan) containing 1 cm/½ in water. Dot the tomatoes with the remaining low-fat spread and replace the lids. Bake in a preheated oven at 190°C/ 375°F/gas mark 5 for 20 minutes until the tomatoes are just tender. Carefully transfer to warmed serving plates and garnish each with a mint sprig.

Normandy Tomatoes

SERVES 8

1 green eating (dessert) apple
Lemon juice
8 large beefsteak tomatoes, halved
225 g/8 oz/2 cups Camembert cheese, chopped
50 g/2 oz/1 cup fresh breadcrumbs
5 ml/1 tsp Kirsch or calvados
A little chopped parsley
Watercress

Core and halve the apple and toss in lemon juice. Scoop the seeds out of the tomatoes. Place the shells in a large shallow flameproof dish. Mix the cheese with the breadcrumbs, Kirsch or calvados and parsley. Spoon into the shells. Place under a moderate grill (broiler) until the cheese melts and bubbles and the tomatoes are hot through. Reduce the heat to low if necessary so the tops do not become too brown. Transfer to warmed plates and garnish with watercress and the apple slices.

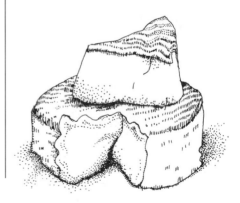

West Country Chicory

SERVES 6

3 heads chicory (Belgian endive)
6 slices low-fat processed cheese
6 thin slices lean ham (from a
    packet)
15 g/½ oz/1 tbsp low-fat spread
1 small cooking (tart) apple, sliced
300 ml/½ pt/1¼ cups medium-
    sweet cider
15 ml/1 tbsp cornflour (cornstarch)
Salt and freshly ground black
    pepper
Chopped parsley

Cut a cone-shaped core out of the base of each chicory head, then halve lengthways. Wrap each in a slice of cheese, then a slice of ham. Lightly grease a large, shallow flameproof dish with the low-fat spread. Spread the apple over. Lay the wrapped chicory in a single layer on top. Pour over the cider. Cover with foil or a lid and bake in a preheated oven at 180°C/350°F/gas mark 4 for about 30 minutes or until the chicory and apples are tender. Carefully transfer the chicory to warmed serving plates. Blend the cornflour with a little water and stir into the cider and apples. Bring to the boil and cook, stirring, for 1 minute until thickened and clear. Season to taste. Spoon over the chicory and serve garnished with chopped parsley.

Mushrooms Moldovia

SERVES 4

450 g/1 lb button mushrooms
300 ml/½ pt/1¼ cups vegetable
    stock, made with 1 stock cube
60 ml/4 tbsp white wine vinegar
1 garlic clove, crushed
15 ml/1 tbsp chopped mint
A few grains of artificial sweetener
45 ml/3 tbsp very low-fat plain
    yoghurt
2 spring onions (scallions),
    chopped
1 green chilli, seeded and chopped
Salt and freshly ground black
    pepper
4 slices wholegrain bread

Put the mushrooms in a saucepan with the stock. Bring to the boil, reduce the heat, cover and simmer for 10 minutes. Turn out into a bowl. Put 60 ml/4 tbsp of the mushroom cooking liquid back into the saucepan with the vinegar, garlic, mint and sweetener. Bring to the boil. Drain any remaining liquid from the mushrooms, then return them to the pan and cook, stirring occasionally, for 10 minutes. Boil rapidly, if necessary, to evaporate any remaining liquid. Leave until cold. Stir in the yoghurt, half the spring onions and the chilli. Season to taste. Spoon into small dishes and sprinkle with the remaining spring onions. Toast the bread on both sides. Cut into triangles and arrange around the edges of the dishes just before serving.

Potted Stilton with Pears

SERVES 8

100 g/4 oz/1 cup ripe Stilton,
  crumbled
75 g/3 oz/⅓ cup low-fat spread
1.5 ml/¼ tsp ground mace
1.5 ml/¼ tsp English made
  mustard
30 ml/2 tbsp port
4 ripe pears
Lemon juice
Watercress sprigs
16 rye crispbreads

Mash the cheese with the low-fat spread in a bowl. Work in the mace, mustard and port. Pack into a small pot and chill. Core and slice the unpeeled pears and toss in lemon juice. Arrange the pear slices attractively on serving plates and add a spoonful of the potted Stilton to one side. Garnish with watercress and serve each with two rye crispbreads.

Baked Stuffed Beetroot

SERVES 6

6 large cooked beetroot (red beets)
20 g/¾ oz/1½ tbsp low-fat spread
100 g/4 oz button mushrooms,
  chopped
20 g/¾ oz/3 tbsp plain (all-
  purpose) flour
200 ml/7 fl oz/scant 1 cup
  skimmed milk
5 ml/1 tsp lemon juice
75 g/3 oz/¾ cup Emmental (Swiss)
  cheese, grated
Salt and freshly ground black
  pepper
30 ml/2 tbsp chopped parsley
90 ml/6 tbsp water
10 ml/2 tsp caraway seeds

Peel the beetroot if necessary and trim the roots. Cut a slice off the top of each. Using a metal spoon, scoop out the flesh leaving a 1 cm/½ in thick wall of beetroot. (Use the remainder for Bortsch, see page 46, or a salad). Stand the beetroot shells in a baking dish. Melt the low-fat spread in a saucepan, add the mushrooms and cook gently, stirring, for 2 minutes. Blend in the flour. Remove from the heat and gradually stir in the milk. Return to the heat and bring to the boil, stirring, until thickened. Simmer for 2 minutes. Stir in the lemon juice and half the cheese and season to taste. Stir in the parsley. Spoon into the beetroot and sprinkle with the remaining cheese. Pour the water around the beetroot and bake in a pre-heated oven at 200°C/400°F/gas mark 6 for about 30 minutes until the cheese is bubbling and golden. Transfer to warmed serving plates and sprinkle with the caraway seeds before serving.

Light Lunches or Suppers

Serve any of these with as much green salad as you want, dressed, if liked, with lemon juice, herbs and pepper or any of the virtually calorie-free dressings on pages 334–6. If you crave salad cream, use just 5 ml/1 tsp of low-calorie dressing.

CALORIES OR LESS

Red Flannel Hash

SERVES 4

1 onion, finely chopped
25 g/1 oz/2 tbsp low-fat spread
350 g/12 oz/1½ cups mashed
    cooked potato
2 cooked beetroot (red beets),
    finely diced
225 g/8 oz corned beef, mashed
30 ml/2 tbsp skimmed milk
Salt and freshly ground black
    pepper
Worcestershire sauce
30 ml/2 tbsp chopped parsley

Fry (sauté) the onion in half the low-fat spread in a frying pan (skillet) until soft and golden. Remove from the pan with a draining spoon and place in a bowl. Work in the potato, beetroot and corned beef. Mix in the milk, a little salt and pepper, Worcestershire sauce to taste and most of the parsley. Heat the remaining low-fat spread in the frying pan. Add the hash and press down well. Cook over a fairly high heat for about 15 minutes until hot through and a rich golden brown underneath. Turn out on to a warmed serving dish and garnish with the remaining parsley.

Bacon-stuffed Onions

SERVES 4

4 large onions, peeled but left whole
50 g/2 oz/1 cup fresh white
    breadcrumbs
100 g/4 oz lean bacon, finely
    chopped
45 ml/3 tbsp low-fat single (light)
    cream
5 ml/1 tsp chopped sage
Salt and freshly ground black pepper
20 ml/4 tsp low-fat spread
4 sage sprigs

Boil the onions in lightly salted water for 30 minutes. Drain, reserving the cooking water. Rinse in cold water. Cut a slice off the top of each onion and scoop out the centres leaving a wall about 1 cm/½ in thick. Chop the scooped-out onion and place in a bowl. Add the breadcrumbs and bacon and mix with the cream. Season with the sage, salt and pepper. Pack into the onion shells and stand the onions in a shallow baking tin (pan). Dot with the low-fat spread. Pour in enough of the onion water to come about 1 cm/½ in up the sides of the pan. Bake in a preheated oven at 190°C/375°F/gas mark 5 for about 40 minutes until tender and golden. Spoon the cooking liquid over the onions once or twice during cooking. Garnish each with a small sage sprig before serving.

Cauliflower Provençale

SERVES 4

1 large cauliflower, cut into florets
1 onion, chopped
1 garlic clove, crushed
1 small green (bell) pepper, sliced
1 red (bell) pepper, sliced
15 g/½ oz/1 tbsp low-fat spread
400 g/14 oz/1 large can tomatoes
2.5 ml/½ tsp dried oregano
15 ml/1 tbsp tomato purée (paste)
100 g/4 oz/1 cup lean cooked ham, diced
Salt and freshly ground black pepper
A little chopped parsley
4 black olives

Cook the cauliflower in boiling, lightly salted water for about 6 minutes or until just tender. Drain. Meanwhile, fry (sauté) the onion, garlic and peppers in the low-fat spread for 2 minutes, stirring. Add the can of tomatoes and break up with a wooden spoon. Add the oregano and tomato purée, bring to the boil and boil rapidly for 5 minutes until reduced and pulpy. Add the ham and season to taste. Spoon the cauliflower into individual warmed bowls and spoon the sauce over. Serve hot, garnished with parsley and an olive.

Courgette Provençale

SERVES 4

Prepare as for Cauliflower Provençale but substitute 450 g/1 lb courgettes (zucchini), sliced, for the cauliflower.

Aubergine Provençale

SERVES 4

Prepare as for Cauliflower Provençale but substitute 2 large aubergines (eggplants), sliced, for the cauliflower.

German Beans with Pears

SERVES 4

4 cooking pears, cored and thickly sliced
450 ml/¾ pt/2 cups vegetable stock, made with 1 stock cube
Thickly pared rind of ½ lime
450 g/1 lb French (green) beans, cut into short lengths
4 very lean rashers (slices) streaky bacon, rinded and diced
2.5 ml/½ tsp artificial sweetener granules
15 ml/1 tbsp cider vinegar
Salt and freshly ground black pepper
2.5 ml/½ tsp dried tarragon

Cook the pears in the stock with the lime rind for 10 minutes. Add the beans to the pan and continue cooking for 5 minutes. Meanwhile, dry-fry (sauté) the bacon in a large frying pan (skillet) until crisp and golden. Remove from the pan with a draining spoon and drain on kitchen paper. Add the artificial sweetener and vinegar to the pears and beans with a little salt and pepper and the tarragon. Boil rapidly until well reduced and syrupy. Spoon on to warmed plates and sprinkle with the bacon before serving.

Sweetcorn, Cheese and Herb-stuffed Onions

SERVES 4

4 large onions
200 g/7 oz/1 small can sweetcorn
(corn)
50 g/2 oz/1 cup fresh white
breadcrumbs
50 g/2 oz/½ cup strong low-fat
Cheddar cheese, grated
30 ml/2 tbsp snipped chives
15 ml/1 tbsp chopped parsley
Salt and freshly ground black
pepper
15 ml/1 tbsp skimmed milk
20 ml/4 tsp low-fat spread
Parsley

Cook the onions in boiling, lightly salted water for 30 minutes. Drain, reserving the cooking water. Rinse with cold water. Cut a slice off the top of each onion and scoop out the centres leaving a wall about 1 cm/½ in thick. Chop the scooped-out onion finely and place in a bowl with the contents of the can of corn, the breadcrumbs, cheese, herbs and a little salt and pepper. Moisten with the milk. Pack into the onion shells and stand the onions in a shallow baking dish. Pour in enough of the onion cooking water to come 1 cm/½ in up the sides of the pan. Dot with the low-fat spread. Bake in a preheated oven at 190°C/375°F/gas mark 5 for about 40 minutes or until tender and golden. Spoon a little of the cooking water over the onions occasionally during cooking. Garnish with parsley and serve hot.

Cauliflower Cheese

SERVES 4

1 cauliflower, cut into florets
15 g/½ oz/2 tbsp cornflour
(cornstarch)
300 ml/½ pt/1¼ cups skimmed
milk
A small knob of low-fat spread
Salt and white pepper
75 g/3 oz/¾ cup low-fat Cheddar
cheese, grated
5 ml/1 tsp English made mustard
A pinch of cayenne
30 ml/2 tbsp cornflakes, crushed

Cook the cauliflower in boiling salted water for about 10 minutes until just tender. Drain and place in a flameproof dish. Meanwhile, blend the cornflour with a little of the milk in a saucepan. Add the remaining milk and the low-fat spread. Bring to the boil and cook for 1 minute, stirring all the time. Season to taste and stir in 50 g/ 2 oz/½ cup of the cheese, the mustard and cayenne. Pour over the cauliflower and sprinkle with the cornflakes and remaining cheese. Flash under a hot grill (broiler) until browning and bubbling.

Cauliflower and Tomato Cheese

SERVES 4

Prepare as for Cauliflower Cheese but spoon a 228 g/8 oz/1 small can chopped tomatoes over the cooked cauliflower before adding the cheese sauce, then continue as before.

Broccoli Cheese

SERVES 4

Prepare as for Cauliflower Cheese (see page 87) but substitute 450 g/ 1 lb broccoli for the cauliflower

Broccoli and Ham Cheese

SERVES 4

Prepare as for Broccoli Cheese (see above) but add 50 g/2 oz/½ cup shredded cooked ham to the cooked broccoli before pouring over the cheese sauce.

Rigatoni with Tomato and Basil Sauce

SERVES 4

175 g/6 oz rigatoni
300 ml/½ pt/1¼ cups passata (sieved tomatoes)
Salt and freshly ground black pepper
15 ml/1 tbsp chopped basil
40 ml/8 tsp grated Parmesan cheese

Cook the rigatoni according to the packet directions. Drain and return to the pan. Add the passata, a little salt, lots of pepper and the basil. Heat through, stirring gently. Pile on to plates and sprinkle each with 10 ml/ 2 tsp of the cheese.

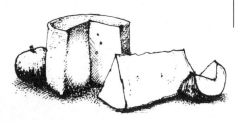

Creamy Cucumber with Crab

SERVES 4

100 g/4 oz/½ cup long-grain rice
50 g/2 oz/½ cup frozen peas
1 large cucumber, diced
40 g/1½ oz/3 tbsp low-fat spread
175 g/6 oz button mushrooms, sliced
10 ml/2 tsp plain (all-purpose) flour
150 ml/¼ pt/⅔ cup vegetable stock, made with ½ stock cube
15 ml/1 tbsp dry sherry
90 ml/6 tbsp low-fat single (light) cream
100 g/4 oz/½ cup white crabmeat
Salt and freshly ground black pepper

Cook the rice in boiling, lightly salted water until tender, adding the peas after 5 minutes. Drain, rinse with boiling water and drain again. Meanwhile, cook the cucumber in lightly salted water for 3 minutes. Drain, rinse with cold water and drain again. Melt the low-fat spread in the cucumber pan, add the mushrooms and cook, stirring, for 2 minutes. Add the cucumber, cover with a lid and cook gently for 2 minutes. Blend in the flour, then gradually stir in the stock, sherry and cream. Bring to the boil, stirring. Add the crab and heat through. Season to taste. Spoon the rice and peas into 'nests' on four warmed plates and spoon the crab mixture in the centres. Serve straight away.

Smoked Haddock and Poached Egg

SERVES 2

**2 smoked haddock fillets, about
175 g/6 oz each
2 eggs
Freshly ground black pepper
Chopped parsley**

L ay the fish in a frying pan (skillet) and cover with water. Cover with a lid, bring to the boil and cook for about 6 minutes or until the fish flakes easily with a fork. Carefully lift out with a fish slice, transfer to warmed plates and keep warm. Break the eggs into a cup and slide into the fish poaching water one at a time. Simmer gently for 3–5 minutes or until cooked to your liking. Carefully lift out with a fish slice and lay on top of the smoked haddock. Sprinkle with freshly ground black pepper and chopped parsley and serve.

Mushroom Omelette

SERVES 1

**50 g/2 oz button mushrooms,
sliced
45 ml/3 tbsp water
2 eggs
Salt and freshly ground black
pepper
5 ml/1 tsp low-fat spread
15 ml/1 tbsp chopped parsley**

C ook the mushrooms in 30 ml/ 2 tbsp of the water until tender, then boil rapidly to evaporate the liquid. Beat the eggs with the remaining water and a little salt and pepper. Melt the low-fat spread in a small omelette pan. Add the egg mixture and cook, lifting and stirring, until the base is golden brown and the egg mixture is nearly set. Spoon the mushrooms over half the omelette and season lightly. Fold the omelette over the filling with the help of a fish slice or palette knife. Slide on to a warmed plate and sprinkle with the chopped parsley.

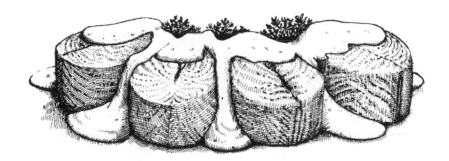

Prawn Omelette

SERVES 1

2 eggs
15 ml/1 tbsp water
Salt and freshly ground black
    pepper
5 ml/1 tsp low-fat spread
25 g/1 oz/¼ cup peeled prawns
    (shrimp)
15 ml/1 tbsp chopped parsley
Worcestershire sauce

Beat the eggs with the water and a little salt and pepper. Melt the low-fat spread in a small omelette pan. Add the eggs and cook, lifting and stirring gently, until the base is golden and the egg mixture is almost set. Scatter the prawns and parsley over half the omelette and heat through for a few minutes. Sprinkle with Worcestershire sauce. Fold the omelette over the filling. Slide on to a warmed plate and serve.

Spinach Omelette

SERVES 1

225 g/8 oz spinach
2 eggs
Salt and freshly ground black
    pepper
A pinch of grated nutmeg
5 ml/1 tsp low-fat spread

Wash the spinach well and discard any thick stalks. Tear the leaves into pieces and place in a saucepan with no added water. Cover and cook for 5 minutes, shaking the pan occasionally until the spinach is cooked. Chop well with scissors. Beat the eggs with a little salt and pepper. Stir in the chopped spinach and any juices. Season lightly and add the nutmeg. Melt the low-fat spread in a small omelette pan. Add the egg mixture and cook gently, lifting and stirring, until the omelette is golden underneath and the egg mixture just set. Fold the omelette in half and continue cooking for a few minutes. Slide on to a warmed plate and serve.

Ham and Tomato Omelette

SERVES 1

2 eggs
15 ml/1 tbsp water
Salt and freshly ground black
    pepper
5 ml/1 tsp low-fat spread
1 thin slice ham (from a packet),
    chopped
1 tomato, finely chopped
A pinch of dried mixed herbs
A parsley sprig

Beat the eggs with the water and a little salt and pepper. Melt the low-fat spread in a small omelette pan. Add the egg mixture and cook, lifting and stirring gently, until the base is golden and the egg is almost set. Scatter the ham and tomato over half the omelette and sprinkle with the herbs. Cook gently for a further 2 minutes. Fold the omelette over the filling. Slide on to a warmed plate and serve garnished with a parsley sprig.

Oven Omelette Wedges

SERVES 4

5 ml/1 tsp low-fat spread
4 eggs, beaten
250 g/9 oz/generous 1 cup very
    low-fat cottage cheese
150 ml/¼ pt/⅔ cup skimmed milk
Salt and freshly ground black
    pepper
100 g/4 oz button mushrooms,
    sliced
1 onion, finely chopped
A pinch of dried mixed herbs
2 tomatoes, sliced
Parsley sprigs

Lightly grease a shallow baking dish with the low-fat spread. Mix together all the remaining ingredients except the tomatoes and parsley in a bowl and pour into the dish. Bake in a preheated oven at 200°C/400°F/ gas mark 6 for 20 minutes until golden brown and firm to the touch. Serve cut into wedges, garnished with tomato slices and parsley sprigs.

Baked Eggs in Tomatoes

SERVES 4

4 beefsteak tomatoes
Salt and freshly ground black
  pepper
1 spring onion (scallion), very
  finely chopped
4 eggs
20 ml/4 tsp low-fat double (heavy)
  cream
20 ml/4 tsp grated Parmesan
  cheese
4 thin slices bread
Low-fat spread
Yeast extract

Cut a slice off the top of each tomato on the rounded side. Scoop out the seeds. Sprinkle with salt on the insides, turn upside-down and drain for 30 minutes on kitchen paper. Transfer to individual, shallow oven-proof dishes. Season the insides with pepper and add the chopped spring onion. Carefully break an egg into each tomato. Spoon over the cream and season again. Sprinkle each with 5 ml/1 tsp Parmesan. Bake in a pre-heated oven at 180°C/350°F/gas mark 4 for 15–20 minutes until just set. Meanwhile, toast the bread and spread very thinly with low-fat spread and yeast extract. Cut into fingers. Arrange beside the tomatoes and serve.

Flippin' Hot Dogs

SERVES 4

4 chipolata sausages
1 onion, thinly sliced
10 ml/2 tsp low-fat spread
4 slices bread
60 ml/4 tbsp tomato ketchup
  (catsup)
A few drops of Tabasco sauce

Grill (broil) the sausages until golden brown and cooked through. Meanwhile, fry (sauté) the onion in the low-fat spread until golden and soft, stirring. Cut the crusts off the bread. Mix the tomato ketchup with Tabasco sauce to taste. Spread on the bread. Top with the onions, then place a sausage on each slice. Roll up and secure with cocktail sticks (toothpicks). Return to the grill (broiler) and cook, turning occasionally, until the bread is golden. Serve straight away.

Tropical Club Sandwich

SERVES 2

3 slices white bread, toasted
10 ml/2 tsp low-fat spread
10 ml/2 tsp low-fat cheese spread
1 thin slice lean ham (from a
  packet)
1 tomato, sliced
Lettuce leaves
1 pineapple ring
4 stuffed olives

Spread two of the toast slices with low-fat spread. Spread the third with the cheese spread. Put one 'buttered' slice on a board. Top with the ham and tomato slices. Top with the cheese-spread toast, then the lettuce and pineapple. Top with the last piece of toast, 'buttered' side down. Press down and cut into four triangles. Push a cocktail stick (toothpick) with an olive on it through each triangle and serve two each.

Cottage Club Sandwich

SERVES 2

3 slices wholemeal bread, toasted
15 ml/1 tbsp low-fat spread
Crisp lettuce leaves
30 ml/2 tbsp very low-fat cottage
cheese with chives
1 thin slice lean roast beef
5 ml/1 tsp horseradish sauce
Thin onion rings
4 cherry tomatoes

Spread the toast thinly with the low-fat spread. Place one slice on a board. Top with lettuce leaves and the cottage cheese. Top with a second slice of toast, then the beef. Spread it with the horseradish. Top with onion rings, then the final slice of toast, spread side down. Cut into four triangles. Spear a cherry tomato on each of four cocktail sticks (toothpicks) and press through each triangle. Serve two each.

Corn on the Cob with Cream Cheese and Herbs

SERVES 4

4 corn on the cob
50 g/2 oz/¼ cup very low-fat soft
cheese
30 ml/2 tbsp skimmed milk
10 ml/2 tsp chopped sage
15 ml/1 tbsp chopped parsley
Salt and freshly ground black pepper

Prepare and cook the corn cobs as for Corn on the Cob with 'Herb Butter'. Meanwhile, put the cheese, milk and herbs in a saucepan and heat gently, stirring, until blended and piping hot. Do not boil. Season to taste. Drain the cobs and place on warmed plates. Insert corn-cob holders if you have them. Spoon the cheese mixture over the cobs and serve.

Corn on the Cob with Herb 'Butter'

SERVES 4

4 corn on the cob
Salt and freshly ground black
pepper
50 g/2 oz/¼ cup low-fat spread
15 ml/1 tbsp chopped parsley
15 ml/1 tbsp snipped chives
A pinch of cayenne
A squeeze of lemon juice

Strip the leaves and silks from the cobs. Put the cobs in boiling, lightly salted water and boil for 15–20 minutes or until a kernel of corn pulls away easily. Meanwhile, melt the low-fat spread with the parsley, chives, lots of black pepper, the cayenne and lemon juice. Drain the cobs and place on warmed serving plates. Insert corn-cob holders if you have them. Drizzle the herb 'butter' over the corn cobs and serve.

Cheesy Corn Cobs

SERVES 4

4 corn on the cob
45 ml/3 tbsp low-fat cheese spread
15 ml/1 tbsp skimmed milk
Paprika

Cook the corn cobs as for Corn on the Cob with Herb 'Butter'. Meanwhile, melt the cheese spread with the milk until well blended. Drain the cobs and place on warmed plates. Insert corn-cob holders if you have them. Spoon the cheese mixture over the corn, dust with paprika and serve.

Pizza Corn Cobs

SERVES 4

4 corn on the cob
45 ml/3 tbsp low-fat cheese spread
15 ml/1 tbsp skimmed milk
2 tomatoes, chopped
2.5 ml/½ tsp dried oregano

Cook the corn as for Corn on the Cob with Herb 'Butter' (see page 93). Meanwhile, heat together the cheese spread and milk. Stir in the tomatoes and oregano and heat through. Drain the cobs and place on warmed serving plates. Insert corn-cob holders if you have them. Spoon the cheese mixture over the corn cobs and serve.

Savoury Eggy Rice

SERVES 4

1 packet savoury vegetable rice
4 eggs

Empty the packet of rice into a large frying pan (skillet). Add water according to the packet directions. Bring to the boil, cover with a lid and cook for 15 minutes. Remove the lid and make four 'wells' in the rice mixture. Break an egg into each. Re-cover and cook for a further 5 minutes or until the eggs are cooked to your liking. Serve straight from the pan.

Hot Ploughman's Lunch

SERVES 1

1 slice bread
5 ml/1 tsp low-fat spread
2 pickled onions, sliced OR
**   15 ml/1 tbsp sweet pickle**
25 g/1 oz/2 tbsp low-fat Cheddar
**   cheese, grated**
Tomato wedges

Toast the bread on both sides. Spread with low-fat spread, then top with pickled onion slices or spread with pickle. Cover with the grated cheese and grill (broil) until melted and bubbling. Serve straight away, garnished with tomato wedges.

Pizza Slice

SERVES 1

1 slice bread
5 ml/1 tsp low-fat spread
1 tomato, sliced
1.5 ml/¼ tsp dried oregano
25 g/1 oz/2 tbsp low-fat Cheddar
**   or Mozzarella cheese, grated**

Toast the bread on both sides. Spread with the low-fat spread. Top with tomato slices and sprinkle with the oregano. Cover with the grated cheese and grill (broil) until melted and bubbling. Serve straight away.

Mega Open Sandwiches

Pastrami with Horseradish Spread: mash 10 ml/2 tsp low-fat spread with 5 ml/1 tsp horseradish sauce. Spread on a slice of rye bread, then cut in half. Top each with a slice of pastrami. Top the pastrami with sliced radishes and a sprinkling of cress.

Pork and Apple Bounty: spread a slice of wholemeal bread with a scraping of low-fat spread. Top with a slice of roast leg of pork, lean only. Cut in half. Top with slices of eating (dessert) apple, dipped in lemon juice. Mix 10 ml/2 tsp low-calorie mayonnaise with two chopped sage leaves. Put a dollop on top of each open sandwich and garnish with a small fresh sage sprig.

Salami and Spinach Special: mash 50 g/2 oz thawed frozen chopped spinach with 15 ml/1 tbsp very low-fat soft cheese. Season with nutmeg. Spread on a slice of pumpernickel. Cut in half. Top each half with two thin slices of German salami, halved and shaped into cornets. Garnish with flat leaf parsley.

Egg and Cress Crisp: cut the crusts off a slice of bread and cut in half. Toast both halves until crisp and golden on both sides. Leave to cool. Spread with a scraping of low-fat spread. Chop a hard-boiled (hard-cooked) egg and mix with 10 ml/2 tsp low-calorie mayonnaise, a pinch of cayenne and a good grinding of black pepper. Season to taste with salt. Spread over the two toast slices. Top with a line of cress and strips of red (bell) pepper.

Liver Sausage Lovely: mash 10 ml/2 tsp low-fat spread with 15 ml/1 tbsp sweet pickle. Spread on a slice of bread, crusts removed. Cut in half. Top each with two thin slices of liver sausage, halved and arranged overlapping on the bread. Top each with a cucumber twist.

Cottage Cheese Corny: cut a slice of wholemeal bread in half and toast both pieces until crisp. Leave until cold. Spread very thinly with low-fat spread. Mix 100 g/4 oz/½ cup very low-fat cottage cheese with 15 ml/1 tbsp corn relish. Pile on the toast and garnish each with halved cherry tomatoes and a sprinkling of snipped chives.

Cheese and Pineapple Pleasure: spread a slice of bread thinly with low-fat spread. Cut in half. Top each with a thin slice of low-fat red Leicester cheese, then a canned pineapple slice in natural juice. Put half a cherry tomato in the centre of the pineapple ring and tuck a slice of cucumber under the ring on each side.

Berlin Beauty: spread a slice of pumpernickel very thinly with low-fat spread, then German mustard. Top with a thin slice of Emmental (Swiss) cheese, then a spoonful of drained sauerkraut. Sprinkle with caraway seeds.

Oriental Bean Sprouts with Prawns: spread a slice of bloomer bread thinly with very low-fat soft cheese. Mix a handful of bean sprouts, 15 ml/1 tbsp peeled prawns (shrimp) and a small piece of chopped cucumber with a few drops of soy sauce and lemon juice. Pile on the bread and add a good grinding of black pepper.

Cheese and Walnut Whopper: mix 15 ml/1 tbsp very low-fat soft cheese with 10 ml/2 tsp chopped walnuts. Spread on a slice of wholemeal bread and cut in half. Grate a chunk of cucumber and squeeze out the excess moisture. Add a dash of vinegar and toss with some freshly ground black pepper. Pile on the nutty cheese and garnish each with a walnut half.

Ham and Salad Pitta Pockets

SERVES 4

4 pitta breads
4 slices ham (from a packet)
60 ml/4 tbsp shredded lettuce
8 cucumber slices
2 tomatoes, sliced
40 ml/8 tsp low-calorie salad
*   cream*
A few coriander (cilantro) leaves
*   (optional)*

Warm the pittas under the grill (broiler) or in the microwave briefly to puff them up. Split along one edge to form a pocket. Fill each with a slice of ham, then add the lettuce, cucumber slices, tomato slices and salad cream. Finish with a few coriander leaves, if liked, for added flavour

Smooth Cheese and Salad Pitta Pockets

SERVES 4

Prepare as for Ham and Salad Pitta Pockets but substitute 15 ml/1 tbsp very low-fat cheese spread for the ham.

Photograph opposite:
Fruity Breakfast Muffins (page 20)

Spicy Potato Cakes

SERVES 2

225 g/8 oz potatoes, grated
1 small onion, grated
2.5 ml/½ tsp garam masala
1.5 ml/¼ tsp chilli powder
1 egg, beaten
5 ml/1 tsp plain (all-purpose)
flour
Salt and freshly ground black
pepper
25 g/1 oz/2 tbsp low-fat spread
Salad and curried fruit chutney, to
serve

Mix together all the ingredients except the low-fat spread in a bowl. Melt the low-fat spread in a frying pan (skillet) and fry (sauté) tablespoonfuls of the mixture until golden brown underneath. Turn over and cook the other sides. Drain on kitchen paper and serve hot with salad and curried fruit chutney.

Soufflé Toasts

SERVES 2

2 slices wholemeal bread
10 ml/2 tsp low-fat spread
Yeast extract
2 tomatoes, sliced
1 egg, separated
2.5 ml/½ tsp English made
mustard
25 g/1 oz/2 tbsp low-fat Cheddar
cheese, grated
Salt and freshly ground black
pepper

Toast the bread lightly on both sides. Place on a baking sheet and spread with the low-fat spread, then yeast extract to taste. Top with the tomato slices. Beat the egg yolk with the mustard and cheese and a little seasoning. Whisk the egg white until stiff and fold into the cheese mixture with a metal spoon. Season to taste. Pile on top of the tomatoes and bake in a preheated oven at 190°C/375°F/gas mark 5 for 10–15 minutes until puffy, golden and set. Serve straight away.

Photograph opposite:
Chinese Prawn Salad (page 59)

········ LIGHT LUNCHES OR SUPPERS ··········

CALORIES OR LESS

Tuna and Sweetcorn Pitta Pockets

SERVES 4

4 pitta breads
85 g/3½ oz/1 small can tuna in
  brine, drained
200 g/7 oz/1 small can sweetcorn
  (corn), drained
30 ml/2 tbsp low-calorie
  mayonnaise
15 ml/1 tbsp snipped chives
Freshly ground black pepper
Shredded lettuce (optional)

Warm the pittas under the grill (broiler) or in the microwave briefly to puff them up. Split along one edge to form a pocket. Mix the tuna with the sweetcorn, mayonnaise and chives and season to taste with pepper. Spoon into the pitta pockets and add shredded lettuce, if liked.

Liver Sausage and Coleslaw Pitta Pockets

SERVES 2

2 pitta breads
4 slices liver sausage
30 ml/2 tbsp low-calorie coleslaw
  (ready-made)
1 spring onion (scallion), finely
  chopped
4 slices beetroot (red beet)

Warm the pitta breads under the grill (broiler) or in the microwave briefly to puff them up. Split along one edge to form a pocket. Fill each pitta with half the liver sausage, coleslaw, spring onion and beetroot slices and serve straight away.

Leek and Apple Pockets

SERVES 2

2 leeks, sliced
150 ml/¼ pt/⅔ cup vegetable stock,
  made with ½ stock cube
1 large eating (dessert) apple,
  chopped
30 ml/2 tbsp shredded lettuce
½ small red (bell) pepper, chopped
60 ml/4 tbsp very low-fat cottage
  cheese
Salt and freshly ground black
  pepper
2 pitta breads

Cook the leeks in the stock until tender. Drain (reserve the stock to add to soup). Leave to cool. When cold, mix with the apple, lettuce, pepper, cheese and seasoning to taste. Grill (broil) or microwave the pitta breads briefly to puff them up. Make a slit along one edge to form a pocket. Fill with the leek and cheese mixture and serve straight away.

American-style Fish Fingers

SERVES 1

2 fish fingers
1 gherkin (cornichon), finely chopped
5 ml/1 tsp chopped parsley
10 ml/2 tsp low-calorie mayonnaise
1 small soft bap, halved
Shredded lettuce
1 slice low-fat processed cheese

Grill the fish fingers according to the packet directions. Mix the gherkin and parsley into the mayonnaise. Spread on the bottom half of the bap. Top with shredded lettuce, then the fish fingers, then the slice of cheese. Flash under a hot grill (broiler) to melt the cheese. Top with the second half of the bap.

Pan Haggerty

SERVES 4

25 g/1 oz/2 tbsp low-fat spread
450 g/1 lb potatoes, thinly sliced
2 onions, thinly sliced
100 g/4 oz/1 cup low-fat Cheddar cheese, grated
Salt and freshly ground black pepper
Lettuce and tomato slices, to serve

Melt the low-fat spread in a frying pan (skillet). Add a layer of half the potatoes and onions, then half the cheese. Season well. Repeat the layers. Cover the pan with foil or a lid and cook over a gentle heat for about 30 minutes or until the potatoes and onions are tender. Uncover and place the pan under a hot grill (broiler) until the cheese is golden and bubbling. Serve cut into wedges on a bed of lettuce, surrounded by tomato slices.

Speedy Cassoulet

SERVES 4

4 chipolata sausages, cut into chunks
2 lean rashers (slices) streaky bacon, rinded and diced
425 g/15 oz/1 large can red kidney beans, drained
400 g/14 oz/1 large can no-added-sugar baked beans
400 g/14 oz/1 large can chopped tomatoes
Worcestershire sauce
Salt and freshly ground black pepper
Chopped parsley

Dry-fry (sauté) the sausages and bacon in a saucepan until well browned and crisp. Remove from the pan with a fish slice and drain thoroughly on kitchen paper. Wipe out the pan with kitchen paper to remove the fat. Add all the remaining ingredients, seasoning to taste with Worcestershire sauce, salt and pepper. Heat through, stirring. Add the sausages and bacon and heat through for a further minute. Spoon into bowls and sprinkle with parsley before serving.

Country Rarebit

SERVES 1

**75 g/3 oz/¾ cup low-fat Cheddar
cheese, grated
2.5 ml/½ tsp English made mustard
15 ml/1 tbsp beer or cider
1 slice toast
A parsley sprig**

Put the cheese, mustard and beer or cider in a small pan and heat gently, stirring, until melted and smooth. Spoon on to the toast and garnish with a parsley sprig before serving.

Yokel Country Rarebit

SERVES 1

Prepare as for Country Rarebit but top the toast with very thinly sliced onion rings before adding the hot cheese topping.

Buck Rarebit

SERVES 2

**15 g/½ oz/1 tbsp low-fat spread
100 g/4 oz/1 cup low-fat red
Leicester cheese, grated
A pinch of salt
A pinch of cayenne
30 ml/2 tbsp milk
Worcestershire sauce
5 ml/1 tsp lemon juice
2 eggs
2 slices toast**

Put the low-fat spread in a saucepan with the cheese, salt, cayenne, milk and a few drops of Worcestershire sauce. Heat gently until melted, stirring occasionally. Meanwhile, bring a frying pan (skillet) of water to the boil with the lemon juice. Break the eggs into a cup, then carefully slide into the water and cook gently for 3–5 minutes until set. Put the toast on two warmed serving plates. Spoon the cheese mixture over and top with a poached egg.

Curried Beans on Toast

SERVES 2

**2 slices bread
10 ml/2 tsp low-fat spread
400 g/14 oz/1 large can no-added-
sugar baked beans
30 ml/2 tbsp sultanas (golden
raisins)
5–10 ml/1–2 tsp curry paste
Chopped coriander (cilantro)**

Toast the bread on both sides and spread with low-fat spread. Meanwhile, heat the beans in a saucepan with the sultanas and curry paste, stirring gently. Spoon on to the bread and serve, sprinkled with a little chopped coriander.

Baked Cheese and Pineapple Open Sandwich

SERVES 4

**4 small slices bread
40 g/1½ oz/3 tbsp low-fat spread
228 g/8 oz/1 small can pineapple
rings in natural juice, drained
4 slices low-fat processed cheese
2 cherry tomatoes, halved
Snipped chives**

Spread the bread with 5 ml/1 tsp low-fat spread on each side. Place on a baking sheet. Drain the pineapple rings on kitchen paper. Lay a cheese slice on each piece of bread and top with a pineapple slice. Bake in a preheated oven at 200°C/400°F/gas mark 6 for 10 minutes, then put half a cherry tomato in the centre of each ring and return to the oven for 5 minutes. Sprinkle with snipped chives and serve straight away.

Baked Ham and Cheese Open Sandwich

SERVES 2

2 small slices bread
20 ml/4 tsp low-fat spread
2 thin slices lean ham (from a
packet)
2 spring onions (scallions), finely
chopped
2 slices low-fat processed cheese
2 tomatoes, sliced
Chopped parsley

Spread the bread with 5 ml/1 tsp low-fat spread on each side. Place on a baking sheet. Top each with a slice of ham, then sprinkle with spring onion. Top with the processed cheese. Bake in a preheated oven at 200ºC/400ºF/gas mark 6 for 10 minutes. Top with tomato slices and return to the oven for 5 minutes. Serve hot, garnished with parsley.

Croque Madame

SERVES 1

2 slices bread
10 ml/2 tsp low-fat spread
40 g/1½ oz/3 tbsp low-fat Cheddar
cheese, grated
½ small onion, thinly sliced and
separated into rings
5 ml/1 tsp chopped sage

Spread one side of each bread slice with 5 ml/1 tsp low-fat spread. Lay one slice, spread side down, on a board. Top with the cheese and onion rings. Sprinkle with the sage. Top with the second bread slice, spread side out. Fry (sauté) or grill (broil) until golden on both sides, pressing down with a fish slice during cooking. Serve cut into quarters.

Croque Monsieur

SERVES 1

2 slices bread
10 ml/2 tsp low-fat spread
25 g/1 oz/2 tbsp low-fat Cheddar
cheese, grated
1 thin slice lean ham (from a
packet)

Spread one side of each bread slice with 5 ml/1 tsp low-fat spread. Put one slice, spread side down, on a board. Top with the cheese and ham. Cover with the remaining bread slice, spread side up. Fry (sauté) or grill (broil) until golden on both sides, pressing down with a fish slice during cooking. Serve cut into quarters.

Croque Tante

SERVES 1

2 slices bread
10 ml/2 tsp low-fat spread
2 lean rashers (slices) streaky
bacon, rinded
1 small banana, mashed
A pinch of cayenne

Spread one side of each bread slice with 5 ml/1 tsp low-fat spread. Put one slice, spread side down, on a board. Grill (broil) the bacon until crisp. Spread the mashed banana on the bread and crumble the bacon on top. Sprinkle with cayenne. Top with the second bread slice, spread side up. Grill or fry (sauté) until golden on both sides, pressing down with a fish slice during cooking. Serve cut into quarters.

Sardine Pyramids

SERVES 2

2 crumpets
10 ml/2 tsp low-fat spread
120 g/4½ oz/1 small can sardines
    in tomato sauce
2.5 cm/1 in piece cucumber, finely
    chopped
Lemon juice
Freshly ground black pepper
Small lemon twists

Toast the crumpets and spread with the low-fat spread. Meanwhile, mash the sardines with their bones and mix with the cucumber and a squeeze of lemon juice. Season to taste with pepper. Pile on the crumpets and garnish each with a small lemon twist.

Tortilla

SERVES 2

1 large potato, grated
1 small onion, thinly sliced
15 g/½ oz/1 tbsp low-fat spread
4 eggs, beaten
Salt and freshly ground black
    pepper
Parsley

Put the potato and onion in a frying pan (skillet) with the low-fat spread. Fry (sauté), stirring, for 5 minutes until the potato is cooked. Beat the eggs with a little salt and pepper and add to the pan. Cook gently, lifting and stirring, until the egg is almost set. Place under a hot grill (broiler) to brown and set the top. Serve hot or cold, cut into wedges.

Ham and Eggs with Watercress Sauce

SERVES 2

1 bunch of watercress, chopped
15 g/½ oz/1 tbsp low-fat spread
15 g/½ oz/2 tbsp plain (all-
    purpose) flour
150 ml/¼ pt/⅔ cup skimmed milk
Salt and freshly ground black
    pepper
5 ml/1 tsp lemon juice
2 eggs
2 thin slices lean ham (from a
    packet)
2 slices toast

Put the watercress, low-fat spread, flour and milk in a saucepan. Whisk over a moderate heat until thickened and smooth. Season to taste. Simmer for 2 minutes. Meanwhile, fill a frying pan (skillet) with water and add the lemon juice. Bring to the boil. Break the eggs into a cup and carefully slide into the water and poach for 3–5 minutes until cooked to your liking. Put a slice of ham on each piece of toast on two warmed plates. Lift the eggs out of the pan with a fish slice and place on top of the ham. Spoon the hot watercress sauce over and serve straight away.

Piperade

SERVES 2

25 g/1 oz/2 tbsp low-fat spread
2 onions, sliced
1 red (bell) pepper, sliced
1 green (bell) pepper, sliced
4 large tomatoes, quartered
1 garlic clove, crushed
4 eggs, beaten
Salt and freshly ground black
pepper

Melt the low-fat spread in a large frying pan (skillet). Add the onion and peppers and fry (sauté) gently, stirring, for 3 minutes. Add the tomatoes and garlic and continue cooking for 5 minutes, stirring. Add the beaten egg and some salt and pepper and cook, stirring gently, until set. Serve straight from the pan.

Beany Spuds

SERVES 4

4 large unpeeled potatoes
400 g/14 oz/1 large can baked
beans
20 ml/4 tsp brown table sauce
50 g/2 oz/½ cup low-fat Cheddar
cheese, grated

Scrub the potatoes and prick all over with a fork. Bake in a preheated oven at 190°C/375°F/gas mark 5 for about 1 hour or until tender when squeezed. Alternatively, cook in the microwave according to the manufacturer's instructions. Meanwhile, heat the beans. Cut a cross cut in the top of each potato and squeeze the sides firmly to open. Place on four flame-proof serving plates. Spoon the beans over, drizzle with brown sauce, top with cheese and flash under a hot grill (broiler) to melt the cheese.

Tuna and Corn Rapsody

SERVES 4

4 large unpeeled potatoes
185 g/6½ oz/1 small can tuna in
brine, drained
200 g/7 oz/1 small can sweetcorn
(corn), drained
30 ml/2 tbsp skimmed milk
Salt and freshly ground black
pepper
25 g/1 oz/2 tbsp strong low-fat
Cheddar cheese, grated

Scrub the potatoes and prick all over with a fork. Bake in a preheated oven at 190°C/375°F/gas mark 5 for about 1 hour or until tender when squeezed. Alternatively, cook in the microwave according to the manufacturer's instructions. Slice the top off each potato and scoop the flesh into a bowl. Add the tuna, sweetcorn and milk and mix well. Season to taste. Pile back into the skins. Sprinkle with cheese and return to the oven for about 15 minutes until piping hot and the cheese has melted and turned golden.

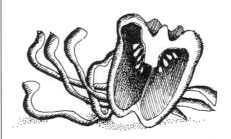

Russian Potatoes

SERVES 4

4 large unpeeled potatoes
275 g/10 oz/1 small can diced
  mixed vegetables, drained
30 ml/2 tbsp low-calorie
  mayonnaise
15 ml/1 tbsp chopped parsley
Freshly ground black pepper
5 m/1 tsp caraway seeds

Scrub the potatoes and prick all over with a fork. Bake in a preheated oven at 190°C/375°F/gas mark 5 for about 1 hour or until the potatoes feel soft when squeezed. Alternatively, cook in the microwave according to the manufacturer's instructions. Meanwhile, mix the vegetables with the mayonnaise, parsley and pepper. Cut a large cross in the top of each potato and squeeze the sides gently to open. Spoon over the vegetable salad and sprinkle with caraway seeds before serving.

Cheese and Herb Melties

SERVES 4

4 large unpeeled potatoes
100 g/4 oz/1 cup low-fat Cheddar
  cheese, grated
25 g/1 oz/2 tbsp low-fat spread
15 ml/1 tbsp chopped parsley
15 ml/1 tbsp snipped chives
10 ml/2 tsp chopped tarragon
Freshly ground black pepper

Scrub the potatoes and prick all over with a fork. Bake in a preheated oven at 190°C/375°F/gas mark 5 for about 1 hour or until the potatoes feel soft when squeezed. Alternatively, cook in the microwave according to the manufacturer's instructions. Meanwhile, mash the cheese with the low-fat spread and herbs and season with pepper. Put the potatoes on four small flameproof serving plates. Cut a cross in the top of each potato and squeeze the sides gently to open. Top with the cheese mixture and place under a hot grill (broiler) until the cheese has melted. Serve straight away.

Cheese, Sage and Onion Melties

SERVES 4

4 large unpeeled potatoes
100 g/4 oz/1 cup low-fat Cheddar
  cheese, grated
25 g/1 oz/2 tbsp low-fat spread
15 ml/1 tbsp chopped sage
½ bunch of spring onions
  (scallions), finely chopped
Freshly ground black pepper

Scrub the potatoes and prick all over with a fork. Bake in a preheated oven at 190°C/375°F/gas mark 5 for about 1 hour or until the potatoes feel soft when squeezed. Alternatively, cook in the microwave according to the manufacturer's instructions. Meanwhile, mash the cheese with the low-fat spread, sage, spring onions and some pepper. Cut a large cross in each potato and squeeze the sides gently to open. Place on four small flameproof plates. Top with the cheese mixture and place under a hot grill (broiler) until the cheese has melted. Serve straight away.

Spaghetti with Garlic and Herbs

SERVES 4

225 g/8 oz spaghetti
50 g/2 oz/¼ cup low-fat spread
1 garlic clove, crushed
15 ml/1 tbsp chopped parsley
15 ml/1 tbsp chopped basil
Salt and freshly ground black
 pepper
60 ml/4 tbsp grated Parmesan
 cheese

Cook the spaghetti according to packet directions. Drain. Melt the low-fat spread in the spaghetti saucepan. Add the garlic and herbs, a little salt and a good grinding of pepper. Return the spaghetti to the pan and toss gently until well coated. Spoon on to plates and sprinkle each portion with 15 ml/1 tbsp Parmesan cheese.

Farmhouse Spaghetti

SERVES 4

175 g/6 oz spaghetti
100 g/4 oz/1 cup strong low-fat
 Cheddar cheese, grated
25 g/1 oz/2 tbsp low-fat spread
Salt and freshly ground black
 pepper
4 tomatoes, chopped
30 ml/2 tbsp chopped parsley

Cook the spaghetti according to packet directions. Drain and return to the saucepan. Add the cheese, low-fat spread and salt and pepper and toss over a gentle heat until melted. Add the tomatoes and parsley. Toss and serve straight away.

Tagliatelle with Mushrooms, Garlic and Herbs

SERVES 4

225 g/8 oz tagliatelle
100 g/4 oz button mushrooms,
 sliced
45 ml/3 tbsp water
50 g/2 oz/¼ cup low-fat spread
1 garlic clove, crushed
15 ml/1 tbsp chopped parsley
15 ml/1 tbsp snipped chives
Salt and freshly ground black
 pepper
60 ml/4 tbsp grated Parmesan
 cheese

Cook the pasta according to the packet directions. Drain. Cook the mushrooms in the water until tender and the liquid has evaporated, stirring all the time. Add the low-fat spread and garlic and cook, stirring, for 1 minute. Add the pasta, herbs, a little salt and lots of pepper and toss together well. Pile on to plates and sprinkle each portion with 15 ml/1 tbsp Parmesan cheese.

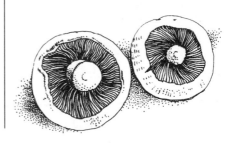

Macaroni Cheese

SERVES 4

175 g/6 oz quick-cook macaroni
20 g/¾ oz/3 tbsp plain (all-
purpose) flour
300 ml/½ pt/1¼ cups skimmed
milk
5 ml/1 tsp English made mustard
A small knob of low-fat spread
75 g/3 oz/¾ cup strong low-fat
Cheddar cheese, grated
Salt and freshly ground black
pepper
2 tomatoes, sliced

Cook the macaroni according to the packet directions. Drain. Whisk together the flour and milk in a saucepan. Add the mustard and low-fat spread and bring to the boil, whisking all the time until thickened and smooth. Stir in nearly all the cheese and season to taste. Mix in the macaroni. Turn into a flameproof dish. Sprinkle with the remaining cheese and arrange the tomato slices around the edge. Grill (broil) until golden and bubbling.

Blue Macaroni Cheese

SERVES 4

Prepare as for Macaroni Cheese but substitute low-fat blue cheese for the Cheddar.

Macaroni and Mushroom Cheese

SERVES 4

Prepare as for Macaroni Cheese but add 100 g/4 oz sliced button mushrooms, previously stewed for 3 minutes in a little water, then boiled rapidly to allow the juices to evaporate.

Macaroni and Spinach Cheese

SERVES 4

Prepare as for Macaroni Cheese but put half the macaroni in cheese sauce in the dish. Top with a layer of drained canned chopped spinach or 225 g/8 oz thawed frozen spinach and a liberal dusting of grated nutmeg. Then add the remaining macaroni cheese and continue as before.

Mighty Macaroni Cheese:

SERVES 4

Prepare as for Macaroni Cheese but add three thin slices ham, chopped, and 50 g/2 oz/½ cup thawed frozen peas to the sauce and heat through before adding the cooked macaroni, then continue as before.

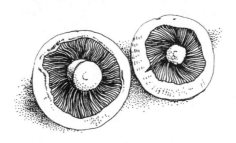

Spaghetti Carbonara Special

SERVES 4

225 g/8 oz spaghetti
4 lean rashers (slices) streaky bacon, rinded and diced
1 onion, finely chopped
1 garlic clove, crushed
2 eggs
60 ml/4 tbsp skimmed milk
Salt and freshly ground black pepper
30 ml/2 tbsp chopped parsley

Cook the spaghetti according to the packet directions. Drain and return to the pan. Meanwhile, dry-fry (sauté) the bacon until the fat runs. Add the onion and garlic and cook, stirring, for 2 minutes. Cover and cook over a gentle heat for 5 minutes until the onion is soft. Add to the cooked spaghetti. Beat together the eggs and milk and add to the pan with a little salt, lots of pepper and most of the parsley. Cook, stirring, over a gentle heat until the egg is creamy but not completely scrambled. Spoon on to serving plates. Sprinkle with the remaining parsley and serve.

Mushrooms and Tomatoes in the Hole

SERVES 4

8 button mushrooms
4 tomatoes, halved
30 ml/2 tbsp sunflower oil
100 g/4 oz/1 cup plain (all-purpose) flour
A pinch of salt
5 ml/1 tsp dried sage
2 eggs
150 ml/¼ pt/⅔ cup skimmed milk
150 ml/¼ pt/⅔ cup water

Arrange the mushrooms and tomatoes in a small roasting tin (pan). Add the oil and place in a preheated oven at 220°C/425°F/gas mark 7 for 5 minutes. Meanwhile, put the flour and salt in a bowl with the sage. Add the eggs and half the milk and water. Beat well until smooth. Stir in the remaining milk and water. Pour into the roasting tin and return to the oven for about 30 minutes until well risen, crisp and golden. Serve straight away.

Cheese Omelette

SERVES 1

2 eggs
15 ml/1 tbsp water
Salt and freshly ground black pepper
5 ml/1 tsp low-fat spread
25 g/1 oz/¼ cup low-fat Cheddar cheese, grated
A parsley sprig

Beat the eggs with the water and a little salt and pepper. Melt the low-fat spread in a small omelette pan. Add the egg mixture and cook, lifting and stirring gently, until the base is golden. Sprinkle the cheese over half the omelette and continue cooking until the mixture is just set. Fold the omelette over the cheese using a fish slice or palette knife. Slide out on to a warmed plate and garnish with parsley.

Cottage Cheese and Chive Omelette

SERVES 1

2 eggs
15 ml/1 tbsp water
Salt and freshly ground black
    pepper
5 ml/1 tsp low-fat spread
50 g/2 oz/¼ cup very low-fat
    cottage cheese with chives
A few chive stalks

Beat the eggs with the water and a little salt and pepper. Melt the low-fat spread in a small omelette pan. Add the egg mixture and cook, lifting and stirring gently, until the base is golden and the mixture is almost set. Spoon the cottage cheese over half the omelette and allow to heat through. Fold over using a fish slice or palette knife. Slide out on to a warmed plate and garnish with a few chive stalks.

Cottage Cheese and Pepper Omelette

SERVES 1

2 eggs
15 ml/1 tbsp water
Salt and freshly ground black
    pepper
5 ml/1 tsp low-fat spread
50 g/2 oz/¼ cup very low-fat
    cottage cheese with chives
½ small red (bell) pepper, finely
    chopped
Chopped parsley

Beat the eggs with the water and a little salt and pepper. Melt the low-fat spread in a small omelette pan. Add the egg mixture and cook, lifting and stirring gently, until the egg is golden underneath and almost set. Mix the cheese with nearly all the pepper, reserving a little for garnish. Spread over half the omelette and heat through for a few minutes. Fold the omelette over the filling using a fish slice or palette knife. Slide out on to a warmed plate. Scatter the remaining red pepper over with the parsley and serve.

Cheese and Asparagus Soufflé

SERVES 4

5 ml/1 tsp low-fat spread
295 g/10½ oz/1 small can cut
    asparagus, drained
295 g/10½ oz/1 small can
    condensed asparagus soup
75 g/3 oz/¾ cup Parmesan cheese,
    grated
4 eggs, separated
Freshly ground black pepper

Grease an 18 cm/7 in soufflé dish with the low-fat spread. Put the drained asparagus in the base. Empty the can of soup into a bowl. Whisk in the cheese and egg yolks. Add pepper to taste. Whisk the egg whites until stiff. Fold into the cheese mixture with a metal spoon. Turn into the dish and bake in a preheated oven at 200°C/400°F/gas mark 6 for 25–30 minutes until well risen and golden brown. Serve straight away.

Cheese and Mushroom Soufflé

SERVES 4

Prepare as for Cheese and Asparagus Soufflé but substitute a drained can of sliced mushrooms and condensed mushroom soup for the asparagus and asparagus soup.

Cheese and Celery Soufflé

SERVES 4

Prepare as for Cheese and Asparagus Soufflé but substitute a drained can of chopped celery and condensed celery soup for the asparagus and asparagus soup.

Golden Pudding

SERVES 4

15 g/½ oz/1 tbsp low-fat spread
2 eggs, separated
300 ml/½ pt/1¼ cups skimmed
* milk*
75 g/3 oz/1½ cups fresh
* breadcrumbs*
100 g/4 oz/1 cup low-fat Cheddar
* cheese, grated*
Salt and freshly ground black
* pepper*
Canned tomatoes, to serve

Grease a 1.2 litre/2 pt/5 cup ovenproof dish with the low-fat spread. Beat the egg yolks with the milk and stir in the breadcrumbs, cheese and a little salt and pepper. Whisk the egg whites until stiff and fold in with a metal spoon. Turn into the prepared dish. Bake in a preheated oven at 200°C/400°F/gas mark 6 for about 35 minutes until risen and a rich golden brown. Serve straight away with canned tomatoes.

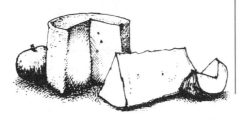

Crunchy Blue Cheese Pudding

SERVES 4

Prepare as for Golden Pudding but substitute crumbled blue cheese for the Cheddar and add 30 ml/2 tbsp finely chopped celery to the mixture before folding in the egg whites.

American-style Beefburgers

SERVES 4

350 g/12 oz/1½ cups very lean
* minced (ground) beef*
Salt and freshly ground black
* pepper*
2 small onions
2.5 ml/½ tsp chilli seasoning
4 soft round baps
4 slices dill pickle
20 ml/4 tsp tomato ketchup
* (catsup)*
10 ml/2 tsp mustard
Shredded lettuce
2 tomatoes, thinly sliced

Put the mince in a bowl and add some salt and pepper. Grate in one of the onions and mix together with the chilli seasoning. Shape into four flat cakes. Grill (broil) for 3–4 minutes on each side until golden brown and cooked through. Meanwhile, split the baps and place on four serving plates. Slice the second onion into thin rings. Put a burger on the base of each bap and top with a slice of dill pickle, 5 ml/1 tsp ketchup, 2.5 ml/½ tsp mustard, some shredded lettuce, tomato slices and onion rings. Add the top of the bap and serve straight away.

Pain Perdu

SERVES 4

4 eggs
Salt and freshly ground black
    pepper
5 ml/1 tsp clear honey
8 slices bread, crusts removed
60 ml/4 tbsp low-fat spread
100 g/4 oz strawberries, sliced
5 ml/1 tsp artificial sweetener
    granules
15 ml/1 tbsp chopped mint

Beat the eggs with a little salt, pepper and the honey. Soak the bread slices in this. Fry (sauté) the soaked bread a piece at a time in a little of the low-fat spread in a frying pan (skillet) until golden on each side. Drain on kitchen paper. Transfer to warmed serving plates. Top with the sliced strawberries. Mix the sweetener with the mint and scatter over. Serve straight away.

Mexican Egg Tacos

SERVES 2

4 taco shells
4 eggs
10 ml/2 tsp low-fat spread
15 ml/1 tbsp skimmed milk
Salt and freshly ground black
    pepper
1 red (bell) pepper, diced
1 small green chilli, seeded and
    chopped
Shredded lettuce

Warm the shells according to the packet directions. Beat the eggs in a saucepan. Add the low-fat spread and milk. Cook, stirring, over a gentle heat until lightly scrambled but still creamy. Season to taste and stir in the red pepper and chilli. Line the taco shells with shredded lettuce, add the egg mixture and serve straight away.

Naan Snackwich

SERVES 4

2 naan breads
225 g/8 oz/1 small can pease
    pudding
10 ml/2 tsp curry paste
30 ml/2 tbsp mango chutney
Lemon juice
Shredded lettuce and cucumber
Thinly sliced onion (optional)

Grill or microwave the naans according to the packet directions. Heat the pease pudding with the curry paste in a saucepan or microwave until piping hot. Spread over the breads. Spread the chutney on top and sprinkle with lemon juice. Add shredded lettuce and cucumber and onion, if liked. Fold into halves, then cut into handy-sized wedges. Serve in paper napkins.

Pear Extravaganza

SERVES 2

2 wholemeal muffins
20 ml/4 tsp low-fat spread
2 thin slices lean Parma (or similar) ham
2 ripe pears, peeled, halved and cored
6 basil leaves, shredded
50 g/2 oz/½ cup Mozzarella cheese, grated
Freshly ground black pepper
2 small basil sprigs

Halve and toast the muffins, then spread with low-fat spread. Put half a slice of Parma ham on each muffin half. Place two halves on each of two flameproof serving plates. Cut a thin slice off the rounded ends of the pears so they will stand up. Place the pears, cored sides up, on the muffin halves and put the pear slices in the core holes. Sprinkle with the torn basil leaves and top with the cheese. Add a good grinding of black pepper. Flash under a hot grill (broiler) until the cheese has melted. Serve each garnished with a small basil sprig.

Scotch Woodcock

SERVES 4

8 canned anchovy fillets
15 g/½ oz/1 tbsp low-fat spread
4 eggs
30 ml/2 tbsp skimmed milk
Freshly ground black pepper
15 ml/1 tbsp chopped parsley
2 slices bread
5 ml/1 tsp capers
4 tomatoes, sliced

Rinse the anchovy fillets under cold water and dry on kitchen paper. Melt the low-fat spread in a saucepan. Remove from the heat and whisk in the eggs, milk and a little pepper. Add the parsley. Cook over a gentle heat, stirring all the time, until scrambled but still creamy. Meanwhile, chop four of the anchovies. Toast the bread and place on two warmed plates. Stir the chopped anchovies into the scrambled egg. Spoon on top of the toast and garnish each with two anchovy fillets in a cross and a few capers. Arrange slices of tomato all round the toast and serve.

Crab and Camembert Heaven

SERVES 4

5 ml/1 tsp low-fat spread
6 slices white bread, crusts
  removed
50 g/2 oz ripe Camembert, thinly
  sliced
170 g/6 oz/1 small can crabmeat,
  drained
30 ml/2 tbsp chopped parsley
2 eggs
250 ml/8 fl oz/1 cup skimmed
  milk
Salt and freshly ground black
  pepper
Parsley sprigs

Grease a 1.2 litre/2 pt/5 cup shallow ovenproof dish with the low-fat spread. Put three of the slices of bread in the base. Cover with the cheese, then the crabmeat and sprinkle with parsley. Top with the remaining bread. Beat the eggs with a little of the milk, then whisk in the remainder. Season well. Pour over the bread and leave to soak for 30 minutes. Bake in a preheated oven at 180°C/350°F/gas mark 4 for about 30 minutes until puffy and golden brown. Serve straight away, garnished with parsley sprigs.

Jansen's Temptation

SERVES 4

50 g/2 oz/¼ cup low-fat spread,
  melted
4 potatoes, thinly sliced
2 onions, thinly sliced
50 g/2 oz/1 small can anchovies,
  drained and chopped
Freshly ground black pepper
150 ml/¼ pt/⅔ cup skimmed milk
40 g/1½ oz/¾ cup breadcrumbs
50 g/2 oz/½ cup Emmental (Swiss)
  cheese, grated
Chopped parsley

Grease a 1.2 litre/2 pt/5 cup ovenproof dish with some of the low-fat spread. Layer the potatoes, onions and anchovies in the dish, sprinkling with black pepper as you go and finishing with a layer of potatoes. Pour over the milk. Cover with foil and bake in a preheated oven at 180°C/350°F/gas mark 4 for 40 minutes. Mix the remaining low-fat spread with the breadcrumbs and cheese. Remove the foil, cover with the breadcrumb mixture and return to the oven, uncovered, for a further 30 minutes or until golden brown and the potatoes and onions are tender. Sprinkle with chopped parsley before serving.

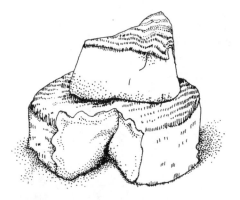

Savoury Chicken Toasts

SERVES 4

**75 g/3 oz button mushrooms,
  sliced
30 ml/2 tbsp water
30 ml/2 tbsp cornflour
  (cornstarch)
250 ml/8 fl oz/1 cup skimmed
  milk
5 ml/1 tsp low-fat spread
Salt and freshly ground black
  pepper
15 ml/1 tbsp chopped parsley
15 ml/1 tbsp chopped thyme
175 g/6 oz/1½ cups cooked chicken,
  skin removed, chopped
4 slices bread
50 g/2 oz/½ cup low-fat Cheddar
  cheese, grated
Parsley sprigs**

Stew the mushrooms in the water until tender. Boil rapidly to evaporate the liquid. Blend the cornflour with a little of the milk, stir in the remaining milk and add to the pan with the low-fat spread. Bring to the boil and cook for 2 minutes, stirring all the time until thick. Season to taste and stir in the chopped herbs and chicken. Heat through. Toast the bread on both sides under a hot grill (broiler). Spoon the chicken mixture on top and cover with the grated cheese. Return to the grill until the cheese melts and bubbles. Serve straight away, garnished with parsley sprigs.

Savoury Turkey Toasts

SERVES 4

Prepare as for Savoury Chicken Toasts but substitute turkey for the chicken and spread each slice of toast with 5 ml/1 tsp cranberry sauce before adding the topping.

Savoury Ham Toasts

SERVES 4

Prepare as for Savoury Chicken Toasts but substitute chopped cooked lean ham for the chicken and low-fat red Leicester for the Cheddar cheese.

Savoury Blue Cheese, Celery and Mushroom Toasts

SERVES 4

225 g/8 oz button mushrooms, sliced
2 celery sticks, finely chopped
300 ml/½ pt/1¼ cups vegetable stock, made with 1 stock cube
Salt and freshly ground black pepper
2.5 ml/½ tsp dried mixed herbs
15 ml/1 tbsp chopped parsley
30 ml/2 tbsp cornflour (cornstarch)
30 ml/2 tbsp skimmed milk powder (non-fat dried milk)
60 ml/4 tbsp cold water
4 slices toast
50 g/2 oz/½ cup blue cheese, crumbled
Tomato slices
Onion rings

Put the mushrooms in a pan with the celery and stock. Bring to the boil, reduce the heat and simmer gently for 10 minutes. Add salt and pepper to taste, the mixed herbs and parsley. Blend the cornflour with the milk powder and water until smooth. Stir into the pan and bring to the boil, stirring until thickened. Simmer for 2 minutes. Place the toast on four serving plates. Spoon the mushroom mixture over. Top with the blue cheese and flash under a hot grill (broiler) until melted and bubbling. Garnish with tomato slices and onion rings and serve.

Potato Gnocchi with Tomato Sauce

SERVES 4

450 g/1 lb potatoes, cut into small pieces
Salt and freshly ground black pepper
1.5 ml/¼ tsp grated nutmeg
100 g/4 oz/1 cup plain (all-purpose) flour
1 egg, beaten
10 ml/2 tsp low-fat spread, melted
300 ml/½ pt/1¼ cups passata (sieved tomatoes)
15 ml/1 tbsp chopped basil
Garlic salt
30 ml/2 tbsp grated Parmesan cheese

Boil the potatoes in lightly salted water for 10 minutes or until tender. Drain thoroughly, mash, then pass through a coarse sieve (strainer) into a bowl. Add a little salt and pepper, the nutmeg and flour. Mix well. Add the egg and mix to form a firm dough. Turn out on to a lightly floured surface and knead gently. Shape into 24 balls. Brush a shallow serving dish with a little of the low-fat spread. Bring a large pan of water to the boil. Add the gnocchi a few at a time and cook for 5 minutes. They will rise to the surface when cooked. Remove from the pan with a draining spoon and place in the dish. Keep warm while cooking the remainder. Meanwhile, heat the passata with the basil and season to taste with garlic salt and pepper. When all the gnocchi are cooked and in the dish, drizzle with the remaining low-fat spread. Pour the warmed passata over and sprinkle with Parmesan. Serve straight away.

Memorable Main Meals

You will see that the recipes for main meals have serving suggestions included in the calorie count as well. If you want to add other accompaniments (see Sumptuous Salads and Side Dishes pages 265–298), you will have to add on the extra calories. Alternatively, if you want to have plain boiled or steamed green, red or yellow vegetables or salad dressed with lemon juice and black pepper or any of the virtually calorie free dressings on pages 347–351, you'll be quids-in with your calories!

·······················POULTRY························

CALORIES OR LESS

Roast Lemon Chicken and Vegetable Platter

SERVES 6

1 oven-ready chicken, about 1.5 kg/3 lb
1 lemon
1 onion
1 garlic clove
A rosemary sprig
5 ml/1 tsp low-fat spread
Salt and freshly ground black pepper
18 small new potatoes, scrubbed
350 g/12 oz French (green) beans
450 g/1 lb carrots, sliced
½ green cabbage, shredded
Chopped parsley
1 chicken stock cube
Artificial sweetener granules (optional)

Pull off any excess fat inside the rim of the body cavity of the chicken. Wipe inside and out with kitchen paper. Place on a trivet (or an old upturned plate) in a roasting tin (pan). Squeeze the lemon, reserving the juice. Push the lemon shell inside the body cavity of the chicken with the onion, garlic and rosemary. Spread the low-fat spread over the breast, drizzle with some of the lemon juice and sprinkle with salt. Roast in a preheated oven at 190°C/375°F/gas mark 5 for 1 hour 20 minutes or until the juices run clear when a skewer is inserted in the thickest part of the thigh. Transfer to a carving dish and keep warm. Meanwhile, boil the vegetables separately until tender in lightly salted water. Drain, reserving the cooking water, arrange on a serving platter, sprinkle with chopped parsley and keep warm. Remove the trivet from the roasting tin and spoon off all fat, leaving any cooking juices. Stir in 600 ml/1 pt/2½ cups of the vegetable cooking water and the stock cube. Bring to the boil and boil until reduced by about a quarter. Add a little more lemon juice and sweeten, if liked, with a few grains of artificial sweetener. Season to taste with salt and pepper. Carve the chicken, cutting the leg joint into thigh and drumstick, cutting off the wings and carving the breast into at least six slices (preferably 12 thin ones). Discard as much skin as possible. Arrange on six warmed plates and spoon a little of the gravy over. Pour the rest into a gravy boat. Serve with the chicken and the hot vegetable platter.

Cheesy Chicken Topper

SERVES 4

4 skinless chicken fillets, about 175 g/6 oz each
20 g/¾ oz/1½ tbsp low-fat spread, melted
4 tomatoes, chopped
4 thin slices lean ham (from a packet)
75 g/3 oz/¾ cup Emmental (Swiss) or low-fat Cheddar cheese, grated
Watercress sprigs
To serve:
Mixed Leaf Salad (see page 265)

Place the chicken breasts one at a time in a plastic bag and beat with a rolling pin or meat mallet to flatten. Brush with the low-fat spread and place on a grill (broiler) rack. Grill (broil) for 3 minutes on each side. Spread the chopped tomato over, then the ham and top with the cheese. Grill until the cheese is melted and golden. Garnish with watercress and serve straight away with a Mixed Leaf Salad.

Chinese-style Chicken with Cashew Nuts and Rice

SERVES 4

225 g/8 oz/1 cup long-grain rice
25 g/1 oz/2 tbsp low-fat spread
225 g/8 oz boneless chicken thighs, skinned and cut into neat strips
1 bunch of spring onions (scallions), diagonally sliced
2 carrots, grated
275 g/10 oz/2½ cups bean sprouts
25 g/1 oz/¼ cup raw cashew nuts
300 ml/½ pt/1¼ cups chicken stock, made with 1 stock cube
15 ml/1 tbsp cornflour (cornstarch)
15 ml/1 tbsp soy sauce

Boil the rice in lightly salted water according to the packet directions. Drain, rinse with boiling water and drain again. Meanwhile, melt the low-fat spread in a large frying pan (skillet) or wok. Add the chicken, onions and carrots and stir-fry for 5 minutes. Add the bean sprouts and cook, stirring, for 3 minutes. Add the cashew nuts and stock. Blend the cornflour with the soy sauce and stir in. Bring to the boil and cook for 2 minutes. Spoon the rice on to four warmed serving plates. Spoon the chicken mixture to one side and serve straight away.

Maybe Chicken Chow Mein

SERVES 4

250 g/9 oz/1 packet quick-cook Chinese egg noodles
225 g/8 oz/2 cups cooked chicken, skin removed, cut into strips
425 g/15 oz/1 large can stir-fry mixed vegetables, drained
1 garlic clove, crushed
30 ml/2 tbsp soy sauce
30 ml/2 tbsp dry sherry
5 ml/1 tsp ground ginger
1.5 ml/¼ tsp artificial sweetener granules, or to taste

Cook the noodles according to the packet directions. Drain. Put the chicken in a large pan or wok. Rinse the drained can of vegetables under cold water, drain again and add to the chicken with the remaining ingredients. Heat through, stirring occasionally, until piping hot. Stir in the drained noodles until well coated. Reheat and serve.

Duck Breasts with Orange

SERVES 4

Salt and freshly ground black
  pepper
2 large duck breasts, skin removed
25 g/1 oz/2 tbsp low-fat spread
15 ml/1 tbsp brandy
150 ml/¼ pt/⅔ cup chicken stock,
  made with ½ stock cube
Grated rind and juice of 1 orange
15 ml/1 tbsp cornflour
  (cornstarch)
A few grains of artificial sweetener
Watercress sprigs
Orange twists
To serve:
450 g/1 lb new potatoes, scrubbed
  and boiled
Mangetout (snow peas)

Season the duck breasts, then fry (sauté) in the low-fat spread, turning occasionally, for 15 minutes or until cooked to your liking. Transfer to a warmed dish and keep warm. Add the brandy to the pan juices and ignite. When the flames have subsided, add the stock. Blend the orange rind and juice with the cornflour and stir into the pan. Bring to the boil and cook for 1 minute, stirring. Season to taste and sweeten with a few grains of artificial sweetener. Cut the duck breasts into neat slices. Arrange attractively on four warmed plates. Add any juices to the sauce. Spoon over the duck and garnish each with watercress sprigs and orange twists. Serve hot with new potatoes and mangetout.

Chicken Liver Nests

SERVES 4

450 g/1 lb potatoes, cut into even-
  sized pieces
40 g/1½ oz/3 tbsp low-fat spread
15 ml/1 tbsp skimmed milk
2 onions, finely chopped
1 wineglass dry vermouth
450 g/1 lb/4 cups chicken livers,
  trimmed
5 ml/1 tsp chopped sage
Salt and freshly ground black
  pepper
350 g/12 oz frozen leaf spinach

Boil the potatoes in lightly salted water until tender. Drain and mash with 15 ml/1 tbsp of the low-fat spread and the milk. Spoon into four 'nests' on flameproof serving plates. Flash under a hot grill (broiler) to brown. Keep warm. Meanwhile, melt the remaining low-fat spread in a frying pan (skillet). Add the onions and fry (sauté), stirring, for 4 minutes until golden and soft. Add the vermouth and boil until nearly all the liquid has evaporated. Stir in the chicken livers, sage and a little salt and pepper and cook, stirring, for about 5 minutes until the livers are browned but still tender. Taste and re-season if necessary. Meanwhile, cook the spinach according to the packet directions. Drain. Spoon the hot livers into the 'nests' and surround with the spinach. Serve straight away.

117

Sweet and Sour Chicken with Oriental Rice and Peas

SERVES 4

225 g/8 oz chicken stir-fry meat
15 g/½ oz/1 tbsp low-fat spread
1 carrot, cut into matchsticks
1 small red (bell) pepper, cut into thin strips
¼ cucumber, cut into matchsticks
430 g/15½ oz/1 large can pineapple pieces in natural juice
30 ml/2 tbsp tomato purée (paste)
45 ml/3 tbsp light soy sauce
2.5 ml/½ tsp ground ginger
60 ml/4 tbsp malt vinegar
10 ml/2 tsp cornflour (cornstarch)
15 ml/1 tbsp water
To serve:
Oriental Rice and Peas (see page 291)

Stir-fry the chicken in the low fat spread in a large frying pan (skillet) or wok for 4 minutes. Remove from the pan. Add the remaining ingredients except the cornflour and water and bring to the boil. Simmer for 5 minutes. Blend the cornflour with the water and stir into the pan. Bring to the boil and cook for 1 minute, stirring, until thickened and clear. Return the chicken to the pan and heat through. Serve with Oriental Rice and Peas.

Baked Chinese Chicken

SERVES 4

30 ml/2 tbsp soy sauce
30 ml/2 tbsp clear honey
Grated rind and juice of 1 large orange
1 small garlic clove, crushed
10 ml/2 tsp chopped fresh root ginger
A pinch of artificial sweetener granules
5 ml/1 tsp ground cumin
4 skinless chicken breasts, about 175 g/6 oz each
25 g/1 oz/2 tbsp low-fat spread, melted
To serve:
175 g/6 oz/¾ cup long-grain rice, boiled
Chinese Leaf and Orange Salad (see page 269)

Mix together all the ingredients except the chicken and low-fat spread in a shallow ovenproof dish. Add the chicken breasts, turn over in the marinade and leave to marinate, preferably overnight, turning occasionally. Drizzle the low-fat spread over, turn the chicken again and bake in a preheated oven at 180°C/350°F/ gas mark 4 for 45 minutes until coated in sauce and cooked through. Serve on a bed of plain boiled rice with Chinese Leaf and Orange Salad.

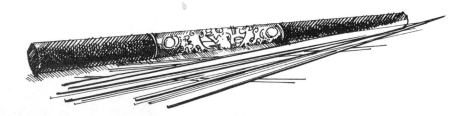

Orchard Chicken

SERVES 4

1 small onion, finely chopped
1 garlic clove, crushed
1.5 ml/¼ tsp artificial sweetener
 granules
15 ml/1 tbsp Dijon mustard
250 ml/8 fl oz/1 cup apple juice
120 ml/4 fl oz/½ cup cider vinegar
15 ml/1 tbsp paprika
5 ml/1 tsp chilli powder
Salt and freshly ground black
 pepper
4 skinless chicken fillets, about
 175 g/6 oz each
15 g/½ oz/1 tbsp low-fat spread,
 melted
Chopped parsley
To serve:
Jacket-baked potatoes
Broccoli

Mix together all the ingredients except the chicken breasts and low-fat spread in a shallow dish. Add the chicken and turn over in the marinade. Leave to marinate for 2 hours. Remove the chicken and place on a grill (broiler) rack. Brush with half the low-fat spread. Grill (broil) for 10–15 minutes, turning once and brushing with the remaining low-fat spread, until golden and cooked through. Meanwhile, boil the marinade until well reduced. Season and sweeten to taste. Transfer the chicken to warmed serving plates and garnish with chopped parsley. Spoon the marinade over and serve each with a jacket-baked potato and a good portion of broccoli.

Chicken and Vegetable Mornay

SERVES 4

30 ml/2 tbsp cornflour
 (cornstarch)
300 ml/½ pt/1¼ cups skimmed
 milk
5 ml/1 tsp low-fat spread
Salt and freshly ground black
 pepper
5 ml/1 tsp English made mustard
75 g/3 oz/¾ cup strong low-fat
 Cheddar cheese, grated
350 g/12 oz/3 cups chopped,
 cooked, mixed leftover or frozen
 vegetables
175 g/6 oz/1½ cups chopped
 cooked chicken, skin removed
1.5 ml/¼ tsp grated nutmeg
To serve:
Tomato and Onion Salad
 (see page 266)

Blend the cornflour in a saucepan with the milk. Add the low-fat spread. Bring to the boil and cook for 1 minute, stirring all the time. Stir in a little salt and pepper, the mustard and two-thirds of the cheese. Fold in the vegetables and chicken and season with the nutmeg and a little more salt and pepper, if necessary. Heat through. Turn into a flameproof scrving dish. Top with the remaining cheese and grill (broil) until golden and bubbling. Serve with Tomato and Onion Salad.

Gorgeous Glazed Chicken

SERVES 4

**4 skinless chicken breasts, about
175 g/6 oz each
25 g/1 oz/2 tbsp low-fat spread
120 ml/4 fl oz/½ cup dry vermouth
Salt and freshly ground black
pepper
15 ml/1 tbsp chopped parsley**
To serve:
**Scalloped Potatoes (see page 289)
Green beans**

Brown the chicken breasts on both sides in the low-fat spread. Add the vermouth and a little salt and pepper and cook for about 15–20 minutes until the chicken is cooked through and stickily glazed, turning the chicken once during cooking. Throw in the parsley after 10 minutes cooking. Serve with Scalloped Potatoes and green beans.

Boozy Red Pasta Chicken

SERVES 4

**1 large onion, finely sliced
1 garlic clove, crushed
25 g/1 oz/2 tbsp low-fat spread
4 skinless chicken breasts, about
175 g/6 oz each
Salt and freshly ground black
pepper
400 g/14 oz/1 large can chopped
tomatoes
60 ml/4 tbsp port
30 ml/2 tbsp chopped parsley
A few grains of artificial sweetener
100 g/4 oz pasta shells
15 ml/1 tbsp chopped basil**
To serve:
Mixed Green Salad (see page 265)

Fry (sauté) the onion and garlic in half the low-fat spread for 3 minutes, stirring until softened and lightly golden. Remove from the pan with a draining spoon. Brown the chicken in the remaining low-fat spread in the same pan. Return the onions and garlic to the pan with the remaining ingredients except the pasta and basil. Bring to the boil, reduce the heat and simmer for 15–20 minutes until the chicken is cooked and the sauce is pulpy, stirring occasionally. Meanwhile, cook the pasta according to packet directions. Drain. When the chicken is cooked, lift out of the pan and transfer to four warmed serving plates. Mix the cooked pasta with the sauce and spoon to one side of the chicken. Sprinkle with the basil and serve with Mixed Green Salad.

Spicy Chicken Wings

SERVES 4

450 g/1 lb chicken wings, as much skin removed as possible
For the marinade:
1 small onion, finely chopped
1.5 ml/¼ tsp artificial sweetener granules, or to taste
30 ml/2 tbsp Worcestershire sauce
15 g/½ oz/1 tbsp low-fat spread, melted
15 ml/1 tbsp paprika
5 ml/1 tsp cayenne
10 ml/2 tsp coarse sea salt
Freshly ground black pepper
For the dip:
150 ml/¼ pt/⅔ cup very low-fat plain yoghurt
30 ml/2 tbsp snipped chives
To serve:
Crispy Baked Potato Skins (see page 275)
Mixed Salad (see page 269)

Put the chicken wings in a single layer in a roasting tin (pan). Mix together the marinade ingredients and pour over, rubbing the mixture into the flesh. Leave to marinate for 2 hours. Lift the wings out of the marinade and grill (broil) for 15–20 minutes until cooked through and crispy, brushing with any remaining marinade. Meanwhile, mix the yoghurt with the chives and a little salt and pepper. Serve the chicken with the dip, Crispy Baked Potato Skins and Mixed Salad.

Sweet and Spicy Duck

SERVES 4

120 ml/4 fl oz/½ cup dry sherry
120 ml/4 fl oz/½ cup strong black tea
120 ml/4 fl oz/½ cup soy sauce
1 garlic clove, crushed
30 ml/2 tbsp clear honey
5 ml/1 tsp ground cloves
Salt and freshly ground black pepper
4 small duck breasts, skin removed
15 g/½ oz/1 tbsp low-fat spread
To serve:
Oriental Bean Sprout Salad (see page 271)

Mix together the sherry, tea, soy sauce, garlic, honey, cloves and a little salt and pepper in a shallow dish. Add the duck and leave to marinate for 1 hour. Remove the duck from the marinade and place on a grill (broiler) rack. Boil the marinade until reduced by half. Stir in the low-fat spread. Brush all over the duck and grill (broil) for 10–12 minutes on each side until golden and cooked through, brushing regularly with the remaining marinade. Serve with Oriental Bean Sprout Salad.

Redcurrant Duck

SERVES 4

2 large duck breasts, skin
  removed, about 275 g/10 oz
  each
25 g/1 oz/2 tbsp low-fat spread
90 ml/6 tbsp port
15 ml/1 tbsp redcurrant jelly
  (clear conserve)
Salt and freshly ground black
  pepper
4 small redcurrant sprigs
  (optional)
Watercress sprigs
To serve:
Parsleyed Potatoes (see page 289)
Cabbage with Celery (see page
  273)

Fry (sauté) the duck breasts in the
low-fat spread for about 10–15
minutes until cooked to your liking.
Remove from the pan and keep warm.
Add the port and redcurrant jelly to the
pan and cook, stirring, until the redcurrant jelly dissolves. Boil rapidly
until reduced by half. Season to taste.
Cut the duck breasts diagonally into
neat slices. Arrange on four warmed
serving plates. Spoon the sauce over
and garnish each with a sprig of redcurrants, if using, and watercress
sprigs. Serve with Parsleyed Potatoes
and Cabbage with Celery.

Chicken with Lime and Garlic

SERVES 4

4 small skinless chicken breasts
50 g/2 oz/¼ cup low-fat spread
1 large garlic clove, crushed
15 ml/1 tbsp chopped parsley
Grated rind and juice of 1 lime
Salt and freshly ground black pepper
Parsley sprigs
To serve:
Yellow Rice (see page 296)
Red Leaf Salad (see page 265)

Make a slit in the side of each
chicken breast to form a pocket.
Mash the low-fat spread with the garlic, chopped parsley, lime rind and a
little salt and pepper. Spoon into the
chicken breasts. Place each on a
square of foil and sprinkle with lime
juice and a little more salt and pepper.
Wrap up. Place on a baking sheet and
bake in a preheated oven at
190°C/375°F/gas mark 5 for 30 minutes. Open up the foil after 20 minutes
to allow the chicken to brown. Garnish
with parsley sprigs and serve with
Yellow Rice and Red Leaf Salad.

Chicken Jalfrezi

SERVES 4

1 garlic clove, crushed
5 ml/1 tsp ground ginger
5 ml/1 tsp ground cumin
10 ml/2 tsp paprika
60 ml/4 tbsp water
30 ml/2 tbsp low-fat spread
2 large onions, thinly sliced
1 large onion, finely chopped
15 ml/1 tbsp curry paste
450 g/1 lb chicken fillets, cut into
    chunky slices
1 large green (bell) pepper, diced
2 courgettes (zucchini), sliced
4 green chillies, seeded and chopped
60 ml/4 tbsp chopped coriander
    (cilantro)
Salt and freshly ground black pepper
A few grains of artificial sweetener
To serve:
225 g/8 oz/1 cup basmati rice,
    boiled

Mix together the garlic, ginger, cumin, paprika and water. Melt the low-fat spread in a large frying pan (skillet). Add the sliced onion and fry (sauté) for 3 minutes until turning golden, stirring all the time. Add the chopped onion and fry for 1 minute. Add the spices in water and curry paste and fry for 1 minute. Add the chicken, diced pepper and courgettes and fry, stirring, for 7 minutes until the chicken and vegetables are tender. Add the chillies, coriander, salt, pepper and just a few grains of sweetener to taste. Cook for a further 2 minutes and serve on a bed of boiled basmati rice.

Grilled Chicken Kiev

SERVES 4

4 boneless chicken breasts, about
    175 g/6 oz each
50 g/2 oz/¼ cup low-fat spread
1 or 2 garlic cloves, crushed
30 ml/2 tbsp chopped parsley
Salt and freshly ground black pepper
A squeeze of lemon juice
To serve:
Yellow Rice (see page 296)
Mixed Salad (see page 269)

Make a slit in the side of each chicken breast to form a pocket. Reserve 5 ml/1 tsp of the low-fat spread. Mash the remainder with the garlic (using more or less to taste), the parsley and a little salt and pepper. Spoon into the chicken breasts and secure thoroughly with cocktail sticks (toothpicks). Place on foil on the grill (broiler) rack. Smear the remaining low-fat spread over and add a squeeze of lemon juice. Place under a hot grill (broiler) for about 15 minutes, turning once until cooked through. Transfer to warmed plates immediately, remove the cocktail sticks and serve with Yellow Rice and Mixed Salad.

Herb-stuffed Chicken Rolls

SERVES 4

40g/1½ oz/¾ cup white breadcrumbs
30 ml/2 tbsp chopped parsley
15 ml/1 tbsp chopped basil
15 ml/1 tbsp chopped thyme
Salt and freshly ground black pepper
1 egg, beaten
4 small skinless chicken breasts
300 ml/½ pt/1¼ cups chicken
  stock, made with 1 stock cube
15 ml/1 tbsp cornflour (cornstarch)
30 ml/2 tbsp low-fat single (light)
  cream
To serve:
450 g/1 lb new potatoes, scrubbed
  and boiled
Garlic Courgettes (see page 276)

Mix the breadcrumbs with the herbs and some salt and pepper. Stir in the egg to bind. Cut each chicken breast in half lengthways with a sharp knife to make eight thinner breasts. Spread the stuffing over each slice and roll up. Secure with cocktail sticks (toothpicks). Place in a saucepan with the stock. Bring to the boil, reduce the heat, cover and poach for 15 minutes or until cooked through. Drain, place on warmed serving plates and remove the cocktail sticks. Keep warm. Blend the cornflour with the cream and stir into the stock. Bring to the boil and simmer for 2 minutes. Taste and add more seasoning if necessary. Pour over the chicken and serve with new potatoes and Garlic Courgettes.

Tempting Turkey Fillets

SERVES 4

4 slices of turkey fillet, about
  150 g/5 oz each
150 ml/¼ pt/⅔ cup dry white wine
150 ml/¼ pt/⅔ cup passata (sieved
  tomatoes)
A few grains of artificial sweetener
16 basil leaves
Salt and freshly ground black
  pepper
4 thin slices lean ham (from a
  packet)
50 g/2 oz/½ cup Mozzarella cheese,
  grated
To serve:
450 g/1 lb baby new potatoes,
  boiled
Italian Green Salad (see page 272)

Put the turkey and wine in a shallow pan. Bring to the boil, reduce the heat, cover and cook gently for about 10 minutes or until the turkey is tender. Remove the turkey and place on foil on a grill (broiler) rack. Boil the wine rapidly until reduced by half. Stir in the passata and a few grains of artificial sweetener. Bring to the boil and simmer for 4 minutes. Chop half the basil leaves and stir in. Season to taste. Put a slice of ham on each turkey fillet and top with cheese. Grill (broil) until the cheese melts and bubbles. Spoon the sauce on to four warmed serving plates. Top each with a turkey fillet and scatter a few torn basil leaves over. Serve with baby new potatoes and Italian Green Salad.

···· FISH ····

350
CALORIES OR LESS

Cod Provençale

SERVES 4

15 g/½ oz/1 tbsp low-fat spread
1 onion, finely chopped
2 garlic cloves, crushed
1 red (bell) pepper, chopped
400 g/14 oz/1 large can chopped
    tomatoes
15 ml/1 tbsp tomato purée (paste)
450 g/1 lb cod fillet, skinned and
    cubed
Salt and freshly ground black
    pepper
4 black olives, stoned (pitted) and
    sliced
15 ml/1 tbsp chopped parsley
To serve:
175 g/6 oz/¾ cup long-grain rice,
    boiled

Melt the low-fat spread in a saucepan. Add the onion and garlic and cook, stirring, for 2 minutes. Add the chopped pepper, tomatoes and purée. Bring to the boil and cook rapidly for 5 minutes until reduced and pulpy. Add the fish and cook gently for 3–5 minutes until tender but still holding its shape. Season to taste. Serve on a bed of boiled rice and garnish with the sliced olives and chopped parsley scattered over.

Hearty Fish Stew

SERVES 4

1 large onion, thinly sliced
2 carrots, thinly sliced
1 large potato, diced
1 parsnip, diced
1 turnip, diced
¼ small green cabbage, shredded
25 g/1 oz/2 tbsp low-fat spread
400 g/14 oz/1 large can chopped
    tomatoes
300 ml/½ pt/1¼ cups water
1 fish stock cube
350 g/12 oz white fish fillet,
    skinned and cubed
Salt and freshly ground black
    pepper
2.5 ml/½ tsp dried mixed herbs
Chopped parsley

Put all the prepared vegetables in a large saucepan with the low-fat spread. Cook, stirring, for 5 minutes. Add the tomatoes, water and crumbled stock cube. Bring to the boil, reduce the heat, part-cover and simmer for 15 minutes or until the vegetables are nearly tender. Add the fish, a little salt and pepper and the herbs and continue cooking for 5 minutes. Taste and re-season if necessary. Ladle into warmed bowls and garnish with chopped parsley.

Tandoori-style Cod

SERVES 4

450 g/1 lb cod fillet, skinned
150 ml/¼ pt/⅔ cup very low-fat
  plain yoghurt
15 ml/1 tbsp lemon juice
5 ml/1 tsp ground coriander
  (cilantro)
5 ml/1 tsp ground cumin
2.5 ml/½ tsp chilli powder
2.5 ml/½ tsp turmeric
Salt
175 g/6 oz/¾ cup basmati rice
400 g/14 oz/1 large can chopped
  tomatoes
300 ml/½ pt/1¼ cups water
1 vegetable stock cube
15 ml/1 tbsp chopped coriander
Lemon wedges
Lettuce leaves
Cucumber slices

Cut the fish into four equal pieces, discarding any bones. Mix together thoroughly the yoghurt, lemon juice, spices and a little salt in a shallow ovenproof dish, just large enough to take the fish in one layer. Add the fish and turn in the mixture to coat well. Leave to stand for 2–3 hours. Place in a preheated oven at 180°C/350°F/gas mark 4 and cook for 20 minutes. Meanwhile, rinse the rice and put in a saucepan with the tomatoes, water and crumbled stock cube. Bring to the boil, stirring, cover, reduce the heat and simmer very gently for 20 minutes until the rice is cooked and has absorbed the liquid. Sprinkle with the chopped coriander and fork in. Spoon on to warmed serving plates. Top with the fish and garnish the plates with lemon wedges, lettuce leaves and cucumber slices.

Hot and Sour Cod

SERVES 4

4 pieces cod fillet, about 175 g/
  6 oz each, skinned
50 g/2 oz/¼ cup low-fat spread
45 ml/3 tbsp lemon juice
5 ml/1 tsp Tabasco sauce
Salt and freshly ground black
  pepper
8 spring onions (scallions),
  trimmed
2 red (bell) peppers, quartered
To serve:
175 g/6 oz/¾ cup basmati rice,
  boiled
Nutty Courgette and Carrot Salad
  (see page 268)

Place the fish in a large, shallow dish. Melt the low-fat spread with the lemon juice, Tabasco and salt and pepper and pour over the fish. Leave to marinate for 1 hour. Transfer to a grill (broiler) rack. Add the spring onions and pepper quarters. Re-melt any remaining marinade and brush over. Grill (broil) for about 5 minutes on each side until the vegetables are golden and the fish is cooked through. Serve hot with boiled basmati rice and Nutty Courgette and Carrot Salad.

Sweet and Sour Monkfish

SERVES 4

Prepare as for Sweet and Sour Chicken with Oriental Rice and Peas (see page 118), but substitute cubed monkfish for the chicken.

350

Peasant-style Swordfish

SERVES 4

4 swordfish steaks, about 175 g/
  6 oz each
5 ml/1 tsp extra virgin olive oil
25 g/1 oz/2 tbsp low-fat spread
1 garlic clove, chopped
30 ml/2 tbsp chopped parsley
Salt and freshly ground black
  pepper
Lemon wedges
To serve:
White Chips (see page 285)
Peasant Salad (see page 284)

Remove and discard the skin from the fish. Fry (sauté) in the oil and low-fat spread for 5 minutes on one side until golden. Turn over. Sprinkle with the garlic, parsley and salt and pepper. Cover the pan with foil or a lid and cook gently for a further 5 minutes until cooked through and fragrant. Serve on warmed plates with the juices from the pan and lemon wedges, with White Chips and Peasant Salad.

Florida Haddock

SERVES 4

25 g/1 oz/2 tbsp low-fat spread
1 orange
1 grapefruit
Freshly grated nutmeg
4 haddock fillets, about 175 g/6 oz
  each, skinned
Salt and freshly ground black
  pepper
15 ml/1 tbsp chopped parsley
1 bunch of watercress
30 ml/2 tbsp Diet Drizzle (see
  page 354)
To serve:
Baby Jackets (see page 287)

Grease four squares of foil with half the low-fat spread. Grate the rind from the orange and grapefruit. Sprinkle half over the foil with a good grating of nutmeg. Season the fish well with salt and pepper and place on the foil. Dot with the remaining low-fat spread, fruit rinds and a little more nutmeg. Close the foil to form parcels and seal the edges by folding them in securely. Transfer to a baking sheet and bake in a preheated oven at 180°C/350°F/gas mark 4 for about 25 minutes until the fish is cooked through. Meanwhile, cut all the pith from the orange and grapefruit, slice thinly and cut each slice in quarters. Trim the watercress and divide between four small salad bowls. Add slices of orange and grapefruit. Sprinkle with the Diet Drizzle. Transfer the fish parcels to warmed plates and open at the table. Serve with Baby Jackets and the salad.

Spicy Haddock with Beans

SERVES 4

25 g/1 oz/2 tbsp low-fat spread
750 g/1½ lb haddock fillet,
  skinned and cut into 4 pieces
228 g/8 oz/1 small can chopped
  tomatoes
15 ml/1 tbsp tomato purée (paste)
275 g/10 oz/1 small can cut green
  beans
2.5 ml/½ tsp chilli powder
A few grains of artificial sweetener
Salt and freshly ground black
  pepper
To serve:
175 g/6 oz/¾ cup long-grain rice,
  boiled

Melt the low-fat spread in a large frying pan (skillet). Fry (sauté) the fish for 5 minutes on one side. Turn over. Add the remaining ingredients and cover with foil or a lid. Simmer for 5 minutes or until the fish is tender. Serve on a bed of boiled rice.

Seafood and Fennel Shells

SERVES 4

225 g/8 oz multi-coloured pasta
  shells
25 g/1 oz/2 tbsp low-fat spread
1 fennel bulb, finely chopped and
  green fronds reserved
1 bunch of spring onions
  (scallions), chopped
30 ml/2 tbsp dry white wine
225 g/8 oz/2 cups frozen seafood
  cocktail, thawed
Salt and freshly ground black
  pepper
15 ml/1 tbsp chopped parsley
4 lemon wedges
To serve:
Mixed Leaf Salad (see page 265)

Cook the pasta according to the packet directions. Drain. Meanwhile, melt the low-fat spread in a saucepan. Add the chopped fennel and spring onions and fry (sauté) for 3 minutes, stirring. Cover with a lid, reduce the heat and cook for a further 5 minutes until tender. Add the wine and seafood. Heat through, stirring gently for about 3 minutes until piping hot. Season to taste and add the parsley. Add the pasta shells and toss gently. Pile on to warmed plates and garnish each with a lemon wedge and fennel frond. Serve with Mixed Leaf Salad.

Photograph opposite:
American Chowder (page 64)

Sharp Spiced Prawn Kebabs with Stir-fry Vegetables

SERVES 4

15 ml/1 tbsp cumin seeds
Grated rind and juice of 1 lemon
15 ml/1 tbsp snipped chives
1 small garlic clove, crushed
15 ml/1 tbsp chopped parsley
A pinch of artificial sweetener
  granules
Salt and freshly ground black
  pepper
50 g/2 oz/¼ cup low-fat spread,
  melted
450 g/1 lb large raw prawns
  (shrimp)
To serve:
Stir-fried Vegetables (see page 278)

Lightly toast the cumin seeds in a dry frying pan (skillet). Crush in a pestle and mortar or in a bowl with the end of a rolling pin. Mix with the remaining ingredients except the prawns. Thread the prawns on soaked wooden skewers and put in a single layer in a shallow dish. Spoon the spice and herb mixture over. Leave to marinate for 2 hours. Transfer to a grill (broiler) rack and grill (broil) for about 8 minutes, turning frequently, until cooked through and sizzling. Heat any remaining marinade and brush over during cooking. Serve with Stir-fried Vegetables.

Prawn and Whiting Parcels

SERVES 4

4 leeks, thinly sliced
4 whiting fillets, about 175 g/6 oz
  each, skinned
100 g/4 oz/1 cup peeled prawns
  (shrimp)
30 ml/2 tbsp chopped dill (dill
  weed)
Salt and freshly ground black
  pepper
Juice of ½ lemon
15 ml/1 tbsp capers
25 g/1 oz/2 tbsp low-fat spread,
  melted
To serve:
Hot Potato and Bean Salad (see
  page 282)

Cut four large circles of baking parchment about 30 cm/12 in diameter. Fold in half, then open out again. Lay the sliced leeks over one half of each piece of parchment. Top with the whiting, then the prawns. Sprinkle with the dill, a little seasoning, the lemon juice and capers. Drizzle with the low-fat spread. Fold over the other halves of the parchment and roll the edges tightly together to seal. Carefully transfer to a baking sheet. Bake in a preheated oven at 200°C/400°F/gas mark 6 for 25 minutes. Transfer to warmed serving plates and open at the table. Serve with Hot Potato and Bean Salad.

Photograph opposite:
Speedy Cassoulet (page 99)

Plaice with Piquant Sauce

SERVES 4

4 plaice fillets
250 ml/8 fl oz/1 cup skimmed
    milk
250 ml/8 fl oz/1 cup water
75 g/3 oz/⅓ cup low-fat spread
Grated rind and juice of 1 lemon
45 ml/3 tbsp capers
Salt and freshly ground black
    pepper
A few grains of artificial sweetener
To serve:
450 g/1 lb baby new potatoes,
    boiled
Green beans

Skin the fillets if the skin is dark, then halve lengthways. Roll them up and put in single layer in a large flameproof casserole (Dutch oven). Pour over the milk and water. Bring to the boil and simmer gently for about 7 minutes or until the fish is cooked but still holds its shape. Meanwhile, melt the low-fat spread with the lemon rind and juice, capers, a little salt and pepper and sweeten to taste with a very few grains of sweetener. Carefully transfer the fish to warmed plates, discarding the cooking liquid. Spoon the piquant sauce over and serve with baby new potatoes and green beans.

Plaice Mornay

SERVES 4

4 plaice fillets
300 ml/½ pt/1¼ cups skimmed
    milk
30 ml/2 tbsp cornflour
    (cornstarch)
50 g/2 oz/½ cup strong, low-fat
    Cheddar cheese, grated
5 ml/1 tsp Dijon mustard
Salt and freshly ground black
    pepper
450 g/1 lb/2 cups mashed cooked
    potatoes
To serve:
Spinach with Tomatoes (see page
    278).

Skin the fillets if the skin is dark, then cut into strips. Put in a saucepan and add all but 30 ml/2 tbsp of the milk. Bring to the boil, reduce the heat and simmer gently for 5 minutes or until the fish is tender. Carefully remove from the pan. Blend the cornflour with the remaining milk and add to the pan. Bring to the boil and cook for 1 minute, stirring. Stir in three-quarters of the cheese and the mustard and season to taste. Spoon the potato round the edge of a shallow flameproof dish. Lay the fish in the centre and pour over the sauce. Sprinkle with the remaining cheese and brown under a hot grill (broiler) Serve with Spinach with Tomatoes.

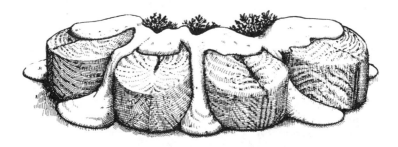

Fish Creole

SERVES 4

**30 ml/2 tbsp plain (all-purpose)
    flour
Salt and freshly ground black
    pepper
2.5 ml/½ tsp chilli powder
4 small white fish fillets, about
    150 g/5 oz each
40 g/1½ oz/3 tbsp low-fat spread
2 bananas, halved lengthways then
    across
To serve:
Lime wedges
175 g/6 oz/¾ cup wild rice mix,
    boiled
Mixed Green Salad (see page 265)**

M ix the flour with a little salt and pepper and the chilli powder and use to coat the fish. Melt two-thirds of the low-fat spread in a large frying pan (skillet) and fry (sauté) the fish on both sides until golden brown and cooked through. Transfer to warmed serving plates and keep warm. Melt the remaining low-fat spread and cook the banana quarters until just cooked but still holding their shape. Lay on top of the fish and serve with lime wedges, boiled wild rice mix and Mixed Green Salad.

Trout with Almonds

SERVES 4

**4 small rainbow trout, cleaned
40 g/1½ oz/3 tbsp low-fat spread
25 g/1 oz /¼ cup flaked (slivered)
    almonds
30 ml/2 tbsp chopped parsley
Salt and freshly ground black pepper
A squeeze of lemon juice
To serve:
450 g/1 lb potatoes, boiled
Peas**

R inse the fish and dry on kitchen paper. Remove the heads, if preferred. Melt 25 g/1 oz/2 tbsp of the low-fat spread in a large frying pan (skillet) and fry (sauté) the fish for 5 minutes on each side until golden brown and cooked through. Transfer to warmed plates and keep warm. Melt the remaining low-fat spread in the juices in the pan. Add the almonds and fry until golden brown. Throw in the parsley, a little salt and pepper and the lemon juice. Spoon over the trout and serve with plain boiled potatoes and peas.

Peppered Trout

SERVES 4

**4 small rainbow trout, cleaned
25 g/1 oz/2 tbsp low-fat spread
75 g/3 oz/⅓ cup very low-fat soft
    cheese
15 ml/1 tbsp coarsely crushed
    black peppercorns
45 ml/3 tbsp skimmed milk
Salt
Chopped parsley
To serve:
Parsleyed Potatoes (see page 289)
Broccoli**

R inse the trout and dry on kitchen paper. Remove the heads, if preferred. Melt the low-fat spread in a large frying pan (skillet) and fry (sauté) the trout for about 5 minutes on each side until golden and cooked through. Transfer to warmed plates and keep warm. Add the cheese to the juices in the pan with the peppercorns and a little of the milk. Heat gently, stirring, until smooth. Thin with more milk until a smooth pouring consistency. Season to taste with salt. Spoon over the trout and sprinkle with chopped parsley. Serve with Parsleyed Potatoes and broccoli.

Minted Trout

SERVES 4

4 small trout, cleaned
15 g/½ oz/1 tbsp low-fat spread
Salt and freshly ground black
pepper
1 lemon, thinly sliced
90 ml/6 tbsp chopped mint
15 ml/1 tbsp artificial sweetener
granules
To serve:
Fluffy Mashed Potatoes (see page
287)
Mangetout (snow peas)

Rinse and dry the trout on kitchen paper. Cut off the heads, if preferred. Grease four large squares of foil with the low-fat spread. Season the fish well. Lay a lemon slice on each piece of foil and sprinkle with half the mint and sweetener. Top with the fish. Lay the remaining lemon slices on top and sprinkle with the remaining mint and sweetener. Season lightly again. Close the foil parcels and seal the edges well. Transfer to a baking sheet and bake in a preheated oven at 190°C/375°F/gas mark 5 for about 25–30 minutes until the fish is cooked through. Transfer the parcels to warmed serving plates and open at the table. Serve with Fluffy Mashed Potatoes and mangetout.

Celtic Scallop Pie

SERVES 4

2 leeks, sliced
25 g/1 oz/2 tbsp low-fat spread
90 ml/6 tbsp fish stock, made with
¼ stock cube
50 g/2 oz/¼ cup very low-fat
fromage frais
3 lean rashers (slices) streaky
bacon, rinded and diced
175 g/6 oz/1½ cups baby scallops
Salt and freshly ground black
pepper
450 g/1 lb/2 cups mashed cooked
potato
15 ml/1 tbsp chopped parsley
To serve:
Crunchy Carrot Salad (see page
271)

Fry (sauté) the leeks in half the low-fat spread for 2 minutes, stirring. Add the stock, cover and simmer gently for 5 minutes until tender. Purée in a blender or food processor, then return to the saucepan. Stir in the fromage frais. Meanwhile, dry-fry the bacon until the juices run. Add the scallops and cook, stirring for 2 minutes until tender. Stir into the leek purée and reheat gently. Season to taste. Meanwhile, spoon the potato into 'nests' in four individual shallow flameproof dishes. Dot with the remaining low-fat spread. Spoon the leek and scallop mixture into the centres. Flash under a hot grill (broiler) until the potato is browning and the top is glazed. Sprinkle with chopped parsley and serve with Crunchy Carrot Salad.

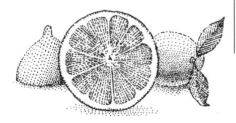

Scallop, Mushroom and Courgette Kebabs

SERVES 4

40 g/1½ oz/3 tbsp low-fat spread
2 onions, finely chopped
400 g/14 oz/1 large can chopped tomatoes
30 ml/2 tbsp chopped basil
Salt and freshly ground black pepper
2 courgettes (zucchini), cut into chunks
100 g/4 oz small button mushrooms
350 g/12 oz/3 cups shelled scallops
To serve:
Caraway Noodles (see page 295)

Melt 25 g/1 oz/2 tbsp of the low-fat spread in a saucepan. Add the onions and fry (sauté), stirring, for 2 minutes. Add the tomatoes and simmer fairly rapidly for about 5 minutes until pulpy. Stir in the basil and season to taste. Meanwhile, thread the courgettes, mushrooms and scallops on to soaked wooden skewers. Place on a grill (broiler) rack. Melt the remaining low-fat spread and brush over. Grill (broil), turning occasionally, for about 10 minutes until cooked through and sizzling, brushing with any remaining low-fat spread during cooking. Transfer to warmed plates and serve with the hot sauce and Caraway Noodles.

Whiting Ragout

SERVES 4

1 onion, finely chopped
1 garlic clove, crushed
15 g/½ oz/1 tbsp low-fat spread
100 g/4 oz button mushrooms, sliced
400 g/14 oz/1 large can chopped tomatoes
15 ml/1 tbsp tomato purée (paste)
50 g/2 oz/½ cup frozen peas
15 ml/1 tbsp chopped parsley
Grated rind and juice of ½ orange
Salt and freshly ground black pepper
450 g/1 lb whiting fillet, skinned and cut into thin strips
To serve:
175 g/6 oz/¾ cup wild rice mix, boiled
40 g/1½ oz/⅓ cup low-fat Cheddar cheese, grated

Fry (sauté) the onion and garlic in the low-fat spread for 3 minutes until softened and lightly golden. Add the remaining ingredients except the fish. Bring to the boil, reduce the heat and simmer for 10 minutes until pulpy. Add the fish and cook for a further 4–5 minutes until the fish flakes easily with a fork. Taste and re-season if necessary. Spoon on to a bed of boiled wild rice mix and sprinkle with the cheese before serving.

·················· PORK, BACON & HAM ··················

350

CALORIES OR LESS

Austrian-style Pork Chops

SERVES 4

4 thin, well-trimmed boneless
 pork chops
15 g/½ oz/1 tbsp low-fat spread
1 onion, thinly sliced
1 garlic clove, crushed
½ small white cabbage, finely
 shredded
150 ml/¼ pt/⅔ cup vegetable stock,
 made with ½ stock cube
15 ml/1 tbsp caraway seeds
Salt and freshly ground black
 pepper
3 potatoes, thinly sliced
Chopped parsley

Fry (sauté) the chops in the low-fat
spread in a flameproof casserole
(Dutch oven) for 2 minutes on each
side to brown. Remove from the pan.
Add the onion and garlic and fry for 2
minutes. Stir in the cabbage and cook
for about 3 minutes until it starts to
soften. Add the stock. Lay the pork on
top and sprinkle with the caraway
seeds. Season lightly. Add the potato
slices, overlapping on top and season
again. Cover with a lid, reduce the heat
and cook for about 20 minutes until
the cabbage, chops and potatoes are
cooked through. Sprinkle with
chopped parsley and serve.

Spaghetti with Bacon, Egg, Tomatoes and Mushrooms

SERVES 4

1 onion, finely chopped
2 garlic cloves, crushed
75 g/3 oz button mushrooms,
 sliced
4 lean rashers (slices) streaky
 bacon, rinded and diced
25 g/1 oz/2 tbsp low-fat spread
225 g/8 oz spaghetti
30 ml/2 tbsp chopped parsley
2 tomatoes, skinned, seeded and
 chopped
2 eggs
60 ml/4 tbsp skimmed milk
Salt and freshly ground black pepper
To serve:
20 ml/4 tsp grated Parmesan Cheese
Mixed Leaf Salad (see page 265)

Fry (sauté) the onion, garlic, mushrooms and bacon in the low-fat
spread, stirring, for 2 minutes. Cover,
reduce the heat and cook gently for
7 minutes. Meanwhile, cook the spaghetti according to the packet directions, drain and return to the pan. Add
the bacon mixture, parsley and tomatoes and toss over a gentle heat. Whisk
together the eggs and milk and add to
the pan with a little salt and lots of
pepper. Toss over a gentle heat until
scrambled but still creamy. Pile on to
warmed plates and serve sprinkled
with Parmesan cheese with Mixed Leaf
Salad.

German-style Frankfurter Supper

SERVES 4

450 g/1 lb potatoes, cut into even-sized pieces
550 g/1¼ lb/1 large jar sauerkraut
15 ml/1 tbsp caraway seeds
16 frankfurters or hot dog sausages
Chopped parsley
German mustard

Cook the potatoes in boiling, lightly salted water until tender but still holding their shape. Drain. Meanwhile, heat the sauerkraut in a saucepan with the caraway seeds. Heat the frankfurters in a separate pan. Spoon the sauerkraut on to four warmed plates. Arrange the frankfurters around and add the potatoes. Garnish with chopped parsley and serve with German mustard.

Grilled Gammon with Spicy Pineapple

SERVES 4

4 all-lean gammon steaks, about 175 g/6 oz each
2 tomatoes, halved
228 g/8 oz/1 small can pineapple slices in natural juice, drained
1 fresh green chilli, seeded and sliced
To serve:
Sesame Seed Wedges (see page 288)
Peas

Place the gammon on a grill (broiler) rack. Snip the edges with scissors to prevent curling up. Grill (broil) for about 3 minutes until golden. Turn over and add the tomato halves to the grill rack. Grill for 2 minutes. Top each steak with a pineapple ring and sprinkle with the chilli. Grill for a further 1–2 minutes until the pineapple is piping hot and the gammon and tomatoes are cooked. Transfer to warmed plates and serve with Sesame Seed Wedges and peas.

Sage and Cheese Pork Fillets

SERVES 4

4 pieces pork fillet, about 100 g/ 4 oz each
10 ml/2 tsp low-fat spread, melted
8 sage leaves, chopped
Salt and freshly ground black pepper
50 g/2 oz/½ cup Gruyère or Emmental (Swiss) cheese, grated
Sage sprigs
To serve:
Baby Potatoes and Onions (see page 285)
Carrot Purée (see page 274)

Put the pork pieces in a plastic bag one at a time and beat flat with a rolling pin or meat mallet. Place on a grill (broiler) rack and brush with half the low-fat spread. Grill (broil) for about 4 minutes until golden. Turn over and brush with the remaining spread. Grill for a further 4 minutes until cooked through. Sprinkle with the chopped sage, a little salt and pepper, then the cheese and return to the grill until the cheese melts and bubbles. Transfer to warmed plates, garnish with sage sprigs and serve with Baby Potatoes and Onions and Carrot Purée.

Oriental Pork Steaks

SERVES 4

**4 pork shoulder steaks, about
150 g/5 oz each
10 ml/2 tsp cornflour (cornstarch)
15 ml/1 tbsp vinegar
250 g/9 oz/1 small can crushed
pineapple
30 ml/2 tbsp tomato ketchup
(catsup)
15 ml/1 tbsp soy sauce
¼ cucumber, chopped**
To serve:
**175 g g/6 oz/¾ cup long-grain rice,
boiled
Bean Sprout and Pepper Salad (see
page 271)**

Grill (broil) the pork steaks for about 8 minutes on each side until golden brown and cooked through. Meanwhile, blend the cornflour with the vinegar in a saucepan. Stir in the remaining ingredients. Bring to the boil and cook for 5 minutes, stirring occasionally. Place the pork on warmed plates. Pour the sauce over and serve with rice and Bean Sprout and Pepper Salad.

Orange-glazed Pork

SERVES 4

**4 lean pork chops, about 150 g/
5 oz each
15 g/½ oz/1 tbsp low-fat spread
15 ml/1 tbsp reduced-sugar orange
marmalade
2.5 ml/½ tsp ground ginger
10 ml/2 tsp pure orange juice
Orange slices
Parsley sprigs**
To serve:
**450 g/1 lb potatoes, boiled
Green beans**

Fry (sauté) the pork in the low-fat spread for about 5 minutes on one side until golden. Turn over. Mix together the marmalade, ginger and orange juice. Spoon over the steaks and continue cooking for 5 minutes, basting with the sticky juices. Flash the pan under a hot grill (broiler) to glaze the tops. Transfer to warmed plates, garnish with orange slices and parsley sprigs and serve with boiled potatoes and green beans.

Cinnamon Pork

SERVES 4

**4 small lean pork steaks, about
150 g/5 oz each
25 g/1 oz/2 tbsp low-fat spread
15 ml/1 tbsp lemon juice
45 ml/3 tbsp chopped mint
5 ml/1 tsp ground cinnamon
Salt and freshly ground black
pepper
Mint sprigs
Lemon slices**
To serve:
**Glazed Carrots (see page 275)
Peas**

Put the pork in a shallow dish. Melt the low-fat spread with the lemon juice and stir in the mint and cinnamon. Season lightly. Pour over the pork and turn over in the mixture. Leave to stand for 1 hour. Grill (broil), brushing with the remaining marinade, for about 10 minutes on each side until golden and cooked through. Transfer to warmed plates, garnish with mint sprigs and lemon slices and serve with Glazed Carrots and peas.

Sweet and Sour Pork

SERVES 4

Prepare as for Sweet and Sour Chicken with Oriental Rice and Peas (see page 118) but substitute 350 g/12 oz diced pork fillet for the chicken.

Pork and Apricot Casserole

SERVES 4

1 onion, chopped
25 g/1 oz/2 tbsp low-fat spread
550 g/1¼ lb lean diced stewing pork
30 ml/2 tbsp plain (all-purpose) flour
Salt and freshly ground black pepper
1 bouquet garni sachet
30 ml/2 tbsp tomato purée (paste)
150 ml/¼ pt/⅔ cup chicken stock, made with ½ stock cube
150 ml/¼ pt/⅔ cup dry white wine
50 g/2 oz dried apricots, chopped
Chopped parsley
To serve:
Jacket-baked potatoes
Mixed Green Salad (see page 265)

Fry (sauté) the onion in the low-fat spread for 2 minutes in a flame-proof casserole (Dutch oven). Toss the pork in the flour with a little salt and pepper and add to the pan. Cook, stirring, for 4 minutes until browned all over. Add the remaining ingredients except the parsley with a little more seasoning and bring to the boil, stirring. Cover and transfer to a preheated oven at 160°C/325°F/ gas mark 3 for 2–2½ hours or until really tender. Garnish with chopped parsley and serve with jacket-baked potatoes and Mixed Green Salad.

Valencian Pork

SERVES 4

40 g/1½ oz/3 tbsp low-fat spread
450 g/1 lb lean diced stewing pork
1 Spanish onion, thinly sliced
2 garlic cloves, crushed
1 green (bell) pepper, sliced
100 g/4 oz button mushrooms, sliced
400 g/14 oz/1 large can tomatoes
250 ml/8 fl oz/1 cup dry white wine
5 ml/1 tsp dried oregano
5 ml/1 tsp dried rosemary
Finely grated rind of 1 lemon
Salt and freshly ground black pepper
450 g/1 lb courgettes (zucchini), sliced
4 stuffed olives, sliced

Melt half the low-fat spread in a large flameproof casserole (Dutch oven). Fry (sauté) the pork on all sides to brown. Remove from the pan with a draining spoon. Melt the remaining low-fat spread and fry the onion, garlic and pepper for 5 minutes, stirring. Add the mushrooms and fry for 1 minute, stirring. Add the tomatoes and break up with a spoon. Return the pork to the pan. Add the wine, herbs, lemon rind and salt and pepper. Bring to the boil. Cover and transfer to a preheated oven at 160°C/325°F/gas mark 3 for 2–2½ hours until the pork is really tender. Meanwhile, boil the courgettes in lightly salted water for 3–4 minutes until almost tender and a rich bright green. Drain. Add to the casserole and return to the oven for a few minutes to heat through. Taste and re-season if necessary. Serve in large soup bowls with the olives sprinkled over.

Liver Hot-pot

SERVES 4

450 g/1 lb pigs' liver, cut into
  bite-sized pieces
30 ml/2 tbsp skimmed milk
40 g/1½ oz/3 tbsp low-fat spread
3 large onions, sliced
2 carrots, sliced
1 cooking (tart) apple, sliced
30 ml/2 tbsp plain (all-purpose)
  flour
450 ml/¾ pt/2 cups beef stock,
  made with 1 stock cube
10 ml/2 tsp Worcestershire sauce
5 ml/1 tsp dried sage
Salt and freshly ground black pepper
450 g/1 lb potatoes, scrubbed and
  thinly sliced
To serve:
Spring greens (spring cabbage)

Soak the liver in the milk for 15 minutes. Drain and dry on kitchen paper. Heat 25 g/1 oz/2 tbsp of the low-fat spread in a flameproof casserole (Dutch oven). Add the onions and carrots and fry (sauté) for 3 minutes until softened and lightly golden. Add the liver and continue frying, stirring, until browned all over. Add the apple and flour and cook, stirring for 1 minute. Blend in the stock, Worcestershire sauce, sage and a little salt and pepper. Bring to the boil, stirring. Remove from the heat. Arrange the potato slices overlapping on top of the meat. Dot with the remaining low-fat spread and cover with a lid or foil. Transfer to a preheated oven at 190°C/375°F/gas mark 5 for 30 minutes. Remove the lid or foil and continue cooking for a further 30 minutes until the potatoes are golden brown and cooked through and the liver is tender. Serve with spring greens.

Fegatini with Vermicelli

SERVES 4

350 g/12 oz pigs' liver
2 onions
1 slice bread
15 ml/1 tbsp chopped sage
1 egg, beaten
Salt and freshly ground black
  pepper
15 g/½ oz/1 tbsp low-fat spread
450 g/1 lb ripe tomatoes, roughly
  chopped
15 ml/1 tbsp tomato purée (paste)
60 ml/4 tbsp water
A few grains of artificial sweetener
175 g/6 oz vermicelli
To serve:
Mixed Leaf Salad (see page 265)

Coarsely mince the liver, one of the onions and the bread. Stir in the sage, egg and a little salt and pepper. Chop the remaining onion. Heat the low-fat spread in a saucepan. Add the chopped onion and fry (sauté) for 2 minutes. Add the tomatoes, purée, water, sweetener and salt and pepper. Simmer, stirring, for about 5 minutes until pulpy. Bring a large pan of salted water to the boil. Drop in tablespoonfuls of the liver mixture and simmer for about 4 minutes until cooked through. Remove with a draining spoon and place in the tomato sauce, over a very low heat. Cook the vermicelli according to the packet directions. Drain. Divide between four warmed serving plates. Top with the fegatini in sauce and serve with Mixed Leaf Salad.

Barbecued Pork and Beans

SERVES 4

2 onions, thinly sliced
225 g/8 oz pork fillet, cubed
15 g/½ oz/1 tbsp low-fat spread
2 x 400 g/2 x 14 oz/2 large cans
    no-added-sugar baked beans
30 ml/2 tbsp bottled barbecue
    sauce
4 slices French bread
10 ml/2 tsp wholegrain mustard
Chopped parsley
To serve:
Mixed Green Salad (see page 265)

Fry (sauté) the onions and pork in the low-fat spread in a saucepan for about 8 minutes until cooked through and golden. Stir in the beans and barbecue sauce and heat through. Meanwhile, toast the French bread and spread with the mustard. Ladle the pork and beans into warmed soup bowls. Top each with a French bread slice and sprinkle with chopped parsley. Serve with Mixed Green Salad.

Irish Bacon with Cabbage

SERVES 4 HOT
THEN 4–6 COLD, SLICED WITH SALAD

1 kg/2¼ lb piece very lean
    unsmoked collar bacon
1 bay leaf
4 onions, peeled but left whole
6 black peppercorns
1 green cabbage, quartered and
    thick stalk removed
450 g/1 lb potatoes, scrubbed and
    cut into large pieces

Place the bacon in a large saucepan and just cover with water. Bring to the boil and throw away the water. Add fresh water, the bay leaf, onions and peppercorns. Bring to the boil, cover, reduce the heat and simmer gently for 1½ hours. Add the cabbage and potatoes and continue cooking for 30 minutes. Lift out the cabbage, potatoes and onions with a draining spoon and keep warm. Carve half the joint, trimming off any remaining fat. Place on warmed plates with the potatoes, cabbage and onions and spoon a little of the broth over.

Boiled Bacon with Carrots

SERVES 4 HOT
THEN 4–6 COLD, SLICED WITH SALAD

Prepare as for Irish Bacon with Cabbage, but substitute 450 g/1 lb carrots, thickly sliced, for the cabbage, sprinkle with chopped parsley before serving and serve with English mustard.

Country-style Pork Pockets

SERVES 4

225 g/8 oz pork fillet, very thinly
 sliced
25 g/1 oz/2 tbsp low-fat spread
1 eating (dessert) apple, thinly
 sliced
8 fresh sage leaves, chopped
15 ml/1 tbsp chopped parsley
A dash of Worcestershire sauce
Salt and freshly ground black
 pepper
6 pitta breads
Shredded lettuce
Thinly sliced cucumber
Thinly sliced red (bell) pepper
Thinly sliced onion rings

Fry (sauté) the pork in the low-fat
spread for 2 minutes. Add the
apple, sage, parsley, Worcestershire
sauce and salt and pepper and fry,
tossing, for about 3 minutes until the
pork is cooked and the apple is soft.
Warm the pitta breads briefly to puff
them up. Slit across the middles and
open up to form pockets. Line with lettuce, cucumber, red pepper and onion
rings. Spoon in the pork and apple
mixture and serve three pockets per
person.

Bangers on a Mound

SERVES 4

450 g/1 lb potatoes, cut into even-
 sized chunks
Salt and freshly ground black
 pepper
25g/1 oz/2 tbsp low-fat spread
15 ml/1 tbsp skimmed milk
2 large onions, sliced
1 small green cabbage, shredded
2 carrots, grated
8 low-fat pork chipolata sausages
Wholegrain mustard

Cook the potatoes in boiling, lightly
salted water until tender. Drain and
mash well with a little pepper, half the
low-fat spread and the milk. Meanwhile, fry (sauté) the onions in the
remaining low-fat spread for about 6
minutes until golden and soft, stirring
all the time. Throw the cabbage into a
pan with just 2.5 cm/1 in boiling, salted water. Cook, pressing down, for 3
minutes, then add the carrots and
cook for a further 3 minutes. Drain
and keep warm. Meanwhile, grill
(broil) the sausages until well browned
and cooked through. Drain on kitchen
paper. Pile the cabbage and carrots
round the edges of four warmed serving plates. Put a mound of potato in
the centre and top with the onions.
Add the sausages on either side of the
potato and serve with wholegrain
mustard.

Fillet of Pork with Red Vermouth

SERVES 4

4 small pieces pork fillet, about 100 g/4 oz each
Salt and freshly ground black pepper
25 g/1 oz/2 tbsp low-fat spread
120 ml/4 fl oz/½ cup chicken stock, made with ½ stock cube
120 ml/4 fl oz/½ cup red vermouth
2 spring onions (scallions), finely chopped
30 ml/2 tbsp chopped parsley
½ small lemon, very thinly sliced
To serve:
Fluffy Mashed Potatoes (see page 287)
Broccoli

Place a piece of pork fillet in a plastic bag and beat with a rolling pin or meat mallet until flattened. Repeat with the remaining slices. Season with salt and pepper. Melt the low-fat spread and fry (sauté) the pork fillets for about 3 minutes on each side until golden and cooked through. Remove from the pan and keep warm. Add the stock and vermouth to the pan. Bring to the boil and boil rapidly until reduced by half. Season to taste. Transfer the pork fillets to warmed serving plates. Spoon the sauce over and scatter with chopped spring onion, the parsley and lemon slices. Serve with Fluffy Mashed Potatoes and broccoli.

French-style Ham and Eggs

SERVES 4

1 onion, chopped
15 g/½ oz/1 tbsp low-fat spread
225 g/8 oz button mushrooms, sliced
1 garlic clove, crushed
150 ml/¼ pt/⅔ cup chicken stock, made with ½ stock cube
100 g/4 oz/1 cup lean cooked ham, diced
10 ml/2 tsp chopped tarragon
15 ml/1 tbsp chopped parsley
Salt and freshly ground black pepper
4 eggs
30 ml/2 tbsp low-fat single (light) cream
8 thin slices French bread
To serve:
Mixed Green Salad (see page 265)

Fry (sauté) the onion in the low-fat spread in a large frying pan (skillet) for 3 minutes, stirring, until soft and lightly golden. Add the mushrooms, garlic and stock. Bring to the boil and simmer for 5 minutes. Add the ham, herbs and a little salt and pepper and continue cooking for 5 minutes. Make four 'wells' in the mixture and break an egg into each. Drizzle the cream over. Cover with foil or a lid and cook gently for 5 minutes or until the eggs are cooked to your liking. Meanwhile, toast the French bread. Stand the toasted slices around the edge of the mixture, resting against the sides and serve straight from the pan with Mixed Green Salad.

·················· LAMB ··················

CALORIES OR LESS

Eastern Yoghurt Lamb

SERVES 4

1 onion, sliced
15 g/½ oz/1 tbsp low-fat spread
225 g/8 oz/2 cups lean cooked
   lamb
1 garlic clove, crushed
2.5 ml/½ tsp grated fresh root
   ginger
2.5 ml/½ tsp ground cumin
2.5 ml/½ tsp ground coriander
   (cilantro)
7.5 ml/1½ tsp turmeric
150 ml/¼ pt/⅔ cup very low-fat
   plain yoghurt
Salt and freshly ground black
   pepper
1 packet pilau rice
20 ml/4 tsp desiccated (shredded)
   coconut
30 ml/2 tbsp currants

Fry (sauté) the onion in the low-fat
spread until turning golden. Add
the lamb and the remaining ingredients except the rice, coconut and currants. Bring to the boil, reduce the
heat and simmer for about 20 minutes.
The mixture will curdle during cooking. Meanwhile, cook the rice according to the packet directions. Pile on to
four warmed plates. Top with the lamb
mixture and sprinkle with the coconut
and currants before serving.

Grilled Redcurrant-glazed Chops

SERVES 4

4 lamb chops, trimmed of any fat
Salt and freshly ground black
   pepper
15 ml/1 tbsp redcurrant jelly
   (clear conserve)
To serve:
Parsleyed Potatoes (see page 289)
Braised Celery (see page 276)

Place the chops on a grill (broiler)
rack and season both sides. Grill
(broil) for 5 minutes on each side. Melt
the redcurrant jelly and brush over.
Continue grilling and brushing for a
few minutes until stickily glazed. Serve
with Parsleyed Potatoes and Braised
Celery.

Grilled Mint-glazed Chops

SERVES 4

Prepare as for Grilled Redcurrant-
glazed Chops but substitute mint
jelly (clear conserve) for the redcurrant
jelly.

Marinated Lamb Kebabs

SERVES 4

350 g/12 oz lamb neck fillet, trimmed and cut into neat cubes
15 ml/1 tbsp lemon juice
15 g/½ oz/1 tbsp low-fat spread
5 ml/1 tsp dried oregano
Salt and freshly ground black pepper
1 small green (bell) pepper, cut into 16 pieces
16 button mushrooms
Lemon wedges
To serve:
Greek Village Salad (see page 283)

Put the meat in a shallow dish. Heat the lemon juice with the low-fat spread until melted and pour over with the oregano and salt and pepper. Toss and leave to marinate for 1 hour. Thread on to soaked wooden skewers alternately with pieces of pepper and the mushrooms. Place on a grill (broiler) rack. Grill (broil), brushing with any remaining marinade for about 10 minutes, turning occasionally, until cooked through. Transfer to warmed plates, garnish with lemon wedges and serve with Greek Village Salad.

Fragrant Lamb Cutlets

SERVES 4

25 g/1 oz/2 tbsp low-fat spread
8 thin lamb cutlets, trimmed of any fat
1 garlic clove, finely chopped
1 large rosemary sprig
60 ml/4 tbsp water
Salt and freshly ground black pepper
Small rosemary sprigs, to garnish
To serve:
Tomato Potatoes (see page 295)
Crisp lettuce dressed with lemon juice and black pepper

Melt the low-fat spread in a large frying pan (skillet). Fry (sauté) the cutlets on both sides to brown. Remove from the pan. Spoon off any fat, leaving any juices. Add the remaining ingredients, cover with foil or a lid and cook gently for 10 minutes until the lamb is really tender. Transfer to warmed serving plates, discarding the large rosemary sprig. Taste and re-season the juices if necessary. Pour over. Garnish with small rosemary sprigs and serve with Tomato Potatoes and a crisp lettuce.

Minted Lemon Chops

SERVES 4

4 lamb chops, trimmed of all fat
15 ml/1 tbsp plain (all-purpose)
  flour
Salt and freshly ground black
  pepper
10 ml/2 tsp chopped mint
25 g/1 oz/2 tbsp low-fat spread
Grated rind and juice of 1 lemon
A pinch of artificial sweetener
  granules, or to taste
Parsley sprigs
To serve:
450 g/1 lb baby new potatoes,
  boiled
Pea Purée (see page 274)

Wipe the chops with kitchen paper. Mix the flour with a little salt and pepper and the mint. Use to coat the chops. Fry (sauté) in the low-fat spread for 10 minutes, turning once, until browned and cooked through. Remove from the pan with a draining spoon and keep warm. Spoon off all the fat, leaving the pan juices. Add the lemon rind and juice and the artificial sweetener and stir, scraping up any pan residue. Taste and season if necessary. Spoon over the chops, garnish with parsley and serve with baby new potatoes and Pea Purée.

Orange Chops

SERVES 4

Prepare as for Minted Lemon Chops but substitute the grated rind and juice of an orange for the lemon.

Sherried Liver Nests

SERVES 4

1 swede (rutabaga), cut into even-
  sized chunks
15 ml/1 tbsp very low-fat fromage
  frais
A good pinch of grated nutmeg
Salt and freshly ground black
  pepper
1 large onion, finely chopped
25 g/1 oz/2 tbsp low-fat spread
1 wineglass medium sherry
350 g/12 oz lambs' liver, trimmed
  and cut into thin strips
100 g/4 oz button mushrooms,
  sliced
15 ml/1 tbsp chopped thyme
Chopped parsley
To serve:
Green beans

Cook the swede in boiling, lightly salted water until tender. Drain and mash thoroughly with the fromage frais, nutmeg and salt and pepper to taste. Spoon into rings on four warmed serving plates and keep warm. Fry (sauté) the onion in the low-fat spread, stirring, until soft but not brown. Add the sherry and simmer until reduced by half. Add the liver, mushrooms and thyme and cook, stirring, for about 3 minutes until cooked but soft. Season to taste. Spoon into the centre of the swede rings and garnish with chopped parsley. Serve with green beans.

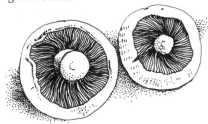

Peppered Liver Deluxe

SERVES 4

15 ml/1 tbsp plain (all-purpose) flour
30 ml/2 tbsp multi-coloured
peppercorns, coarsely crushed
225 g/8 oz lambs' liver, very thinly
sliced
25 g/1 oz/2 tbsp low-fat spread
15 ml/1 tbsp lemon juice
1 small onion, grated
30 ml/2 tbsp chopped parsley
45 ml/3 tbsp Worcestershire sauce
To serve:
Puréed Potatoes (see page 287)
Parsleyed Carrots (see page 277)

Mix the flour with the peppercorns and use to coat the liver slices. Melt the low-fat spread in a large frying pan (skillet) and fry (sauté) the liver on one side until golden underneath. Turn over and cook until the pink juices rise to the surface. Remove from the pan and transfer to warmed serving plates. Add the remaining ingredients to the juices in the pan and cook, stirring, for 1 minute, scraping up any residue in the pan. Spoon over the liver and serve with Puréed Potatoes and Parsleyed Carrots.

Tiddley Kiddleys

SERVES 4

25 g/1 oz/2 tbsp low-fat spread
8 lambs' kidneys, cored and
quartered
100 g/4 oz button mushrooms, sliced
2 onions, thinly sliced
45 ml/3 tbsp low-fat single (light)
cream
15 ml/1 tbsp sherry
Chopped parsley, to garnish
To serve:
100 g/4 oz flat noodles, boiled
Mixed Green Salad (see page 265)

Melt the low-fat spread in a large frying pan (skillet). Add the kidneys, mushrooms and onions and stir. Cover with foil or a lid and cook gently for 10 minutes, stirring occasionally. Add the remaining ingredients and heat through. Spoon on to warmed plates with the boiled noodles to one side. Sprinkle with chopped parsley and serve with Mixed Green Salad.

Brittany Lamb

SERVES 4

1 onion, thinly sliced
1 cooking (tart) apple, thinly sliced
15 g/½ oz/1 tbsp low-fat spread
4 lamb chump chops, trimmed of
fat
300 ml/½ pt/1¼ cups cider or apple
juice
15 ml/1 tbsp chopped mint
Salt and freshly ground black
pepper
15 ml/1 tbsp chopped parsley
To serve:
Dieters' Rosti (see page 286)
Rocket Salad (see page 273)

Fry (sauté) the onion and apple in the low-fat spread for 4 minutes until softened and lightly golden. Remove from the pan with a draining spoon and keep warm. Add the chops and fry for 10–15 minutes until cooked to your liking, turning once. Remove from the pan and add to the onion and apple. Spoon off all fat, leaving the juices. Add the cider or apple juice and mint. Bring to the boil and boil rapidly until reduced by half. Season to taste. Arrange the chops on four warmed serving plates and top with the onion and apple mixture. Spoon the sauce over and sprinkle with the chopped parsley. Serve with Dieters' Rosti and Rocket Salad.

Far Eastern Lamb

SERVES 4

2 lamb neck fillets, about
    275 g/10 oz each, trimmed of
    all fat and sinews
Grated rind and juice of 1 lime
30 ml/2 tbsp soy sauce
2 garlic cloves, chopped
15 g/½ oz/1 tbsp low-fat spread
A few artificial sweetener granules
    (optional)
To serve:
175 g/6 oz/¾ cup Thai fragrant
    rice, boiled
Mustard Carrot Salad (see page 268)

Wipe the meat and place in a shallow dish. Mix together the lime rind and juice, soy sauce and garlic. Pour over the lamb and turn to coat completely. Cover and chill for at least 6 hours, preferably overnight. Remove from the marinade and place in a roasting tin (pan), reserving the marinade. Dot with the low-fat spread. Roast in a preheated oven at 230°C/450°F/gas mark 8 for 20 minutes. Transfer to a warmed carving dish and leave to rest for 5 minutes before carving into slices. Meanwhile, spoon off any fat in the roasting tin. Add the reserved marinade and bring to the boil, stirring. Taste and add a few grains of artificial sweetener, if liked. Arrange the lamb on four warmed plates. Spoon the juices over and serve with Thai fragrant rice and Mustard Carrot Salad.

Spiced Lamb with Prunes

SERVES 4

450 g/1 lb boned leg or neck fillets
    of lamb
Salt and freshly ground black
    pepper
1.5 ml/¼ tsp turmeric
2.5 ml/½ tsp grated fresh root
    ginger
1 garlic clove, crushed
1 bunch of spring onions
    (scallions), chopped
45 ml/3 tbsp chopped parsley
225 g/8 oz prunes, stoned (pitted)
    and chopped
5 ml/1 tsp ground cinnamon
15 ml/1 tbsp clear honey
20 ml/4 tsp orange flower water
15 ml/1 tbsp flaked (slivered)
    almonds
To serve:
1 small baguette
Cucumber with Yoghurt Dressing
    (see page 267)

Cut the lamb into chunks and trim it of all fat and sinew. Put in a saucepan with a little salt, lots of pepper, the turmeric, ginger, garlic, spring onions and parsley. Add just enough water to cover. Bring to the boil, reduce the heat, cover and simmer gently for 1½ hours until the lamb is very tender. Add the prunes and cinnamon and cook uncovered for a further 15 minutes. Add the honey and orange flower water and simmer for 5 minutes, stirring. Dry-fry (sauté) the almonds until golden. Ladle the lamb into four warmed soup bowls. Sprinkle with the almonds and serve with the baguette and Cucumber with Yoghurt Dressing.

French Braised Lamb

SERVES 6

½ small leg of lamb, about 900 g/
2 lb, trimmed of all fat
1 large onion, cut into thick
wedges
2 garlic cloves, crushed
5 ml/1 tsp dried Herbes de
Provence
600 ml/1 pt/2½ cups lamb or
chicken stock, made with
2 stock cubes
60 ml/4 tbsp red wine
Salt and freshly ground black
pepper
3 large leeks, cut into chunks
2 turnips, cut into chunks
450 g/1 lb carrots, cut into chunks
450 g/1 lb small potatoes,
scrubbed

Put the lamb in a flameproof casserole (Dutch oven) with the onion, garlic, herbs, stock, wine and seasoning. Bring to the boil, cover and transfer to a preheated oven at 180ºC/ 350ºF/gas mark 4. Cook for 1½ hours. Add the remaining vegetables and return to the oven for a further 45 minutes or until the meat is falling off the bones and the vegetables are tender. Remove the meat from the bones and cut into neat pieces, discarding any remaining fat. Skim any fat from the surface of the casserole. Spoon everything into six warmed soup bowls and serve.

Leftover Lamb Biryani

SERVES 4

100 g/4 oz/½ cup basmati rice,
rinsed thoroughly
25 g/1 oz/2 tbsp low-fat spread
2 onions, thinly sliced
10 ml/2 tsp curry paste
30 ml/2 tbsp water
100 g/4 oz/1 cup cooked lamb,
diced
2.5 ml/½ tsp ground coriander
(cilantro)
2.5 ml/½ tsp ground cumin
1 tomato, finely chopped
Salt and freshly ground black
pepper
30 ml/2 tbsp sultanas (golden
raisins)
45 ml/3 tbsp chopped coriander
leaves
15 ml/1 tbsp desiccated (shredded)
coconut
Lettuce leaves, tomato wedges,
cucumber slices, lemon wedges

Cook the rice according to the packet directions. Drain, rinse with cold water and drain again. Melt the low-fat spread in a saucepan and fry (sauté) the onions until golden brown. Stir in the curry paste, water, lamb, ground spices, tomato and a little salt and pepper. Stir-fry for about 5 minutes. Add the sultanas, rice and coriander leaves, mix well and heat through. Spoon on to four warmed plates, sprinkle with the coconut and serve garnished with lettuce, tomato, cucumber and lemon wedges.

BEEF

CALORIES OR LESS

Braised Beef in Wine

SERVES 4

450 g/1 lb lean braising steak,
    trimmed of any fat and diced
50 g/2 oz lean bacon pieces, diced
1 garlic clove, crushed
225 g/8 oz button onions, peeled
    but left whole
3 carrots, sliced
175 g/6 oz button mushrooms
1 bay leaf
300 ml/½ pt/1¼ cups red wine
150 ml/¼ pt/⅔ cup beef stock,
    made with ½ stock cube
15 ml/1 tbsp tomato purée (paste)
Salt and freshly ground black
    pepper
15 ml/1 tbsp cornflour
    (cornstarch)
15 ml/1 tbsp water
3 courgettes (zucchini), sliced
To serve:
4 jacket-baked potatoes

Put all the ingredients except the
cornflour, water and courgettes in a
flameproof casserole (Dutch oven).
Bring to the boil, then transfer to a preheated oven at 150°C/300°F/gas mark
2. Cook for 3 hours. Discard the bay
leaf. Blend the cornflour with the
water. Stir in a little of the cooking
liquid, then stir back into the casserole.
Add the courgettes. Return to the oven
for a further 30 minutes. Taste and re-
season if necessary and serve each
portion with a jacket-baked potato.

Steak Diane

SERVES 4

4 tenderised top-rump steaks,
    about 150 g/5 oz each
10 ml/2 tsp lemon juice
25 g/1 oz/2 tbsp low-fat spread
1 small onion, grated
15 ml/1 tbsp chopped parsley
30 ml/2 tbsp Worcestershire sauce
4 tomatoes
4 tiny parsley sprigs
To serve:
Fluffy Mashed Potatoes (see page
    287)
Runner beans

Rub the steaks with the lemon juice.
Melt the low-fat spread in a large
frying pan (skillet) and fry (sauté) the
steaks for 2–3 minutes on each side
until cooked through. Remove from
the pan and place on warmed serving
plates. Keep warm. Add the remaining
ingredients except the tomatoes and
parsley sprigs to the pan and cook,
stirring, for 1 minute. Pour over the
steaks. With stalk sides down, cut the
tomatoes almost in quarters but not
right through the base. Open out gently to form 'lilies'. Put a tiny sprig of
parsley in the centre of each and use
to garnish the steaks. Serve with Fluffy
Mashed Potatoes and runner beans.

Pasta Grill

SERVES 4

175 g/6 oz pasta shapes
1 onion, chopped
225 g/8 oz/2 cups very lean
  minced (ground) beef
400 g/14 oz/1 large can tomatoes
2.5 ml/½ tsp dried oregano
Salt and freshly ground black
  pepper
45 ml/3 tbsp grated low-fat
  Cheddar cheese
To serve:
Mixed Green Salad (see page 265)

Cook the pasta according to the packet directions. Drain. Meanwhile, fry (sauté) the onion and beef together in a pan until the grains of meat are brown and separate. Pour off any fat. Add the tomatoes and break up with a wooden spoon. Stir in the oregano and a little salt and pepper. Bring to the boil, reduce the heat and simmer for 10 minutes. Stir in the pasta. Spoon into a flameproof dish. Top with the cheese and flash under a hot grill (broiler) to brown the top. Serve with Mixed Green Salad.

Chilli con Carne

SERVES 4

1 onion, chopped
1 garlic clove, crushed
225 g/8 oz/2 cups very lean
  minced (ground) beef
2.5 ml/½ tsp hot chilli powder
5 ml/1 tsp ground cumin
2.5 ml/½ tsp dried oregano
400 g/14 oz/1 large can tomatoes
425 g/15 oz/1 large can red kidney
  beans, drained, rinsed and
  drained again
15 ml/1 tbsp tomato purée (paste)
Salt and freshly ground black
  pepper
Shredded lettuce
Lemon wedges
To serve:
175 g/6 oz/¾ cup long-grain rice,
  boiled

Put the onion, garlic and meat in a saucepan. Fry (sauté), stirring, until the grains of meat are brown and separate. Pour off any fat. Add the remaining ingredients except the lettuce and lemon wedges and break up the tomatoes with a wooden spoon. Bring to the boil, reduce the heat and simmer for 20 minutes until a rich colour and reduced. Spoon on to warmed serving plates with the rice, garnish with shredded lettuce and lemon wedges and serve.

Sesame Beef with Mushrooms

SERVES 4

30 ml/2 tbsp sesame seeds
3 garlic cloves, crushed
120 ml/4 fl oz/½ cup red wine
60 ml/4 tbsp soy sauce
10 ml/2 tsp red wine vinegar
Salt and freshly ground black
 pepper
350 g/12 oz lean, tender rump
 steak, all fat discarded and
 cubed
175 g/6 oz button mushrooms
To serve:
Crispy Baked Potato Skins (see
 page 275)
Mixed Leaf Salad (see page 265)

Dry-fry (sauté) the sesame seeds in a frying pan (skillet) until golden. Put in a shallow dish with the garlic, wine, soy sauce, vinegar and a little salt and pepper. Add the steak and mushrooms. Toss and leave to marinate for at least 2 hours. Thread the steak and mushrooms on to soaked wooden skewers and place on a grill (broiler) rack. Grill (broil) for about 5 minutes, turning occasionally, until cooked to your liking. Serve with Crispy Baked Potato Skins and Mixed Leaf Salad.

Grilled Steak with Peppers

SERVES 4

15 g/½ oz/1 tbsp low-fat spread
1 garlic clove, crushed
15 ml/1 tbsp chopped parsley
15 ml/1 tbsp chopped basil
15 ml/1 tbsp lemon juice
Salt and freshly ground black
 pepper
4 thin fillet steaks, about 100 g/
 4 oz each
1 each of red, green, yellow and
 orange (bell) peppers, cut into
 sixths
To serve:
Stewed Herby Mushrooms (see
 page 278)
Mixed Salad (see page 269)

Melt the low-fat spread and stir in the garlic, herbs, lemon juice and a little salt and pepper. Lay the steaks and peppers on a grill (broiler) rack. Brush all over with the garlic mixture. Grill (broil), brushing and turning once, until the steaks and peppers are cooked through. If you like your steak rare, remove after about 4 minutes of cooking and keep warm while continuing to cook the peppers. Transfer to warmed plates and serve with Stewed Herby Mushrooms and Mixed Salad.

Peppered Steak Madeira

SERVES 4

4 small fillet steaks, about 150 g/
  5 oz each
15 ml/1 tbsp multi-coloured
  peppercorns, crushed
25 g/1 oz/2 tbsp low-fat spread
1 bunch of spring onions
  (scallions), finely chopped
90 ml/6 tbsp Madeira
Salt and freshly ground black
  pepper
Parsley sprigs
To serve:
Mushroom Wild Rice Mix
  (see page 297)

Wipe the steaks and press the peppercorns into the surfaces. Melt
the low-fat spread and fry (sauté) the
steaks for 4–6 minutes or until cooked
to your liking. Lift them out of the pan
and keep warm on warmed plates. Add
the spring onions to the pan and cook
for 3 minutes, stirring. Add the
Madeira and cook until bubbling.
Season to taste and spoon over the
steaks. Garnish with parsley sprigs
and serve with Mushroom Wild Rice
Mix.

Keema Curry

SERVES 4

1 onion, finely chopped
1 garlic clove, crushed
450 g/1 lb/4 cups very lean minced
  (ground) beef
5 ml/1 tsp grated fresh root ginger
15 ml/1 tbsp garam masala
2.5 ml/½ tsp hot chilli powder
5 ml/1 tsp ground cumin
5 ml/1 tsp turmeric
228 g/8 oz/1 small can chopped
  tomatoes
30 ml/2 tbsp tomato purée (paste)
150 ml/¼ pt/⅔ cup beef stock,
  made with ½ stock cube
50 g/2 oz/½ cup peas
150 ml/¼ pt/⅔ cup very low-fat
  plain yoghurt
Salt and freshly ground black
  pepper
To serve:
175 g/6 oz/¾ cup basmati rice,
  rinsed and boiled
Coriander (cilantro) leaves

Put the onion and garlic in a pan
with the meat. Cook, stirring, until
the grains are brown and separate.
Pour off any fat. Add all the remaining
ingredients. Bring to the boil, reduce
the heat, cover and cook gently for 40
minutes, stirring occasionally. Remove
the lid after 20 minutes. Taste and re-
season if necessary. Serve on a bed of
basmati rice, garnished with coriander
leaves.

Beef and Vegetable Loaf

SERVES 6

1 onion, grated
2 carrots, grated
1 parsnip, grated
1 turnip, grated
A pinch of ground cinnamon
450 g/1 lb/4 cups very lean minced
    (ground) beef
50 g/2 oz/1 cup fresh wholemeal
    breadcrumbs
Salt and freshly ground black pepper
1 egg, beaten
330 ml/12 fl oz/1 can mixed
    vegetable juice
10 ml/2 tsp low-fat spread
15 ml/1 tbsp cornflour
    (cornstarch)
15 ml/1 tbsp water
15 ml/1 tbsp tomato purée (paste)
15 ml/1 tbsp chopped basil
Small basil sprigs
To serve:
Winter Slaw (see page 272)

Mix the prepared vegetables with the cinnamon, mince, breadcrumbs and some salt and pepper. Stir in the egg to bind with 60 ml/4 tbsp of the vegetable juice. Grease a 900 g/2 lb loaf tin (pan) with the low-fat spread. Turn the mixture into the tin and press down well. Cover with foil. Bake in the oven at 190°C/375°F/gas mark 5 for 1¼ hours. Remove the foil after 45 minutes. Meanwhile, empty the remaining vegetable juice into a saucepan. Blend the cornflour with the water and tomato purée. Add to the juice. Bring to the boil and cook for 1 minute, stirring, until thickened. Add the chopped basil and season to taste. Turn out the meat loaf and slice thickly. Spoon the hot sauce on to six warmed plates. Add a slice of loaf and garnish each with a basil sprig. Serve with Winter Slaw.

No-nonsense Meat Loaf

SERVES 4

5 ml/1 tsp low-fat spread
450 g/1 lb/4 cups very lean minced
    (ground) beef
1 onion, finely chopped
30 ml/2 tbsp chopped parsley
2.5 ml/½ tsp dried mixed herbs
Grated rind and juice of ½ lemon
10 ml/2 tsp Worcestershire sauce
45 ml/3 tbsp red wine
15 ml/1 tbsp tomato purée (paste)
Salt and freshly ground black
    pepper
1 egg, beaten
To serve:
300 ml/½ pt/1¼ cups passata
    (sieved tomatoes), heated
Mixed Salad (see page 269)

Lightly grease a 450 g/1 lb loaf tin (pan) or similar sized dish with the low-fat spread. Mix together all the ingredients and press into the tin. Cover with foil and bake in a preheated oven at 180°C/350°F/gas mark 4 for about 1 hour or until firm to the touch. Cool slightly, then turn out and serve sliced with the passata spooned over and Mixed Salad. This is also delicious served cold with a little chutney instead of the sauce.

·····················MEATLESS MEALS·····················

CALORIES OR LESS

Asparagus and Smoked Tofu Kebabs

SERVES 4

225 g/8 oz thick asparagus spears, cut into short lengths
250 g/9 oz/1 block smoked tofu, cubed
100 g/4 oz button mushrooms
1 lime, thinly sliced
25 g/1 oz/2 tbsp low-fat spread
10 ml/2 tsp lime juice
Salt and freshly ground black pepper
To serve:
Savoury Vegetable Rice (see page 292)

Blanch the asparagus in boiling water for 2 minutes. Drain, rinse with cold water and drain again. Thread the tofu, asparagus and mushrooms on soaked wooden skewers, interspersed with the lime slices. Melt the low-fat spread with the lime juice and season well. Lay the kebabs on the grill (broiler) rack and brush with the melted mixture. Grill (broil) for about 8 minutes or until the asparagus and mushrooms are cooked through, turning occasionally and brushing with the melted mixture during cooking. Serve with Savoury Vegetable Rice.

Swedish Saucy Pasta

SERVES 4

1 onion, thinly sliced
100 g/4 oz mushrooms, quartered
175 g/6 oz quorn pieces
450 ml/¾ pt/2 cups vegetable stock, made with 1 stock cube
2.5 ml/½ tsp soy sauce
5 ml/1 tsp yeast extract
15 ml/1 tbsp chopped basil
Salt and freshly ground black pepper
15 ml/1 tbsp plain (all-purpose) flour
100g/4 oz/½ cup very low-fat quark
100 g/4 oz rotelli or other pasta shapes
Basil sprigs
To serve:
Beetroot and Orange Salad (see page 269)

Put the onions, mushrooms and quorn in a saucepan with 300 ml/ ½ pt/1¼ cups of the stock. Bring to the boil. Add the soy sauce, yeast extract, chopped basil and salt and pepper and simmer for 1 hour. Blend the remaining stock with the flour and quark. Stir into the pan, bring back to the boil and cook, stirring, for 2 minutes. Meanwhile, cook the pasta according to the packet directions. Drain. Add to the pan and toss well. Spoon on to warmed plates and garnish with basil sprigs. Serve with Beetroot and Orange Salad.

Broccoli and Cider Cheese

SERVES 4

350 g/12 oz broccoli florets
45 ml/3 tbsp plain (all-purpose)
flour
60 ml/4 tbsp skimmed milk
powder (non-fat dried milk)
150 ml/¼ pt/⅔ cup cider
A small knob of low-fat spread
50 g/2 oz/½ cup low-fat Cheddar
cheese, grated
Salt and freshly ground white
pepper
1 eating (dessert) apple, halved,
cored and sliced
Lemon juice
To serve:
Poached Tomatoes with Basil (see
page 279)
4 slices crusty bread

Cook the broccoli in lightly salted boiling water until just tender. Drain, reserving 150 ml/¼ pt/⅔ cup of the cooking water. Place the broccoli in a flameproof serving dish. Blend the flour and milk powder with the cider in the broccoli saucepan until smooth. Stir in the reserved cooking water. Add the low-fat spread. Bring to the boil and cook for 2 minutes, stirring all the time. Stir in three-quarters of the cheese and salt and pepper to taste. Pour over the broccoli. Sprinkle with the remaining cheese and brown under a hot grill (broiler). Dip the apple slices in lemon juice to prevent browning. Arrange attractively around the top of the cheese and serve with Poached Tomatoes with Basil and crusty bread.

Alpine Aubergines

SERVES 4

2 large aubergines (eggplants),
halved lengthways and stalks
removed
Salt and freshly ground black
pepper
25 g/1 oz/2 tbsp low-fat spread,
melted
1 red (bell) pepper, chopped
1 onion, chopped
175 g/6 oz goat's cheese, chilled
and then sliced
175 g/6 oz cherry tomatoes,
halved
10 ml/2 tsp chopped basil
To serve:
Mixed Green Salad (see page 265)

Sprinkle the aubergines with salt and leave to stand for 30 minutes. Rinse, then dry on kitchen paper. Place in a roasting tin (pan). Brush with a little of the melted low-fat spread. Bake in a preheated oven at 200°C/400°F/ gas mark 6 for 35–40 minutes or until tender. Scoop out most of the flesh, leaving a wall about 1 cm/½ in thick. Chop the scooped-out flesh. Put half the remaining low-fat spread in a frying pan (skillet) and fry (sauté) the pepper and onion for 3 minutes. Add the aubergine pulp and a little salt and pepper and continue cooking for 2 minutes. Pile into the aubergine shells. Arrange the cheese and tomato slices in alternate rows along the tops. Drizzle with the remaining low-fat spread and sprinkle with the basil. Return to the oven for 20–25 minutes until the tomatoes and cheese are sizzling and soft. Serve straight away with Mixed Green Salad.

Middle Eastern Aubergine Slippers

SERVES 4

2 large aubergines (eggplants),
    stalks removed
40 g/1½ oz/3 tbsp low-fat spread,
    melted
2 large onions, chopped
1 garlic clove, crushed
4 tomatoes, skinned and chopped
1.5 ml/¼ tsp ground cinnamon
A few grains of artificial sweetener
15 ml/1 tbsp chopped parsley
Salt and freshly ground black
    pepper
60 ml/4 tbsp pine nuts
To serve:
4 slices rye bread
Mixed Leaf Salad (see page 265)

Boil the aubergines whole in lightly salted water for 10 minutes. Drain, rinse thoroughly with cold water and drain again. Dry on kitchen paper. Halve lengthways. Scoop out most of the flesh, leaving a wall about 1 cm/½ in thick. Chop the scooped-out flesh. Grease a shallow ovenproof dish with a little of the low-fat spread. Put the shells in this and brush the insides with a little more of the melted spread. Bake in a preheated oven at 180°C/350°F/gas mark 4 for about 30 minutes. Meanwhile, fry (sauté) the onions and garlic in the remaining low-fat spread for about 5 minutes until soft and golden. Add the tomatoes, cinnamon, a few grains of sweetener and the parsley and season to taste. Simmer, uncovered, for 15 minutes. Add the chopped aubergine and pine nuts and cook for a further 15 minutes. Remove the aubergine shells from the oven. Spoon in the tomato and pine nut mixture and serve with rye bread and Mixed Leaf Salad.

Cheesy-topped Vegetable Stew

SERVES 4

1 onion, sliced
15 g/½ oz/1 tbsp low-fat spread
175 g/6 oz/1 cup split red lentils,
    soaked for 2 hours and drained
2 carrots, cut into chunks
½ small swede (rutabaga), cut into
    chunks
2 turnips, cut into chunks
4 leeks, cut into chunks
225 g/8 oz small waxy potatoes,
    scrubbed
450 ml/¾ pt/2 cups vegetable
    stock, made with 1 stock cube
1 bouquet garni sachet
Salt and freshly ground black
    pepper
¼ small green cabbage, shredded
2 slices wholemeal toast
10 ml/2 tsp yeast extract
50 g/2 oz/½ cup low-fat Cheddar
    cheese, grated

Fry (sauté) the onion in the low-fat spread in a large flameproof casserole (Dutch oven) for 2 minutes to soften. Stir in the lentils and all the remaining prepared vegetables except the cabbage and stir for 1 minute. Add the stock, bouquet garni and a little salt and pepper. Bring to the boil, reduce the heat, part-cover and simmer gently for 30 minutes. Add the cabbage and cook for a further 20 minutes until all the vegetables are really tender. Discard the bouquet garni. Meanwhile, spread the toast with the yeast extract and cut in quarters diagonally. Top each with cheese. Lay on top of the casserole and place under a hot grill (broiler) until the cheese melts.

Egg and Vegetable Curry

SERVES 4

100 g/4 oz French (green) beans
2 carrots, sliced
1 small cauliflower, cut into
    florets
1 potato, cut into small chunks
2 courgettes (zucchini), thickly
    sliced
100 g/4 oz/1 cup frozen peas
25 g/1 oz/2 tbsp low-fat spread
1 small onion, finely chopped
30 ml/2 tbsp mild curry paste
25 g/1 oz/¼ cup plain (all-purpose)
    flour
300 ml/½ pt/1¼ cups coconut milk
Salt and freshly ground black
    pepper
5 ml/1 tsp garam masala
4 hard-boiled (hard-cooked) eggs,
    halved
Torn coriander (cilantro) leaves

Top and tail the beans and cut into short lengths. Cook the carrots, cauliflower and potato in lightly salted boiling water for 5 minutes. Add the beans and peas and cook for a further 5 minutes until all the vegetables are tender. Drain, reserving 150 ml/¼ pt/ ⅔ cup of the cooking water. Melt the low-fat spread in the same saucepan. Add the onion and fry (sauté) for 3 minutes, stirring, until softened. Add the curry paste and flour and cook for 1 minute. Blend in the reserved cooking water and the coconut milk. Bring to the boil and cook for 2 minutes, stirring. Season to taste and stir in the garam masala. Fold in the cooked vegetables and simmer for 2–3 minutes. Spoon on to warmed plates and top each with a halved hard-boiled egg and a few torn coriander leaves.

Quorn-stuffed Marrow

SERVES 4

1 small marrow (squash), about
    1 kg/2¼ lb
Salt and freshly ground black pepper
30 ml/2 tbsp water
25 g/1 oz/2 tbsp low-fat spread
1 onion, finely chopped
1 carrot, finely chopped
1 celery stick, finely chopped
225 g/8 oz mushrooms, roughly
    chopped
200 g/7 oz/1¾ cups minced
    (ground) quorn
30 ml/2 tbsp tomato purée (paste)
150 ml/¼ pt/⅔ cup vegetable stock,
    made with ½ stock cube
2.5 ml/½ tsp dried mixed herbs
50 g/2 oz/½ cup low-fat Cheddar
    cheese, grated
To serve:
Baked Tomatoes with Spring
    Onions (see page 279)

Peel the marrow and cut into eight slices. Discard the pith and seeds (pits). Place in a single layer in a baking tin (pan) and sprinkle with salt and pepper. Add the water. Cover with foil and bake in a preheated oven at 180°C/350°F/gas mark 4 for 30 minutes. Meanwhile, make the filling. Melt the low-fat spread in a saucepan. Add the onion, carrot and celery and cook, stirring, for 2 minutes. Add the mushrooms, quorn, tomato purée, stock, herbs and a little salt and pepper and stir well. Bring to the boil, reduce the heat and simmer gently for 20 minutes until the mixture is tender and the liquid is well reduced, stirring occasionally. Spoon the mixture into the marrow rings, top each with a little grated cheese and bake uncovered in the oven for a further 25 minutes or until tender and golden. Serve hot with Baked Tomatoes with Spring Onions.

Simple Stuffed Peppers

SERVES 4

4 red (bell) peppers
227 g/8 oz/1 small packet diced
  frozen mixed vegetables
1 spring onion (scallion), finely
  chopped
50 g/2 oz button mushrooms,
  chopped
25 g/1 oz/½ cup fresh wholemeal
  or rye breadcrumbs
50 g/2 oz/½ cup low-fat Cheddar
  cheese, grated
1 small egg
15 ml/1 tbsp light soy sauce
Salt and freshly ground black
  pepper
To serve:
Poppy Seed and Oregano Wedges
  (see page 288)
Mixed Green Salad (see page 265)

Cut the tops off the peppers and discard the seeds and membranes inside. Trim the bases so they stand up but don't make holes. Cook the peppers and the tops in boiling water for 8 minutes. Drain and stand in a roasting tin (pan). Meanwhile, cook the vegetables according to the packet directions, but using only enough water to cover the vegetables. Add the onion and mushrooms for the last minute of the cooking time. Drain and mix with the breadcrumbs and cheese. Beat the egg with the soy sauce and stir into the vegetable mixture. Season lightly. Pack into the peppers. Top with the 'lids' and bake in a preheated oven at 190°C/375°F/gas mark 5 for about 20 minutes until tender. Serve with Poppy Seed and Oregano Wedges and Mixed Green Salad.

Sweet and Sour Stir-fry with Green Noodles

SERVES 4

15 g/½ oz/1 tbsp low-fat spread
1 onion, sliced
1 red (bell) pepper, cut into thin
  strips
1 green (bell) pepper, cut into thin
  strips
1 carrot, cut into thin matchsticks
175 g/6 oz button mushrooms,
  sliced
430 g/15½ oz/1 large can
  pineapple pieces in natural
  juice, drained
100 g/4 oz bean sprouts
30 ml/2 tbsp tomato ketchup
  (catsup)
30 ml/2 tbsp soy sauce, plus extra
  to serve
30 ml/2 tbsp red wine vinegar
15 ml/1 tbsp clear honey
2.5 ml/½ tsp ground ginger
60 ml/4 tbsp water
15 ml/1 tbsp cornflour
  (cornstarch)
100 g/4 oz/1 slab quick-cook
  green Chinese noodles

Melt the low-fat spread in a large frying pan (skillet) or wok. Add the onion, peppers and carrot and stir-fry for 3 minutes. Add the mushrooms and stir-fry (sauté) for a further 2 minutes. Add the contents of the can of pineapple and the bean sprouts. Blend together the remaining ingredients except the noodles, stir into the pan and cook, stirring, for 2 minutes. Meanwhile, cook the noodles according to the packet directions. Drain. Add to the stir-fry and toss for 1 minute. Serve with extra soy sauce.

Oven-baked Pilau

SERVES 4

**1 bunch of spring onions
(scallions), chopped
1 garlic clove, crushed
25 g/1 oz/2 tbsp low-fat spread
225 g/8 oz/1 cup long-grain rice
600 ml/1 pt/2½ cups vegetable
stock, made with 2 stock cubes
1 bouquet garni sachet
175 g/6 oz button mushrooms
225 g/8 oz/2 cups frozen peas with
sweetcorn (corn)
Salt and freshly ground black
pepper
30 ml/2 tbsp pine nuts
4 tomatoes, cut into wedges
Parsley sprigs**

Fry (sauté) the spring onions and
garlic in the low-fat spread in a
flameproof casserole (Dutch oven) for
2 minutes, stirring. Stir in the rice and
cook for 1 minute. Add the stock, bouquet garni, mushrooms and the peas
and sweetcorn. Season well. Bring to
the boil, cover and cook in a preheated oven at 200ºC/400ºF/gas mark 6 for
20 minutes until the rice is tender and
has absorbed the liquid. Taste and re-
season if necessary. Discard the bouquet garni. Fluff up with a fork and
sprinkle with the pine nuts. Arrange
the tomato wedges around and garnish with a few parsley sprigs. Serve
straight away.

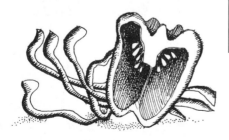

Chakchouka

SERVES 4

**2 onions, chopped
2 garlic cloves, crushed
40 g/1½ oz/3 tbsp low-fat spread
1 small cauliflower, cut into
florets
225 g/8 oz broccoli, cut into
florets
1 green (bell) pepper, diced
450 g/1 lb tomatoes, skinned and
chopped
60 ml/4 tbsp water
Salt and freshly ground black
pepper
10 ml/2 tsp paprika
1.5 ml/¼ tsp chilli powder
1.5 ml/¼ tsp ground cumin
4 eggs
Chopped parsley**
To serve:
1 small wholemeal baguette

Fry (sauté) the onions and garlic in
the low-fat spread in a large frying
pan (skillet) for 2 minutes until slightly softened. Add the cauliflower, broccoli, green pepper, tomatoes, water, a
little salt and pepper, the paprika, chilli
and cumin. Cover and simmer for
about 20 minutes or until the vegetables are tender and bathed in
sauce, stirring from time to time. Make
four 'wells' in the mixture and break
an egg into each. Cover and continue
cooking for about 5 minutes or until
the eggs are set. Alternatively, stir the
mixture to break the eggs up during
cooking. Sprinkle with parsley and
serve straight from the pan with the
wholemeal bread.

Golden Stuffed Courgettes

SERVES 4

175 g/6 oz/1½ cups sweetcorn
  (corn)
100 g/4 oz/½ cup very low-fat
  cottage cheese
1 small yellow (bell) pepper, finely
  chopped
Salt and freshly ground black
  pepper
1 small onion, finely chopped
15 ml/1 tbsp chopped parsley
4 large courgettes (zucchini)
5 ml/1 tsp low-fat spread
45 ml/3 tbsp grated Parmesan
  cheese (fresh if possible)
Tomato slices
To serve:
Nutty Wild Rice Mix (see page 297)

Mix together the corn, cottage cheese, yellow pepper, a little salt and pepper, the onion and parsley. Halve the courgettes lengthways and scoop out the seeds with a teaspoon. Spoon the cottage cheese mixture into the courgettes, piling them up a little. Grease a shallow baking dish with the low-fat spread and place the stuffed courgettes in it in a single layer. Sprinkle the Parmesan over. Bake in a preheated oven at 200°C/400°F/gas mark 6 for about 20 minutes until the courgettes are tender and the topping slightly golden. Transfer to warmed plates, garnish with tomato slices and serve with Nutty Wild Rice Mix.

Blue Cheese Vegetarian Hot-pot

SERVES 4

2 carrots, sliced
1 turnip, diced
2 celery sticks, sliced
8 small leeks, quartered
25 g/1 oz/2 tbsp low-fat spread
25 g/1 oz/¼ cup plain (all-purpose)
  flour
450 ml/¾ pt/2 cups vegetable
  stock, made with 1 stock cube
5 ml/1 tsp yeast extract
425 g/15 oz/1 large can haricot
  (navy) beans, drained
Salt and freshly ground black
  pepper
45 ml/3 tbsp chopped parsley
450 g/1 lb potatoes, thinly sliced
50 g/2 oz/½ cup blue cheese,
  crumbled

Fry (sauté) the carrots, turnip, celery and leeks in the low-fat spread in a flameproof casserole (Dutch oven) for 3 minutes, stirring. Stir in the flour. Remove from the heat and gradually blend in the stock and yeast extract. Return to the heat, bring to the boil and cook for 2 minutes, stirring. Stir in the beans, salt and pepper to taste and the parsley. Cover with the potatoes in a layer. Cover with a lid and bake in a preheated oven at 180°C/350°F/gas mark 4 for 1 hour. Remove the lid, sprinkle with the cheese and continue cooking, uncovered, for a further 30 minutes. Serve straight from the pot.

Broccoli with Feta and Tomato Sauce

SERVES 4

450 g/1 lb broccoli, cut into
 florets
25 g/1 oz/2 tbsp low-fat spread
1 large onion, finely chopped
3 garlic cloves, crushed
2 x 400 g/2 x 14 oz/2 large cans
 chopped tomatoes
5 ml/1 tsp dried oregano
1 piece of cinnamon stick
Salt and freshly ground black
 pepper
15 ml/1 tbsp lemon juice
100 g/4 oz/1 cup Feta cheese,
 crumbled
100 g/4 oz/1 cup Emmental
 (Swiss) cheese, grated
To serve:
4 thick slices crusty bread

Cook the broccoli in lightly salted boiling water for 5 minutes until just tender. Drain and place in an ovenproof serving dish. Melt the low-fat spread in the saucepan. Fry (sauté) the onion and garlic for 3 minutes, stirring. Add the tomatoes, oregano and cinnamon. Season with a little salt and pepper. Bring to the boil and simmer for 5 minutes. Discard the cinnamon stick. Pour the sauce over the broccoli and sprinkle with the lemon juice, then cover with the cheeses. Bake in a preheated oven at 190°C/375°F/gas mark 5 for 25 minutes. Serve immediately with the crusty bread.

Mixed Vegetable Curry

SERVES 4

25 g/1 oz/2 tbsp low-fat spread
1 onion, sliced
30 ml/2 tbsp curry powder
1 small cauliflower, cut into
 florets
2 carrots, sliced
2 courgettes (zucchini), sliced
1 green (bell) pepper, sliced
1 potato, cut into chunks
50 g/2 oz/⅓ cup red lentils, rinsed
150 ml/¼ pt/⅔ cup coconut milk
150 ml/¼ pt/⅔ cup vegetable stock,
 made with ½ stock cube
100 g/4 oz/1 cup frozen peas
15 ml/1 tbsp mango chutney,
 chopped
15 ml/1 tbsp tomato purée (paste)
Salt and freshly ground black
 pepper
Chopped coriander (cilantro)
To serve:
175 g/6 oz/¾ cup basmati rice,
 boiled

Melt the low-fat spread in a large saucepan. Fry (sauté) the onion for 2 minutes, stirring. Stir in the curry powder and cook for 1 minute. Add the remaining ingredients except the coriander. Bring to the boil, part-cover and simmer for 30 minutes until tender and the sauce is thickened by the lentils. If necessary, boil rapidly without a lid to reduce the liquid slightly. Taste and re-season if necessary and serve with the rice, garnished with chopped coriander.

Photograph opposite:
Tagliatelle with Mushrooms, Garlic and Herbs (page 105)

················ **POULTRY** ················

450

CALORIES OR LESS

Chicken Pesto

SERVES 4

**4 boneless chicken breasts, about
175 g/6 oz each
25 g/1 oz/2 tbsp low-fat spread
1 bunch of spring onions
(scallions), chopped
4 large, ripe tomatoes, skinned
and chopped
300 ml/½ pt/1¼ cups dry white
wine
15 ml/1 tbsp tomato purée (paste)
Salt and ground black pepper
30 ml/2 tbsp pesto sauce
30 ml/2 tbsp chopped parsley
30 ml/2 tbsp grated Mozzarella
cheese**
To serve:
**4 slices ciabatta bread
Italian Pepper Salad (see page 282)**

Fry (sauté) the chicken breasts in the low-fat spread for 5 minutes until golden on each side. Remove from the pan. Add the remaining ingredients except the pesto, parsley and cheese. Bring to the boil, stirring. Return the chicken to the pan and season. Cover and simmer for 15 minutes. Stir in the pesto and parsley. Cook uncovered for a further 5 minutes. Transfer to warmed plates. Sprinkle the cheese over and flash under a hot grill (broiler) to melt the cheese. Serve with ciabatta bread and Italian Pepper Salad.

Photograph opposite:
*Scallop, Mushroom and Courgette
Kebabs (page 133)*

Chicken Liver Risotto

SERVES 4

**350 g/12 oz/3 cups chicken livers
40 g/1½ oz/3 tbsp low-fat spread
2 onions, chopped
2 garlic cloves, crushed
4 lean rashers (slices) streaky
bacon, rinded and diced
2 carrots, chopped
225 g/8 oz/1 cup long-grain rice
600 ml/1 pt/2½ cups chicken
stock, made with 2 stock cubes
2.5 ml/½ tsp dried mixed herbs
Salt and freshly ground black
pepper
50 g/2 oz/½ cup frozen peas
30 ml/2 tbsp chopped parsley
30 ml/2 tbsp grated Parmesan
cheese**

Trim the chicken livers and cut into bite-sized pieces if necessary. Melt the low-fat spread in a heavy-based saucepan. Add the onions, garlic, bacon and carrots and fry (sauté), stirring, for 3 minutes. Add the livers and cook for a further 3 minutes or until browned but still very soft. Stir in the rice, then add the stock, herbs and a little salt and pepper. Bring to the boil, reduce the heat, cover and simmer very gently for 15 minutes. Add the peas and cook for a further 5 minutes or until the rice is tender and has absorbed the liquid. Spoon on to warmed plates and sprinkle with the parsley and Parmesan. Serve hot.

161

Spicy Chicken Tacos

SERVES 4

For the filling:
100 g/4 oz/1 cup cooked chicken, finely chopped
4 spring onions (scallions), chopped
213 g/7½ oz/1 small can red kidney beans, drained
4 tomatoes, skinned and chopped
1 small red (bell) pepper, chopped
Salt and freshly ground black pepper
5 ml/1 tsp ground cumin
2.5 ml/½ tsp dried oregano
15 ml/1 tbsp chopped parsley
For the dressing:
1 small avocado, halved and stoned (pitted)
10 ml/2 tsp lemon juice
1 green chilli, seeded and chopped
1 garlic clove, crushed
150 ml/¼ pt/⅔ cup very low-fat plain yoghurt
A dash of Worcestershire sauce
To serve:
Shredded lettuce
8 taco shells
15 g/½ oz Parmesan cheese, thinly shaved with a potato peeler

Thoroughly mix together all the filling ingredients. Scoop the avocado flesh into a blender or food processor and discard the skin. Add the remaining dressing ingredients and blend until smooth. Season to taste. Put some lettuce in the taco shells. Spoon the filling into the taco shells and drizzle in the dressing. Top each with a few slivers of Parmesan cheese and serve.

Zingy Turkey Steaks

SERVES 4

Salt and freshly ground black pepper
4 slices turkey steak, about 175 g/6 oz each
15 g/½ oz/1 tbsp low-fat spread
150 ml/¼ pt/⅔ cup ginger wine
10 ml/2 tsp lemon juice
1 piece of stem ginger in syrup, chopped
45 ml/3 tbsp soured (dairy sour) cream
Salt and freshly ground black pepper
450 g/1 lb baby new potatoes, quartered
450 g/1 lb spring greens (spring cabbage), shredded
Paprika

Season the turkey steaks and fry (sauté) in the low-fat spread for about 5 minutes on each side until golden and cooked through. Remove from the pan and keep warm. Add the ginger wine to the pan. Bring to the boil and boil for 5 minutes. Stir in the lemon juice, chopped ginger and soured cream. Bring to the boil and simmer for 2–3 minutes. Taste and re-season if necessary. Meanwhile, cook the potatoes in lightly salted boiling water for 4 minutes. Add the greens and continue boiling until both are tender. Drain thoroughly and add a good grinding of black pepper. Spread the potato and greens on to four warmed plates. Top each with a turkey steak, then spoon the sauce over. Garnish with a dusting of paprika and serve straight away.

Sherried Chicken Casserole

SERVES 4

4 chicken portions, skinned
25 g/1 oz/2 tbsp low-fat spread
1 large onion, finely chopped
100 g/4 oz button mushrooms, quartered
400 g/14 oz/1 large can chopped tomatoes
1 sherry glass of sherry
30 ml/2 tbsp tomato purée (paste)
1 bouquet garni sachet
Salt and freshly ground black pepper
A few snipped chives
To serve:
Jacket-baked potatoes with Yoghurt and Chive Dressing (see page 356)
Cabbage with Celery and Walnuts (see page 285)

Brown the chicken portions in the low-fat spread in a flameproof casserole (Dutch oven). Remove from the pan with a draining spoon. Add the onion and fry (sauté) for 2 minutes, stirring. Add the mushrooms and cook for 1 minute. Return the chicken to the pan. Add the can of tomatoes. Blend the sherry with the tomato purée and stir in. Add the bouquet garni and salt and pepper. Bring to the boil. Cover and cook in a preheated oven at 180°C/350°F/gas mark 4 for 1½ hours or until the chicken is really tender. Spoon off any fat. Garnish with the snipped chives and serve with jacket-baked potatoes with Yoghurt and Chive Dressing and Cabbage with Celery and Walnuts.

Citrus Chicken

SERVES 4

1 large orange
4 chicken portions, skinned as much as possible
45 ml/3 tbsp plain (all-purpose) flour
Salt and freshly ground black pepper
25 g/1 oz/2 tbsp low-fat spread
2 leeks, sliced
1 small onion, sliced
1 chicken stock cube
175 g/6 oz button mushrooms
5 ml/1 tsp dried thyme
Chopped parsley
To serve:
Sesame Seed Wedges (see page 288)
Glazed Carrots (see page 275)

Thinly pare the rind from the orange. Cut into thin strips and reserve. Halve the orange and squeeze out all the juice. Make up to 600 ml/1 pt/2½ cups with water. Toss the chicken in the flour with a little salt and pepper. Melt the low-fat spread in a flameproof casserole (Dutch oven), add the chicken and brown all over. Remove from the pan with a draining spoon. Add the leeks and onion and fry (sauté) quickly to brown. Blend any remaining flour with a little of the orange juice and water. Stir in the remainder and add to the pan. Crumble in the stock cube. Bring to the boil, stirring. Return the chicken to the pan. Add the mushrooms, half the orange rind, the thyme and a little more salt and pepper. Cover and cook in a preheated oven at 180°C/350°F/gas mark 4 for 1½ hours or until the chicken is really tender. Taste and re-season if necessary. Sprinkle over the remaining orange rind and the parsley and serve with Sesame Seed Wedges and Glazed Carrots.

Turkey and Pineapple Stir-fry with Noodles

SERVES 4

225 g/8 oz turkey pieces
25 g/1 oz/2 tbsp low-fat spread
1 garlic clove, finely chopped
300g/11 oz/1 packet ready-
  prepared fresh stir-fry mixed
  vegetables
100 g/4 oz button mushrooms,
  sliced
228 g/8 oz/1 small can pineapple
  pieces in natural juice
175 g/6 oz bean sprouts
2 tomatoes, roughly chopped
30 ml/2 tbsp soy sauce
Salt and freshly ground black
  pepper
100 g/4 oz/1 slab quick-cook
  Chinese egg noodles
To serve:
A handful of prawn crackers

Trim the turkey and cut into even-sized thin strips. Melt the low-fat spread in a large frying pan (skillet) or wok. Add the turkey and stir-fry for 3 minutes until browned and almost cooked through. Add the garlic, mixed vegetables and mushrooms and stir-fry for 3 minutes. Add the pineapple and its juice, the bean sprouts, tomatoes, soy sauce and a little salt and pepper. Stir well, then cover and cook for 5 minutes. Meanwhile, cook the noodles according to the packet directions. Drain and add to the stir-fry. Mix well, then spoon on to warmed plates and serve each with a few prawn crackers on the side.

Spanish Rice

SERVES 4

175 g/6 oz boneless chicken meat,
  diced
1 small green (bell) pepper, diced
1 small red (bell) pepper, diced
1 onion, chopped
25 g/1 oz/2 tbsp low-fat spread
225 g/8 oz/1 cup long-grain rice
5 ml/1 tsp turmeric or saffron
  powder
600 ml/1 pt/2½ cups chicken
  stock, made with 2 stock cubes
2 tomatoes, roughly chopped
100 g/4 oz/1 cup frozen peas
100 g/4 oz/1 cup peeled prawns
  (shrimp)
Salt and freshly ground black
  pepper
4 black olives, halved and stoned
  (pitted)
Chopped parsley
To serve:
Mixed Leaf Salad (see page 265)

Fry (sauté) the chicken, peppers and onion in the low-fat spread, stirring, for 4 minutes. Stir in the rice and cook for 1 minute. Add the turmeric or saffron and the stock, bring to the boil, stirring, cover and simmer for 10 minutes. Stir in the tomatoes, peas, prawns and a little salt and pepper. Cover and continue cooking for a further 10 minutes over a low heat until the rice is cooked and has absorbed all the liquid. Fluff up with a fork, spoon on to warmed plates and garnish each with halved olives and chopped parsley. Serve with Mixed Leaf Salad.

Indonesian Supper

SERVES 4

225 g/8 oz/1 cup long-grain rice
50 g/2 oz/½ cup frozen peas
2 onions, sliced
40 g/1½ oz/3 tbsp low-fat spread
15 ml/1 tbsp curry powder
2.5 ml/½ tsp ground cinnamon
175 g/6 oz chicken stir-fry meat
50 g/2 oz/½ cup cooked ham, diced
Salt and freshly ground black
  pepper
1 egg
30 ml/2 tbsp water
30 ml/2 tbsp chopped coriander
  (cilantro)
To serve:
**Bean Sprout and Pepper Salad
  (see page 271)**

Cook the rice according to the packet directions, adding the peas for the last 5 minutes' cooking time. Drain, rinse with cold water and drain again. Meanwhile, fry (sauté) the onions in 25 g/1 oz/2 tbsp of the low-fat spread in a large frying pan (skillet) or wok for 2 minutes until softened but not browned. Add the curry powder, cinnamon and chicken and stir-fry for 5 minutes until the chicken is tender and cooked through. Add the ham, rice and peas and toss over a gentle heat for 4 minutes. Season to taste. Meanwhile, beat the eggs and water with a little salt and pepper and stir in the coriander. Melt the remaining low-fat spread in an omelette pan and fry the egg mixture until set underneath. Turn over and cook the other side. Roll up and cut into shreds. Pile the rice mixture on to four warmed plates and top with the shredded omelette. Serve with Bean Sprout and Pepper Salad.

Spiced Chicken Casserole

SERVES 4

4 chicken portions, skinned as
  much as possible
30 ml/2 tbsp plain (all-purpose)
  flour
Salt and freshly ground black
  pepper
5 ml/1 tsp paprika
25 g/1 oz/2 tbsp low-fat spread
5 ml/1 tsp curry powder
295 g/10½ oz/1 small can
  condensed mushroom soup
10 ml/2 tsp gherkins (cornichons),
  chopped
Lemon wedges
Gherkin 'fans'
To serve:
175 g/6 oz/¾ cup basmati rice,
  boiled
**Mustard Carrot Salad (see page
  268)**

Toss the chicken portions in the flour seasoned with a little salt and pepper and the paprika. Melt the low-fat spread in a flameproof casserole (Dutch oven) and brown the chicken on all sides. Remove from the pan. Drain off any excess fat. Sprinkle the curry powder into the casserole and add the condensed soup. Add a little more pepper. Bring to the boil, stirring. Add the chicken, sprinkle over the gherkins, cover and cook in a preheated oven at 180°C/350°F/gas mark 4 for 1½–2 hours. Spoon on to warmed plates, garnish with lemon wedges and gherkin fans and serve with the rice and Mustard Carrot Salad.

Nutty Chicken with Water Chestnuts

SERVES 4

4 chicken portions, skinned as
  much as possible
15 ml/1 tbsp sherry
A few grains of artificial sweetener
25 g/1 oz/2 tbsp low-fat spread
1 bunch of spring onions
  (scallions), diagonally sliced
175 g/6 oz button mushrooms,
  quartered
225 g/8 oz/1 small can water
  chestnuts, drained and quartered
600 ml/1 pt/2½ cups chicken
  stock, made with 2 stock cubes
15 ml/1 tbsp soy sauce
30 ml/2 tbsp cornflour (cornstarch)
30 ml/2 tbsp walnuts, chopped
To serve:
Chinese Leaf and Mango Salad
  (see page 269)

Place the chicken in a shallow dish. Drizzle with sherry and add a few grains of artificial sweetener. Toss to coat and leave to marinate for 2 hours. Melt the low-fat spread in a flameproof casserole (Dutch oven). Add the chicken and brown on all sides. Remove from the pan with a draining spoon. Add the spring onions and mushrooms and cook, stirring, for 2 minutes. Add the water chestnuts, stock and soy sauce. Return the chicken to the pan and bring to the boil. Cover and transfer to a preheated oven at 180°C/350°F/gas mark 4 for 1½ hours or until really tender. Lift out the chicken on to warmed plates and keep warm. Blend the cornflour with a little water and stir into the cooking liquid. Bring to the boil and cook for 2 minutes, stirring. Spoon over the chicken, sprinkle with the chopped walnuts and serve with Chinese Leaf and Mango Salad.

Pheasant with Calvados and Apples

SERVES 4

1 pheasant, quartered and skinned
  as much as possible
40 g/1½ oz/3 tbsp low-fat spread
2 large cooking (tart) apples,
  sliced thinly
Salt and freshly ground black
  pepper
15 ml/1 tbsp calvados or brandy
75 ml/5 tbsp low-fat single (light)
  cream
8 baby onions, peeled but left
  whole
Chopped parsley
To serve:
Fluffy Mashed Potatoes
  (see page 287)
Stir-fried Greens (see page 280)

Rinse the pheasant under cold running water and dry on kitchen paper. Melt half the low-fat spread in a flameproof casserole (Dutch oven) and brown the pheasant all over. Remove with a draining spoon. Put half the apple slices in the base of the casserole and toss in the juices. Lay the pheasant on top and season well. Add the remaining apple slices. Mix the calvados with the cream and pour over. Cover tightly and cook in a preheated oven at 180°C/350°F/gas mark 4 for 1 hour. Meanwhile, boil the onions in water for 5 minutes. Drain, dry on kitchen paper and fry (sauté) in the remaining low-fat spread to brown. Arrange around the top of the casserole and return to the oven for 15 minutes. Sprinkle with chopped parsley and serve with Fluffy Mashed Potatoes and Stir-fried Greens.

Winter Chicken Stew

SERVES 4

4 chicken portions, skinned as
   much as possible
25 g/1 oz/2 tbsp low-fat spread
1 onion, sliced
4 carrots, sliced
1 small swede (rutabaga), sliced
100 g/4 oz/⅔ cup pearl barley
900 ml/1½ pts/3¾ cups chicken
   stock, made with 2 stock cubes
Salt and freshly ground black
   pepper
3 unpeeled potatoes, scrubbed and
   cut into bite-sized chunks
1 small green cabbage, shredded

Brown the chicken portions in the low-fat spread in a large saucepan. Remove from the pan with a draining spoon. Add the onion, carrots and swede and fry (sauté) for 2 minutes, stirring. Add the barley and stock and return the chicken to the pan. Season to taste. Bring to the boil, reduce the heat and simmer for 45 minutes. Add the potatoes and cabbage, cover and continue cooking for 20 minutes or until everything is tender. Serve in large open soup bowls.

Fijian Chicken

SERVES 4

4 chicken portions, skinned as
   much as possible
25 g/1 oz/2 tbsp low-fat spread
425 g/15 oz/1 large can pineapple
   pieces in natural juice, drained,
   reserving the juice
15 ml/1 tbsp soy sauce
4 celery sticks, sliced
1 carrot, chopped
1 green (bell) pepper, cut into thin
   strips
3 tomatoes, quartered
Salt and freshly ground black
   pepper
15 ml/1 tbsp cornflour
   (cornstarch)
To serve:
175 g/6 oz/¾ cup long-grain rice,
   boiled
Melon and Cucumber Salad
   (see page 267)

Brown the chicken in the low-fat spread in a saucepan. Remove from the pan with a draining spoon. Make the pineapple juice up to 300 ml/ ½ pt/1¼ cups with water. Add to the pan with the soy sauce, celery and carrot. Add the chicken. Bring to the boil, reduce the heat, cover and simmer for 20 minutes. Add the pineapple pieces, green pepper, tomatoes and a little salt and pepper and cook for a further 20 minutes or until the chicken is tender. Lift out the chicken and transfer to warmed plates. Blend the cornflour with 30 ml/2 tbsp water and stir into the pan. Bring to the boil and cook for 1 minute, stirring. Taste and re-season if necessary. Spoon over the chicken and serve with the rice and Melon and Cucumber Salad.

Chicken Paprika

SERVES 4

2 onions, sliced
25 g/1 oz/2 tbsp low-fat spread
4 boneless chicken breasts, about
    175 g/6 oz each
30 ml/2 tbsp paprika
400 g/14 oz/1 large can chopped
    tomatoes
228 g/8 oz/1 small can pimientos,
    drained and chopped
Salt and freshly ground black
    pepper
45 ml/3 tbsp very low-fat plain
    yoghurt
Chopped parsley
To serve:
Caraway Noodles (see page 295)
Mixed Green Salad (see page 265)

Fry (sauté) the onions in the low-fat spread in a large saucepan for 2 minutes. Add the chicken breasts and fry on each side to brown. Add the remaining ingredients except the yoghurt and parsley. Bring to the boil, reduce the heat, part-cover and simmer for 20 minutes. Remove the lid after 10 minutes. Taste and re-season if necessary. Remove the chicken and transfer to warmed serving plates. Stir the yoghurt into the sauce. Spoon over, garnish with chopped parsley and serve with Caraway Noodles and Plain Green Salad.

Chicken and Broccoli Cheese

SERVES 4

350 g/12 oz broccoli, cut into
    florets
225 g/8 oz/2 cups cooked chicken,
    cut into bite-sized pieces
25 g/1 oz/2 tbsp low-fat spread
1 green (bell) pepper, chopped
1 onion, chopped
20 g/¾ oz/3 tbsp plain (all-
    purpose) flour
300 ml/½ pt/1¼ cups skimmed
    milk
50 g/2 oz/1 cup low-fat Cheddar
    cheese, grated
Salt and freshly ground black
    pepper
25 g/1 oz/1 cup bran flakes,
    crushed
1.5 ml/¼ tsp chilli powder
To serve:
Bacon and Onion Topped
    Tomatoes (see page 291)

Cook the broccoli in lightly salted boiling water until just tender. Drain and transfer to an ovenproof serving dish. Scatter the chicken over. Melt the low-fat spread in the broccoli saucepan. Stir in the chopped pepper and onion and cook, stirring, for 3 minutes. Stir in the flour. Remove from the heat and blend in the milk. Return to the heat and bring to the boil stirring all the time. Cook for 2 minutes. Stir in the cheese and season to taste. Pour over the chicken and broccoli. Mix the bran flakes with the chilli powder and sprinkle over. Bake in a preheated oven at 190°C/375°F/gas mark 5 for 20 minutes. Serve hot with Bacon and Onion Topped Tomatoes.

Turkey and Cranberry Burgers

SERVES 4

450 g/1 lb/4 cups minced (ground) turkey
1 small onion, finely chopped
15 ml/1 tbsp chopped parsley
45 ml/3 tbsp fresh breadcrumbs
Grated rind of ½ lemon
2.5 ml/½ tsp dried thyme
1.5 ml/¼ tsp grated nutmeg
Salt and freshly ground black pepper
1 egg, beaten
40 ml/8 tsp cranberry sauce
4 small slices bread
Low-fat spread
4 parsley sprigs
To serve:
Brussels Spouts with Almonds (see page 292)

Mix the turkey with the onion, parsley, breadcrumbs, lemon rind, thyme and nutmeg and season with salt and pepper. Mix with the egg to bind. Shape into eight flat cakes. Put 10 ml/2 tsp cranberry sauce on each of four patties. Top with the remaining ones and press the edges together well to seal. Grill (broil) on each side for about 5 minutes or until golden brown and cooked through. Meanwhile, cut large rounds from the slices of bread and spread very thinly on both sides with low-fat spread. Fry (sauté) in a frying pan (skillet) until golden brown on both sides. Transfer to four warmed plates. Top each slice with a burger, garnish with a parsley sprig and serve with Brussels Sprouts with Almonds.

Easy Tandoori Chicken

SERVES 4

8 chicken drumsticks, skin removed
300 ml/½ pt/1¼ cups very low-fat plain yoghurt
1 small garlic clove, crushed
15 ml/1 tbsp tandoori powder
5 ml/1 tsp chopped coriander (cilantro)
Salt and freshly ground black pepper
Shredded lettuce
Lemon wedges
Tomato wedges
Coriander sprigs
To serve:
175 g/6 oz/¾ cup basmati rice, boiled
Mustard Carrot Salad (see page 268)

Make several slashes in the flesh of the chicken legs. Mix together the yoghurt, garlic, tandoori powder, chopped coriander and seasoning in a large, shallow dish. Add the chicken and rub the mixture well into the slits. When well coated, leave to marinate for at least 3 hours. Place the chicken in a baking tin (pan). Spoon any remaining marinade over. Cover with foil. Bake in a preheated oven at 200°C/400°F/gas mark 6 for 45 minutes. Remove the foil, pour off any liquid and bake uncovered for 15 minutes or until well browned and cooked through. Garnish with lettuce, lemon wedges, tomato wedges and coriander leaves and serve with boiled basmati rice and Mustard Carrot Salad.

Mediterranean Jellied Chicken

15 ml/1 tbsp powdered gelatine
300 ml/½ pt/1¼ cups chicken
    stock, made with 1 stock cube
45 ml/3 tbsp lemon juice
75 ml/5 tbsp low-calorie
    mayonnaise
1 spring onion (scallion), finely
    chopped
3 celery sticks, chopped
1 green (bell) pepper, chopped
1 red (bell) pepper, chopped
5 cm/2 in piece cucumber, chopped
5 ml/1 tsp chopped basil
6 stuffed olives, sliced
350 g/12 oz/3 cups cooked
    chicken, chopped
Salt and freshly ground black
    pepper
Lollo rosso lettuce leaves
A basil sprig
To serve:
450 g/1 lb baby new potatoes,
    boiled
Mixed Salad (see page 269)

Dissolve the gelatine in the stock according to the packet directions. Stir in the lemon juice. Leave to cool. When cold, whisk in the mayonnaise and chill until the consistency of egg white, then fold in the prepared vegetables, the basil, olives and chicken. Season to taste. Turn into a fluted mould. Chill until set. Loosen the edges and turn out on to a bed of lollo rosso leaves. Garnish with a basil sprig and serve with boiled new potatoes and Mixed Salad.

Chicken Supreme Salad

4 small boneless chicken breasts
300 ml/½ pt/1¼ cups chicken
    stock, made with 1 stock cube
175 g/6 oz/¾ cup long-grain rice
Salt and freshly ground black
    pepper
½ cucumber, diced
2 red skinned eating (dessert)
    apples, diced
5 ml/1 tsp lemon juice
120 ml/4 fl oz/½ cup very low-fat
    plain yoghurt
75 ml/5 tbsp low-calorie
    mayonnaise
5 ml/1 tsp curry paste
10 ml/2 tsp smooth mango chutney
Torn coriander (cilantro) leaves
To serve:
Banana and Chicory Salad
    (see page 281)

Put the chicken in a saucepan with the stock. Bring to the boil, reduce the heat and poach gently for about 10–15 minutes until the chicken is tender. Remove from the pan with a draining spoon and leave until cold. Meanwhile, make the stock up to 600 ml/1 pt/2½ cups with water. Bring to the boil, add a little salt and cook the rice for about 10 minutes until tender. Drain, rinse with cold water, drain again and leave until cold. Mix in the cucumber and apple, tossed in the lemon juice, and pile on to four serving plates. Place the cold chicken breasts on top. Mix the yoghurt with the mayonnaise and curry paste. Stir in the chutney and season to taste. Spoon over the chicken and garnish with a few torn coriander leaves. Serve with Banana and Chicory Salad.

FISH

CALORIES OR LESS

Tuna Gnocchi

SERVES 4

600 ml/1 pt/2½ cups skimmed milk
5 ml/1 tsp salt
Freshly ground black pepper
1 bay leaf
1.5 ml/¼ tsp grated nutmeg
150 g/5 oz/scant 1 cup semolina (cream of wheat)
2 eggs
100 g/4 oz/1 cup low-fat Cheddar cheese, grated
185 g/6½ oz/1 small can tuna in brine, drained
295 g/10½ oz/1 small can condensed cream of mushroom soup
15 g/½ oz/1 tbsp low-fat spread, melted
Tomato wedges
Chopped coriander (cilantro) leaves
To serve:
Italian Celeriac Salad (see page 270)

Put the milk, salt, some pepper, the bay leaf and nutmeg in a saucepan. Blend in the semolina. Bring to the boil and cook for 10 minutes, stirring all the time, until really thick. Discard the bay leaf. Beat in the eggs and three-quarters of the cheese. Spread out on non-stick baking parchment on a baking sheet to about 2 cm/¾ in thick, using a wet palette knife. Leave to cool, then chill for 1 hour. Cut into 4 cm/1½ in squares. Meanwhile, mix the tuna with the soup and turn into a 1.2 litre/2 pt/5 cup ovenproof dish. Arrange the gnocchi overlapping around the top. Brush with the low-fat spread and sprinkle with the remaining cheese. Bake in a preheated oven at 200°C/400°F/gas mark 6 for 30 minutes until golden and sizzling. Garnish with tomato wedges and chopped coriander and serve with Italian Celeriac Salad.

Midweek Paella

SERVES 4

1 packet savoury vegetable rice
450 ml/¾ pt/2 cups boiling water
100 g/4 oz/1 cup cooked chicken, diced
250 g/9 oz/1 small can mussels in brine, drained
100 g/4 oz/1 cup peeled prawns (shrimp)
Chopped parsley
To serve:
Hot Herb Bread (see page 293)
Mixed Green Salad (see page 265)

Put the rice in a pan with the boiling water. Stir, cover and simmer for 12 minutes. Add the remaining ingredients except the parsley and cook for a further 8 minutes until all the liquid has been absorbed and the rice is tender. Spoon on to warmed plates and sprinkle with chopped parsley. Serve with Hot Herb Bread and Mixed Green Salad.

Salmon Gnocchi

SERVES 4

Prepare as for Tuna Gnocchi (see page 171) but substitute a small can of pink salmon, skin and bones removed, for the tuna and celery soup for mushroom. For added texture, blanch 2 chopped sticks of celery in boiling water for 2 minutes and mix in with the soup and salmon before topping with the gnocchi.

Scandinavian Trout

SERVES 4

4 trout, cleaned
Salt and freshly ground black pepper
25 g/1 oz/2 tbsp low-fat spread
150 ml/¼ pt/⅔ cup buttermilk
5 ml/1 tsp cornflour (cornstarch)
15 ml/1 tbsp snipped chives
15 ml/1 tbsp chopped parsley
30 ml/2 tbsp flaked (slivered) almonds
To serve:
Parsleyed Potatoes (see page 289)
Curly Endive Salad (see page 265)

Rinse the fish and pat dry with kitchen paper. Remove the heads, if preferred. Season lightly. Melt the low-fat spread in a large frying pan (skillet) and fry (sauté) the fish for 3 minutes on each side. Blend the buttermilk with the cornflour and add to the pan with the herbs and a little more salt and pepper. Cover with foil or a lid and cook gently for about 8 minutes until the fish is cooked through. Meanwhile, dry-fry the almonds in a frying pan until golden. Transfer the fish to warmed serving plates. Stir the creamy juices well and spoon over. Garnish with the toasted almonds and serve with Parsleyed Potatoes and Curly Endive Salad.

Crab Soufflé

SERVES 4

35 g/1¼ oz/2½ tbsp low-fat spread
2 courgettes (zucchini), sliced
50 g/2 oz button mushrooms, sliced
Salt and freshly ground black pepper
2.5 ml/½ tsp dried mixed herbs
15 g/½ oz/2 tbsp plain (all-purpose) flour
150 ml/¼ pt/⅔ cup skimmed milk
15 ml/1 tbsp low-calorie mayonnaise
30 ml/2 tbsp grated Parmesan cheese
3 eggs, separated
170 g/6 oz/1 small can white crabmeat, drained
To serve:
Herby Potatoes (see page 289)
Mixed Salad (see page 269)

Use 10 ml/2 tsp of the low-fat spread to grease an 18 cm/7 in soufflé dish. Melt 15 g/½ oz/1 tbsp of the spread in a frying pan (skillet). Add the courgettes and mushrooms and cook, stirring, for 2 minutes. Cover with a lid and cook gently for 5 minutes until softened and the juices have run. Season to taste with salt and pepper and add the herbs. Turn into the soufflé dish. Melt the remaining low-fat spread in a saucepan. Add the flour and milk and bring to the boil, stirring all the time. Beat in the mayonnaise, Parmesan and egg yolks. Stir in the crabmeat. Season. Whisk the egg whites until stiff and fold in with a metal spoon. Spoon on top of the mushrooms and courgettes and bake in a preheated oven at 200°C/400°F/gas mark 6 for 25–30 minutes until well risen, golden and just set. Serve straight away with Herby Potatoes and Mixed Salad.

Poached Hake in Velvet Lemon Sauce

SERVES 4

2 lemons
4 hake fillets, about 175 g/6 oz
 each, skinned
150 ml/¼ pt/⅔ cup fish or vegetable
 stock, made with ½ stock cube
150 ml/¼ pt/⅔ cup skimmed milk
1 small bay leaf
15 g/½ oz/1 tbsp low-fat spread
150 ml/¼ pt/⅔ cup very low-fat
 plain yoghurt
15 ml/1 tbsp cornflour
 (cornstarch)
Salt and white pepper
A few grains of artificial sweetener
 (optional)
A few coriander (cilantro) leaves
To serve:
Parsleyed Potatoes (see page 289)
Baby Asparagus Spears
 (see page 280)

Pare the rind off one of the lemons and cut into thin strips. Boil in water for 2 minutes. Drain, rinse with cold water, drain again and reserve for garnish. Grate the rind off the second lemon and squeeze the juice from both. Put the fish in a flameproof casserole (Dutch oven) with the stock, milk, most of the lemon rind, the lemon juice and the bay leaf. Bring to the boil, reduce the heat, cover and cook gently for 6 minutes or until the fish is tender and just cooked through. Carefully lift out the fish with a fish slice. Transfer to warmed plates and keep warm. Blend the low-fat spread into the juices. Blend together the yoghurt and cornflour and stir into the pan. Bring to the boil and cook for 2 minutes, stirring. Season to taste with salt, pepper and a few grains of sweetener, if liked. Discard the bay leaf.

Spoon the sauce over the fish and sprinkle with the reserved lemon rind. Lay a few coriander leaves to the side of each piece and serve with Parsleyed Potatoes and Baby Asparagus Spears.

Smoked Mussel and Potato Bake

SERVES 4

450 g/1 lb potatoes, sliced
100 g/4 oz/1 small can smoked
 mussels
225 g/8 oz/1 cup very low-fat soft
 cheese
Lemon juice
15 ml/1 tbsp snipped chives
15 ml/1 tbsp chopped parsley
Salt and freshly ground black pepper
150 ml/¼ pt/⅔ cup skimmed milk
1 egg, beaten
50 g/2 oz/½ cup Emmental (Swiss)
 cheese, grated
A parsley sprig
To serve:
Baked Tomatoes with Spring
 Onions (see page 279)
Crisp Green Salad (see page 265)

Par-boil the potatoes in lightly salted water for 4 minutes until almost tender. Drain. Drain the oil from the mussels and roughly chop. Mix with the soft cheese. Layer the potatoes with the cheese mixture, sprinkling each layer of cheese with lemon juice, the herbs and a little salt and pepper. Finish with a layer of potatoes. Beat together the egg and milk and pour over. Sprinkle with the Gruyère. Bake in a preheated oven at 190°C/375°F/gas mark 5 for about 45 minutes or until set and golden brown and the potatoes are tender. Garnish with a parsley sprig and serve with Baked Tomatoes with Spring Onions and Crisp Green Salad.

Cod Steaks with Fennel

SERVES 4

450 g/1 lb potatoes, cut into
    chunks
100 g/4 oz French (green) beans,
    cut into short lengths
25 g/1 oz/2 tbsp low-fat spread
1 onion, sliced
1 garlic clove, crushed
1 fennel head, sliced
225 g/8 oz button mushrooms
400 g/14 oz/1 large can chopped
    tomatoes
4 cod steaks, skinned
150 ml/¼ pt/⅔ cup dry white wine
Salt and freshly ground black
    pepper
Lemon twists
Chopped parsley
To serve:
1 small French stick

Cook the potatoes in lightly salted boiling water for 5 minutes. Add the beans half-way through cooking. The vegetables should be almost cooked. Drain. Meanwhile, melt the low-fat spread in a flameproof casserole (Dutch oven) and fry (sauté) the onion, garlic and fennel for 4 minutes, stirring. Add the mushrooms and tomatoes and bring to the boil. Add the potatoes and beans, then lay the fish on top and pour over the wine. Season. Transfer to a preheated oven at 190°C/375°F/gas mark 5 for 40 minutes until the fish and vegetables are tender. Garnish the fish steaks with lemon twists and chopped parsley and serve with a small French stick to mop up the juices.

Warm Summer Seafood

SERVES 4

450 g/1 lb baby squid, cleaned and
    sliced into rings
15 ml/1 tbsp olive oil
25 g/1 oz/2 tbsp low-fat spread
1 garlic clove, crushed
5 ml/1 tsp fresh dill (dill weed)
15 ml/1 tbsp chopped parsley
15 ml/1 tbsp lemon juice
Salt and freshly ground black
    pepper
4 crab sticks, cut into chunks
225 g/8 oz cooked tiger prawns
    (jumbo shrimp), peeled but the
    tails left on
225 g/8 oz/2 cups peeled prawns
    (shrimp)
1 lollo rosso lettuce, torn into
    pieces
½ cucumber, peeled, seeded and
    cut into matchsticks
8 cherry tomatoes, halved
A few dill sprigs
4 green olives
Lemon wedges

Put the squid in a frying pan (skillet) with the oil and low-fat spread and the garlic and cook gently, stirring, for about 5 minutes until pink and tender. Stir in the herbs, lemon juice and some salt and pepper. Add the crab and both types of prawns and toss for 2 minutes. Turn into a large salad bowl and add the lettuce, cucumber and tomatoes. Toss and re-season if necessary. Serve straight away, garnished with dill sprigs, olives and lemon wedges.

Kedgeree

SERVES 4

175 g/6 oz/¾ cup long-grain rice
2 eggs, scrubbed under the cold
*   tap*
50 g/2 oz/½ cup frozen peas
175 g/6 oz smoked haddock
150 ml/¼ pt/⅔ cup skimmed milk
25 g/1 oz/2 tbsp low-fat spread
1 small onion, finely chopped
Salt and freshly ground black
*   pepper*
1.5 ml/¼ tsp grated nutmeg
30 ml/2 tbsp chopped parsley
15 ml/1 tbsp low-fat single (light)
*   cream*
To serve:
Poached Tomatoes with
**   Mushrooms (see page 279)**

Bring a pan of lightly salted water to the boil. Add the rice and the eggs in their shells and boil for 10 minutes or until the rice is tender. Add the peas after 5 minutes. Drain and plunge the eggs immediately into cold water. Shell and roughly chop the eggs. Meanwhile, poach the fish in the milk for 5 minutes or until tender. Remove the fish from the pan, reserving the milk. Flake the fish roughly and remove the skin and any bones. Meanwhile, melt the low-fat spread in the rice saucepan and fry (sauté) the onion for 3 minutes, stirring until softened and only lightly golden. Stir in the rice and peas, the flaked fish, eggs, salt and pepper to taste and the nutmeg. Toss over a gentle heat. Stir in the parsley and cream and moisten to taste with the reserved milk (I use about 30 ml/2 tbsp). When piping hot, spoon on to warmed plates and serve with Poached Tomatoes with Mushrooms.

Cheese and Garlic-topped Haddock

SERVES 4

25 g/1 oz/2 tbsp low-fat spread
4 pieces haddock fillet, about
*   175 g/6 oz each, skinned*
50 g/2 oz/½ cup low-fat red
*   Leicester cheese, grated*
15 ml/1 tbsp skimmed milk
15 ml/1 tbsp chopped parsley
1 small garlic clove, crushed
Salt and freshly ground black
*   pepper*
Parsley sprigs
To serve:
White Chips (see page 285)
Tomatoes with Courgettes (see
**   page 275)**

Grease a shallow flameproof dish with a little of the low-fat spread. Put the fish in it, skinned sides up. Grill (broil) for 3 minutes. Turn over. Mix the remaining low-fat spread with the cheese, milk, parsley, garlic and a little salt and pepper. Spread over the fish and return to the grill (broiler) for about 10 minutes until golden and bubbling and the fish is cooked through. Carefully transfer to warmed serving plates, garnish with parsley sprigs and serve with White Chips and Tomatoes with Courgettes.

Tasty Whiting Bake

SERVES 4

100 g/4 oz/½ cup long-grain rice
40 g/1½ oz/3 tbsp low-fat spread
2 large onions, sliced
30 ml/2 tbsp chopped parsley
5 ml/1 tsp paprika
450 g/1 lb tomatoes, skinned and chopped
Salt and freshly ground black pepper
450 g/1 lb whiting fillet, cut into thick strips
15 ml/1 tbsp cornflour (cornstarch)
5 ml/1 tsp dried dill (dill weed)
150 ml/¼ pt/⅔ cup soured (dairy sour) cream
25 g/1 oz/½ cup wholemeal breadcrumbs
1.5 ml/¼ tsp cayenne
To serve:
Spinach with Mushrooms (see page 277)

Cook the rice according to the packet directions. Drain, rinse with cold water and drain again. Lightly grease a 1.5 litre/2½ pt/6 cup ovenproof dish with a very little of the low-fat spread. Spoon the rice into the base and spread out. Melt 25 g/1 oz/2 tbsp of the remaining low-fat spread in the rice saucepan and fry (sauté) the onions for 5 minutes, stirring, until browned and softened. Mix in the parsley, paprika, tomatoes and some salt and pepper. Spoon over the rice. Toss the fish in the cornflour with a little salt and pepper. Lay on top of the tomato mixture and sprinkle with the dill. Pour over the soured cream. Cover and bake in a preheated oven at 190°C/375°F/gas mark 5 for 30 minutes. Meanwhile, melt the remaining low-fat spread in a frying pan (skillet) and fry the crumbs, stirring, until golden brown. Mix with the cayenne. Scatter over the cooked fish dish and serve straight away with Spinach with Mushrooms.

Prawn Supper

SERVES 4

100 g/4 oz/½ cup long-grain rice
225 g/8 oz/2 cups peeled prawns (shrimp)
295 g/10½ oz/1 small can condensed cream of mushroom soup
50 g/2 oz/½ cup low-fat Cheddar cheese, grated
25 g/1 oz/¼ cup blue cheese, crumbled
10 ml/2 tsp tomato ketchup (catsup)
For the garnish:
1 celery stick
5 cm/2 in piece cucumber
1 carrot
15 ml/1 tbsp chopped parsley
To serve:
Garlic Bread (see page 293)

Boil the rice according to the packet directions. Drain and mix with the remaining ingredients. Spoon into an ovenproof dish and bake in a preheated oven at 180°C/350°F/gas mark 4 for about 30 minutes until piping hot. Meanwhile, prepare the garnish. Cut the celery stick into three and cut each piece into very thin matchsticks. Cut the cucumber into very thin matchsticks. Cut the carrot into two or three pieces, then into very thin matchsticks. Mix together with the parsley. Spoon the prawn mixture on to warmed plates and garnish with a small pile of the celery mixture. Serve hot with Garlic Bread.

Fish Pie

SERVES 4

**225 g/8 oz cod or haddock fillet,
skinned**
375 ml/13 fl oz/1½ cups milk
**50 g/2 oz button mushrooms,
sliced**
50 g/2 oz/½ cup frozen peas
**20 g/¾ oz/3 tbsp plain (all-
purpose) flour**
40 g/1½ oz/3 tbsp low-fat spread
**Salt and freshly ground black
pepper**
30 ml/2 tbsp chopped parsley
**450 g/1 lb potatoes, cut into small
pieces**
**2 eggs, scrubbed under the cold
tap**
To serve:
**Green Beans with Cherry
Tomatoes (see page 267)**

Put the fish in a saucepan with
300 ml/½ pt/1¼ cups of the milk.
Add the mushrooms and peas. Bring to
the boil, cover, reduce the heat and
simmer gently for about 8 minutes or
until the fish is tender. Lift out the fish,
mushrooms and peas with a draining
spoon and transfer to a flameproof
serving dish. Flake the fish roughly
with a fork, discarding any bones.
Blend half the remaining cold milk
with the flour and stir into the fish
milk with a third of the low-fat spread.
Bring to the boil and cook for 2 minutes, stirring all the time. Season to
taste and stir in the parsley. Pour over
the fish mixture in the dish and mix in.
Boil the potatoes and the eggs in their
shells in salted water for ten minutes
until the potatoes are tender. Drain
and plunge the eggs into cold water.
Mash the potatoes with the remaining
milk and half the remaining low-fat
spread. Shell and chop the eggs and
add to the fish mixture. Pile the potato
on top and dot with the remaining
low-fat spread. Place under a hot grill
(broiler) until the potato is browned
and the mixture is piping hot. Serve
with Green Beans with Cherry
Tomatoes.

Tempting Baked Haddock

SERVES 4

**4 small haddock fillets, about
150 g/5 oz each, skinned**
5 ml/1 tsp extra virgin olive oil
25 g/1 oz/2 tbsp low-fat spread
60 ml/4 tbsp dry vermouth
**30 ml/2 tbsp tomato ketchup
(catsup)**
2.5 ml/½ tsp dried mixed herbs
**Salt and freshly ground black
pepper**
30 ml/2 tbsp white breadcrumbs
15 ml/1 tbsp chopped parsley
1 garlic clove, very finely chopped
To serve:
Fennel Potatoes (see page 288)
Mixed Leaf Salad (see page 265)

Lay the fish in a shallow flameproof
dish. Heat the oil with the low-fat
spread and drizzle over. Blend the vermouth with the ketchup and drizzle
over. Sprinkle with the herbs and salt
and pepper. Mix the breadcrumbs with
the parsley and garlic. Scatter over,
then bake in a preheated oven at
180°C/350°F/gas mark 4 for about 30
minutes until cooked through and
golden on top. Serve with Fennel
Potatoes and Mixed Leaf Salad.

Golden-topped Tuna and Sweetcorn

SERVES 4

175 g/6 oz penne or other pasta shapes
20 g/¾ oz/3 tbsp plain (all-purpose) flour
300 ml/½ pt/1¼ cups skimmed milk
20 g/¾ oz/1½ tbsp low-fat spread
75 g/3 oz/¾ cup strong low-fat Cheddar cheese, grated
Salt and freshly ground black pepper
185 g/6½ oz/1 small can tuna in brine, drained
200 g/7 oz/1 small can sweetcorn (corn), drained
30 ml/2 tbsp chopped parsley
25 g/1 oz/1 cup cornflakes, crushed
To serve:
Iceberg Boats (see page 270)

Cook the pasta according to the packet directions. Drain. Whisk together the flour and milk in a saucepan until smooth. Add the low-fat spread. Bring to the boil and cook for 2 minutes, stirring, until thickened and smooth. Stir in two-thirds of the cheese, a little salt and pepper, the tuna, sweetcorn and parsley. Mix well. Stir in the pasta. Taste and add more seasoning if necessary. Heat through. Spoon into a flameproof dish. Mix the remaining cheese with the crushed cornflakes and sprinkle over the top. Place under a moderate grill (broiler) until golden and bubbling. Serve hot with Iceberg Boats.

Fishermen's Crumble

SERVES 4

75 g/3 oz/¾ cup plain (all-purpose) flour
10 ml/2 tsp paprika
40 g/1½ oz/3 tbsp low-fat spread
50 g/2 oz/½ cup Edam cheese, grated
450 g/1 lb white fish fillets, skinned and cubed
295 g/10½ oz/1 small can condensed celery soup
100 g/4 oz/1 cup frozen diced mixed vegetables
2.5 ml/½ tsp dried mixed herbs
15 ml/1 tbsp snipped chives
To serve:
Broccoli

Put the flour in a bowl with the paprika. Add the low-fat spread and rub in with the fingertips or a fork until the mixture resembles breadcrumbs. Stir in the cheese. Put the fish in an ovenproof dish and stir in the soup, vegetables and herbs. Spoon the crumble mixture over and press down lightly. Bake in a preheated oven at 200°C/400°F/gas mark 6 for about 30 minutes until golden brown and cooked through. Serve with broccoli.

Mushroom-stuffed Plaice

SERVES 4

**100 g/4 oz button mushrooms,
 finely chopped
25 g/1 oz/2 tbsp low-fat spread
50 g/2 oz/1 cup fresh breadcrumbs
15 ml/1 tbsp chopped coriander
 (cilantro) or parsley, or half and
 half
Salt and freshly ground black
 pepper
4 plaice fillets, skinned if dark
150 ml/¼ pt/⅔ cup low-fat single
 (light) cream
Coriander or parsley sprigs**
To serve:
**Tomato Potatoes (see page 295)
Crisp Green Salad (see page 265)**

Cook the mushrooms in the low-fat spread for 2 minutes, stirring. Add the breadcrumbs and chopped herbs and season with a little salt and pepper. Halve the plaice fillets lengthways. Divide the stuffing between the centres of the fillets and fold over the two ends to form parcels. Transfer to individual ovenproof dishes. Spoon the cream over. Season very lightly again with pepper and bake in a preheated oven at 180°C/350°F/gas mark 4 for 20 minutes until cooked through. Garnish each with a small coriander or parsley sprig and serve with Tomato Potatoes and Crisp Green Salad.

Cod with Cheese and Anchovies

SERVES 4

**4 pieces of cod fillet, about
 150 g/5 oz each, skinned
25 g/1 oz/2 tbsp low-fat spread
2 ripe tomatoes, sliced
100 g/4 oz Mozzarella cheese,
 thinly sliced
50 g/2 oz/1 small can anchovies,
 drained
A few torn basil leaves**
To serve:
**1 small ciabatta loaf
Italian Celeriac Salad (see page
 270)**

Fry (sauté) the fish in the low-fat spread for 1 minute on each side. Top with tomato slices, then the cheese. Rinse the anchovy fillets and pat dry. Arrange attractively on top. Cover the pan with foil or a lid and cook gently for about 6–7 minutes until the fish is cooked and the cheese has melted. Transfer to warmed serving plates. Throw a few torn basil leaves over each and serve with a small ciabatta loaf and Italian Celeriac Salad.

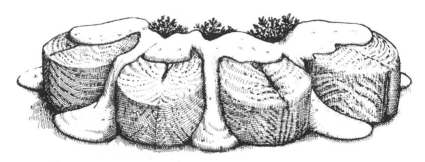

Fish Rosti

SERVES 4

25 g/1 oz/2 tbsp low-fat spread
450 g/1 lb potatoes, grated
Salt and freshly ground black
    pepper
450 g/1 lb white fish fillets,
    skinned and cut into small
    pieces
Grated rind of ½ lemon
15 ml/1 tbsp chopped parsley
300 ml/½ pt/1¼ cups passata
    (sieved tomatoes)
5 ml/1 tsp chopped basil
Lemon wedges
To serve:
Mangetout (snow peas)

Melt the low-fat spread in a frying pan (skillet). Add half the potatoes and press down well. Season with salt and pepper. Add the fish in an even layer and sprinkle with the lemon rind, parsley and a little seasoning. Top with the remaining potatoes, press down well again and season lightly. Cover with foil or a lid and cook gently for 30 minutes until cooked through. Meanwhile, heat the passata with the basil in a small saucepan. Turn the fish cake out on to a warmed serving plate. Garnish with lemon wedges and serve, cut into quarters, with the tomato sauce and mangetout.

Smoked Salmon and Broccoli Papardelle

SERVES 4

225 g/8 oz papardelle (wide ribbon
    noodles)
175 g/6 oz broccoli, cut into tiny
    florets
100 g/4 oz smoked salmon pieces,
    cut up if necessary
50 g/2 oz/¼ cup very low-fat quark
2 eggs
60 ml/4 tbsp skimmed milk
Salt and freshly ground black
    pepper
A squeeze of lemon juice
25 g/1 oz fresh Parmesan cheese,
    thinly shaved with a potato
    peeler

Cook the pasta according to the packet directions. Add the broccoli for the last 5 minutes cooking time. Drain and return to the saucepan. Add the salmon and quark. Toss gently. Beat together the eggs and milk and add to the pan with some salt and pepper. Cook over a gentle heat until creamy but not totally scrambled. Taste and add lemon juice and a little more seasoning if necesssary. Pile on to warmed plates and top with Parmesan shavings.

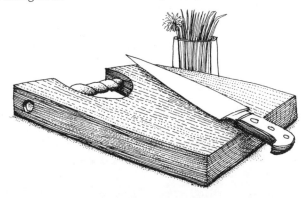

···············PORK, BACON & HAM ···············

CALORIES OR LESS

Bacon-topped Liver Bake

SERVES 4

5 ml/1 tsp low-fat spread
350 g/12 oz pigs' liver, trimmed
1 onion, quartered
1 slice bread
8 sage leaves
2 parsley sprigs
Salt and freshly ground black
  pepper
1 egg, beaten
8 lean rashers (slices) streaky
  bacon, rinded
300 ml/½ pt/1¼ cups chicken
  stock, made with 1 stock cube
75 g/3 oz button mushrooms,
  sliced
15 ml/1 tbsp cornflour
  (cornstarch)
15 ml/1 tbsp sherry or water
To serve:
450 g/1 lb potatoes, boiled
Peas

Lightly grease a 1.2 litre/2 pt/5 cup ovenproof serving dish with the low-fat spread. Mince (grind) the liver, onion, bread and herbs into a bowl. Alternatively, put in a food processor but don't process too finely. Season with salt and pepper and mix with the egg. Press into the dish. Lay the bacon on top and spoon over 45 ml/3 tbsp of the stock. Cover with foil and bake in a preheated oven at 190°C/375°F/gas mark 5 for 30 minutes. Remove the foil after 20 minutes to allow the top to brown. Meanwhile, put the remaining stock in a saucepan. Add the mushrooms and simmer gently for 5 minutes. Blend the cornflour with the sherry or water and stir into the stock. Bring to the boil and simmer for 1 minute, stirring. Serve the bake with the sauce and plain boiled potatoes and peas.

Fireside Supper

SERVES 4

2 x 400 g/2 x 14 oz/2 large cans
  no-added-sugar baked beans
1 packet onion soup mix
30 ml/2 tbsp tomato purée (paste)
30 ml/2 tbsp water
15 ml/1 tbsp honey
15 ml/1 tbsp Dijon mustard
16 hot-dog sausages, cut into
  short lengths
25 g/1 oz/½ cup fresh breadcrumbs
5 ml/1 tsp dried mixed herbs
A pinch of garlic salt
To serve:
Celery and Apple Slaw
  (see page 273)

Blend the first six ingredients in an ovenproof dish. Stir in the hot dogs. Cover and bake in a preheated oven at 180°C/350°F/gas mark 4 for 1 hour. Meanwhile, toss the breadcrumbs, herbs and a little garlic salt over a moderate heat in a frying pan (skillet) until golden brown and crispy. Sprinkle over the casserole and serve piping hot in bowls with Celery and Apple Slaw to follow.

Saucy Braised Celery and Ham

SERVES 4

430 g/15½ oz/1 large can celery
    hearts (4 in all), drained
4 lean slices ham
100 g/4 oz/1 cup frozen peas
228 g/8 oz/1 small can chopped
    tomatoes
2.5 ml/½ tsp dried oregano
25 g/1 oz/¼ cup plain (all-purpose)
    flour
450 ml/¾ pt/2 cups skimmed milk
25 g/1 oz/2 tbsp low-fat spread
40 g/1½ oz/⅓ cup low-fat Cheddar
    cheese, grated
40 g/1½ oz/⅓ cup Emmental
    (Swiss) cheese, grated
To serve:
Crunchy Spinach Salad
    (see page 268)

Dry the celery on kitchen paper. Wrap a piece of ham round each celery heart. Spread the peas in the base of an ovenproof serving dish. Lay the celery on top. Spoon over the tomatoes and sprinkle with the oregano. Blend the flour with the milk in a saucepan. Add the low-fat spread. Bring to the boil and cook for 2 minutes, stirring. Stir in two-thirds of the cheeses and season to taste. Spoon into the dish to cover the tomatoes completely. Sprinkle with the remaining cheese. Bake in a preheated oven at 190°C/375°F/gas mark 5 for about 25 minutes until golden brown and piping hot. Serve with Crunchy Spinach Salad.

Pork with Creamy Orange Sauce

SERVES 4

4 boneless pork chops, about
    150 g/5 oz each, trimmed of all
    fat
30 ml/2 tbsp plain (all-purpose)
    flour
Salt and freshly ground black
    pepper
A good pinch of ground ginger
25 g/1 oz/2 tbsp low-fat spread
Grated rind and juice of 2 oranges
Chicken stock, made with 1 stock
    cube
A few grains of artificial sweetener
75 ml/5 tbsp soured (dairy sour)
    cream
Snipped chives
To serve:
Parsleyed Potatoes (see page 289)
Mangetout (snow peas)

Coat the chops in the flour, seasoned with a little salt and pepper and the ginger. Melt the low-fat spread in a large frying pan (skillet). Brown the chops on both sides. Remove from the pan. Make up the orange juice to 300 ml/½ pt/1¼ cups with the stock. Sprinkle any remaining flour into the pan, then blend in the juice and stock. Add a few grains of artificial sweetener and a little more salt and pepper to taste. Bring to the boil, stirring. Return the chops to the pan, cover, reduce the heat and simmer gently for 45 minutes or until the meat is really tender. Transfer the meat to four warmed plates. Stir in the soured cream and simmer for 5 minutes until slightly thickened. Taste and re-season if necessary. Spoon over the chops, garnish with snipped chives and serve with Parsleyed Potatoes and mangetout.

Kowloon Fried Rice

SERVES 4

100 g/4 oz/½ cup long-grain rice
2 carrots, diced
50 g/2 oz/¼ cup low-fat spread
3 eggs
Salt and freshly ground black
  pepper
100 g/4 oz/1 cup peeled prawns
  (shrimp)
225 g/8 oz/2 cups cooked lean
  pork, diced
100 g/4 oz button mushrooms,
  sliced
100 g/4 oz/1 cup frozen peas
60 ml/4 tbsp boiling water
¼ vegetable stock cube
30 ml/2 tbsp sherry
15 ml/1 tbsp soy sauce
To serve:
Chinese Leaf and Watercress Salad
  (see page 266)

Cook the rice and carrots in plenty of boiling, salted water for about 10–12 minutes until the rice is just tender. Drain, rinse with cold water and drain again. Meanwhile, heat half the low-fat spread in a frying pan (skillet). Beat two of the eggs with a little salt and pepper. Add to the pan and fry (sauté), lifting and stirring, until the mixture forms a flat omelette. Roll up and cut into strips when cool enough to handle. Heat the remaining low-fat spread in a wok or large frying pan. Add the rice, prawns, pork, mushrooms and peas and cook, tossing and stirring, for 5 minutes until piping hot. Mix together the water and stock cube until dissolved. Add to the pan with the sherry, soy sauce and a little more salt and pepper. Push the mixture to one side of the pan. Beat the third egg and pour in. Cook, stirring, until scrambled, then toss back into the rice. Pile on to warmed plates and serve topped with the omelette strips and with Chinese Leaf and Watercress Salad.

Pork Chilli

SERVES 4

450 g/1 lb/4 cups minced (ground)
  pork
2 onions, finely chopped
1 garlic clove, crushed
2.5 ml/½ tsp chilli powder
5 ml/1 tsp ground cumin
5 ml/1 tsp dried sage
400 g/14 oz/1 large can chopped
  tomatoes
15 ml/1 tbsp tomato purée (paste)
425 g/15 oz/1 large can white
  kidney or cannellini beans,
  drained
Salt and freshly ground black
  pepper
Chopped parsley
To serve:
Cheesy-topped Rice (see page 295)
Lettuce dressed with lemon juice
  and black pepper

Put the pork in a large saucepan with the onions and garlic. Fry (sauté), stirring, until the meat is brown and all the grains are separate. Pour off any fat. Stir in the chilli and cumin and cook for 1 minute. Add the remaining ingredients except the parsley and bring to the boil, stirring. Reduce the heat and simmer gently for 30 minutes, stirring occasionally. Taste and re-season if necessary. Serve on warmed plates, garnished with parsley with Cheesy-topped Rice and lettuce dressed with lemon juice and black pepper.

Parma Ham and Mushroom Ribbons

SERVES 4

225 g/8 oz papardelle (wide ribbon
  noodles)
25 g/1 oz/2 tbsp low-fat spread
100 g/4 oz button mushrooms,
  sliced
1 small garlic clove, crushed
90 ml/6 tbsp very low-fat crème
  fraîche
Salt and freshly ground black
  pepper
1.5 ml/¼ tsp grated nutmeg
30 ml/2 tbsp chopped parsley
75 g/3 oz wafer-thin slices lean
  Parma ham, cut into thin strips
20 ml/4 tsp grated Parmesan
  cheese
To serve:
Mixed Leaf Salad (see page 265)

Cook the pasta according to the
packet directions. Drain and return
to the pan. Meanwhile, melt the low-
fat spread in a saucepan and add the
mushrooms and garlic. Cook gently,
stirring, for 3 minutes until soft and
the juices run. Stir in the crème
fraîche, a little salt and pepper, the
nutmeg and parsley and blend well.
Add to the papardelle with the Parma
ham and toss gently until piping hot.
Pile on to warmed plates, sprinkle
with the Parmesan and serve with
Mixed Leaf Salad.

Pisa Pasta Prima

SERVES 4

225 g/8 oz rigatoni
225 g/8 oz/2 cups lean cooked
  ham pieces
2 onions, finely chopped
75 g/3 oz/⅓ cup low-fat spread
100 g/4 oz/1 cup frozen peas
5 ml/1 tsp dried mint
50 g/2 oz/½ cup Parmesan cheese,
  grated
Salt and freshly ground black
  pepper
30 ml/2 tbsp skimmed milk
To serve:
*Tomato and Basil Salad
  (see page 266)*

Cook the pasta according to the
packet directions. Drain and return
to the pan. Trim every bit of fat and
gristle from the ham and cut into small
dice. Fry (sauté) the onions gently in
half the low-fat spread until softened
but not browned. Add the ham, peas
and mint. Cover and cook very gently
for 5 minutes, stirring occasionally.
Add the remaining low-fat spread, half
the cheese and a little salt and pepper.
Add to the pasta and toss well.
Moisten with the milk. Taste and add
more seasoning if necessary. Pile on to
warmed plates and sprinkle with the
remaining Parmesan. Serve with
Tomato and Basil Salad.

Turkish Pork Rolls

SERVES 4

**4 lean pork steaks, about 100 g/
4 oz each, trimmed of any fat**
For the stuffing:
**50 g/2 oz lean raw cured ham
such as Parma, Westphalian or
Serrano, chopped
30 ml/2 tbsp pine nuts, chopped
25 g/1 oz/2 tbsp raisins, chopped
30 ml/2 tbsp fresh breadcrumbs
15 ml/1 tbsp capers, chopped
Salt and freshly ground black
pepper**
For the sauce:
**25 g/1 oz/2 tbsp low-fat spread
45 ml/3 tbsp dry white wine
30 ml/2 tbsp tomato purée (paste)
30 ml/2 tbsp water
1 piece of cinnamon stick**
To garnish:
**60 ml/4 tbsp very low-fat yoghurt
Chopped parsley**
To serve:
**175 g/6 oz/¾ cup long-grain rice,
boiled
Crisp Green Salad (see page 265)**

Place the pork steaks in a plastic bag one at a time and beat with a rolling pin or meat mallet until flattened and thin. Mix together the stuffing ingredients and spread over the pork. Roll up and secure with cocktail sticks (toothpicks). To make the sauce, heat the low-fat spread in a flameproof casserole (Dutch oven). Add the pork and brown on all sides. Reduce the heat. Blend the wine with the tomato purée and the water. Pour into the pan with a little salt and pepper. Add the cinnamon stick. Cover and cook over a very gentle heat for 1 hour or until tender and bathed in sauce. Remove the cinnamon stick. Transfer to warmed plates and top each with 15 ml/1 tbsp yoghurt and a sprinkling of parsley. Serve with boiled rice and Crisp Green Salad.

Gingered Pork with Apples and Cider

SERVES 4

**450 g/1 lb pork fillet, thinly sliced
1.5 ml/¼ tsp ground ginger
A good pinch of mixed (apple-pie)
spice
1 small onion, thinly sliced
2 eating (dessert) apple, cored and
sliced
25 g/1 oz/2 tbsp low-fat spread
150 ml/¼ pt/⅔ cup cider
150 ml/¼ pt/⅔ cup low-fat single
(light) cream
Salt and freshly ground black
pepper
1 green (bell) pepper, cut into thin
rings**
To serve:
**Fluffy Mashed Potatoes
(see page 287)
Green beans**

Sprinkle the meat with the spices. Fry (sauté) the onion and apple in the low-fat spread for 2 minutes. Add the pork and stir-fry for 3 minutes until browned on all sides. Add the cider and simmer for about 5 minutes until the pork is tender. Boil rapidly for 1 minute, if necessary, to reduce the cider by half. Stir in the cream and season to taste. Do not allow to boil again. Meanwhile, cook the pepper rings in boiling water for 3 minutes. Drain. Spoon the pork and sauce on to warmed plates and garnish with the pepper rings. Serve with Fluffy Mashed Potatoes and green beans.

Glazed Nutty Pork

SERVES 4

4 lean pork chops, trimmed of any fat
10 ml/2 tsp English made mustard
15 ml/1 tbsp clear honey
15 ml/1 tbsp raw peanuts, chopped
5 ml/1 tsp Worcestershire sauce
2.5 ml/½ tsp salt
Freshly ground black pepper
5 ml/1 tsp melted low-fat spread
To serve:
Braised Celery (see page 276)
Peas

Grill (broil) the chops for 5 minutes on each side until nearly cooked. Mix together the remaining ingredients and spread over the chops. Grill until golden brown and bubbling. Transfer to warmed plates and serve with Braised Celery and peas.

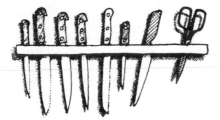

Creamy Sherried Pork with Mushrooms

SERVES 4

450 g/1 lb pork fillet, cut into 4 thick slices
40 g/1½ oz/3 tbsp low-fat spread
1 garlic clove, crushed
10 ml/2 tsp chopped sage
1 onion, thinly sliced
15 ml/1 tbsp lemon juice
175 g/6 oz button mushrooms, sliced
30 ml/2 tbsp sherry
75 ml/5 tbsp low-fat double (heavy) cream
Salt and freshly ground black pepper
Chopped parsley
To serve:
Caraway Noodles (see page 295)
Mixed Green Salad (see page 265)

Put the slices of pork one at a time in a plastic bag and beat with a rolling pin or meat mallet until flattened. Melt half the low-fat spread in a large frying pan (skillet) and fry (sauté) the meat on both sides to brown. Remove from the pan. Melt the remaining low-fat spread and fry the garlic, sage and onion, stirring, for 3 minutes until softened. Add the lemon juice and mushrooms and fry, stirring, for a further 2 minutes. Return the meat to the pan and add the sherry and cream. Season, cover and cook very gently for 5 minutes until the pork is cooked through. Transfer the meat to four warmed plates. Stir the juices well, taste and re-season if necessary. Spoon over the pork, sprinkle with parsley and serve with Caraway Noodles and Mixed Green Salad.

Sausage and Bacon Kebabs

SERVES 4

8 rashers (slices) lean streaky
　bacon, rinded and halved
16 low-fat pork cocktail sausages
1 courgette (zucchini), cut into 8
　small pieces
8 cherry tomatoes
8 button mushrooms
15 ml/1 tbsp low-fat spread
5 ml/1 tsp dried oregano
To serve:
Mexican Rice (see page 298)
60 ml/4 tbsp chilli salsa from a jar
Crisp lettuce, dressed with lemon
　juice and black pepper

Wrap a piece of bacon round each
sausage. Thread a piece of courgette on each of eight skewers, add a
sausage wrapped in bacon, then a
tomato, then another sausage, then a
mushroom. Place on a grill (broiler)
rack. Melt the low-fat spread with the
oregano and brush over the kebabs.
Grill (broil) for about 10 minutes until
cooked through, turning occasionally
and brushing with the herby spread.
Transfer to four warmed plates and
serve with Spicy Rice, chilli salsa and
crisp lettuce.

Cockle-warming Sausage Stew

SERVES 4

450 g/1 lb low-fat pork sausages
2 leeks, sliced
450 g/1 lb carrots, thinly sliced
2 celery sticks, sliced
400 g/14 oz/1 large can chopped
　tomatoes
300 ml/½ pt/1¼ cups vegetable
　stock, made with 1 stock cube
30 ml/2 tbsp tomato purée (paste)
Salt and freshly ground black
　pepper
1 small bay leaf
450 g/1 lb potatoes, diced
To serve:
4 not-too-thick slices crusty bread

Dry-fry (sauté) the sausages in a
heavy-based saucepan until well
browned all over. Remove from the
pan and drain on kitchen paper. Drain
off all the fat in the pan and wipe out
with kitchen paper. Add the remaining
ingredients except the potatoes.
Return the sausages. Bring to the boil,
reduce the heat, cover and simmer
gently for 35 minutes. Add the potatoes and continue cooking for a
further 30 minutes until the mixture is
a rich stew with very little liquid. Taste
and re-season if necessary. Remove
the bay leaf and serve with a little
crusty bread.

Ham Hot-pot

SERVES 4

**225 g/8 oz/2 cups cooked ham
pieces
6 leeks, sliced
450 g/1 lb potatoes, sliced
425 g/15 oz/1 large can butter
beans, drained
Salt and freshly ground black
pepper
300 ml/½ pt/1¼ cups ham stock,
made with 1 stock cube
5 ml/1 tsp low-fat spread
30 ml/2 tbsp chopped parsley**
To serve:
Carrots Cressy (see page 274)

Trim the ham pieces of any fat or gristle and cut into bite-sized pieces. Boil the leeks and potatoes separately in lightly salted water for 4 minutes. Drain. Layer the leeks, ham, butter beans and potatoes in a casserole dish (Dutch oven), seasoning each layer lightly and finishing with potatoes. Pour over the stock. Dot with the low-fat spread, cover and bake in a preheated oven at 190ºC/375ºF/gas mark 5 for 40 minutes. Remove the lid and continue cooking for a further 30 minutes or until golden on top and cooked through. Sprinkle with the parsley and serve with Carrots Cressy.

Bacon-stuffed Cabbage

SERVES 4

**12 large cabbage leaves
1 large onion, chopped
8 lean rashers (slices) streaky
bacon, rinded and finely
chopped
225 g/8 oz mushrooms, chopped
25 g/1 oz/2 tbsp low-fat spread
75 g/3 oz/⅓ cup long-grain rice
Salt and freshly ground black
pepper
2.5 ml/½ tsp dried mixed herbs
2 tomatoes, skinned and chopped
300 ml/½ pt/1¼ cups water
300 ml/½ pt/1¼ cups passata
(sieved tomatoes)
60 ml/4 tbsp very low-fat quark**
To serve:
450 g/1 lb potatoes, plain boiled

Cook the cabbage leaves in lightly salted boiling water for 2 minutes. Drain, rinse with cold water and drain again. Cut out any very thick central stalk. Fry (sauté) the onion, bacon and mushrooms in the low-fat spread in a large flameproof casserole (Dutch oven) for 5 minutes. Add the rice, a little salt and pepper, the herbs, tomatoes and half the water and cook for a further 5 minutes, stirring, until all the water has been absorbed. Divide the filling between the cabbage leaves. Fold in the sides and roll up. Pack into the casserole in a single layer. Blend the passata with the remaining water and pour over. Bring to the boil, reduce the heat, cover and simmer gently for 1 hour or until the cabbage parcels are really tender and the rice has absorbed a lot of the liquid so the parcels are bathed in a rich sauce. Spoon on to warmed plates and garnish each with 15 ml/1 tbsp quark. Serve with plain boiled potatoes.

Pork Chops in Red Wine

SERVES 4

25 g/1 oz/2 tbsp low-fat spread
2 onions, thinly sliced
2 large carrots, thinly sliced
2 courgettes (zucchini), thinly sliced
4 pork loin chops, trimmed of all fat
150 ml/¼ pt/⅔ cup red wine
150 ml/¼ pt/⅔ cup pork or chicken stock, made with ½ stock cube
Salt and freshly ground black pepper
1 bouquet garni sachet
15 ml/1 tbsp redcurrant jelly (clear conserve)
15 ml/1 tbsp cornflour (cornstarch)
15 ml/1 tbsp water
Chopped parsley
To serve:
Fluffy Mashed Potatoes (see page 287)
Broccoli

Melt the low-fat spread in a flame-proof casserole (Dutch oven). Add the onions, carrots and courgettes and fry (sauté) for 2 minutes, stirring. Remove from the pan with a draining spoon. Add the chops to the pan and brown on both sides. Return the vegetables on top of the pork. Pour in the wine, stock, a little salt and pepper and the bouquet garni sachet. Bring to the boil, cover and transfer to a pre-heated oven at 200°C/400°F/gas mark 6 for about 40 minutes or until the pork and vegetables are tender. Lift the pork and vegetables out of the casserole with a draining spoon and keep warm. Discard the bouquet garni. Stir in the redcurrant jelly until dissolved. Blend the cornflour with the water and a little of the cooking liquor. Return to the pan, bring to the boil and cook for

1 minute, stirring, until thickened. Taste and re-season if necessary. Return the chops and vegetables to the casserole. Garnish with parsley and serve with Fluffy Mashed Potatoes and Broccoli.

Liver and Macaroni Casserole

SERVES 4

350 g/12 oz pigs' liver, thinly sliced
25 g/1 oz/2 tbsp low-fat spread
2 onions, thinly sliced
20 g/¾ oz/3 tbsp plain (all-purpose) flour
400 g/14 oz/1 large can chopped tomatoes
150 ml/¼ pt/⅔ cup chicken or pork stock, made with ½ stock cube
10 ml/2 tsp chopped sage
Salt and freshly ground black pepper
100 g/4 oz macaroni
To serve:
Tangy Shredded Cabbage (see page 274)

Brown the liver in half the low-fat spread in a flameproof casserole (Dutch oven) for 1 minute on each side. Remove from the pan with a draining spoon. Add the remaining low-fat spread and fry (sauté) the onions for 3 minutes until softened and lightly golden. Add the flour and cook, stirring, for 1 minute. Blend in the can of tomatoes and stock. Bring to the boil, stirring. Return the liver to the pan and add the sage and a little salt and pepper. Cover and cook in a preheated oven at 180°C/350°F/gas mark 4 for 1 hour. Meanwhile, cook the macaroni according to the packet directions. Drain. Stir into the casserole and serve with Tangy Shredded Cabbage.

Bacon and Mushroom Soufflé Pie

SERVES 4

2 large potatoes, scrubbed
50 g/2 oz/¼ cup low-fat spread
4 lean rashers (slices) streaky bacon, rinded and diced
100 g/4 oz button mushrooms, sliced
20 g/¾ oz/3 tbsp plain (all-purpose) flour
150 ml/¼ pt/⅔ cup skimmed milk
2.5 ml/½ tsp dried thyme
15 ml/1 tbsp chopped parsley
30 ml/2 tbsp grated Parmesan cheese
Salt and freshly ground black pepper
3 eggs, separated
To serve:
Saucy Runner Beans (see page 277)

Prick the potatoes with a fork and either boil in lightly salted water until tender, then drain or cook in the microwave according to the manufacturer's instructions. Cool slightly, then slice and arrange overlapping in the base of a large ovenproof dish, greased with a little of the low-fat spread. Meanwhile, fry (sauté) the bacon and mushrooms in the remaining low-fat spread for 3 minutes. Remove from the heat and stir in the flour, then blend in the milk. Return to the heat and bring to the boil, stirring until very thick. Add the herbs, cheese and a little salt and pepper, then beat in the egg yolks. Whisk the egg whites until stiff and fold into the mixture with a metal spoon. Spoon over the potatoes. Bake in a preheated oven at 190°C/375°F/gas mark 5 for about 25 minutes or until risen, golden and just set. Serve straight away with Saucy Runner Beans.

Porky Pie

SERVES 4

350 g/12 oz/3 cups minced (ground) pork
2 onions, chopped
100 g/4 oz button mushrooms, sliced
2 carrots, finely diced
50 g/2 oz/½ cup frozen peas
30 ml/2 tbsp plain (all-purpose) flour
300 ml/½ pt/1¼ cups chicken stock, made with 1 stock cube
2.5 ml/½ tsp dried mixed herbs
Salt and freshly ground black pepper
450 g/1 lb potatoes, thinly sliced
10 ml/2 tsp low-fat spread
To serve:
Chopped spinach

Put the pork in a flameproof casserole (Dutch oven) with the onions, mushrooms and carrots. Fry (sauté), stirring, until the meat is brown and all the grains are separate. Drain off any fat. Add the peas and stir in the flour. Cook for 1 minute, stirring. Remove from the heat and blend in the stock. Return to the heat and bring to the boil, stirring. Add the herbs and salt and pepper to taste. Reduce the heat, part-cover and simmer gently for 30 minutes, stirring from time to time to prevent sticking. Meanwhile, cook the potatoes in lightly salted boiling water for about 4 minutes until just tender but still holding their shape. Drain. When the meat mixture is cooked, arrange the potato slices overlapping all over the top. Dot with the low-fat spread and place under a hot grill (broiler) until well browned. Serve straight from the pan with chopped spinach.

Pork Schnitzels

SERVES 4

**4 pork fillet steaks, about 150 g/
5 oz each**
20 ml/4 tsp German mustard
4 thin slices ham (from a packet)
**100 g/4 oz Emmental (Swiss)
cheese, sliced**
Lemon wedges
Parsley sprigs
To serve:
**Crunchy-topped Tagliatelle (see
page 293)**
**Green Bean and Onion Salad (see
page 268)**

Put the steaks one at a time in a plastic bag and beat with a rolling pin or meat mallet to flatten. Grill (broil) on one side for 3 minutes until golden brown. Turn over. Grill for a further 2 minutes, then spread with the mustard. Top each with a slice of ham, then the cheese. Grill until the cheese has melted and bubbles. Transfer to warmed plates, garnish with lemon wedges and parsley sprigs and serve with Crunchy-topped Tagliatelle and Green Bean and Onion Salad.

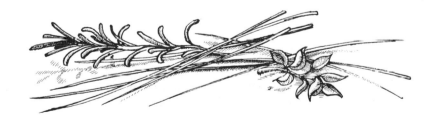

····················· LAMB ·····················

CALORIES OR LESS

Spring Lamb Casserole

SERVES 4

450 g/1 lb neck fillet, trimmed and
    cut into small pieces
25 g/1 oz/2 tbsp low-fat spread
1 garlic clove, crushed
8 button (pearl) onions
16 baby carrots, scrubbed
4 small turnips, quartered
30 ml/2 tbsp plain (all-purpose)
    flour
450 ml/¾ pt/2 cups lamb or chicken
    stock, made with 1 stock cube
30 ml/2 tbsp tomato purée (paste)
1 bouquet garni sachet
12 baby new potatoes, scraped
Chopped parsley

Brown the lamb in the low-fat
spread with the garlic added in a
flameproof casserole (Dutch oven).
Remove from the pan with a draining
spoon. Add the onions, carrots and
turnips and toss for 3 minutes until
lightly browned. Remove from the pan.
Stir the flour into the pan, then remove
from the heat and gradually blend in
the stock and tomato purée. Return to
the heat and bring to the boil, stirring.
Add the bouquet garni. Return the
meat and browned vegetables to the
pan and add the potatoes. Season
lightly. Cover and transfer to a preheated oven at 180°C/350°F/gas mark
4 for 1¼ hours or until the lamb and
vegetables are really tender. Taste and
re-season if necessary. Garnish with
parsley and serve.

Spicy Lamb Cutlets

SERVES 4

8 small lamb cutlets, trimmed of
    any fat
25 g/1 oz/2 tbsp low-fat spread
2 garlic cloves, crushed
30 ml/2 tbsp soy sauce
15 ml/1 tbsp tomato ketchup
    (catsup)
15 ml/1 tbsp red wine vinegar
1.5 ml/¼ tsp chilli powder
Salt and freshly ground black
    pepper
2 spring onions (scallions),
    chopped
To serve:
Almost Fried Rice with Bean
    Sprouts (see page 294)

Place the cutlets in a shallow dish.
Melt half the low-fat spread and
mix in the remaining ingredients
except the spring onions, adding just a
very little salt but lots of pepper. Leave
to marinate for 2 hours. Heat the
remaining low-fat spread in a large
frying pan (skillet). Remove the chops
from the marinade and fry (sauté) for 6
minutes, turning once. Add the
remaining marinade and continue
cooking for 4 minutes, turning once.
Transfer to warmed plates, sprinkle
with the chopped spring onion and
serve with Almost Fried Rice with Bean
Sprouts.

Photograph opposite:
Valencian Pork (page 137)

Saucy Lamb with Capers

SERVES 4

225 g/8 oz/2 cups cooked lamb
40 g/1½ oz/3 tbsp low-fat spread
2 slices bread, cubed
4 courgettes (zucchini), diced
30 ml/2 tbsp plain (all-purpose)
   flour
200 ml/7 fl oz/scant 1 cup chicken
   or lamb stock, made with 1
   stock cube
30 ml/2 tbsp capers, chopped
10 ml/2 tsp liquid from the jar of
   capers
30 ml/2 tbsp chopped parsley
Salt and freshly ground black
   pepper
2 eggs, beaten
To serve:
Grated Winter Salad (see page 268)

Trim the lamb of all fat and cut into small pieces. Melt 25 g/1 oz/2 tbsp of the low-fat spread in a saucepan. Remove from the heat. Add the bread and toss to coat. Remove from the pan with a draining spoon and put to one side. Melt the remaining low-fat spread in the saucepan. Add the courgettes and cook, stirring, for 2 minutes until softened. Add the lamb, reduce the heat, cover and cook gently for 5 minutes or until the courgettes are tender. Stir in the flour and cook for 1 minute. Remove from the heat and stir in the stock. Return to the heat and bring to the boil, stirring. Simmer for 2 minutes. Stir in the chopped capers and their liquid and the parsley. Add seasoning and stir in the beaten eggs until creamy. Turn into four individual flameproof dishes and top with the bread cubes. Place under a hot grill (broiler) until the bread is crisp and golden. Serve hot with Grated Winter Salad.

Spicy Lamb Balls

SERVES 4

450 g/1 lb/4 cups minced (ground)
   lamb
25 g/1 oz/½ cup fresh breadcrumbs
1 egg, beaten
2.5 ml/½ tsp chilli powder
15 ml/1 tbsp grated Parmesan
   cheese
30 ml/2 tbsp water
2.5 ml/½ tsp dried basil
Salt and freshly ground black
   pepper
15 g/½ oz/1 tbsp low-fat spread
1 onion, finely chopped
400 g/14 oz/1 large can chopped
   tomatoes
45 ml/3 tbsp tomato purée (paste)
30 ml/2 tbsp chopped parsley
2.5 ml/½ tsp dried oregano
To serve:
Hot Bulgar Salad (see page 297)

Mix the meat with the breadcrumbs, egg, chilli, cheese, water, basil and a little salt and pepper. Shape into about 20 small balls. Melt the low-fat spread in a large frying pan (skillet). Add the meatballs and cook gently, turning occasionally, until golden brown all over. Pour off any fat. Mix together the remaining ingredients with a little salt and pepper. Pour over the meatballs, cover and simmer very gently for 1½ hours. Serve hot with Hot Bulgar Salad.

Photograph opposite:
Blue Cheese Vegetarian Hot-pot
(page 159)

Rich Savoury Lamb Steaks

SERVES 4

4 lamb leg steaks, all fat removed
30 ml/2 tbsp plain (all-purpose) flour
Salt and freshly ground black pepper
25 g/1 oz/2 tbsp low-fat spread
3 leeks, sliced
295 g/10½ oz/1 small can condensed cream of tomato soup
5 ml/1 tsp dried basil
To serve:
Herby Pasta (see page 296)
Crisp Green Salad (see page 265)

Wipe the lamb and toss in the flour, seasoned with a little salt and pepper. Melt the low-fat spread in a flameproof casserole (Dutch oven) and fry (sauté) the leeks for 2 minutes until softened and lightly browned. Add the lamb and brown on both sides. Pour off any excess fat. Add the soup and basil and a little more salt and pepper. Cover and cook in a preheated oven at 160°C/325°F/gas mark 3 for 1½ hours. Serve with Herby Pasta and Crisp Green Salad.

French-style Lamb and Peas

SERVES 4

40 g/1½ oz/3 tbsp low-fat spread
1 small round lettuce, shredded
1 bunch of spring onions (scallions), cut into short lengths
15 ml/1 tbsp chopped mint
15 ml/1 tbsp chopped parsley
450 g/1 lb/4 cups frozen peas
150 ml/¼ pt/⅔ cup chicken stock, made with ½ stock cube
Salt and freshly ground black pepper
A few grains of artificial sweetener
4 loin lamb chops, trimmed of excess fat
Parsley and mint sprigs
To serve:
450 g/1 lb baby new potatoes, boiled
Glazed Carrots (see page 275)

Melt the low-fat spread in a saucepan. Add the lettuce, spring onions, mint, parsley, peas, stock, a little salt and pepper and a very few grains of artificial sweetener. Bring to the boil, cover tightly, reduce the heat and simmer gently for 20 minutes. Boil rapidly until the liquid is well reduced and the peas are bathed in sauce. Meanwhile, wipe the lamb and place on a grill (broiler) rack. Season lightly. Grill (broil) for about 6 minutes on each side until golden brown, tender and just cooked through. Spoon the peas on to four warmed serving plates and top each with a lamb chop. Garnish with parsley and mint sprigs and serve with baby new potatoes and Glazed Carrots.

Crusty Baked Lamb Cutlets

SERVES 4

8 lamb cutlets, trimmed of all fat
100 g/4 oz/2 cups fresh
breadcrumbs
Grated rind of 1 lime
5 ml/1 tsp celery seeds
15 ml/1 tbsp chopped parsley
2.5 ml/½ tsp dried basil
Salt and freshly ground black
pepper
1 egg, beaten
50 g/2 oz/¼ cup low-fat spread
Cutlet frills, to garnish
Lemon wedges
To serve:
Baby Jackets (see page 287)
Tomatoes with Courgettes (see
page 275)

Wipe the cutlets and scrape the ends of the bones free from all meat. Mix the breadcrumbs with the lime rind, celery seeds, herbs and a little salt and pepper. Dip the cutlets in the beaten egg, then coat in the flavoured crumbs. Chill for 30 minutes. Melt the low-fat spread in a roasting tin (pan). Lay the cutlets in the tin and turn over so both sides are coated. Bake in a preheated oven at 220°C/425°F/gas mark 7 for about 45 minutes until crisp and golden. Drain on kitchen paper. Put a cutlet frill on the end of each bone and lay on warmed plates. Garnish with lemon wedges and serve with Baby Jackets and Tomatoes with Courgettes.

Lamb Haricot

SERVES 4

8 small lamb cutlets, trimmed of
all fat
25 g/1 oz/2 tbsp low-fat spread
2 onions, sliced
4 carrots, peeled and sliced
1 bouquet garni sachet
228 g/8 oz/1 small can chopped
tomatoes
Salt and freshly ground black
pepper
600 ml/1 pt/2½ cups lamb or
chicken stock, made with 2
stock cubes
425 g/15 oz/1 large can haricot
(navy) beans, drained
1 small green cabbage, cut into
8 wedges
Chopped parsley
To serve:
Jacket-baked potatoes with Quark
and Sun-dried Tomato Dressing
(see page 356)

Wipe the meat. Brown in the low-fat spread in a flameproof casserole (Dutch oven). Remove from the pan. Add the onions and carrots and fry (sauté) for 3 minutes, stirring. Pour off any excess fat. Return the meat to the casserole and add the remaining ingredients except the cabbage and parsley. Bring to the boil, cover and cook in a preheated oven at 160°C/325°F/gas mark 3 for 2 hours. Add the cabbage wedges and return to the oven for a further 1 hour. Discard the bouquet garni. Taste and re-season if necessary. Sprinkle with chopped parsley and serve with Jacket-baked potatoes with Quark and Sun-dried Tomato Dressing.

Italian-style Kidneys

SERVES 4

25 g/1 oz/2 tbsp low-fat spread
8 lambs' kidneys, quartered, cores
  removed
1 large onion, chopped
2 wafer-thin slices lean Parma
  ham, cut into thin strips
100 g/4 oz button mushrooms,
  sliced
1 green (bell) pepper, sliced
1 red (bell) pepper, sliced
30 ml/2 tbsp plain (all-purpose)
  flour
300 ml/½ pt/1¼ cups chicken or
  lamb stock, made with 1 stock
  cube
15 ml/1 tbsp dry vermouth
30 ml/2 tbsp tomato purée (paste)
Salt and freshly ground black
  pepper
45 ml/3 tbsp low-fat single (light)
  cream
4 black olives, stoned (pitted) and
  sliced
To serve:
175 g/6 oz/¾ cup long-grain rice,
  cooked

Melt the low-fat spread in a large frying pan (skillet). Add the kidneys, onion, ham, mushrooms and peppers and fry (sauté) stirring, for 5 minutes. Stir in the flour and cook for 1 minute. Remove from the heat and blend in the stock, vermouth and tomato purée. Return to the heat, bring to the boil, stirring, reduce the heat, cover and simmer gently for 15 minutes. Season to taste. Stir in the cream and serve immediately, garnished with sliced olives on a bed of plain boiled rice.

Fruity Lamb Stew

SERVES 4

1 lemon
450 g/1 lb lean diced lamb
20 ml/4 tsp plain (all-purpose)
  flour
Salt and freshly ground black pepper
1.5 ml/¼ tsp ground cinnamon
2 onions, chopped
3 carrots, chopped
15 g/½ oz/1 tbsp low-fat spread
50 g/3 oz/⅓ cup raisins
150 ml/¼ pt/⅔ cup cider
150 ml/¼ pt/⅔ cup lamb or chicken
  stock, made with ½ stock cube
2.5 ml/½ tsp dried mixed herbs
Chopped parsley
To serve:
Fluffy Mashed Potatoes (see page
  287)
Green beans

Thinly pare the rind off half the lemon. Cut into thin strips and boil in water for 2 minutes. Drain, rinse with cold water and drain again. Reserve for a garnish. Grate the remaining rind and squeeze the juice. Toss the meat in the flour, seasoned with a little salt, pepper and the cinnamon. Fry (sauté) the onions and carrots in the low-fat spread for 2 minutes in a flameproof casserole (Dutch oven). Add the meat and continue frying, tossing until golden brown. Stir in the grated lemon rind, 5 ml/1 tsp of the juice and the remaining ingredients except the parsley. (Reserve the remaining lemon juice for another recipe.) Bring to the boil, stirring. Reduce the heat, cover and simmer gently for 1 hour or until the lamb and vegetables are tender. Taste and re-season if necessary. Garnish with the shredded lemon rind and chopped parsley and serve with Fluffy Mashed Potatoes and green beans.

450

Lamb Goulash

SERVES 4

2 onions, thinly sliced
2 carrots, sliced
1 green (bell) pepper, thinly sliced
25 g/1 oz/2 tbsp low-fat spread
450 g/1 lb lean lamb, cubed
15 ml/1 tbsp paprika, or to taste
30 ml/2 tbsp plain (all-purpose)
  flour
400 g/14 oz/1 large can chopped
  tomatoes
300 ml/½ pt/1¼ cups lamb or
  chicken stock, made with 1
  stock cube
2.5 ml/½ tsp dried mixed herbs
450 g/1 lb potatoes, diced
Salt and freshly ground black
  pepper
30 ml/2 tbsp very low-fat crème
  fraîche
Chopped parsley
To serve:
½ small French stick
Crisp Green Salad (see page 265)

Fry (sauté) the onions, carrots and green pepper in the low-fat spread for 3 minutes in a large saucepan. Add the lamb and paprika and continue cooking for 3 minutes, stirring. Stir in the flour, tomatoes, stock and herbs and bring to the boil, stirring. Add the potatoes and season to taste. Cover, reduce the heat and simmer gently for 1–1½ hours or until the meat and vegetables are really tender. Taste and re-season if necessary. Ladle into warmed bowls and garnish with a swirl of crème fraîche and chopped parsley. Serve with French bread and Crisp Green Salad.

Moussaka

SERVE 4

1 onion, finely chopped
1 garlic clove, crushed
350 g/12 oz/3 cups minced
  (ground) lamb
150 ml/¼ pt/⅔ cup lamb or chicken
  stock, made with ½ stock cube
30 ml/2 tbsp tomato purée (paste)
5 ml/1 tsp ground cinnamon
2.5 ml/½ tsp dried oregano
Salt and freshly ground black
  pepper
1 large aubergine (eggplant),
  sliced
150 ml/¼ pt/⅔ cup very low-fat
  plain yoghurt
1 egg
50 g/2 oz/½ cup low-fat Cheddar
  cheese, grated
To serve:
Cucumber with Yoghurt Dressing
  (see page 267)

Put the onion, garlic and mince in a saucepan and fry (sauté) for 4 minutes, stirring, until the lamb is brown and all the grains are separate. Drain off any excess fat. Add the stock, tomato purée, cinnamon, oregano and a little salt and pepper. Bring to the boil, and boil for about 5 minutes until nearly all the liquid has evaporated. Meanwhile, boil the aubergine slices in lightly salted water for 5 minutes or until tender. Drain. Layer the meat mixture and aubergine in a 1.5 litre/2½ pt/6 cup ovenproof dish, finishing with a layer of aubergine. Beat the yoghurt with the egg and cheese and add a little salt and pepper. Spoon over. Place under a moderately hot grill (broiler) until the top is set and golden brown. Serve hot with Cucumber with Yoghurt Dressing.

Lamb, Corn and Sun-dried Tomato Kebabs

SERVES 4

350 g/12 oz lamb neck fillet,
  trimmed of any fat and sinews
15 ml/1 tbsp olive oil
15 ml/1 tbsp lemon juice
2.5 ml/½ tsp dried oregano
2.5 ml/½ tsp dried mint
1 garlic clove, crushed
Salt and freshly ground black
  pepper
2 corn cobs, each cut into 6 pieces
1 jar sun-dried tomatoes, drained
To serve:
Tomato Rice (see page 296)
Greek Village Salad (see page 283)

Cut the meat into neat cubes and place in a shallow bowl. Drizzle with the oil and lemon juice, and sprinkle with the oregano, mint, garlic and a little salt and pepper. Toss well and leave to marinate for at least 1 hour. Plunge the corn cobs into boiling water for 3 minutes to soften slightly. Drain. Thread the meat, corn and sun-dried tomatoes on eight skewers. Brush with any remaining marinade. Place on a grill (broiler) rack. Grill (broil) for about 10 minutes, turning once or twice and brushing with any leftover marinade during cooking. Transfer to warmed plates and serve with Tomato Rice and Greek Village Salad.

Saucy Liver and Onions

SERVES 4

8 lean streaky bacon rashers
  (slices), rinded
15 g/½ oz/1 tbsp low-fat spread
8 thin slices lambs' liver, about
  275 g/10 oz in all
3 large onions, sliced
150 ml/¼ pt/⅔ cup water
20 g/¾ oz/3 tbsp plain (all-
  purpose) flour
150 ml/¼ pt/⅔ cup skimmed milk
Salt and freshly ground black
  pepper
30 ml/2 tbsp chopped parsley
To serve:
450 g/1 lb potatoes, boiled
Spring Green Toss (see page 277)

Dry-fry (sauté) the bacon until crisp. Remove from the pan, drain on kitchen paper and keep warm. Wipe out the pan. Melt the low-fat spread and fry the liver for about 2 minutes on each side until golden and just cooked through. Transfer to a warmed plate and keep warm. Meanwhile, put the onions in a saucepan with the water, cover, bring to the boil and cook for 4 minutes. Blend the flour with the milk until smooth. Add to the pan, bring back to the boil and cook, stirring, for 2 minutes. Season to taste and stir in half the parsley. Spoon the onion sauce on to four warmed plates. Top with the bacon and liver and sprinkle with the remaining parsley. Serve with boiled potatoes and Spring Green Toss.

Lamburgers

SERVES 4

450 g/1 lb/4 cups minced (ground) lamb
1 onion, finely chopped
1 garlic clove, crushed
10 ml/2 tsp dried mint
Salt and freshly ground black pepper
1 egg, beaten
2 muffins, halved
1 onion, sliced into thin rings
20 ml/4 tsp low-calorie mayonnaise
Chopped mint
Lettuce, tomato slices and cucumber slices, to garnish
To serve:
Poppy Seed and Oregano Wedges (see page 288)

Mix the mince with the onion, garlic, mint and a little salt and pepper. Mix with the egg to bind. Shape into four patties. Grill (broil) for about 5 minutes on each side until golden brown and cooked through. Drain on kitchen paper. Meanwhile, toast the halved muffins. Place a burger on each muffin half. Top with onion rings and the mayonnaise. Sprinkle with chopped mint. Place on warmed plates, garnish with the salad ingredients and serve with Poppy Seed and Oregano Wedges.

·····BEEF·····

450

CALORIES OR LESS

Ginger Crusty Mustard Beef

SERVES 4

550 g/1¼ lb lean braising steak
30 ml/2 tbsp plain (all-purpose) flour
Salt and freshly ground black pepper
3 onions, sliced
3 carrots, sliced
1 garlic clove, crushed
40 g/2 oz/¼ cup low-fat spread
2.5 ml/½ tsp grated fresh root ginger
200 ml/7 fl oz/1 cup beef stock, made with 1 stock cube
150 ml/¼ pt/⅔ cup American ginger ale
1 bay leaf
A few drops of gravy browning
8 thin slices French bread
30 ml/2 tbsp French wholegrain mustard
To serve:
Spring Green Toss (see page 277)

Cube the meat and trim away all fat and gristle. Toss the meat in 15 ml/ 1 tbsp of the flour with a little salt and pepper. Fry (sauté) the onions, carrots and garlic in 30 ml/2 tbsp of the low-fat spread for 2 minutes, stirring, in a flameproof casserole (Dutch oven). Remove from the pan with a draining spoon. Add a further 15 g/½ oz/1 tbsp of the spread to the casserole and brown the meat quickly. Remove from the pan. Stir the remaining flour into the juices. Add the ginger, stock and ginger ale and bring to the boil, stirring and scraping up any residue from the pan. Return the vegetables and meat to the pan and add the bay leaf and gravy browning. Season lightly. Cover and place in a preheated oven at 160°C/325°F/gas mark 3 for 1½–2 hours or until tender. Stir well, taste and re-season if necessary. Discard the bay leaf. Meanwhile, toast the French bread. Mash the remaining low-fat spread with the mustard and spread on top. When the meat is tender, arrange the bread around the top and return uncovered to the oven for 10 minutes. Serve with Spring Green Toss.

450

Golden-topped Cottage Pie

SERVES 4

1 onion, finely chopped
2 carrots, chopped
450 g/1 lb/4 cups minced (ground)
   beef
15 ml/1 tbsp plain (all-purpose)
   flour
300 ml/½ pt/1¼ cups beef stock,
   made with 1 stock cube
75 g/3 oz/¾ cup frozen peas
2.5 ml/½ tsp dried mixed herbs
Salt and freshly ground black
   pepper
450 g/1 lb potatoes, cut into small
   chunks
30 ml/2 tbsp skimmed milk
A small knob of low-fat spread
50 g/2 oz/½ cup low-fat Cheddar
   cheese, grated
To serve:
Savoy cabbage, steamed or very
   lightly boiled

Put the onion and carrots in a saucepan with the meat. Fry (sauté), stirring, until the meat is brown and all the grains are separate. Pour off any fat. Stir in the flour and stock. Bring to the boil, stirring. Add the peas and herbs and simmer uncovered for about 30 minutes or until tender and the meat is bathed in a rich gravy. Season to taste. Meanwhile, cook the potatoes in lightly salted boiling water until tender. Drain and mash with the milk and low-fat spread. Turn the meat mixture into a flameproof serving dish. Top with the mashed potato and rough up with a fork. Sprinkle with the cheese and grill (broil) until golden. Serve hot with Savoy cabbage.

Beef and Vegetable Stew

SERVES 4

550 g/1¼ lb lean stewing beef
2 onions, cut into wedges
3 carrots, cut into chunks
1 small swede (rutabaga), cut into
   chunks
8 potatoes, scrubbed
600 ml/1 pt/2½ cups beef stock,
   made with 2 stock cubes
Salt and freshly ground black
   pepper
1 bouquet garni sachet
100 g/4 oz green beans, cut into
   short lengths

Cut the meat into small cubes and trim away any fat or gristle. Place all the ingredients except the beans in a large saucepan. Bring to the boil and skim the surface. Cover, reduce the heat and simmer gently for 2 hours. Remove the lid for the last 30 minutes. Add the beans for the last 15 minutes. Discard the bouquet garni sachet. Taste and re-season if necessary. Ladle into large soup bowls and serve.

International Beef Pot

SERVES 4

550 g/1¼ lb lean braising steak
3 large onions, sliced
450 ml/¾ pt/2 cups beef stock,
    made with 1 stock cube
1 small bay leaf
Salt and freshly ground black
    pepper
175 g/6 oz button mushrooms
A few drops of gravy browning
225 g/8 oz/1 small can water
    chestnuts, drained and sliced
450 g/1 lb potatoes, thinly sliced
295 g/10½ oz/1 small can condensed
    cream of mushroom soup
A parsley sprig
To serve:
Fruity Red Cabbage (see page 290)

Trim the meat of any fat or sinews and cut into small cubes. Place in a saucepan with the onions, stock, bay leaf and a little salt and pepper. Bring to the boil and skim the surface. Reduce the heat, part-cover and simmer very gently for 2 hours or until the meat is really tender. Add the mushrooms for the last 15 minutes. Taste and re-season if necessary. Remove the bay leaf and add a few drops of gravy browning. Drain off the stock and reserve. Put half the meat and mushroom mixture into a fairly large, shallow ovenproof dish. Top with the water chestnuts, then the remaining meat mixture. Arrange the potatoes overlapping on the top. Spoon the mushroom soup over, then pour over as much or all, if necessary, of the stock to moisten thoroughly. Bake in a preheated oven at 160°C/325°F/gas mark 3 for 2 hours or until the top is golden and the potatoes are cooked. Garnish with the parsley sprig and serve hot with Fruity Red Cabbage.

Beef Stroganoff

SERVES 4

40 g/1½ oz/3 tbsp low-fat spread
2 onions, thinly sliced
175 g/6 oz button mushrooms,
    sliced
350 g/12 oz fillet steak, cut into
    short, thin strips
Salt and freshly ground black
    pepper
15 ml/1 tbsp brandy
150 ml/¼ pt/⅔ cup soured (dairy
    sour) cream
225 g/8 oz short flat noodles
Chopped parsley
To serve:
Mixed Leaf Salad (see page 265)

Melt half the low-fat spread in a large frying pan (skillet). Add the onions and mushrooms and fry (sauté) for 5 minutes until the onions are soft and lightly golden. Remove from the pan. Melt the remaining low-fat spread and brown the steak on all sides. Season well and continue frying for about 3 minutes until cooked through. Return the onions and mushrooms to the pan. Add the brandy and ignite. Shake the pan until the flames subside. Stir in the soured cream and allow to bubble for a few minutes. Taste and re-season if necessary. Meanwhile, cook the noodles according to the packet directions. Drain and spoon on to four warmed plates. Spoon the stroganoff to one side and sprinkle with chopped parsley. Serve with Mixed Leaf Salad.

Redcurrant Fillet

SERVES 4

10 ml/2 tsp pink peppercorns,
  coarsely crushed
450 g/1 lb fillet steak, cut into
  4 slices
25 g/1 oz/2 tbsp low-fat spread
1 onion, finely chopped
2 wafer-thin slices lean Parma
  ham, cut into thin strips
150 ml/¼ pt/⅔ cup red wine
A squeeze of lemon juice
30 ml/2 tbsp redcurrant jelly
  (clear conserve)
Salt
To serve:
Puréed Potatoes (see page 287)
Crunchy-topped Broccoli and
  Cauliflower (see page 279)

Press the peppercorns into the
steaks on both sides. Heat half the
low-fat spread and brown the steaks
on each side. Remove from the pan
and keep warm. Add the onion and
Parma ham and fry (sauté) for 4 minutes until soft and golden. Add the
wine and lemon juice. Bring to the boil
and stir in the redcurrant jelly until
dissolved. Season with salt. Add the
steak and simmer for 5–10 minutes
until cooked to your liking. Transfer
the steaks to warmed serving plates.
Spoon the sauce over and serve with
Puréed Potatoes and Crunchy-topped
Broccoli and Cauliflower.

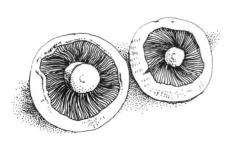

Creamy Tarragon and Mushroom Steaks

SERVES 4

1 onion, finely chopped
25 g/1 oz/2 tbsp low-fat spread
225 g/8 oz button mushrooms,
  sliced
200 ml/7 fl oz/scant 1 cup white
  wine
450 g/1 lb fillet steak, cut into
  4 slices
150 ml/¼ pt/⅔ cup low-fat double
  (heavy) cream
1 garlic clove, crushed
15 ml/1 tbsp chopped tarragon
10 ml/2 tsp Dijon mustard
Salt and freshly ground black
  pepper
Tarragon sprigs
To serve:
450 g/1 lb baby new potatoes,
  boiled
Crisp Green Salad (see page 265)

Fry (sauté) the onion in half the low-
fat spread until softened and slightly golden. Add the mushrooms and
wine and simmer for 5 minutes.
Meanwhile, put the steaks one at a
time in a plastic bag and beat briefly
with a rolling pin or meat mallet to
flatten. Melt the remaining low-fat
spread. Brush all over and grill (broil)
for 2–5 minutes on each side until
cooked to your liking. Transfer to
warmed plates and keep warm. Stir
the remaining ingredients except the
tarragon sprigs into the mushroom
mixture, seasoning to taste. Bring to
the boil and allow to bubble for 4–5
minutes until rich and thick. Spoon
over the steaks, garnish with tarragon
sprigs and serve hot with baby new
potatoes and Crisp Green Salad.

Rich Tomato Beef

SERVES 4

45 ml/3 tbsp plain (all-purpose)
flour
Salt and freshly ground black
pepper
550 g/1¼ lb lean braising steak
4 large onions, sliced
40 g/1½ oz/3 tbsp low-fat spread
1 garlic clove, crushed
400 g/14 oz/1 large can chopped
tomatoes
45 ml/3 tbsp tomato purée (paste)
30 ml/2 tbsp very low-fat plain
yoghurt
Snipped chives
To serve:
Jacket-baked potatoes with
Yoghurt and Chive Dressing
(see page 356)
Broccoli

Mix the flour with a little salt and pepper. Cut the meat into four steaks, discarding any fat or gristle. Toss in the flour. Fry (sauté) the onions in half the low-fat spread in a flame-proof casserole (Dutch oven) for 4 minutes until softened and lightly browned. Remove from the pan. Melt the remaining low-fat spread and brown the meat on both sides. Return the onions to the pan with the remaining ingredients except the yoghurt and chives. Stir well. Bring to the boil, cover and transfer to a preheated oven at 160°C/325°F/gas mark 3 for 2 hours or until the beef is very tender. Stir and re-season if necessary. Spoon the yoghurt on top in a swirl and sprinkle with snipped chives. Serve hot with jacket-baked potatoes with Yoghurt and Chive Dressing and broccoli.

Hungarian Goulash

SERVES 4

40 g/1½ oz/3 tbsp low-fat spread
3 onions, chopped
550 g/1¼ lb lean braising steak,
cubed, discarding any fat or
gristle
15 ml/1 tbsp paprika
5 ml/1 tsp caraway seeds
1 garlic clove, crushed
1 potato, grated
1 parsnip, grated
30 ml/2 tbsp tomato purée (paste)
300 ml/½ pt/1¼ cups beef stock,
made with 1 stock cube
2 tomatoes, skinned, seeded and
chopped
1 green (bell) pepper, thinly sliced
Salt and freshly ground black
pepper
To serve:
Caraway Noodles (see page 295)
Lettuce, dressed with lemon juice
and black pepper

Melt the low-fat spread in a flame-proof casserole (Dutch oven). Add the onions and fry (sauté) for 2 minutes, stirring. Add the beef and paprika and fry for 2 minutes, stirring, to seal. Stir in the remaining ingredients, seasoning with a little salt and pepper. Bring to the boil, reduce the heat, cover and simmer very gently for 2 hours or until the meat is very tender. Remove the lid for the last 30 minutes cooking to thicken the liquid. Stir well, taste and re-season if necessary. Spoon on to the Caraway Noodles and serve with lettuce.

English-style Beef Curry

SERVES 4

550 g/1¼ lb lean braising steak
40 g/1½ oz/3 tbsp low-fat spread
3 onions, sliced
1 eating (dessert) apple, diced
30 ml/2 tbsp curry powder
15 ml/1 tbsp plain (all-purpose)
flour
300 ml/½ pt/1¼ cups beef stock,
made with 1 stock cube
Salt and freshly ground black
pepper
50 g/2 oz/⅓ cup sultanas (golden
raisins)
175 g/6 oz/¾ cup basmati rice
To garnish:
1 banana, sliced and tossed in
lemon juice
Desiccated (shredded) coconut
Chopped cucumber and tomato
Shredded lettuce
Onion rings
Lemon wedges
60 ml/4 tbsp mango chutney or
sweet pickle

Cut the meat into small cubes and trim away any fat or gristle. Melt half the low-fat spread in a heavy-based saucepan. Add the meat and brown on all sides. Remove from the pan with a draining spoon. Add the onions and apple and fry (sauté) for 3 minutes, stirring. Stir in the curry powder and flour and cook for 1 minute. Blend in the stock, a little salt and pepper and the sultanas. Bring to the boil, stirring. Reduce the heat, cover and simmer over the lowest heat for 2–3 hours, stirring occasionally. If too thick add a little water. About 20 minutes before eating, rinse the rice and cook in boiling, salted water for 12–15 minutes until just tender but all the grains are still separate. Drain, rinse with boiling water and drain again. Pile on to warmed plates. Taste and re-season the curry if necessary. Spoon on to the plates and serve with all the garnishes.

MEATLESS MEALS

CALORIES OR LESS

Tagliatelle with Two-bean Sauce

SERVES 4

40 g/1½ oz/3 tbsp low-fat spread
1 bunch of spring onions
  (scallions), chopped
425 g/15 oz/1 large can haricot
  (navy) beans, drained
425 g/15 oz/1 large can red kidney
  beans, drained
400 g/14 oz/1 large can chopped
  tomatoes
15 ml/1 tbsp clear honey
5 ml/1 tsp wholegrain mustard
Salt and freshly ground black
  pepper
15 ml/1 tbsp pumpkin seeds
225 g/8 oz green tagliatelle
To serve:
Crisp Green Salad (see page 265)

Melt the low-fat spread in a saucepan. Add the spring onions and fry (sauté) for 3 minutes. Add the remaining ingredients except the pasta. Bring to the boil and simmer for 8 minutes until pulpy. Taste and re-season if necessary. Meanwhile, cook the pasta according to the packet directions. Pile on to plates, top with the sauce and serve with Crisp Green Salad.

Baked Bean Loaf

SERVES 4

10 ml/2 tsp low-fat spread
400 g/14 oz/1 large can no-added-
  sugar baked beans
1 small onion, finely chopped
50 g/2 oz/1 cup wholemeal
  breadcrumbs
30 ml/2 tbsp tomato ketchup
  (catsup)
1 egg, beaten
5 ml/1 tsp yeast extract
5 ml/1 tsp dried mixed herbs
Salt and freshly ground black
  pepper
Lettuce leaves and tomato wedges,
  to garnish
To serve:
Baby Jackets (see page 287)
**Beetroot and Chive Salad (see
  page 270)**

Wet a 450 g/1 lb loaf tin (pan) and line with non-stick baking parchment. Mix together all the ingredients. Turn into the prepared tin. Level the surface. Bake in a preheated oven at 180°C/350°F/gas mark 4 for 30–40 minutes until firm to the touch. Leave to cool in the tin for a few minutes then turn out, remove the paper and serve warm or cold, sliced, garnished with lettuce leaves and tomato wedges, with Baby Jackets and Beetroot and Chive Salad.

Lentil and Baby Vegetable Platter

SERVES 4

150 g/5 oz/scant 1 cup green lentils
40 g/1½ oz/3 tbsp low-fat spread
2 garlic cloves, crushed
Salt and freshly ground black pepper
15 ml/1 tbsp red wine vinegar
1 bunch of spring onions (scallions), trimmed but left whole
16 baby carrots, scraped
4 baby corn cobs
120 ml/4 fl oz/½ cup vegetable stock, made with ½ stock cube
20 ml/4 tsp clear honey
100 g/4 oz mangetout (snow peas), topped and tailed
60 ml/4 tbsp soured (dairy sour) cream
15 ml/1 tbsp toasted pine nuts

Soak the lentils in boiling water for 30 minutes, then drain and place in a saucepan. Cover with water. Bring to the boil, reduce the heat and simmer for 20 minutes or until tender but still holding their shape. Drain. Add a third of the low-fat spread, half the garlic, a little salt and pepper and the vinegar. Mix well. In a large frying pan (skillet) or wok, heat the remaining low-fat spread and stir-fry the remaining garlic, the onions, carrots and corn for 2 minutes. Add the stock and boil for 5 minutes until the liquid has evaporated. Add the honey and mangetout and cook for a further 2 minutes. Spoon the lentils in piles on four warmed serving plates and arrange the vegetables attractively around. Top the lentils with a little soured cream and the toasted pine nuts. Serve.

Instant Veggie Supper

SERVES 4

400 g/14 oz/1 large can ratatouille
425 g/15 oz/1 large can butter beans
2.5 ml/½ tsp dried mixed herbs
Salt and freshly ground black pepper
50 g/2 oz/1 cup breadcrumbs
50 g/2 oz/½ cup low-fat Cheddar cheese, grated
2 eggs
30 ml/2 tbsp skimmed milk
15 ml/1 tbsp chopped parsley
5 ml/1 tsp low-fat spread
Parsley sprigs

Mix the ratatouille with the beans, herbs and some pepper in a flameproof casserole (Dutch oven). Heat until piping hot. Mix the breadcrumbs and cheese and sprinkle over. Place under a hot grill (broiler) until golden brown. Meanwhile, beat together the eggs and milk with a little salt and pepper and the chopped parsley. Melt the low-fat spread in an omelette pan and fry (sauté) the egg mixture until set. Cut into four wedges. Spoon the ratatouille mixture on to four warmed plates. Put an omelette wedge to one side and garnish with parsley sprigs.

Root Vegetable Satay

SERVES 4

1 large turnip, cut into bite-sized
   pieces
2 large carrots, cut into bite-sized
   pieces
1 small swede (rutabaga), cut into
   bite-sized pieces
1 parsnip, cut into bite-sized pieces
8 whole, baby waxy potatoes
15 g/½ oz/1 tbsp low-fat spread
15 ml/1 tbsp honey
Grated rind of ½ lime
Salt and freshly ground black pepper
150 ml/¼ pt/⅔ cup skimmed milk
75 ml/5 tbsp peanut butter
1 green chilli, seeded and finely
   chopped
50 g/2 oz/⅓ cup raw peanuts,
   chopped
½ ungrated lime, sliced and twisted
To serve:
Oriental Rice and Peas (see page
   291)

Boil the prepared vegetables in
lightly salted water until just tender. Drain. When cool enough to handle, thread alternately on soaked
wooden skewers. Melt together the
low-fat spread, honey and lime rind.
Add a little salt and pepper. Lay the
skewers on foil on a grill (broiler) rack
and brush with the lime mixture. Grill
(broil), turning occasionally, until
golden brown. Meanwhile put the milk
and peanut butter in a small saucepan
and warm through, stirring, until well
blended. Add the chilli. Spoon into
four small bowls and sprinkle with the
chopped peanuts. Transfer the vegetable skewers to warmed serving
plates, garnish with the lime twists
and place a small bowl of the satay
sauce on the side. Serve with Oriental
Rice and Peas.

Vegetarian Slab Supper

SERVES 4

400 g/14 oz/1 large can whole
   lentils, drained
425 g/15 oz/1 large can haricot
   (navy) beans, drained
100 g/4 oz/1 cup frozen peas
40 g/1½ oz/⅓ cup blue cheese,
   crumbled
A pinch of celery salt
40 g/1½ oz/3 tbsp low-fat spread
40 g/1½ oz/⅓ cup raw peanuts,
   chopped
3 eggs, beaten
Salt and freshly ground black
   pepper
Coriander (cilantro) sprigs
To serve:
Mixed Leaf Salad (see page 265)
Tomato and Onion Salad (see page
   266)

Put the lentils, beans and peas in a
blender or food processor and
purée to a paste. Add the cheese, celery salt, three-quarters of the low-fat
spread, the nuts and eggs and blend
briefly. Season to taste. Grease a shallow baking tin (pan) with the remaining low-fat spread. Fill with the mixture and spread out. Top with a piece
of baking parchment. Bake in a preheated oven at 200°C/400°F/gas mark
6 for 30 minutes or until firm. Cool and
turn out on to a board. Slice thickly
and serve with Mixed Leaf Salad and
Tomato and Onion Salad.

Cashew-crumbed Spinach with Eggs

SERVES 4

900 g/2 lb spinach
40 g/1½ oz/3 tbsp low-fat spread
1 bunch of spring onions (scallions), chopped
Salt and freshly ground black pepper
2.5 ml/½ tsp grated nutmeg
150 ml/¼ pt/⅔ cup very low-fat plain yoghurt
100 g/4 oz/2 cups wholemeal breadcrumbs
50 g/2 oz/⅓ cup raw cashew nuts, chopped
10 ml/2 tsp lemon juice
4 eggs
50 g/2 oz/½ cup low-fat red Leicester cheese, finely grated
Cayenne
To serve:
Baby Jackets (see page 287)

Thoroughly wash the spinach under running water and remove any tough stalks. Shake off the excess water, then place in a saucepan. Cover and cook for about 5 minutes until tender. Drain and chop. Heat 15 g/ ½ oz/1 tbsp of the low fat spread in a frying pan (skillet) and fry (sauté) the spring onions for 3 minutes, stirring. Return the spinach to the pan and add a little salt, pepper and the nutmeg. Stir for 2 minutes. Stir in the yoghurt. Place in four individual ovenproof dishes. Melt the remaining low-fat spread and stir in the breadcrumbs and nuts. Sprinkle over the spinach and bake in a preheated oven at 190°C/375°F/gas mark 5 for 20 minutes or until golden on top. Meanwhile, fill a frying pan with water and add the lemon juice. Bring to the boil, then reduce to simmering. Break the eggs into a cup, then carefully slide into simmering water. Poach for 3–4 minutes to your liking. Remove from the pan with a draining spoon. Slide on top of the crumb mixture, sprinkle with the cheese and flash under a very hot grill (broiler) to melt the cheese. Sprinkle with cayenne and serve straight away with Baby Jackets.

Monday Pie

SERVES 4

450 g/1 lb potatoes, cut into small even-sized pieces
15 g/½ oz/1 tbsp low-fat spread
30 ml/2 tbsp skimmed milk
450 g/1 lb any cooked vegetables such as cabbage, peas, carrots, swede (rutabaga), parsnips, or use cooked frozen casserole mix
400 g/14 oz/1 large can no-added-sugar baked beans
2 slices wholemeal bread, cut into small dice
10 ml/2 tsp yeast extract
30 ml/2 tbsp boiling water
Salt and freshly ground black pepper
50 g/2 oz/½ cup low-fat Cheddar cheese, grated
To serve:
Creamed Spinach (see page 289)

Cook the potatoes in lightly salted boiling water until tender. Drain and mash with the low-fat spread and milk. Meanwhile, chop the vegetables, if necessary, and place in an ovenproof dish with the beans and bread. Dissolve the yeast extract in the water and stir into the dish. Season well and mix thoroughly. Cover with the potato, then sprinkle with the cheese. Bake in a preheated oven at 220°C/425°F/gas mark 7 for 35 minutes until golden brown and piping hot. Serve with Creamed Spinach.

Sumptuous Stuffed Onions

SERVES 4

4 large Spanish onions
1 egg, scrubbed under the cold tap
50 g/2 oz/¼ cup low-fat spread
12 black olives, stoned (pitted)
 and sliced
6 mushrooms, chopped
30 ml/2 tbsp chopped nuts
45 ml/3 tbsp breadcrumbs
2 garlic cloves, crushed
30 ml/2 tbsp chopped basil
25 g/1 oz/2 tbsp strong low-fat
 Cheddar cheese, grated
Salt and freshly ground black
 pepper
1 egg, beaten
120 ml/4 fl oz/½ cup vegetable
 stock, made with ½ stock cube
30 ml/2 tbsp grated Mozzarella
 cheese
To serve:
Hot Walnut Bread (see page 294)
Italian Green Salad (see page 272)

Peel the onions and cut a slice off the root end of each. Boil for 15 minutes in lightly salted water. Add the egg after 5 minutes cooking. Drain. Plunge the onions and egg into cold water. Leave the egg, remove the onions and dry on kitchen paper. Squeeze out most of the insides, leaving a shell about 1 cm/½ in thick. Finely chop the squeezed-out centres. Melt the low-fat spread in a saucepan. Add the chopped onion and the remaining ingredients except the stock and Mozzarella cheese. Mix thoroughly, seasoning to taste. Shell and chop the cooked egg and add. Pack tightly into the onion skins and stand each in an individual ovenproof dish. Pour the stock over, cover with foil and bake in a preheated oven at 190°C/ 375°F/gas mark 5 for 20 minutes. Remove the foil, top each with Mozzarella and return to the oven until the cheese has melted and is turning lightly golden. Serve straight away with Hot Walnut Bread and Italian Green Salad.

Chestnut and Vegetable Tagliatelle

SERVES 4

1 onion, chopped
2 leeks, sliced
15 g/½ oz/1 tbsp low-fat spread
2 carrots, chopped
2 celery sticks, chopped
175 g/6 oz button mushrooms,
 quartered
2.5 ml/½ tsp dried mixed herbs
15 ml/1 tbsp chopped parsley
15 ml/1 tbsp soy sauce
Salt and freshly ground black pepper
320 g/12 oz/1 large can
 unsweetened chestnut purée
450 ml/¾ pt/2 cups vegetable
 stock, made with 1 stock cube
225 g/8 oz tagliatelle
30 ml/2 tbsp grated Parmesan
 cheese
To serve:
Mixed Green Salad (see page 265)

Fry (sauté) the onion and leeks in the low-fat spread in a flameproof casserole (Dutch oven) for 3 minutes, stirring. Add the remaining vegetables and cook for a further 5 minutes, stirring from time to time. Stir in the remaining ingredients except the pasta and Parmesan and mix well. Cover and cook in a preheated oven at 180°C/ 350°F/gas mark 4 for about 40 minutes until cooked through. Meanwhile, cook the tagliatelle according to the packet directions. Drain. Pile on to warmed serving plates. Top with the chestnut mixture, sprinkle with the Parmesan and serve with Mixed Green Salad.

Carrot and Spinach Tofu Cakes

SERVES 4

2 carrots, sliced
250 g/9 oz/1 packet firm tofu
100 g/4 oz/1 cup plain (all-purpose) flour
Chilli powder
225 g/8 oz frozen chopped spinach, thawed and drained well
5 ml/1 tsp grated nutmeg
Salt and freshly ground black pepper
1 large egg, beaten
175 g/6 oz/3 cups fresh breadcrumbs
350 g/12 oz tomatoes, skinned, seeded and chopped
10 ml/2 tsp soy sauce
10 ml/2 tsp malt vinegar
5 ml/1 tsp honey
50 g/2 oz/¼ cup low-fat spread
Coriander (cilantro) sprigs
To serve:
Baby Carrot and Corn Crunch (see page 284)

Boil the carrots in lightly salted water until tender. Drain and mash thoroughly with half the tofu and 25 g/ 1 oz/¼ cup of the flour to form a stiff paste. Season with a pinch of chilli powder. Squeeze the spinach as dry as possible and mash with the remaining tofu, the nutmeg and a further 25 g/ 1 oz/¼ cup of the flour. Season both pastes lightly. Shape each paste into eight balls. Press one of each type together to form flattish cakes. Chill for at least 30 minutes. Mix the remaining flour with a little salt and pepper. Dip the cakes in seasoned flour, then beaten egg, then breadcrumbs to coat completely. Purée the tomatoes with the soy sauce, vinegar, honey, a pinch of chilli and salt and pepper to taste. Place in a saucepan and simmer for 5 minutes. Heat the low-fat spread in a large frying pan (skillet) and fry (sauté) the cakes until golden brown on both sides. Drain on kitchen paper and serve, garnished with coriander sprigs, with the tomato sauce spooned on the side and Baby Carrot and Corn Crunch.

Greek-style Chick Pea Casserole

SERVES 4

450 g/1 lb spinach
25 g/1 oz/2 tbsp low-fat spread
1 garlic clove, crushed
400 g/14 oz/1 large can chick peas (garbanzos), drained
100 g/4 oz/1 cup Feta cheese, cubed
Salt and freshly ground black pepper
A pinch of ground cinnamon
4 tomatoes, skinned, seeded and chopped
120 ml/4 fl oz/1 cup very low-fat crème fraîche
To serve:
8 small pitta breads
Mixed Green Salad (see page 265)

Wash the spinach thoroughly under running water and remove any tough stems. Cut into shreds. Heat the low-fat spread in a saucepan and fry (sauté) the spinach and garlic, stirring, for 4 minutes. Add the chick peas, cheese, salt and pepper and the cinnamon. Toss over a gentle heat for 2 minutes. Add the tomatoes and crème fraîche and heat through, tossing and stirring. Warm the pitta breads briefly to puff them up. Make a slit along the top of each one to form a pocket. Fill with the spinach mixture and serve with Mixed Green Salad.

Quorn and Bean Bake

SERVES 4

25 g/1 oz/2 tbsp low-fat spread
1 bunch of spring onions
  (scallions), finely chopped
1 garlic clove, crushed
175 g/6 oz quorn pieces
100 g/4 oz button mushrooms,
  quartered
425 g/15 oz/1 large can flageolet
  beans, drained
300 ml/½ pt/1¼ cups vegetable
  stock, made with 1 stock cube
20 ml/4 tsp redcurrant jelly (clear
  conserve)
A rosemary sprig
Salt and freshly ground black
  pepper
450 g/1 lb potatoes, thinly sliced
To serve:
Sir-fried Greens (see page 280)

Melt half the low-fat spread in a flameproof casserole (Dutch oven). Add the spring onions and garlic clove and fry (sauté) for 2 minutes. Stir in the quorn and mushrooms and fry, stirring, for 2 minutes. Stir in the beans, stock and redcurrant jelly. Add the rosemary and season lightly. Bring to the boil and simmer for 5 minutes. Remove from the heat and discard the rosemary. Lay the potatoes overlapping on top. Dot with the remaining low-fat spread and season again. Bake in a preheated oven at 180ºC/350ºF/ gas mark 4 for about 50 minutes or until the potatoes are cooked and golden. Serve with Stir-fried Greens.

Mediterranean Haricots

SERVES 4

2 large onions, sliced
2 garlic cloves, crushed
25 g/1 oz/2 tbsp low-fat spread
2 x 415 g/2 x 15 oz/2 large cans
  haricot (navy) beans, drained
400 g/14 oz/1 large can chopped
  tomatoes
2 sun-dried tomatoes, chopped
15 ml/1 tbsp chopped basil
Salt and freshly ground black
  pepper
A few torn basil leaves
8 black olives, stoned (pitted) and
  halved
To serve:
225 g/8 oz plain pasta, cooked
Mixed Salad (see page 269)

Fry (sauté) the onions and garlic in the low-fat spread for 3 minutes. Add the remaining ingredients except the torn basil leaves and olives. Bring to the boil, reduce the heat and simmer for about 10 minutes until pulpy. Serve, garnished with torn basil leaves and olives, on a bed of pasta with Mixed Salad.

Lentil and Mushroom Curry

SERVES 4

225 g/8 oz/1⅓ cups whole brown lentils
1 onion, chopped
1 garlic clove, crushed
25 g/1 oz/2 tbsp low-fat spread
30 ml/2 tbsp curry paste
900 ml/1½ pts/3¾ cups vegetable stock, made with 2 stock cubes
100g/4 oz cup mushrooms, quartered
100 g/4 oz oyster mushrooms, quartered
100 g/4 oz chestnut mushrooms, quartered
150 ml/¼ pt/⅔ cup very low-fat plain yoghurt
15 ml/1 tbsp curried peach chutney, chopped if necessary
Salt and freshly ground black pepper
Roughly chopped coriander (cilantro)
Lemon wedges
Shredded lettuce
Cucumber and tomato slices
To serve:
4 small individual coriander naan breads

Soak the lentils in cold water for several hours, then drain thoroughly. Fry (sauté) the onion and garlic in the low-fat spread in a large saucepan, stirring, for 2 minutes. Stir in the curry paste and cook for 1 minute. Blend in the stock and bring to the boil. Stir in the lentils, cover, reduce the heat and simmer gently for 1½ hours. Add all the mushrooms and continue cooking for 30 minutes until the mushrooms are tender and nearly all the liquid has been absorbed. Stir in the yoghurt and chutney and season to taste. Pile on to warmed serving plates. Sprinkle with coriander and garnish on the side with lemon wedges, lettuce and cucumber and tomato slices. Serve with warmed individual naan breads.

·······················POULTRY·······················

CALORIES OR LESS

Chicken Masala

SERVES 4

350 g/12 oz boneless chicken
   meat, diced
1 onion, chopped
1 small green (bell) pepper, diced
15 ml/1 tbsp curry paste
25 g/1 oz/2 tbsp low-fat spread
450 ml/¾ pt/2 cups chicken stock,
   made with 1 stock cube
½ block creamed coconut
225 g/8 oz/1 small can pease
   pudding
15 ml/1 tbsp raisins
Salt and freshly ground black
   pepper
15 ml/1 tbsp chopped coriander
   (cilantro)
Shredded lettuce, tomato wedges,
   lemon wedges
To serve:
Yellow Rice (see page 296)
Nutty Courgette and Carrot Salad
   (see page 268)

Fry (sauté) the chicken, onion, diced
pepper and curry paste in the low-
fat spread for 4 minutes, stirring. Add
the stock, coconut, pease pudding and
raisins. Bring to the boil, stirring,
reduce the heat and simmer gently for
10 minutes, stirring to prevent sticking. Season to taste and stir in the
coriander. Spoon on to warmed plates,
garnish with shredded lettuce, tomato
and lemon wedges and serve with
Yellow Rice and Nutty Courgette and
Carrot Salad.

Tender Turkey Breasts in Smooth Cider Sauce

SERVES 4

4 small turkey breast fillets, about
   200 g/7 oz each
150 ml/¼ pt/⅔ cup cider
150 ml/¼ pt/⅔ cup chicken stock,
   made with ½ stock cube
2.5 ml/½ tsp dried basil
2.5 ml/½ tsp dried oregano
Salt and freshly ground black
   pepper
20 ml/4 tsp cornflour (cornstarch)
30 ml/2 tbsp skimmed milk
100 g/4 oz/½ cup very low-fat
   fromage frais
15 ml/1 tbsp chopped parsley
To serve:
Onion-topped Mash (see page 287)
Runner beans
Baby carrots

Place the turkey breasts in a
saucepan and add the cider, stock,
herbs and a little salt and pepper.
Bring to the boil, reduce the heat,
cover and poach gently for about
10–15 minutes until really tender.
Remove from the pan with a draining
spoon and keep warm. Blend the cornflour with the milk. Stir into the pan
and bring to the boil, stirring. Blend in
the fromage frais, taste and re-season.
Simmer for 4–5 minutes. Transfer the
turkey to warmed plates. Spoon the
sauce over and garnish with the parsley. Serve with Onion-topped Mash,
runner beans and baby carrots.

Chicken Veronica

SERVES 4

**150 ml/¼ pt/⅔ cup chicken stock,
made with ½ stock cube**
1 bay leaf
1 small onion, halved
150 ml/¼ pt/⅔ cup red wine
40 g/1½ oz/3 tbsp low-fat spread
**4 small skinless chicken breasts,
about 150 g/5 oz each**
**25 g/1 oz/¼ cup plain (all-purpose)
flour**
**150 ml/¼ pt/⅔ cup low-fat single
(light) cream**
**75 g/3 oz/½ cup seedless red
grapes, halved**
**Salt and freshly ground black
pepper**
Watercress
To serve:
Herby Potatoes (see page 289)
Carrots Cressy (see page 274)

Put the stock, bay leaf, onion and wine in a saucepan. Bring to the boil, remove from the heat and leave to infuse. Meanwhile, melt the low-fat spread in a large frying pan (skillet). Add the chicken and fry (sauté) on both sides for about 8–10 minutes until golden and cooked through. Remove from the pan and keep warm. Stir the flour into the pan and cook for 1 minute, stirring. Strain in the stock and wine, discarding the bay leaf and onion. Blend until smooth, then bring to the boil, stirring. Blend in the cream, grapes and salt and pepper to taste. Simmer for 2 minutes. Transfer the chicken to warmed plates. Spoon the sauce over and garnish with watercress. Serve with Herby Potatoes and Carrots Cressy.

Savoury Turkey Escalopes

SERVES 4

**4 small turkey breast fillets, about
175 g/6 oz each**
**85 g/3½ oz/1 small packet sage
and onion stuffing mix**
1 egg
15 ml/1 tbsp skimmed milk
50 g/2 oz/¼ cup low-fat spread
Lemon wedges
Parsley or sage sprigs
To serve:
Puréed Potatoes (see page 287)
**Tomatoes with Courgettes (see
page 275)**

Put the fillets one at a time in a plastic bag and beat with a rolling pin or meat mallet until flattened and fairly thin. Put the stuffing mix in a shallow dish and beat the egg and milk in a separate dish. Dip the turkey in the beaten egg, then in the stuffing to coat completely. Melt half the low-fat spread in a large frying pan (skillet). Add the escalopes and fry (sauté) for 3–4 minutes until golden brown underneath. Add the remaining low fat spread and fry the other sides until cooked through and golden. Drain on kitchen paper. Garnish with lemon wedges and sprigs of parsley or fresh sage and serve with Puréed Potatoes and Tomatoes with Courgettes.

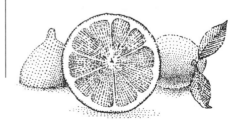

Peking-style Turkey

SERVES 4

*1 bunch of spring onions
(scallions)
¼ cucumber
350 g/12 oz turkey stir-fry pieces
45 ml/3 tbsp soy sauce
5 ml/1 tsp grated fresh root ginger
1 garlic clove, crushed
10 ml/2 tsp red wine vinegar
Freshly ground black pepper
45 ml/3 tbsp plum jam (conserve),
reduced-sugar preferably
5 ml/1 tsp lemon juice
8 Chinese pancakes or small
tortillas
15 g/½ oz/1 tbsp low-fat spread*
To serve:
**Oriental Bean Sprout Salad (see
page 271)**

Cut the roots and the green tops off the spring onions, leaving onions about 7.5 cm/3 in long. Make a series of cuts through the white bulb to a depth of about 2.5 cm/1 in. Place in a bowl of cold water and chill to allow the ends to open out. Cut the cucumber into thin strips. Place in a serving bowl and chill. Put the turkey in a shallow dish. Mix together half the soy sauce and ginger and all the garlic, vinegar and a good grinding of pepper. Pour over the turkey and toss well. Leave to stand for at least 1 hour to absorb the flavours. Meanwhile, mix the plum jam with the remaining soy sauce and ginger and the lemon juice. Put in a small serving bowl. Warm the pancakes or tortillas according to the packet directions. Heat the low-fat spread in a large frying pan (skillet). Lift the turkey out of the marinade with a draining spoon and fry (sauté) for about 5 minutes until cooked through. Turn on to a warmed serving dish. To serve, use a spring onion 'brush' to dip in the plum sauce and spread over a Chinese pancake or tortilla. Add a spoonful of meat and some cucumber. Roll up and eat with Oriental Bean Sprout Salad.

Spaghetti with Chicken and Mushrooms

SERVES 4

*40 g/1½ oz/3 tbsp low-fat spread
225 g/8 oz boneless chicken,
skinned and diced
2 carrots, finely chopped
1 celery stick, finely chopped
1 large onion, finely chopped
1 garlic clove, crushed
175 g/6 oz button mushrooms,
sliced
6 tomatoes, skinned and chopped
50 g/2 oz/½ cup frozen peas
Salt and freshly ground black
pepper
5 ml/1 tsp dried mixed herbs
350 g/12 oz spaghetti
20 ml/4 tsp grated Parmesan
cheese*
To serve:
Crisp Green Salad (see page 265)

Melt the low-fat spread in a saucepan. Add the remaining ingredients except the spaghetti and cheese and fry (sauté), stirring, for 3 minutes. Reduce the heat, cover and simmer gently for 15 minutes until the vegetables and chicken are tender. Meanwhile, cook the spaghetti according to the packet directions. Drain and return to the pan. Add the chicken mixture and toss well. Pile on to warmed plates and sprinkle with the Parmesan. Serve with Crisp Green Salad.

Pan-roast Pheasant with Italian Sauce

SERVES 4

1 cock pheasant, quartered, skin removed
25 g/1 oz/2 tbsp low-fat spread
15 ml/1 tbsp plain (all-purpose) flour
150 ml/¼ pt/⅔ cup chicken stock, made with ½ stock cube
6 tomatoes, skinned, seeded and chopped
Artificial sweetener granules
150 ml/¼ pt/⅔ cup low-fat double (heavy) cream
50 g/2 oz/½ cup Parmesan cheese, grated
Salt and freshly ground black pepper
A few basil leaves
To serve:
Parsleyed Potatoes (see page 289)
Mixed Leaf Salad (see page 265)

Fry (sauté) the pheasant in a flame-proof casserole (Dutch oven) in the low-fat spread on all sides to brown. Cover, reduce the heat and cook gently for 30 minutes or until tender (depending on the toughness of the bird). Remove from the pan and keep warm. Drain off the fat. Blend the flour with the stock and stir into the pan. Bring to the boil, stirring. Add the tomatoes, a few grains of artificial sweetener, the cream and cheese and simmer for 3 minutes, stirring. Season to taste. Return the pheasant to the pan and simmer for a further 5 minutes. Transfer to warmed plates. Scatter a few basil leaves over and serve with Parsleyed Potatoes and Mixed Leaf Salad.

Chicken Tuscany

SERVES 4

40 g/1½ oz/3 tbsp low-fat spread
1 onion, finely chopped
2 garlic cloves, crushed
1 green (bell) pepper, chopped
1 red (bell) pepper, chopped
400 g/14 oz/1 large can chopped tomatoes
75 g/3 oz/½ cup green olives, stoned (pitted) and chopped
2.5 ml/½ tsp cayenne
A few drops of Worcestershire sauce
Salt and freshly ground black pepper
4 skinless chicken breasts, about 175 g/6 oz each
225 g/8 oz short ribbon noodles
To serve:
Crisp Green Salad (see page 265)

Melt 15 g/½ oz/1 tbsp of the low-fat spread in a saucepan. Add the onion, garlic and peppers and fry (sauté) fairly gently for 5 minutes until soft but not browned. Add the tomatoes, olives, cayenne, Worcestershire sauce and a little salt and pepper. Bring to the boil, reduce the heat and simmer for 10 minutes. Meanwhile, melt half the remaining low-fat spread. Brush over the chicken and place on a grill (broiler) rack. Grill (broil) for about 10 minutes until golden on both sides and cooked through. Meanwhile, cook the noodles according to the the packet directions. Drain and toss with the remaining low-fat spread. Transfer the chicken to warmed plates and spoon the sauce over. Spoon the noodles to one side and serve with Crisp Green Salad.

French-style Stewed Duck

SERVES 4

1 oven-ready duck, about
    1.75 kg/4 lb
25 g/1 oz/2 tbsp low-fat spread
12 button onions, peeled but left
    whole
600 ml/1 pt/2½ cups chicken
    stock, made with 2 stock cubes
Salt and freshly ground black
    pepper
225 g/8 oz/2 cups frozen peas
15 ml/1 tbsp chopped mint
15 ml/1 tbsp chopped oregano
15 ml/1 tbsp chopped parsley
1.5 ml/¼ tsp grated nutmeg
1 round lettuce, shredded
30 ml/2 tbsp plain (all-purpose)
    flour
Mint sprigs
To serve:
Baby Jackets (see page 287)
Glazed Carrots (see page 275)

Remove the giblets (use for the stock, if liked) and wipe the duck inside and out with kitchen paper. Prick all over with a fork. Melt the low-fat spread in a flameproof casserole (Dutch oven) and brown the duck on all sides. Remove the duck and brown the onions. Pour off any fat. Return the duck to the pan. Add the stock and a little salt and pepper. Bring to the boil, cover and transfer to a preheated oven at 200°C/400°F/gas mark 6 for 30 minutes. Skim the surface of any fat, then add the remaining ingredients except the flour. Reduce the oven to 180°C/350°F/gas mark 4 and cook for a further 1½ hours. Remove the duck and keep warm. Skim off any fat. Blend the 30 ml/2 tbsp flour with water. Stir into the casserole, place on top of the stove and simmer for 3 minutes, stirring. Taste and re-season if necessary.

Carve the duck, discarding the skin, and transfer to warmed plates. Spoon the pea sauce over each portion, garnish with mint sprigs and serve with Baby Jackets and Glazed Carrots.

Peasant Chicken

SERVES 4

450 g/1 lb small new potatoes,
    scraped but left whole
50 g/2 oz/¼ cup low-fat spread
4 chicken portions, skinned as
    much as possible
100 g/4 oz button mushrooms
150 ml/¼ pt/⅔ cup chicken stock,
    made with ½ stock cube
Salt and freshly ground black
    pepper
2 garlic cloves, chopped
30 ml/2 tbsp chopped parsley
To serve:
Rustic Salad (see page 283)

Fry (sauté) the potatoes in a flameproof casserole (Dutch oven) in half the low-fat spread, turning until golden brown. Remove from the pan. Melt the remaining low-fat spread and fry the chicken pieces on all sides to brown. Return the potatoes to the pan and add the mushrooms, stock and a little salt and pepper. Cover tightly, reduce the heat and cook very gently for about 40 minutes until the chicken and potatoes are tender. Sprinkle over the garlic and most of the parsley, recover and cook gently for a further 5 minutes. Transfer the chicken, potatoes and mushrooms to warmed serving plates. Keep warm. Boil the liquid rapidly, if necessary, to reduce a little. Taste and adjust the seasoning. Spoon over the chicken and vegetables and sprinkle with the remaining parsley. Serve with Rustic Salad.

Old English Country Duck

SERVES 4

**1 oven-ready duck, about
    1.75 kg/4 lb
25 g/1 oz/2 tbsp low-fat spread
2 onions, sliced
2 lean rashers (slices) streaky
    bacon, rinded and diced
1 carrot, finely diced
600 ml/1 pt/2½ cups chicken
    stock, made with 2 stock cubes
Salt and freshly ground black
    pepper
1 bouquet garni sachet
45 ml/3 tbsp port
450 g/1 lb baby turnips, peeled
    but left whole**
To serve:
**Parsleyed Potatoes (see page 289)
Mangetout (snow peas)**

Remove the giblets from the duck (use for the stock if liked) and wipe the duck inside and out with kitchen paper. Prick all over with a fork. Melt the low-fat spread in a flameproof casserole (Dutch oven). Brown the duck all over. Remove from the pan. Add the onions, bacon and carrot and fry (sauté), stirring, for 2 minutes. Remove from the pan with a draining spoon and skim off all the fat. Return the duck to the pan with the onion mixture. Pour on the stock. Add a little salt and pepper, the bouquet garni and the port. Surround with the turnips. Bring to the boil, cover and transfer to a preheated oven at 180°C/350°F/gas mark 4. Cook for 2 hours or until the duck and turnips are tender. Remove the duck and turnips from the casserole and keep warm. Skim the surface again, then boil rapidly until reduced by half. Taste and re-season if necessary. Carve the duck, discarding as much skin as possible, and arrange on warmed plates. Spoon a little of the sauce over

and arrange the turnips to one side. Serve with the remaining sauce, Parsleyed Potatoes and mangetout.

Garlic and Lemon Chicken

SERVES 4

**1 oven-ready chicken about
    1.25 kg/2¾ lb
Salt and freshly ground black
    pepper
1 large rosemary sprig
2 garlic cloves, halved
30 ml/2 tbsp lemon juice
15 g/½ oz/1 tbsp low-fat spread
Salt and freshly ground black
    pepper
300 ml/½ pt/1¼ cups chicken
    stock, made with 1 stock cube
Rosemary sprigs
Lemon twists**
To serve:
**Dauphine Potatoes (see page 294)
Green beans**

Wipe the chicken inside and out with kitchen paper. Remove any excess fat from just inside the body cavity. Season inside with a little salt and pepper and push in the large rosemary sprig and garlic. Place in a casserole (Dutch oven). Sprinkle all over with the lemon juice and spread the low-fat spread over the breast. Season with a little salt. Pour the stock around. Cook in a preheated oven at 190°C/375°F/ gas mark 5 for 1¼ hours. Transfer the chicken to a carving dish. Spoon off any fat, then boil the juices rapidly until reduced by half. Season to taste. Cut the chicken into four portions, discarding the skin. Transfer to warmed plates and spoon the pan juices over. Garnish with rosemary and lemon twists and serve with Dauphine Potatoes and green beans.

Thai Chicken

SERVES 4

4 small skinless chicken breasts,
  about 150 g/5 oz each
60 ml/4 tbsp lime juice
10 ml/2 tsp curry powder
175 ml/6 fl oz/¾ cup canned
  coconut milk
75 g/3 oz/⅓ cup peanut butter
30 ml/2 tbsp white wine vinegar
15 ml/1 tbsp soy sauce
10 ml/2 tsp cornflour (cornstarch)
1 small green chilli, seeded and
  finely chopped
4 ml/¾ tsp artificial sweetener
  granules
20 g/¾ oz/1½ tbsp low-fat spread,
  melted
Torn coriander (cilantro) leaves
To serve:
175 g/6 oz/¾ cup Thai fragrant
  rice, boiled
Chinese Leaf and Mango Salad
  (see page 269)

Cut the chicken into bite-sized
pieces. Place in a shallow dish and
sprinkle with the lime juice and half the
curry powder. Leave to marinate for at
least 1 hour, stirring occasionally. Put
the coconut milk, peanut butter, vinegar, soy sauce, cornflour, remaining
curry powder and chilli in a saucepan.
Heat gently, stirring, until melted, then
bring to the boil and simmer for 3 minutes, stirring. Sweeten to taste with
artificial sweetener (add just a few
grains at a time). Thread the chicken on
to soaked wooden skewers. Brush with
the low-fat spread and grill (broil) for
8–10 minutes until tender and cooked
through. Transfer to warmed plates.
Spoon a little sauce over and sprinkle
with torn coriander leaves. Serve with
Thai fragrant rice, Chinese Leaf and
Mango Salad and the remaining sauce.

Chicken Fajitas

SERVES 4

1 garlic clove, crushed
15 ml/1 tbsp clear honey
150 ml/¼ pt/⅔ cup apple juice
150 ml/¼ pt/⅔ cup lager
60 ml/4 tbsp red wine vinegar
2.5 ml/½ tsp chilli powder
350 g/12 oz chicken stir-fry meat
25 g/1 oz/2 tbsp low-fat spread
1 bunch of spring onions
  (scallions), diagonally sliced
1 red (bell) pepper, cut into thin
  strips
1 green (bell) pepper, cut into thin
  strips
Salt and freshly ground black
  pepper
8 tortillas
To serve:
Mexican Salad (see page 282)

Put the garlic, honey, apple juice,
lager, vinegar and chilli powder in a
pan. Bring to the boil, reduce the heat
and simmer for 5 minutes. Put the
chicken in a shallow dish. Pour over
the marinade and leave to marinate for
1 hour. Heat half the low-fat spread in
a large frying pan (skillet). Add the
spring onions and peppers and stir-fry
for 4 minutes until softened. Remove
from the pan and reserve. Add the
remaining low-fat spread to the pan.
Remove the chicken from the marinade and stir-fry the chicken for 5
minutes until cooked through. Return
the spring onions and peppers to the
pan with 30 ml/2 tbsp of the marinade
and toss until piping hot and glazed.
Season to taste. Warm the tortillas
according to the packet directions.
Divide the chicken mixture between
the tortillas. Roll up and serve with
Mexican Salad.

Chicken and Asparagus Bake

SERVES 4

225 g/8 oz conchiglie or other
  pasta shapes
298 g/10½ oz/1 small can
  asparagus spears, drained
225 g/8 oz/2 cups cooked chicken
  (skin removed), cut into bite-
  sized pieces
Salt and freshly ground black
  pepper
A pinch of grated nutmeg
295 g/10½ oz/1 small can
  condensed cream of chicken
  soup
120 ml/4 fl oz/½ cup skimmed
  milk
150 ml/¼ pt/⅔ cup very low-fat
  crème fraîche
50 g/2 oz/½ cup low-fat Cheddar
  cheese, grated
50 g/2 oz/1 cup fresh breadcrumbs
15 g/½ oz/1 tbsp low-fat spread,
  melted
Parsley sprigs
To serve:
Garlic Bread (see page 293)
Lettuce dressed with lemon juice
  and black pepper

Cook the pasta according to the
packet directions. Drain and transfer to a large ovenproof dish. Top with
the drained asparagus, then the chick-
en. Season lightly with salt, pepper
and the nutmeg. Blend the soup with
the milk, crème fraîche and cheese.
Spoon over. Mix the breadcrumbs with
the low-fat spread and sprinkle over.
Bake in a preheated oven at
190°C/375°F/gas mark 5 for about 35
minutes until piping hot and golden
on top. Serve with Garlic Bread and
lettuce. Garnish with parsley sprigs.

Chicken and Celery Bake

SERVES 4

Prepare as for Chicken and
Asparagus Bake but substitute a
can of chopped celery for the asparagus. Spoon 228 g/8 oz/1 small can
chopped tomatoes over the celery
before adding the soup mixture and
omit the nutmeg.

Chicken with Cointreau Sauce

SERVES 4

4 skinless chicken breasts, about
  175 g/6 oz each
50 g/2 oz/¼ cup low-fat spread,
  melted
Salt and freshly ground black
  pepper
120 ml/4 fl oz/½ cup low-fat
  double (heavy) cream
60 ml/4 tbsp Cointreau
Grated rind and juice of 1 orange
1 egg
Chopped parsley
To serve:
Pan Scalloped Potatoes (see page
  289)
Broccoli

Brush the chicken with a little of the
low-fat spread and season lightly.
Grill (broil) for about 6 minutes on
each side or until golden and cooked
through. Meanwhile, put the remaining low-fat spread in a saucepan with
the remaining ingredients. Whisk
together thoroughly. Heat gently,
whisking all the time, until thickened.
Do not boil. Season to taste. Spoon
the sauce on to four warmed plates.
Top with a chicken breast and sprinkle
with parsley. Serve with Pan Scalloped
Potatoes and broccoli.

Chicken and Spiced Almond Salad

SERVES 4

1 oven-ready chicken about
  1.25 kg/2¾ lb
1 garlic clove
25 g/1 oz/2 tbsp low-fat spread
Salt and freshly ground black pepper
For the sauce:
75 ml/5 tbsp low-calorie
  mayonnaise
75 ml/5 tbsp very low-fat yoghurt
15 ml/1 tbsp tomato purée (paste)
5 ml/1 tsp Worcestershire sauce
5 cm/2 in piece cucumber, chopped
50 g/2 oz/½ cup blanched almonds
1.5 ml/¼ tsp chilli powder
1.5 ml/¼ tsp mixed (apple-pie) spice
1 small lollo rosso lettuce
Lemon wedges
To serve:
Garlic Potatoes (see page 286)
Tomato, Chicory and Orange Salad
  (see page 271)

Wipe the chicken inside and out with kitchen paper. Pull off any excess fat just inside the body cavity. Place in a roasting tin (pan) and put the garlic clove inside. Spread half the low-fat spread over. Sprinkle with a little salt and pepper. Cover and roast in a preheated oven at 190°C/375°F/gas mark 5 for 1¼ hours or until the juices run clear when a skewer is inserted in the thickest part of the thigh. Remove from the pan and drain on kitchen paper. Leave to cool a little while preparing the sauce. Mix together the mayonnaise, yoghurt, tomato purée and Worcestershire sauce. Season lightly. Stir in the cucumber. Melt the remaining low-fat spread in a frying pan (skillet). Fry (sauté) the almonds until golden brown. Sprinkle with the spices and toss well. Drain on kitchen paper. Transfer the chicken to a carving dish, discard the skin and cut into quarters. Lay the lettuce leaves on four serving plates. Top with a piece of warm chicken. Spoon the sauce over and garnish with lemon wedges and the almonds. Serve with Garlic Potatoes and Tomato, Chicory and Orange Salad.

Creamy Tarragon Chicken

SERVES 4

4 skinless chicken breasts
25 g/1 oz/2 tbsp low-fat spread
10 ml/2 tsp plain (all-purpose)
  flour
15 ml/1 tbsp chopped tarragon
5 ml/1 tsp Dijon mustard
120 ml/4 fl oz/½ cup dry white
  wine
120 ml/4 fl oz/½ cup very low-fat
  crème fraîche
Salt and freshly ground black
  pepper
Tarragon sprigs
To serve:
450 g/1 lb baby new potatoes,
  boiled
Polonaise-style Cauliflower and
  Broccoli (see page 290)

Fry (sauté) the chicken in the low-fat spread for about 15 minutes until golden brown on both sides and cooked through. Remove from the pan and keep warm. Stir the flour, chopped tarragon, mustard and wine into the pan. Bring to the boil and boil for 3 minutes or until reduced by half. Stir in the crème fraîche and season to taste. Return the chicken to the pan with any juices and simmer gently for 5 minutes. Transfer to warmed plates. Garnish with tarragon sprigs and serve with baby new potatoes and Polonaise-style Cauliflower and Broccoli.

Brown Rice and Chicken Slow-pot

SERVES 4

1 oven-ready chicken, about
  1.25 kg/2¾ lb
225 g/8 oz/1 cup brown long-grain
  rice
8 button onions, peeled but left
  whole
2 carrots, cut into chunks
2 turnips, cut into chunks
A pinch of grated nutmeg
5 ml/1 tsp chopped sage
Salt and freshly ground black
  pepper
600 ml/1 pt/2½ cups hot chicken
  stock, made with 2 stock cubes
60 ml/4 tbsp low-fat single (light)
  cream
Sage sprigs
To serve:
Spring Green Toss (see page 277)

Wipe the chicken inside and out with kitchen paper. Pull off any excess fat from just inside the body cavity. Place in a casserole (Dutch oven). Wash the rice thoroughly in several changes of water. Drain and surround the chicken. Add the vegetables, nutmeg, sage and a little salt and pepper. Pour the hot stock over. Cover tightly and cook in a preheated oven at 140°C/275°F/gas mark 1 for 2 hours. Check and add a little more stock if the rice is becoming too dry. Re-cover and continue cooking for a further 2 hours. Turn up the heat to 200°C/400°F/gas mark 6 and cook for a further 30 minutes, adding a little more stock if necessary. Remove the chicken and ease it apart into portions, discarding the skin. Stir the cream into the rice. Taste and add more seasoning if necessary. Spoon on to warmed plates, top with the chicken and garnish with a few sage sprigs. Serve with Spring Green Toss.

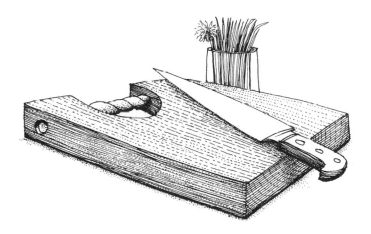

·······FISH·······

CALORIES OR LESS

Soused Mackerel

SERVES 4

4 small mackerel, cleaned
Salt and freshly ground black
  pepper
2 onions, thinly sliced
300 ml/½ pt/1¼ cups tarragon
  vinegar
150 ml/¼ pt/⅔ cup water
5 ml/1 tsp artificial sweetener
  granules
1 bay leaf
3 cloves
8 peppercorns
Low-fat spread, for greasing
Lettuce leaves
Parsley sprigs
To serve:
Hot Potato and Bean Salad (see
  page 282)
Beetroot and Orange Salad
  (see page 269)

Rinse the fish under cold water. Drain and dry on kitchen paper. Cut off the heads, remove the fins and trim the tails. Slit down the stomachs and open out flat, skin sides up. Run the thumb firmly up and down the backbone. Turn over and lift off the backbone and any loose bones.

Season the flesh with salt and pepper and cover with half the onion rings. Roll up from head to tail. Place in a shallow ovenproof dish with the tails upwards. Scatter the remaining onion over. Boil the remaining ingredients in a pan for 5 minutes. Strain over the fish. Grease some foil with a little low-fat spread and use to cover the fish. Bake in a preheated oven at 180ºC/350ºF/gas mark 4 for 45 minutes until cooked through. Leave in the liquid to cool, then chill. Drain and transfer to a bed of lettuce on serving plates with the onion rings scattered over. Garnish with parsley sprigs and serve with Hot Potato and Bean Salad and Beetroot and Orange Salad.

Soused Orange Herrings

SERVES 4

Prepare as for Soused Mackerel but substitute herrings for the mackerel. Make sure you remove any loose bones before rolling up. Add the grated rind and juice of an orange to the sousing mixture and garnish with orange twists.

Photograph opposite:
Fijian Chicken (page 167)

Golden Cheese Custard

SERVES 4

350 g/12 oz cod fillet, skinned
175 g/6 oz smoked cod fillet,
skinned
600 ml/1 pt/2½ cups fish stock,
made with 2 stock cubes
1 onion, finely chopped
1 garlic clove, crushed
1.5 ml/¼ tsp grated nutmeg
Salt and freshly ground black
pepper
20 g/¾ oz/3 tbsp plain (all-
purpose) flour
150 ml/¼ pt/⅔ cup skimmed milk
40g/1½ oz/3 tbsp low-fat spread
450 g/1 lb tomatoes, skinned and
chopped
30 ml/2 tbsp chopped parsley
2 eggs
150 ml/¼ pt/⅔ cup low-fat single
(light) cream
50 g/2 oz/½ cup Parmesan cheese,
grated
To serve:
Parsleyed Potatoes (see page 289)
Broccoli

Put the fish in a pan with the stock, onion, garlic and nutmeg. Season lightly. Cover, bring to the boil, reduce the heat and simmer gently for 10 minutes until tender. Remove the fish from the pan, flake with a fork and place in a 1.5 litre/2½ pt/6 cup oven-proof dish. Boil the fish liquid until reduced by half. Blend the flour with 45 ml/3 tbsp of the milk and stir into the pan with half the low-fat spread. Bring to the boil and cook for 2 minutes, stirring all the time, until thickened. Season to taste. Spoon over the fish and mix well. Top with the tomatoes, then the parsley. Beat the eggs with the remaining milk, the cream and the cheese. Season lightly. Pour over the tomatoes and parsley. Dot with the remaining low-fat spread and bake in a preheated oven at 180°C/350°F/gas mark 4 for 40 minutes or until the custard is set. Serve with Parsleyed Potatoes and broccoli.

Ceviche with Avocado

SERVES 4

450 g/1 lb cod fillet, skinned and
cut into bite-sized pieces
Juice of 2 limes
4 tomatoes, skinned, seeded and
diced
1 green (bell) pepper, diced
1 small green chilli, seeded and
chopped
1 small onion, thinly sliced and
separated into rings
15 ml/1 tbsp olive oil
15 ml/1 tbsp chopped parsley
10 ml/2 tsp white wine vinegar
2 ripe avocados, sliced
Salt and freshly ground black
pepper
2.5 ml/½ tsp dried oregano
½ curly endive (frisée lettuce)
Cucumber twists
To serve:
Hot Herb Bread (see page 293)

Put the fish in a large container. Add the lime juice and toss gently. Chill for at least 3 hours, tossing occasionally until completely white as if it has been cooked. Add the remaining ingredients except the endive and cucumber twists, toss gently and chill for a further 1 hour to allow the flavours to develop. Pile on to curly endive leaves and garnish with cucumber twists. Serve with Hot Herb Bread.

Photograph opposite:
Warm Summer Seafood (page 174)

Portuguese Salt Cod with Potatoes

SERVES 4

450 g/1 lb salt cod, soaked for 24
  hours in several changes of cold
  water
10 ml/2 tsp lemon juice
45 ml/3 tbsp plain (all-purpose)
  flour
A good pinch of cayenne
30 ml/2 tbsp olive oil
4 large onions, thinly sliced
450 g/1 lb waxy potatoes, sliced
450 g/1 lb ripe tomatoes, skinned
  and chopped
2 garlic cloves, chopped
30 ml/2 tbsp chopped parsley
450–600 ml/¾–1 pt/2–2½ cups fish
  or chicken stock, made with 2
  stock cubes
Freshly ground black pepper
5 ml/1 tsp powdered saffron
To serve:
Mixed Green Salad (see page 265)

Drain the cod and place in a saucepan. Just cover with fresh water with the lemon juice added. Cover, bring to the boil and simmer for 3 minutes. Leave to cool. Lift out of the liquid and pat dry. Cut into bite-sized pieces. Dust with flour to which the cayenne has been added. Fry (sauté) in the oil in a flameproof casserole (Dutch oven) until golden on all sides. Remove from the pan with a draining spoon. Add the onions, potatoes, tomatoes and garlic and cook, stirring, for 3 minutes. Add half the parsley and enough stock to just cover the ingredients. Season with pepper. Cover and simmer gently until the potatoes are just tender. Take out 30 ml/2 tbsp of the cooking liquid and stir in the saffron. Add the fish to the pan and pour over the saffron liquid. Cover and continue cooking for 10 minutes until the fish is tender. Ladle into warm bowls and garnish with the remaining parsley. Serve with Mixed Green Salad to follow.

Saucy Smoked Mackerel

SERVES 4

40 g/1½ oz/3 tbsp low-fat spread
20 g/¾ oz/3 tbsp plain (all-
  purpose) flour
300 ml/½ pt/1¼ cups skimmed milk
Grated rind and juice of ½ lemon
15 ml/1 tbsp horseradish sauce
Salt and freshly ground black
  pepper
4 smoked mackerel fillets
Lemon wedges
Parsley sprigs
To serve:
450 g/1 lb potatoes, scrubbed and
  boiled
Spinach with Tomatoes (see page
  278)

Put half the low-fat spread in a saucepan with the flour and milk. Whisk until smooth, then bring to the boil and cook for 2 minutes, stirring all the time. Stir in the lemon rind, horseradish and salt and pepper to taste. Cover with a circle of wet greaseproof (waxed) paper to stop a skin forming. Put the mackerel fillets on the grill (broiler) rack. Dot with the remaining low-fat spread and drizzle with the lemon juice. Grill (broil) for 3–5 minutes on each side until cooked through, basting with the pan juices during cooking. Transfer to warmed plates and keep warm. Strain the juices and stir into the sauce. Heat through. Spoon over the mackerel and garnish with lemon wedges and parsley sprigs. Serve hot with plain boiled potatoes and Spinach with Tomatoes.

Lobster Thermidor

SERVES 6

**3 small cooked lobsters, about
550 g/1¼ lb each**
**300 ml/½ pt/1¼ cups fish stock,
made with ½ stock cube**
150 ml/¼ pt/⅔ cup dry white wine
1 bay leaf
A pinch of onion salt
450 ml/¾ pt/2 cups skimmed milk
**50 g/2 oz/½ cup plain (all-purpose)
flour**
100 g/4 oz/½ cup low-fat spread
10 ml/2 tsp Dijon mustard
**Salt and freshly ground black
pepper**
1 egg, beaten
**150 ml/¼ pt/⅔ cup low-fat single
(light) cream**
5 ml/1 tsp lemon juice
15 ml/1 tbsp brandy
**50 g/2 oz/½ cup Parmesan cheese,
grated**
**50 g/2 oz/1 cup fresh white
breadcrumbs**
Lemon twists
To serve:
1 French stick, heated
**French-style Green Salad (see page
272)**

Remove the claws from the lobsters. Split along the backs and open out into two halves. Remove the black thread and grey sack behind the head. Remove the meat from the shells and claws, cut into neat pieces and mix with any coral. Boil the stock and wine together with the bay leaf and onion salt until reduced to 150 ml/¼ pt in all. Whisk the milk with the flour until smooth. Whisk into the reduced wine mixture. Add half the low-fat spread. Bring to the boil and cook for 2 minutes, stirring. Stir in the mustard and season to taste. Whisk in the egg, cream and lemon juice. Keep warm. Melt the remaining low-fat spread in a frying pan (skillet). Add the lobster meat and toss for 2 minutes. Add the brandy and ignite. Shake the pan until the flames subside. Spoon a little of the sauce into each of the lobster shells. Mix the lobster with the remaining sauce and spoon into the shells. Blend the Parmesan with the breadcrumbs and sprinkle over. Place under a hot grill (broiler) until the tops are golden brown. Garnish with lemon twists and serve with French bread and French-style Green Salad.

Fresh Baked Sardines with Tomatoes

SERVES 4

900 g/2 lb ripe tomatoes, sliced
15 ml/1 tbsp chopped basil
30 ml/2 tbsp chopped parsley
1 garlic clove, finely chopped
50 g/2 oz/¼ cup low-fat spread,
 melted
Salt and freshly ground black
 pepper
8 fresh sardines, heads discarded
 and cleaned
2 lemons
To serve:
1 French stick, warmed
Mixed Green Salad (see page 265)

Arrange half the tomato slices in a shallow ovenproof dish. Sprinkle with half the herbs, garlic, low-fat spread and some salt and pepper. Wash the sardines under cold running water and pat dry. Lay the fish on the tomatoes. Slice one of the lemons thinly and lay over the fish. Season and top with the remaining tomatoes, herbs and low-fat spread. Season again. Squeeze the juice from the remaining lemon and sprinkle over. Bake in a preheated oven at 190°C/ 375°F/gas mark 5 for about 20 minutes until cooked through and browning on top. Serve straight from the dish with hot French bread and Mixed Green Salad.

Mackerel with Mustard 'Butter' Boats

SERVES 4

4 mackerel, cleaned
Salt and freshly ground black pepper
75 g/3 oz/⅓ cup low-fat spread
10 ml/2 tsp English made mustard
A few grains of artificial sweetener
5 ml/1 tsp lemon juice
1 small baguette
Parsley sprigs
To serve:
Green Beans with Cherry
 Tomatoes (see page 267)
Mixed Leaf Salad (see page 265)

Rinse the fish and cut off the heads. Wipe inside and out with kitchen paper. Make several slashes in the fish on each side and season with salt and pepper. Heat 25 ml/1 oz/2 tbsp of the low-fat spread in a large frying pan (skillet). Add the fish and fry (sauté) for about 5 minutes on each side until browned and cooked through. Remove from the pan and keep warm. Melt the remaining low-fat spread in the pan and add the mustard, artificial sweetener and lemon juice. Heat, stirring, until well blended. Taste and season if necessary. Meanwhile, cut the baguette lengthways into four slices. Toast under the grill (broiler) on both sides. Place on four warmed plates. Spoon a little of the mustard 'butter' on the toast. Top each with a cooked mackerel. Spoon the rest of the 'butter' over, garnish with parsley sprigs and serve with Green Beans with Cherry Tomatoes and Mixed Leaf Salad.

Salmon in Filo Pastry

SERVES 4

**4 small salmon steaks, about
150 g/5 oz each
4 filo pastry (paste) sheets
15 g/½ oz/1 tbsp low-fat spread,
melted
2 tomatoes, skinned and chopped
2 mushrooms, skinned and
chopped
5 ml/1 tsp chopped basil
A little extra low-fat spread for
greasing
120 ml/4 fl oz/½ cup passata
(sieved tomatoes)
Salt and freshly ground black
pepper
A few basil leaves**
To serve:
**Parsleyed Potatoes (see page 289)
Green Beans with Mushrooms
(see page 276)**

Remove any skin and bones from the fish. Lay the pastry sheets on a work surface and brush very lightly with some of the low-fat spread. Fold in halves and brush again. Mix together the tomatoes and mushrooms and spoon on to the centres of the pastry. Top each with a piece of fish and sprinkle with the chopped basil. Draw the pastry up over the filling to form parcels, pinching the folds together. Transfer to a lightly greased baking sheet. Brush with any remaining melted low-fat spread. Bake in a preheated oven at 200°C/400°F/gas mark 6 for 10–15 minutes until golden. Meanwhile, warm the passata and season lightly. Spoon on to four warmed plates. Put a parcel in the centre of each and garnish with basil leaves. Serve with Parsleyed Potatoes and Green Beans with Mushrooms.

Smoked Haddock Bake

SERVES 4

**40 g/1½ oz/3 tbsp low-fat spread
450 g/1 lb smoked haddock fillet,
skinned and cut into 4 pieces
3 hard-boiled (hard-cooked) eggs,
sliced
20 g/¾ oz/3 tbsp plain (all-
purpose) flour
300 ml/½ pt/1¼ cups skimmed
milk
30 ml/2 tbsp chopped parsley
75 g/3 oz/¾ cup low-fat Cheddar
cheese, grated
25 g/1 oz/½ cup fresh white
breadcrumbs
2 tomatoes, sliced
A parsley sprig**
To serve:
**Jacket-baked potatoes with Quark
and Sun-dried Tomato Dressing
(see page 356)
Mixed Leaf Salad (see page 265)**

Grease a 1.2 litre/2 pt/5 cup oven-proof dish with a little of the low-fat spread. Lay the fish in the dish and top with egg slices. Put half the remaining low-fat spread in a saucepan with the flour and milk. Whisk until smooth. Bring to the boil and cook for 2 minutes, whisking all the time. Stir in the chopped parsley and cheese and season to taste. Spoon over the fish. Melt the remaining low-fat spread. Stir in the breadcrumbs. Sprinkle over the sauce and bake in a preheated oven at 190°C/375°F/gas mark 5 for about 45 minutes until the fish is tender and the top is golden brown. Garnish with a parsley sprig and serve hot with Jacket-baked potatoes with Quark and Sun-dried Tomato Dressing and Mixed Leaf Salad.

Oriental Fish

SERVES 4

40 g/1½ oz/3 tbsp low-fat spread
1 green (bell) pepper, cut into thin
**   strips**
1 red (bell) pepper, cut into thin
**   strips**
2 celery sticks, thinly sliced
2 carrots, cut into matchsticks
1 bunch of spring onions
**   (scallions), diagonally sliced**
750 g/1½ lb cod fillet, skinned and
**   cut into 4 pieces**
2 tomatoes, skinned and quartered
228 g/8 oz/1 small can pineapple
**   pieces in natural juice**
300 ml/½ pt/1¼ cups fish or
**   chicken stock, made with 1**
**   stock cube**
Salt and freshly ground black
**   pepper**
225 g/8 oz ribbon noodles
15 ml/1 tbsp chopped coriander
**   (cilantro)**
15 ml/1 tbsp cornflour
**   (cornstarch)**
30 ml/2 tbsp water
A few coriander leaves
To serve:
Oriental Bean Sprout Salad
**   (see page 271)**

Melt half the low-fat spread in a flameproof casserole (Dutch oven). Add the peppers, celery, carrots and spring onions and fry (sauté), stirring, for 2 minutes. Cover, reduce the heat and cook for 10 minutes. Add the fish, tomatoes, pineapple with the juice, and stock to the pan. Season well. Bring to the boil, reduce the heat, cover and simmer gently for 10 minutes until the fish and vegetables are tender. Meanwhile, cook the noodles according to the packet directions. Drain and return to the pan. Add the remaining low-fat spread, the chopped coriander and a good grinding of pepper. Toss well and pile on to warmed plates. Carefully lift out the fish and transfer to the noodles. Blend the cornflour with the water and stir into the vegetables in the pan. Bring to the boil and cook for 2 minutes, stirring. Taste and re-season if necessary. Spoon over the fish, garnish with a few torn coriander leaves and serve with Oriental Bean Sprout Salad.

St Clements Cod with Lentils

SERVES 4

225 g/8 oz/1⅓ cups red lentils
1 bunch of spring onions
  (scallions), chopped
450 ml/¾ pt/2 cups fish or chicken
  stock, made with 1 stock cube
1 bay leaf
25 g/1 oz/2 tbsp low-fat spread
450 g/1 lb cod fillet, skinned and
  cut into chunks
Grated rind and juice of 1 large
  lemon
Grated rind and juice of 1 orange
10 ml/2 tsp cornflour (cornstarch)
45 ml/3 tbsp clear honey
Salt and freshly ground black pepper
To serve:
**Fluffy Mashed Potatoes
  (see page 287)**
French-style Peas (see page 291)

Put the lentils in a saucepan with the spring onions, stock and bay leaf. Bring to the boil, reduce the heat and simmer gently for 15–20 minutes until the lentils are tender and the liquid has been absorbed. Remove the bay leaf. Meanwhile, melt the low-fat spread in a frying pan (skillet). Add the fish and fry (sauté) for 4–5 minutes until golden and cooked through. Spoon the lentils into a serving dish and top with the fish. Stir the remaining ingredients together and add to the pan juices. Cook, stirring, until thickened. Taste and re-season if necessary. Pour over the fish and serve with Fluffy Mashed Potatoes and French-style Peas.

Halibut with Egg and Lemon Dressing

SERVES 4

4 halibut steaks, about 175 g/6 oz
  each, skinned
3 onions, thinly sliced
150 ml/¼ pt/⅔ cup white wine
150 ml/¼ pt/⅔ cup water
Grated rind and juice of 2 lemons
Salt and white pepper
2 eggs
Artificial sweetener granules
Lettuce leaves
Watercress
To serve:
Nutty Rice Salad (see page 292)
**Tomato and Onion Salad
  (see page 266)**

Place the fish in a saucepan with the onions, wine, water, lemon rind and juice and a little salt and pepper. Bring to the boil, reduce the heat, cover and simmer gently for 10 minutes or until the fish is tender. Carefully lift the fish and onions out of the pan and leave to cool. Whisk the eggs in a bowl. Strain the cooking liquor and gradually whisk into the eggs. Stand the bowl over a pan of gently simmering water and cook, whisking, until thickened. Do not allow to boil. Sweeten to taste and re-season if necessary. Leave until cold. Lay the fish on a bed of lettuce and watercress and arrange the onions over. Spoon on the lemon dressing and chill. Serve with Nutty Rice Salad and Tomato and Onion Salad.

Red Mullet Fillets with Vegetables

SERVES 4

225 g/8 oz/1 cup wild rice mix
2 carrots, cut into thin
    matchsticks
2 courgettes (zucchini), cut into
    thin matchsticks
100 g/4 oz short, thin asparagus
    spears
100 g/4 oz baby corn cobs
300 ml/½ pt/1¼ cups fish or
    chicken stock, made with 1
    stock cube
4 red mullet, filleted
25 g/1 oz/2 tbsp low-fat spread
75 ml/5 tbsp white wine
75 ml/5 tbsp very low-fat crème
    fraîche
30 ml/2 tbsp snipped chives
Salt and freshly ground black
    pepper
To serve:
Avocado and Watercress Salad
    (see page 283)

Cook the wild rice mix according to the packet directions. Drain. Meanwhile, poach the vegetables in the stock until just tender. Drain, reserving the stock. Fry (sauté) the mullet in the low-fat spread for 3–4 minutes on each side until browned and cooked through. Spoon the rice on to warmed plates. Top with the fish and vegetables. Keep warm. Add the wine and reserved stock to the pan juices and boil rapidly until syrupy. Stir in the crème fraîche, half the chives and some salt and pepper. Spoon over the fish and scatter with the remaining chives. Serve hot with Avocado and Watercress Salad.

Grilled Plaice with Prawn and Mushroom Sauce

SERVES 4

100 g/4 oz button mushrooms,
    sliced
1 onion, finely chopped
50 g/2 oz/¼ cup low-fat spread
15 g/½ oz/2 tbsp plain (all-
    purpose) flour
150 ml/¼ pt/⅔ cup skimmed milk
150 ml/¼ pt/⅔ cup low-fat single
    (light) cream
100 g/4 oz/1 cup peeled prawns
    (shrimp)
15 ml/1 tbsp chopped parsley
Salt and freshly ground black
    pepper
4 whole plaice, trimmed
A few capers
Torn flatleaf parsley leaves
To serve:
Potato Pudding (see page 295)
Peas

Fry (sauté) the mushrooms and onion in half the low-fat spread for 3 minutes until soft but not browned. Stir in the flour and cook for 1 minute. Remove from the heat and blend in the milk and cream. Return to the heat, bring to the boil and cook for 2 minutes, stirring. Stir in the prawns, parsley and seasoning to taste. Cover with a circle of wet greaseproof (waxed) paper and keep warm. Place the fish on the grill (broiler) rack. Melt the remaining low-fat spread and brush half over the fish. Season lightly. Grill (broil) for 3 minutes on each side or until cooked through, brushing with the remaining low-fat spread during cooking. Transfer to warmed plates. Spoon the sauce over, sprinkle with a few capers and garnish with flatleaf parsley leaves. Serve with Potato Pudding and peas.

Gourmet Crab Omelette

SERVES 2

1 onion, thinly sliced
1 garlic clove, crushed
25 g/1 oz/2 tbsp low-fat spread
1 large potato, grated
1 green (bell) pepper, thinly sliced
6 eggs
Salt and freshly ground black
   pepper
30 ml/2 tbsp water
2 x 40 g/2 x 1½ oz/2 small cans
   dressed crab
170 g/6 oz/1 small can white
   crabmeat, drained
Parsley sprigs
Lemon wedges
Sliced tomatoes
To serve:
Garlic Bread (see page 293)
Mixed Green Salad (see page 265)

Fry (sauté) the onion and garlic in the low-fat spread for 2 minutes to soften. Add the potato and green pepper and cook, stirring, for 5 minutes until soft. Beat the eggs with a little salt and pepper and the water and pour into the pan. Add the dressed crab. Cook, lifting and stirring, until almost set and the underside is golden brown. Add the white crabmeat to one half of the omelette and fold over the other half. Continue cooking for 2–3 minutes until piping hot. Cut in half. Slide on to warmed plates and garnish with parsley sprigs, lemon wedges and sliced tomatoes. Serve with Garlic Bread and Mixed Green Salad.

Golden Stack

SERVES 4

450 g/1 lb smoked haddock,
   skinned
150 ml/¼ pt/⅔ cup skimmed milk
225 g/8 oz/1 cup long-grain rice
5 ml/1 tsp turmeric
320 g/12 oz/1 large can sweetcorn
   (corn) with (bell) peppers
1 yellow (bell) pepper, thinly
   sliced
Salt and freshly ground black
   pepper
4 eggs
5 ml/1 tsp lemon juice
50 g/2 oz/¼ cup low-fat Cheddar
   cheese, grated
Cayenne
To serve:
1 French stick, warmed
Green Beans with Cherry
   Tomatoes (see page 267)

Put the fish in a saucepan with the milk. Bring to the boil, reduce the heat and simmer for 15 minutes until the fish is tender. Drain, reserving the cooking liquid. Flake the fish roughly with a fork. Cook the rice in plenty of boiling water to which the turmeric has been added for about 10 minutes or until just tender. Drain and return to the pan. Add the corn, yellow pepper, fish and about 60 ml/4 tbsp of the fish cooking liquid. Heat through, stirring gently, until piping hot. Season to taste. Poach the eggs in water to which the lemon juice has been added for 3–5 minutes until cooked to your liking. Pile the fish mixture on to four warmed plates. Top each with a poached egg, then the cheese and dust with cayenne. Flash under a hot grill to melt the cheese. Serve straight away with warm French bread and Green Beans with Cherry Tomatoes.

Tuscan Tuna and Bean Salad

SERVES 4

225 g/8 oz small waxy potatoes,
    scrubbed and cut into bite-sized
    pieces
3 eggs, scrubbed under cold
    running water
225 g/8 oz French (green) beans
425 g/15 oz/1 large can cannellini
    beans, drained, rinsed and
    drained again
225 g/8 oz cherry tomatoes,
    halved
185 g/6½ oz/1 small can tuna in
    brine, drained
1 cos (romaine) lettuce, torn into
    pieces
60 ml/4 tbsp olive oil
15 ml/1 tbsp red wine vinegar
1 garlic clove, finely chopped
30 ml/2 tbsp chopped parsley
Salt and freshly ground black pepper
50 g/2 oz/1 small can anchovies,
    drained
1 onion, thinly sliced and
    separated into rings
50 g/2 oz/⅓ cup black olives

Cook the potatoes and the eggs in their shells in boiling, lightly salted water for 10 minutes until the potatoes are tender. Add the French beans half-way through cooking. Drain, rinse with cold water and drain again. Shell the eggs and cut into quarters. Place the French beans and potatoes in a bowl with the beans, tomatoes, tuna and lettuce. Whisk together the oil, vinegar, garlic, half the parsley and salt and pepper. Pour into the bowl and toss gently. Pile into four serving bowls. Arrange the egg wedges around. Top with criss-crossed anchovies, onion rings and olives. Sprinkle with the remaining parsley and serve.

Gingered Fish and Special Fried Rice

SERVES 4

225 g/8 oz/1 cup long-grain rice
15 ml/1 tbsp sunflower oil
1 carrot, finely diced
1 red (bell) pepper, finely diced
1 bunch of spring onions
    (scallions), chopped
50 g/2 oz/½ cup frozen peas
225 g/8 oz/2 cups peeled prawns
    (shrimp)
2 eggs, beaten
30 ml/2 tbsp soy sauce
Salt and freshly ground black
    pepper
4 tail piece haddock fillets,
    skinned
25 g/1 oz/2 tbsp low-fat spread
5 ml/1 tsp grated fresh root ginger
Grated rind of 1 lime

Cook the rice in plenty of boiling, salted water until just tender. Drain. Heat the oil in a large frying pan (skillet) or wok. Add the carrot, red pepper and spring onions and stir-fry for 5 minutes. Add the rice and toss for 2 minutes. Stir in the peas and prawns. Push to one side of the pan. Add the beaten eggs and stir until cooked. Gradually work into the rice. Season with soy sauce, salt and pepper. Meanwhile, place the fish on a grill (broiler) rack. Melt the low-fat spread with the ginger and lime rind and brush over the fish. Grill (broil) for 4–5 minutes on each side until cooked through, brushing with more of the ginger mixture during cooking. Spoon the fried rice on to four warmed plates. Top each with a fish fillet and spoon any remaining ginger mixture over. Serve straight away.

550

Mackerel with Sweet Mustard Sauce

SERVES 4

4 mackerel, cleaned
Salt and freshly ground black
** pepper**
Lemon juice
20 g/¾ oz/1½ tbsp low-fat spread
20 g/¾ oz/3 tbsp cup plain (all-
** purpose) flour**
300 ml/½ pt/1¼ cups skimmed
** milk**
15 ml/1 tbsp English made
** mustard**
15 ml/1 tbsp malt vinegar
Artificial sweetener granules
Chopped parsley
Lettuce wedges
Lemon wedges
To serve:
Herby Potatoes (see page 289)
Glazed Carrots (see page 275)

Rinse the mackerel under running water. Dry with kitchen paper. Cut off the heads, if preferred. Make several slashes along the body on both sides. Place on a grill (broiler) rack. Season with a little salt and pepper and sprinkle with lemon juice. Grill (broil) for about 6 minutes on each side or until golden and cooked through. Transfer to warmed plates. Meanwhile, melt the low-fat spread in a saucepan. Stir in the flour and whisk in the milk until smooth. Bring to the boil and cook for 2 minutes, stirring all the time, until thickened and smooth. Stir in the mustard and vinegar and sweeten with the artificial sweetener (the sauce should taste both sweet and sharp). Season to taste. Spoon over the mackerel, sprinkle with chopped parsley and add a side garnish of lettuce and lemon wedges. Serve with Herby Potatoes and Glazed Carrots.

···············PORK, BACON & HAM···············

CALORIES OR LESS

Barbecued Pork with Savoury Rice

SERVES 4

15 g/½ oz/1 tbsp low-fat spread
4 pork shoulder steaks, about 175 g/6 oz each
15 ml/1 tbsp lemon juice, plus extra for sprinkling
15 ml/1 tbsp malt vinegar
30 ml/2 tbsp tomato purée (paste)
15 ml/1 tbsp Worcestershire sauce
15 ml/1 tbsp soy sauce
30 ml/2 tbsp clear honey
Fresh bean sprouts
Parsley sprigs
To serve:
1 packet savoury vegetable rice
Mixed Green Salad (see page 265)

Melt the low-fat spread in a frying pan (skillet). Add the pork and fry (sauté) for 3 minutes on each side to brown. Mix together the remaining ingredients except the bean sprouts and parsley and pour over the pork. Cook over a moderate heat for about 10 minutes, turning the pork occasionally, until stickily glazed in the sauce. Put a pile of bean sprouts on four serving plates and sprinkle with a little lemon juice. Top with a piece of pork. Garnish with parsley sprigs. Serve with savoury rice and Mixed Green Salad.

Mustard-glazed Gammon

SERVES 6

1.1 kg/2½ lb piece very lean gammon
300 ml/½ pt/1¼ cups cider
1 bay leaf
Salt and freshly ground black pepper
10 ml/2 tsp thick honey
15 ml/1 tbsp wholegrain mustard
15 ml/1 tbsp cornflour (cornstarch)
15 ml/1 tbsp water
To serve:
Stock-roast Potatoes (see page 286)
Parsleyed Carrots (see page 277)

Place the gammon in a casserole (Dutch oven) or roasting tin (pan) with a lid. Add the cider and bay leaf and a good grinding of pepper. Cover and cook in a preheated oven at 190°C/375°F/gas mark 5 for 1 hour. Remove the lid and peel the rind off the gammon. Mix together the honey and mustard and spread over the surface. Return to the oven for 20 minutes or until golden brown. Remove from the tin and transfer to a carving dish. Blend the cornflour with the water and stir into the juices in the pan. Bring to the boil and cook for 2 minutes, stirring. Season to taste. Carve the meat and arrange on warmed plates. Spoon the sauce over and serve with Stock-roast Potatoes and Parsleyed Carrots.

Rustic Pork Casserole

SERVES 4

4 lean pork chops, trimmed of fat
40 g/1½ oz/3 tbsp low-fat spread
450 g/1 lb potatoes, cut into
   walnut-sized pieces
100 g/4 oz button mushrooms,
   sliced
425 g/15 oz/1 large can butter
   beans, drained
1 garlic clove, chopped
300 ml/½ pt/1¼ cups chicken or
   pork stock, made with 1 stock
   cube
Salt and freshly ground black pepper
15 ml/1 tbsp cornflour
   (cornstarch)
15 ml/1 tbsp water
30 m/2 tbsp chopped parsley
To serve:
Cabbage with Celery (see page
   273)

Fry (sauté) the chops in half the low-fat spread on both sides to brown in a flameproof casserole (Dutch oven). Remove from the pan. Add the remaining low-fat spread and fry the potatoes quickly for about 3 minutes until golden all over. Add the mushrooms and stir well. Return the meat to the pan, arranging the potatoes on top. Add the butter beans and sprinkle on the garlic. Pour in the stock and season well. Cover with a lid and cook in a pre-heated oven at 180°C/350°F/ gas mark 4 for 1½ hours until the potatoes and pork are really tender. Transfer the meat and vegetables to warmed serving plates. Blend the cornflour with the water and stir into the juices in the pan. Bring to the boil and cook for 1 minute, stirring. Taste and re-season if necessary. Spoon over the pork and vegetables. Sprinkle with chopped parsley and serve with Cabbage with Celery.

Pork with Herby Prune Stuffing

SERVES 4

75 g/3 oz/½ cup no-need-to-soak
   prunes, halved, stoned (pitted)
   and roughly chopped
50 g/2 oz/1 cup fresh breadcrumbs
40 g/1½ oz/3 tbsp low-fat spread,
   melted
15 ml/1 tbsp finely chopped sage
Salt and freshly ground black
   pepper
1 egg, beaten
2 pork fillets, about 350 g/12 oz
   each
Sage sprigs
To serve:
Scalloped Potatoes (see page 289)
French-style Peas (see page 291)

Mix the prunes with the bread-crumbs, 25 g/1 oz/2 tbsp of the low-fat spread, the chopped sage and some salt and pepper. Mix with the egg to bind. Cut the fillets lengthways through the middle. Open out and flatten slightly with a meat mallet. Cover with the stuffing. Roll up and tie securely with string or secure with cocktail sticks (toothpicks). Brush with the remaining low-fat spread and wrap loosely in foil, sealing the edges well. Place in a roasting tin (pan) and roast in a preheated oven at 190°C/375°F/gas mark 5 for about 45 minutes or until tender and cooked through. Leave to rest for 5 minutes, then carve into thick slices and spoon any juices over. Garnish with sage sprigs and serve with Scalloped Potatoes and French-style Peas.

Pork Fried Rice

SERVES 4

225 g/8 oz/1 cup long-grain rice
225 g/8 oz pork fillet, finely diced
50 g/2 oz/¼ cup low-fat spread
2 carrots, diced
1 bunch of spring onions
   (scallions), chopped
2 courgettes (zucchini), chopped
1 red (bell) pepper, chopped
100 g/4 oz/1 cup frozen peas
1 garlic clove, finely chopped
30 ml/2 tbsp soy sauce
5 ml/1 tsp grated fresh root ginger
Salt and freshly ground black
   pepper
2.5 ml/½ tsp Chinese five spice
   powder
2 eggs
30 ml/2 tbsp water
To serve:
Chinese Leaf and Orange Salad
   (see page 269)

Cook the rice in plenty of boiling, lightly salted water for about 10 minutes or until just tender. Drain, rinse with cold water and drain again. Fry (sauté) the pork in half the low-fat spread in a wok or large frying pan (skillet) for 4 minutes until almost cooked. Add half the remaining low-fat spread and the vegetables and continue stir-frying for a further 5 minutes. Add the cooked rice and toss well. Add the garlic, soy sauce, ginger, salt, pepper and five spice powder and cook, stirring, for 3 minutes. Melt the remaining low-fat spread in a small frying pan. Beat together the eggs and water with a little salt and pepper. Pour into the pan and fry until golden underneath and just set. Either place under the grill (broiler) to brown the top or carefully flip over and cook the other side. Roll up and cut into slices.

Pile the fried rice on to warmed serving plates and top with the egg strips. Serve with Chinese Leaf and Orange Salad.

Smokies

SERVES 4

8 even-sized courgettes (zucchini),
   halved lengthways
40 g/1½ oz/3 tbsp low-fat spread
4 lean smoked streaky bacon
   rashers (slices), rinded and diced
1 garlic clove, crushed
50 g/2 oz/1 cup fresh breadcrumbs
Salt and freshly ground black
   pepper
2.5 ml/½ tsp dried oregano
100 g/4 oz/1 barrel Austrian
   smoked cheese, thinly sliced
300 ml/½ pt/1¼ cups passata
   (sieved tomatoes)
30 ml/2 tbsp low-fat single (light)
   cream
To serve:
Poppy Seed and Oregano Wedges
   (see page 288)
Mixed Leaf Salad (see page 265)

Scoop the seedy centres out of the courgette halves with a teaspoon, leaving the shells. Chop the scooped-out flesh. Boil the shells in lightly salted water for 5 minutes. Drain and place in a shallow ovenproof dish. Melt 15 g/½ oz/1 tbsp of the low-fat spread in a frying pan (skillet). Add the bacon and chopped courgettes and stir-fry for 10 minutes. Remove from the pan with a draining spoon and drain on kitchen paper. Heat the remaining low-fat spread in the pan and add the garlic and breadcrumbs. Fry (sauté), stirring, for 3 minutes, until golden. Remove from the pan and drain on kitchen paper. Mix with the bacon and courgette mixture and season with salt, pepper and the oregano. Spoon into the cooked courgette shells. Lay the slices of smoked cheese attractively over the stuffing. Bake in a preheated oven at 190°C/375°F/gas mark 5 for about 20 minutes until piping hot and the cheese is turning golden. Meanwhile, warm the passata and spoon on to four warmed plates. Drizzle the cream over and draw the point of a knife or a cocktail stick (toothpick) through it several times to form a 'feathered' effect. Lay the courgettes on top and serve with Poppy Seed and Oregano Wedges and Mixed Leaf Salad.

Faggots 'n' Peas

SERVES 4

225 g/8 oz lean boneless pork
225 g/8 oz pigs' liver, trimmed of
  any sinews
2 onions
2 thick slices bread
1 egg, beaten
15 ml/1 tbsp chopped sage,
  or 5 ml/1 tsp dried sage
Salt and freshly ground black
  pepper
25 g/1 oz/2 tbsp low-fat spread
225 g/8 oz/2 cups frozen peas
A pinch of nutmeg
5 ml/1 tsp dried mint
30 ml/2 tbsp plain (all-purpose)
  flour
300 ml/½ pt/1¼ cups water
1 beef stock cube
To serve:
Potato Potch (see page 288)

Mince (grind) the pork, then the liver, then the onions, then the bread (or use a food processor but don't process too finely). Stir in the egg and sage and season well. Chill for

2 hours. Put large spoonfuls of the mixture tightly together in a roasting tin (pan) greased with half the low-fat spread. Dot with the remaining low-fat spread. Cover with foil and bake in a preheated oven at 180°C/350°F/gas mark 4 for 30 minutes. Remove the foil and cook for a further 15 minutes. Meanwhile, cook the peas for 5 minutes in a little boiling, salted water to which the nutmeg and mint have been added. Drain. When the faggots are cooked, transfer to warmed plates and keep warm. Blend the flour with a little of the water and stir into the juices in the tin. Add the remaining water. Crumble in the stock cube. Bring to the boil and cook for 2 minutes, stirring. Add more seasoning if necessary. Spoon over the faggots, add the peas to one side and serve with Potato Potch.

Savoury Pork Escalopes

SERVES 4

Prepare as for Savoury Turkey Escalopes (see page 215) but substitute lean pork steaks or pork fillet for the turkey breasts and garnish with slices of unpeeled eating (dessert) apple, dipped in lemon juice to prevent browning.

Sumptuous Sausage Bake

SERVES 4

175 g/6 oz tagliatelle
450 g/1 lb lean pork sausagemeat
1 small onion, finely chopped
1 garlic clove, crushed
15 ml/1 tbsp plain (all-purpose)
    flour
150 ml/¼ pt/⅔ cup skimmed milk
5 ml/1 tsp dried Herbes de
    Provence
Salt and freshly ground black
    pepper
30 ml/2 tbsp low-fat double
    (heavy) cream
25 g/1 oz/¼ cup low-fat Cheddar
    cheese, grated
25 g/1 oz/¼ cup Parmesan cheese,
    grated
50 g/2 oz/1 cup fresh breadcrumbs
Watercress
To serve:
Fruity Red Cabbage (see page 290)

Cook the pasta according to the packet directions. Drain and return to the saucepan. Meanwhile, shape the sausagemeat into small balls and fry (sauté) in a frying pan (skillet) until golden brown all over. Drain on kitchen paper. Pour off all but 15 ml/ 1 tbsp of the fat in the pan. Add the onion and garlic to the pan and fry for 3 minutes until soft but not browned. Stir in the flour and cook for 1 minute. Remove from the heat and blend in the milk. Bring to the boil and cook for 2 minutes, stirring. Stir in the herbs and salt and pepper to taste. Stir in the cream and half of each cheese. Mix in the tagliatelle. Spoon into four individual ovenproof dishes and top with the sausagemeat balls. Mix the breadcrumbs with the remaining cheeses and sprinkle over. Bake in a preheated oven at 200°C/400°F/gas mark 6 for 25 minutes until piping hot and golden brown. Garnish with watercress and serve straight away with Fruity Red Cabbage.

Savoury Sausage Burgers

SERVES 4

85 g/3½ oz/1 small packet sage
    and onion stuffing mix
350 g/12 oz lean pork
    sausagemeat
1 small cooking (tart) apple,
    grated
Salt and freshly ground black
    pepper
25 g/1 oz/2 tbsp low-fat spread
4 soft white baps
20 ml/4 tsp Dijon mustard
20 ml/4 tsp cucumber relish
1 small onion, sliced into thin
    rings
Lettuce, cucumber slices, pickled
    onions, baby beetroot (red
    beets), tomato wedges, to
    garnish

Make up the stuffing according to the packet directions. Leave to cool, then mix in the sausagemeat, apple and a little salt and pepper. Shape into four rounds. Melt the low-fat spread in a frying pan (skillet). Add the sausage burgers and fry (sauté) over a moderate heat for about 10–15 minutes, turning once, until golden brown and cooked through. Drain on kitchen paper. Place in the baps and top the burgers with mustard, cucumber relish and onion rings. Place on plates and garnish generously with lettuce, cucumber, pickled onions, baby beetroot and tomato wedges and tuck in!

Hearty Sausage Salad

SERVES 4

450 g/1 lb lean pork sausages
225 g/8 oz new potatoes, scrubbed
and cut into bite-sized pieces
2 slices bread
25 g/1 oz/2 tbsp low-fat spread
1 garlic clove, halved
320 g/12 oz/1 large can sweetcorn
(corn) with (bell) peppers
425 g/15 oz/1 large can black-eyed
beans, drained, rinsed and
drained again
½ cucumber, diced
1 bunch of radishes, quartered
100 g/4 oz cherry tomatoes,
halved
1 bunch of spring onions
(scallions), cut into short
lengths
For the dressing:
150 ml/¼ pt/⅔ cup very low-fat
plain yoghurt
Salt and freshly ground black
pepper
15 ml/1 tbsp chopped parsley
Cayenne

Grill (broil) the sausages for about 10 minutes until browned all over and cooked through. Drain on kitchen paper, cool and slice thickly. Meanwhile, boil the potatoes in lightly salted water until tender. Drain, rinse with cold water and drain again. Spread both sides of the bread with low-fat spread. Cut the slices into dice and fry (sauté) in a frying pan (skillet) with the garlic added, tossing until golden brown and crisp. Drain on kitchen paper. Place the cold sausages and potatoes in a large salad bowl. Add the remaining salad ingredients and toss gently. To make the dressing, mix the yoghurt with a little salt and pepper and the parsley. Add to the bowl and toss gently. Dust with cayenne, scatter the garlic croûtons over and serve.

Pasta Quiche

SERVES 4

100 g/4 oz elbow macaroni
4 leeks, sliced
1 onion, finely chopped
1 red (bell) pepper, finely chopped
25 g/1 oz/2 tbsp low-fat spread
Salt and freshly ground black
pepper
1 chorizo sausage, skinned and
chopped
4 eggs
60 ml/4 tbsp low-fat single (light)
cream
100 g/4 oz/1 cup Gouda cheese,
grated
15 ml/1 tbsp chopped parsley
To serve:
Mixed Salad (see page 265)

Cook the macaroni according to the packet directions. Drain, rinse with cold water and drain again. Fry (sauté) the leeks, onion and pepper in half the low-fat spread for 2 minutes, stirring. Reduce the heat, add some salt and pepper, cover and cook very gently for 6 minutes until fairly soft. Remove from the heat. Add the pasta and chorizo. Beat the eggs with the cream, cheese and a little more salt and pepper. Stir in the parsley. Add to the pasta mixture. Grease a 23 cm/9 in flan dish (pie pan) with the remaining low-fat spread. Add the pasta mixture. Bake in a preheated oven at 180°C/350°F/gas mark 4 for about 30 minutes until golden brown and set. Serve hot or cold, cut into wedges with Mixed Salad.

Bacon-wrapped Cheese Loaf

SERVES 6

175 g/6 oz lean streaky bacon
    rashers (slices), rinded
25 g/1 oz/2 tbsp low-fat spread
100 g/4 oz/1 cup mixed nuts and
    raisins, finely chopped
1 onion, finely chopped
2 carrots, grated
100 g/4 oz/2 cups fresh wholemeal
    breadcrumbs
175 g/6 oz/1½ cups low-fat
    Cheddar cheese, grated
20 ml/4 tsp peach chutney,
    chopped if necessary
Salt and freshly ground black
    pepper
1 egg
150 ml/¼ pt/⅔ cup skimmed milk
A pinch of cayenne
Lettuce leaves
Cherry tomatoes
To serve:
1 French stick, warmed
Mixed Salad (see page 265)

Stretch the rashers slightly with the back of a knife. Grease a 900 g/2 lb loaf tin (pan) with the low-fat spread and line with the bacon rashers, laid widthways. Thoroughly mix together the nuts and raisins, onion, carrots, breadcrumbs, cheese and chutney. Season thoroughly. Beat together the egg and milk with the cayenne and use to bind the mixture. Turn into the prepared tin and level the surface. Cover with foil, twisting under the rim to secure. Bake in a preheated oven at 190ºC/375ºF/gas mark 5 for about 1½ hours or until firm to the touch. Leave to cool in the tin, then turn out on to a bed of lettuce. Arrange cherry tomatoes around and serve sliced with warm French bread and Mixed Salad.

Pork Chops with Oyster Mushroom Sauce

SERVES 4

4 pork chops, trimmed of fat
100 g/4 oz oyster mushrooms,
    sliced
Juice of 1 lemon
30 ml/2 tbsp sunflower oil
10 ml/2 tsp chopped thyme
15 ml/1 tbsp chopped parsley
Salt and freshly ground black
    pepper
25 g/1 oz/2 tbsp low-fat spread
10 ml/2 tsp cornflour (cornstarch)
45 ml/3 tbsp water
150 ml/¼ pt/⅔ cup very low-fat
    crème fraîche
Parsley sprigs
To serve:
Golden Rice (see page 296)
Mangetout (snow peas)

Wipe the chops and place in a shallow dish in a single layer. Add the mushrooms. Mix together the lemon juice, oil, herbs and a little salt and pepper and spoon over. Leave to marinate for at least 3 hours, turning occasionally. Melt the low-fat spread in a large frying pan (skillet). Lift the chops out of the marinade and fry (sauté) for about 10 minutes on each side until golden brown and cooked through. Transfer to warmed plates and keep warm. Add the marinade and mushrooms to the pan. Cook, stirring, for 3 minutes. Blend the cornflour with the water and stir into the pan. Bring to the boil and cook for 2 minutes, stirring. Stir in the crème fraîche and season to taste. Spoon over the chops and garnish with parsley sprigs. Serve with Golden Rice and mangetout.

Warm Bacon, Egg and Avocado Salad

SERVES 4

4 eggs
Lemon juice
2 ripe avocados
350 g/12 oz/1 large packet ready-prepared mixed salad leaves
8 cherry tomatoes, quartered
¼ cucumber, diced
2 small red onions, sliced and separated into rings
2 slices bread
25 g/1 oz/2 tbsp low-fat spread
8 lean streaky bacon rashers (slices), rinded and diced
30 ml/2 tbsp olive oil
30 ml/2 tbsp Worcestershire sauce
Salt and freshly ground black pepper
To serve:
Garlic Bread (see page 293)

Poach the eggs in water to which 5 ml/1 tsp lemon juice has been added for 3–5 minutes according to taste. Carefully lift out using a fish slice and put in a bowl of cold water. Halve, stone (pit) and peel the avocados and cut into slices. Dip in lemon juice to prevent browning. Place the salad leaves in four large individual bowls. Add the tomatoes, cucumber, onion rings and avocado slices. Lift the eggs out of the cold water and lay one on top of each salad. Spread the bread on both sides with the low-fat spread and cut into dice. Place in a large frying pan (skillet) and fry (sauté) until golden all over. Drain on kitchen paper. Add the bacon to the pan and fry until crisp. Remove from the pan and scatter over the salads. Add the oil, Worcestershire sauce and 15 ml/1 tbsp lemon juice to the pan and season with salt and pepper. Bring to the boil. Spoon over the salads, top with the croûtons and add a good grinding of pepper. Serve straight away with Garlic Bread.

Herby Roast Pork

SERVES 6

5 ml/1 tsp dried mixed herbs
1.1 kg/2½ lb lean pork loin, boned and rolled
5 ml/1 tsp sunflower oil
Salt and freshly ground black pepper
12 small onions, peeled but left whole
60 ml/4 tbsp dry white vermouth
150 ml/¼ pt/⅔ cup vegetable stock, made with ½ stock cube
150 ml/¼ pt/⅔ cup very low-fat crème fraîche
Artificial sweetener granules
15 ml/1 tbsp chopped parsley
To serve:
Glazed Carrots (see page 275)
Broccoli

Sprinkle the mixed herbs over the flesh of the pork. Place on a trivet or upturned saucer in a roasting tin (pan). Score the rind and rub with the oil and salt. Surround with the onions. Roast in a preheated oven at 220°C/425°F/gas mark 7 for 1 hour. Reduce the heat to 190°C/375°F/gas mark 5 and continue cooking for a further 45–60 minutes or until the pork is tender and the crackling is crisp. Transfer the pork and onions to a carving dish. Pour off all the fat from the roasting tin, leaving the juices. Add the vermouth and the stock and bring to the boil, stirring and scraping up any meat juices. Boil rapidly until well reduced. Stir in the crème fraîche, sweeten and season to taste. Stir in the parsley. Carve the meat, spoon the sauce over and serve with Glazed Carrots and broccoli.

Winter Bacon Stew with Caraway Potato Cakes

SERVES 4

4 small all-lean bacon steaks, diced
1 large onion, sliced
2 leeks, sliced
2 carrots, sliced
65 g/2½ oz/generous ¼ cup low-fat spread
1 eating (dessert) apple, sliced
225 g/8 oz Brussels sprouts, trimmed but left whole
750 ml/1¼ pts/3 cups chicken or ham stock, made with 2 stock cubes
Salt and freshly ground black pepper
1 bouquet garni sachet
30 ml/2 tbsp chopped parsley
450 g/1 lb potatoes, grated
1 egg
10 ml/2 tsp caraway seeds

Fry (sauté) the bacon, onion, leeks and carrots in 15 g/½ oz/1 tbsp of the low-fat spread for 2 minutes in a large saucepan. Add the apple, sprouts, stock, some salt and pepper and the bouquet garni sachet. Bring to the boil, reduce the heat and simmer for 20 minutes. Discard the bouquet garni and add half the parsley. Taste and re-season if necessary. Meanwhile, mix the potatoes with the egg, caraway seeds and the remaining parsley. Season well. Melt the remaining low-fat spread in a large frying pan (skillet). Divide the mixture into eight portions and add to the pan. Press down with a fish slice. Fry until golden underneath. Turn over and cook the other sides, pressing down well again, until golden and cooked through. Drain on kitchen paper. Ladle the stew into warmed shallow bowls, top with the potato cakes and serve straight away.

Pork and Aubergine Pasta Special

SERVES 4

1 aubergine (eggplant), sliced
350 g/12 oz/3 cups lean minced (ground) pork
1 onion, finely chopped
2 garlic cloves, crushed
150 ml/¼ pt/⅔ cup dry white vermouth
400 g/14 oz/1 large can chopped tomatoes
2.5 ml/½ tsp dried oregano
Salt and freshly ground black pepper
350 g/12 oz tagliatelle
60 ml/4 tbsp grated Mozzarella cheese
30 ml/2 tbsp grated Parmesan cheese
To serve:
Italian Celeriac Salad (see page 270)

Boil the aubergine in lightly salted water until tender. Drain thoroughly. Put the pork in a large saucepan with the onion and garlic. Cook, stirring, until the grains are brown and separate. Pour off excess fat. Add the vermouth, tomatoes, oregano and a little salt and pepper. Bring to the boil, reduce the heat, part-cover and simmer for about 20 minutes or until nearly all the liquid has evaporated. Taste and re-season. Meanwhile, cook the pasta according to the packet directions. Drain and return to the saucepan. Add the pork mixture and toss. Spoon into a flameproof serving dish. Top with a layer of aubergine, then sprinkle with the cheeses. Flash under a hot grill (broiler) until the cheese melts and bubbles. Serve straight away with Italian Celeriac Salad.

Sicilian Baked Pork

SERVES 4

**550 g/1¼ lb pork fillet, trimmed
and cut into chunks
2 small eggs, beaten
50 g/2 oz/½ cup Parmesan cheese,
grated
40 g/1½ oz/⅓ cup plain (all-
purpose) flour
25 g/1 oz/2 tbsp low-fat spread
1 red onion, chopped
1 garlic clove, crushed
3 lean streaky bacon rashers
(slices), rinded and diced
450 g/1 lb ripe tomatoes, skinned
and chopped
30 ml/2 tbsp tomato purée (paste)
1 sun-dried tomato, chopped
5 ml/1 tsp dried basil
175 ml/6 fl oz/¾ cup chicken
stock, made with ½ stock cube
Salt and freshly ground black pepper
A pinch of cayenne
50 g/2 oz/½ cup Bel Paese cheese,
sliced**
To serve:
Italian Green Salad (see page 272)

Dip the meat in the egg. Mix half the Parmesan with the flour and use to coat the meat. Fry (sauté) in half the low-fat spread in a saucepan until golden. Remove from the pan with a draining spoon. Drain on kitchen paper. Fry the onion in the remaining low-fat spread with the garlic and bacon for 3 minutes, stirring. Pour off any fat. Add the chopped tomatoes, tomato purée, sun-dried tomato, the basil and stock. Bring to the boil and cook for about 10 minutes until pulpy. Season to taste with salt, pepper and the cayenne. Layer the meat and sauce in an oven-proof dish. Add the Bel Paese before the last layer of sauce. Top with the remaining Parmesan. Bake in a preheated oven at 190°C/375°F/gas mark 5 for 1¼ hours. Serve with Italian Green Salad.

Polish Noodles

SERVES 4

**15 ml/1 tbsp olive oil
50 g/2 oz/¼ cup low-fat spread
2 leeks, sliced
2 garlic cloves, crushed
450 g/1 lb spring greens (spring
cabbage), shredded
1 smoked pork ring, sliced
45 ml/3 tbsp water
12 stoned (pitted) black olives
Salt and freshly ground black pepper
10 ml/2 tsp caraway seeds
2.5 ml/½ tsp paprika
225 g/8 oz short ribbon noodles
50 g/2 oz goat's cheese, cut into
small pieces**
To serve:
**4 slices rye bread
Beetroot and Chive Salad (see
page 270)**

Heat the oil in a large saucepan with half the low-fat spread. Add the leeks and garlic. Cover and cook gently for 5 minutes until softened but not browned. Add the greens and cook, stirring, until they begin to soften. Add the sausage and water. Cover and cook very gently for about 6 minutes until the greens are soft, stirring occasionally. Throw in the olives, some salt and pepper, the caraway and paprika. Meanwhile, cook the noodles according to the packet directions. Drain and add to the greens. Toss together well, then pile into a flameproof serving dish. Top with the pieces of goat's cheese and place under a hot grill (broiler) until it begins to melt. Serve straight away with rye bread and Beetroot Salad.

Paprikash with Noodles

SERVES 4

3 onions
50 g/2 oz/¼ cup low-fat spread
450 g/1 lb pork fillet, cut into thin
    strips
15 ml/1 tbsp paprika
190g/6½ oz/1 small can pimientos,
    drained and sliced
150 ml/¼ pt/⅔ cup chicken or pork
    stock, made with ½ stock cube
Salt and freshly ground black
    pepper
45 ml/3 tbsp plain (all-purpose)
    flour
A pinch of cayenne
15 ml/1 tbsp water
150 ml/¼ pt/⅔ cup very low-fat
    crème fraîche
225 g/8 oz green ribbon noodles
Chopped coriander (cilantro)
To serve:
Crisp Green Salad (see page 265)

Chop one of the onions. Fry (sauté) in a saucepan in 15 g/½ oz/1 tbsp of the low-fat spread for 2 minutes until softened but not browned. Add the pork and cook, stirring, for 4 minutes. Add the paprika, pimientos and stock. Season with a little salt and pepper. Bring to the boil, reduce the heat, part-cover and simmer gently for 15 minutes or until the pork is tender. Meanwhile, slice the remaining two onions and separate into rings. Dip in 30 ml/2 tbsp of the flour, seasoned with salt, pepper and the cayenne. Heat the remaining low-fat spread in a frying pan (skillet) and fry the onion rings until golden brown. Drain on kitchen paper and keep warm. Blend the remaining flour with the water and stir into the pork. Cook, stirring, for 2 minutes. Stir in the crème fraîche, taste and re-season if necessary. Meanwhile, cook the noodles according to the packet directions. Pile on to plates and sprinkle with coriander. Spoon over the paprikash, garnish with the onion rings and serve with Crisp Green Salad.

Pan Sizzler

SERVES 4

450 g/1 lb small, waxy potatoes,
    scrubbed and thinly sliced
1 onion, thinly sliced
1 garlic clove, crushed
1 celery stick, chopped, reserving
    the leaves
1 leek, chopped
40 g/1½ oz/3 tbsp low-fat spread
120 ml/4 fl oz/½ cup apple juice
1 red (bell) pepper, diced
1 green (bell) pepper, diced
1 yellow (bell) pepper, diced
2 peperami sticks, chopped
100 g/4 oz lean smoked bacon,
    diced
Salt and freshly ground black
    pepper
To serve:
Garlic Bread (see page 293)

Fry (sauté) the potatoes, onion, garlic, chopped celery and leek in the low-fat spread in a large frying pan (skillet) or wok for 10 minutes, stirring occasionally. Add the apple juice, peppers, peperami and bacon and cook for a further 10 minutes, stirring occasionally, until cooked through and the liquid has evaporated. Season to taste and sprinkle with the reserved torn celery leaves. Serve straight from the pan with Garlic Bread.

·····LAMB·····

550

CALORIES OR LESS

Lamb Shanks with Mediterranean Vegetables

SERVES 4

4 lamb shanks, about 225 g/8 oz each
Salt and freshly ground black pepper
5 ml/1 tsp dried thyme
5 ml/1 tsp dried rosemary
15 ml/1 tbsp chopped parsley
15 ml/1 tbsp extra virgin olive oil
60 ml/4 tbsp red wine
40 g/1½ oz/3 tbsp low-fat spread
1 onion, sliced
1 aubergine (eggplant), sliced
2 courgettes (zucchini), sliced
1 red (bell) pepper, sliced
450 g/1 lb tomatoes, sliced
To serve:
Tomato Rice (see page 296)
Mixed Leaf Salad (see page 265)

Slash the lamb in several places and put in a large roasting tin (pan). Rub in a little salt and pepper and the herbs. Whisk together the oil and wine and pour over. Leave to marinate for 1 hour, turning occasionally. Drain off the marinade and reserve. Spread the low-fat spread over the lamb and bake in a preheated oven at 180°C/350°F/gas mark 4 for 45 minutes until browned, turning once. Arrange the prepared vegetables around the lamb and drizzle with the marinade. Toss and season. Return to the oven and bake for a further 45 minutes, basting occasionally, until the vegetables and lamb are golden and cooked through. Serve hot with Tomato Rice and Mixed Leaf Salad.

Greek-style Lamb

SERVES 6

1 small leg of lamb, about 1.6 kg/ 3½ lb, trimmed of excess fat
750 g/1½ lb potatoes, halved if very large
2 garlic cloves, finely chopped
300 ml/½ pt/1¼ cups chicken or lamb stock, made with 1 stock cube
Salt and freshly ground black pepper
5 ml/1 tsp dried oregano
Chopped parsley
To serve:
3 pitta breads, warmed and cut into fingers
Greek Village Salad (see page 283)

Place the lamb in a roasting tin (pan) with a lid or a large casserole dish (Dutch oven). Arrange the potatoes around. Sprinkle the garlic over the lamb. Pour the stock around. Season all over with salt and pepper and sprinkle the oregano over the meat. Cover tightly and cook in a preheated oven at 160°C/325°F/gas mark 3 for 4 hours until the lamb is almost falling off the bones. Carefully lift the lamb out on to a carving dish. Cut into chunky pieces, discarding any fat and skin. Put on warmed plates with the potatoes. Spoon off any fat, then taste and re-season the cooking juices if necessary. Spoon over and sprinkle with parsley. Serve with pitta bread fingers and Greek Village Salad.

Kidneys Turbigo-style

SERVES 4

12 button (pearl) onions, peeled
but left whole
2 chipolata sausages, quartered
40 g/1½ oz/3 tbsp low-fat spread
8 lamb's kidneys, halved and
cored
15 ml/1 tbsp plain (all-purpose)
flour
150 ml/¼ pt/⅔ cup lamb or chicken
stock, made with ½ stock cube
150 ml/¼ pt/⅔ cup dry white wine
15 ml/1 tbsp tomato purée (paste)
15 ml/1 tbsp brandy
Salt and freshly ground black
pepper
1 bouquet garni sachet
2 slices bread, crusts removed
30 ml/2 tbsp low-fat single (light)
cream
Chopped parsley
To serve:
Fluffy Mashed Potatoes (see page
287)
Broccoli

Boil the onions in water for 5 minutes until just soft. Drain. Gently
fry (sauté) the sausages in a flameproof casserole (Dutch oven) until
browned, remove and drain on kitchen
paper. Wipe out the casserole with
kitchen paper to remove the fat. Melt
15 g/½ oz/1 tbsp of the low-fat spread
in the casserole and fry the kidneys
gently until browned. Remove with a
draining spoon. Stir the flour into the
juices in the casserole and cook, stirring, for 1 minute. Remove from the
heat and gradually blend in the stock,
wine, tomato purée, brandy and some
salt and pepper. Return to the heat and
bring to the boil, stirring. Return the
kidneys and sausages to the casserole,
add the bouquet garni and onions and
simmer gently for 20 minutes.
Meanwhile, spread both sides of the
bread with the remaining low-fat
spread and fry in a frying pan (skillet)
until golden on both sides. Cut each
piece into four triangles. Discard the
bouquet garni from the casserole.
Taste and re-season if necessary. Stir
in the cream, sprinkle with chopped
parsley and arrange the bread triangles around the edge. Serve with
Fluffy Mashed Potatoes and broccoli.

Lamb and Leek Stew

SERVES 4

8 small lamb cutlets, trimmed of
all fat
450 g/1 lb leeks, thickly sliced
3 carrots, thickly sliced
2 turnips, cut into chunks
900 ml/1½ pts/3¾ cups lamb or
chicken stock, made with 2
stock cubes
Salt and freshly ground black
pepper
1 bouquet garni sachet
450 g/1 lb potatoes, cut into large
chunks
30 ml/2 tbsp chopped parsley
To serve:
1 French stick, warmed

Put all the ingredients except the
potatoes and parsley in a large
saucepan. Bring to the boil and skim
the surface. Reduce the heat, part-
cover and simmer gently for 1 hour.
Add the potatoes and a little more seasoning and simmer for a further 30
minutes or until the potatoes and
meat are tender. Remove the bouquet
garni sachet. Taste and re-season if
necessary. Sprinkle with the parsley
and serve with French bread.

Lamb Moussaka

SERVES 4

2 aubergines (eggplants), sliced
450 g/1 lb potatoes, sliced
1 large onion, chopped
1 garlic clove, crushed
350 g/12 oz/3 cups lean minced
    (ground) lamb
150 ml/¼ pt/⅔ cup lamb or chicken
    stock, made with ½ stock cube
30 ml/2 tbsp tomato purée (paste)
5 ml/1 tsp dried oregano
2.5 ml/½ tsp ground cinnamon
Salt and freshly ground black
    pepper
40 g/1½ oz/⅓ cup plain (all-
    purpose) flour
600 ml/1 pt/1¼ cups skimmed
    milk
40 g/1½ oz/3 tbsp low-fat spread
1 bay leaf
2 eggs, beaten
50 g/2 oz/½ cup Parmesan cheese,
    grated
To serve:
Greek Village Salad (see page 283)

Boil the aubergines and potatoes separately in lightly salted water until just tender. Drain, rinse with cold water and drain again. Put the onion, garlic and meat in a large saucepan and fry (sauté), stirring, until all the grains of meat are brown and separate. Drain off the excess fat. Add the stock, tomato purée, oregano, cinnamon and some salt and pepper. Bring to the boil, reduce the heat, part-cover and simmer gently, stirring occasionally, for about 15 minutes until the liquid has almost been absorbed. Put a layer of potatoes in the base of a large fairly shallow ovenproof dish. Then add a layer of meat, then aubergine. Continue layering, finishing with a layer of aubergine. Put the flour in a saucepan. Whisk in the milk gradually until smooth. Add the low-fat spread and bay leaf. Bring to the boil, whisking all the time, and cook for 2 minutes until thickened. Remove the bay leaf and whisk in the eggs and cheese. Season to taste. Pour over the aubergines. Bake in a preheated oven at 180°C/350°F/gas mark 4 for about 45–50 minutes until the top is set and golden brown. Cool for 10 minutes, then serve with Greek Village Salad.

Roast Lamb with Mint Sauce

SERVES 6

1 small leg of lamb, about 1.6 kg/
   3½ lb
Salt and freshly ground black pepper
45 ml/3 tbsp chopped mint
450 ml/¾ pt/2 cups lamb stock,
   made with 1 stock cube
30 ml/2 tbsp cornflour (cornstarch)
75 ml/5 tbsp apple juice
15 ml/1 tbsp artificial sweetener
   granules
30 ml/2 tbsp boiling water
Red wine vinegar
To serve:
Stock-roast Potatoes (see page 286)
Braised Celery (see page 276)
Peas

Trim off and discard any visible excess fat from the lamb. Place in a roasting tin (pan) and sprinkle with pepper and 15 ml/1 tbsp of the mint. Cover with foil or a lid and roast in a preheated oven at 190°C/375°F/gas mark 5 for 2 hours. Remove the lid for the last 30 minutes cooking time. Remove from the pan and transfer to a warm carving dish. Pour off all the fat from the tin, leaving the pan juices. Blend in the stock and simmer, stirring and scraping, for 5 minutes. Blend the cornflour with the apple juice and stir into the pan. Bring to the boil and cook for 2 minutes, stirring, until thickened. Season to taste. Meanwhile, put the remaining mint in a small bowl. Add the artificial sweetener granules and the water and leave to stand for at least 30 minutes to infuse. Stir in red wine vinegar to taste. Carve the lamb, discarding any fat or skin. Serve with Stock-roast Potatoes, Braised Celery and peas, with the gravy and mint sauce handed separately.

Almost Lancashire Hot Pot

SERVES 4

½ small shoulder of lamb
1 onion, quartered
45 ml/3 tbsp plain (all-purpose)
   flour
Salt and freshly ground black pepper
40 g/1½ oz/3 tbsp low-fat spread
750 g/1½ lb potatoes, sliced
2 onions, sliced
2 carrots, sliced
2 leeks, sliced
2.5 ml/½ tsp dried mixed herbs
To serve:
Fruity Red Cabbage (see page 290)

Bone the lamb and discard as much fat as possible. Put the bones in a saucepan with the onion and cover with water. Bring to the boil, skim the surface, cover and simmer while preparing the rest of the dish. Cut the meat into bite-sized pieces. Toss in the flour, seasoned with a little salt and pepper. Melt half the low-fat spread in a flameproof casserole (Dutch oven) and brown the meat on all sides. Take the pan off the heat and remove the meat from the pan. Put a layer of half the potatoes in the base of the casserole. Mix together the sliced onions, carrots, leeks and herbs with some salt and pepper. Put a layer of meat over the potatoes, then a layer of vegetables. Continue layering the meat and vegetables, then top with a layer of the remaining potatoes. Strain in the lamb stock, to come just up to the potatoes. Dot with the remaining low-fat spread. Cover with greaseproof (waxed) paper, then the lid and bake in a preheated oven at 180°C/350°F/gas mark 4 for 2 hours. Remove the lid and paper, turn up the heat to 200°C/400°F/gas mark 6 and cook for a further 30 minutes until golden brown. Serve hot with Fruity Red Cabbage.

Overnight Hunter's Lamb

SERVES 6

1 small leg of lamb, about
*   1.6 kg/3½ lb*
Rosemary sprigs
3 garlic cloves, cut into slivers
12 juniper berries, crushed
1 onion, sliced
1 carrot, sliced
60 ml/4 tbsp port
30 ml/2 tbsp red wine vinegar
30 ml/2 tbsp sunflower oil
Salt and freshly ground black
*   pepper*
45 ml/3 tbsp plain (all-purpose)
*   flour*
450 ml/¾ pt/2 cups lamb or
*   chicken stock, made with 1*
*   stock cube*
30 ml/2 tbsp redcurrant jelly
*   (clear conserve)*
To serve:
Parsleyed Potatoes (see page 289)
Mangetout (snow peas)

Trim off any excess fat from the lamb. Make deep slits in the flesh all over. Push a small rosemary sprig and a sliver of garlic in each slit. Place in a large shallow dish. Add the juniper berries, onion and carrot slices. Mix together the port, vinegar, oil and a little salt and pepper and pour over. Chill overnight to marinate, turning occasionally. Transfer the meat to a roasting tin (pan), preferably with a lid. Strain the marinade and pour over. Cover the tin with the lid or foil, twisting it under the rim to secure. Roast in a preheated oven at 180°C/350°F/gas mark 4 for 2½ hours. Uncover for the last 30 minutes. Transfer to a carving dish and discard the rosemary. Spoon off any fat in the pan, leaving the juices. Blend in the flour and cook, stirring, for 1 minute. Stir in the remaining ingredients. Bring to the boil and cook for 2 minutes, stirring all the time, until thickened. Taste and re-season. Carve the lamb, discarding the fat and skin. Serve with the sauce, Parsleyed Potatoes and mangetout.

Asparagus Lamb

SERVES 4

750 g/1½ lb thin asparagus
750 g/1½ lb lamb neck fillet,
  trimmed and diced
20 ml/4 tsp plain (all-purpose)
  flour
Salt and freshly ground black
  pepper
40 g/1½ oz/3 tbsp low-fat spread
2 onions, chopped
100 ml/3½ fl oz/6½ tbsp very low-
  fat crème fraîche
Chopped parsley
To serve:
Herby Potatoes (see page 289)
Glazed Carrots (see page 275)

Tie the asparagus in small bundles and stand in a pan of simmering, lightly salted water. Cover and cook for 5 minutes. Turn off the heat and leave to stand for 5 minutes. Carefully remove the bundles, reserving the cooking water. Cut off the heads about 5 cm/2 in down the stalks and reserve. Purée the stalks in a blender or food processor with a little of the cooking water. Pass through a sieve (strainer) to remove any stringy bits. Reserve the purée. Meanwhile, toss the meat in the flour, seasoned with a little salt and pepper. Melt the low-fat spread in a flameproof casserole (Dutch oven). Fry (sauté) the onions for 3 minutes to soften. Remove from the pan with a draining spoon. Add the meat and brown on all sides. Return the onions to the pan. Blend in 250 ml/8 fl oz/1 cup of the asparagus cooking water and bring to the boil, stirring. Cover, reduce the heat and simmer gently for 45 minutes or until the lamb is tender, skimming off any fat from time to time. Stir in the asparagus purée and season to taste. Stir in the crème fraîche. Taste and re-season if necessary. Sprinkle with chopped parsley and serve with Herby Potatoes and Glazed Carrots.

··· **BEEF**·······································

550

CALORIES OR LESS

Spaghetti Bolognese

SERVES 4

350 g/12 oz/3 cups extra-lean
  minced (ground) beef
2 onions, chopped
1 carrot, finely chopped
1 garlic clove, crushed
400 g/14 oz/1 large can chopped
  tomatoes
15 ml/1 tbsp tomato purée (paste)
45 ml/3 tbsp red wine
Salt and freshly ground black
  pepper
5 ml/1 tsp dried oregano
225 g/8 oz spaghetti
30 ml/2 tbsp grated Parmesan
  cheese
To serve:
Mixed Green Salad (see page 265)

Dry-fry (sauté) the mince with the onions, carrot and garlic in a large saucepan, stirring, until the grains are brown and separate. Pour off any excess fat. Add the remaining ingredients except the spaghetti and cheese. Bring to the boil, stirring. Reduce the heat, part-cover and simmer gently for 30 minutes until the mixture has formed a rich sauce. Taste and re-season if necessary. Meanwhile, cook the spaghetti according to the packet directions. Drain. Pile on to warmed plates. Spoon the sauce over, sprinkle with the Parmesan cheese and serve with Mixed Green salad.

Lasagne al Forno

SERVES 4

1 quantity Bolognese sauce (see
  Spaghetti Bolognese left)
6 sheets no-need-to-precook
  lasagne
300 ml/½ pt/1¼ cups skimmed
  milk
45 ml/3 tbsp plain (all-purpose)
  flour
A small knob of low-fat spread
Salt and freshly ground black
  pepper
2.5 ml/½ tsp dried mixed herbs
50 g/2 oz/½ cup low-fat Cheddar
  cheese, grated
To serve:
Italian Green Salad (see page 272)

Prepare the Bolognese sauce. Spread a little in the base of a fairly shallow ovenproof dish. Top with 2 sheets of lasagne. Add half the remaining meat. Add another layer of lasagne sheets, the remaining meat, then the remaining lasagne. Whisk a little of the milk in a saucepan with the flour. Whisk in the remaining milk and add the low fat spread, some salt and pepper and the herbs. Bring to the boil and cook for 2 minutes, whisking all the time until thickened. Stir in the cheese. Spoon on top of the lasagne and bake in a preheated oven at 190ºC/375ºF/gas mark 5 for 35 minutes or until cooked through and golden on top. Serve with Italian Green Salad.

Cannelloni al Forno

SERVES 4

Prepare as for Lasagne al Forno (see page 253), but substitute half the beef with minced (ground) chicken livers. Use the Bolognese mixture to fill eight cannelloni tubes, place in an ovenproof dish and cover with the cheese sauce. Bake as for Lasagne al Forno.

Corned Beef Hash

SERVES 4

450 g/1 lb potatoes, diced
350 g/12 oz/1 large can corned beef
2 onions, chopped
25 g/1 oz/2 tbsp low-fat spread
400 g/14 oz/1 large can no-added-sugar baked beans
15 ml/1 tbsp Worcestershire sauce
Salt and freshly ground black pepper
To serve:
English Country Garden Salad (see page 282)

Boil the potatoes in lightly salted water until tender. Drain. Meanwhile, dice the corned beef, discarding any excess fat. Melt the low-fat spread in a large frying pan (skillet) and fry (sauté) the onions for 3 minutes until soft but not brown. Add the remaining ingredients, the potatoes and corned beef and fry, turning occasionally, for 5 minutes. Press down the mixture with a fish slice and continue cooking for about 5 minutes until golden brown underneath. Flash under a hot grill (broiler) to brown the top. Loosen and turn out on to a warmed plate. Serve cut into quarters with English Country Garden Salad.

Kebabs with Walnut Sauce

SERVES 4

100 g/4 oz/1 cup walnut pieces
2 spring onions (scallions), chopped
60 ml/4 tbsp beef stock, made with ¼ stock cube
45 ml/3 tbsp lemon juice
1.5 ml/¼ tsp ground ginger
Salt and freshly ground black pepper
450 g/1 lb tender rump steak, trimmed of any fat and cubed
250 ml/8 fl oz/1 cup very low-fat fromage frais
To serve:
Mexican Rice (see page 298)

Put the walnuts, spring onions, stock, lemon juice, ginger and a little salt and pepper in a blender or food processor. Purée until smooth. Thread the meat on skewers and place on a grill (broiler) rack. Brush with a little of the sauce. Grill (broil) until cooked to your liking. Transfer to warmed plates. Blend the fromage frais with the remaining walnut sauce. Spoon into small pots and serve with the steak and Mexican Rice.

Beef Moussaka

SERVES 4

Prepare as for Lamb Moussaka (see page 249) but substitute extra-lean minced (ground) beef for the lamb and 4 courgettes (zucchini) for the aubergines (eggplants).

Stifado

SERVES 4

750 g/1½ lb lean braising steak,
    trimmed of all fat and cubed
40 g/1½ oz/⅓ cup plain (all-
    purpose) flour
Salt and freshly ground black
    pepper
15 ml/1 tbsp extra virgin olive oil
25 g/1 oz/2 tbsp low-fat spread
1.5 ml/¼ tsp cumin seeds, crushed
A small piece of cinnamon stick
30 ml/2 tbsp tomato purée (paste)
15 ml/1 tbsp red wine vinegar
750 ml/1¼ pts/3 cups beef stock,
    made with 2 stock cubes
5 ml/1 tsp dried thyme
225 g/8 oz button (pearl) onions,
    peeled but left whole
50 g/2 oz/½ cup Feta cheese, cubed
To serve:
**Green Beans with Cherry
    Tomatoes (see page 267)**

Toss the meat in the flour, seasoned with a little salt and pepper. Heat the oil and low-fat spread in a flame-proof casserole (Dutch oven) and brown the meat on all sides. Pour off any excess fat. Add the remaining ingredients except the onions and cheese. Bring to the boil, stirring. Cover and transfer to a preheated oven at 160°C/325°F/gas mark 3 for 2½ hours. Meanwhile, boil the onions in water for 3 minutes. Drain. Add to the casserole and return to the oven for a further 30 minutes until cooked through. Add the cheese and return to the oven for a few minutes to melt. Serve straight from the dish with Green Beans with Cherry Tomatoes.

Savoury Beef Crumble

SERVES 4

2 onions, chopped
1 leek, chopped
2 carrots, chopped
450 g/1 lb/4 cups extra-lean
    minced (ground) beef
75 g/3 oz/¾ cup plain (all-purpose)
    flour
600 ml/1 pt/2½ cups beef stock,
    made with 2 stock cubes
5 ml/1 tsp yeast extract
Salt and freshly ground black
    pepper
85 g/3½ oz/1 small packet sage
    and onion stuffing mix
75 g/3 oz/⅓ cup low-fat spread
50 g/2 oz/½ cup low-fat Cheddar
    cheese, grated
To serve:
**Tomatoes with Courgettes
    (see page 275)**

Put the chopped vegetables in a flameproof casserole (Dutch oven) with the meat. Cook, stirring, until the grains of meat are brown and separate. Pour off any excess fat. Stir in 25 g/1 oz/¼ cup of the flour and cook for 2 minutes. Remove from the heat and blend in the stock and yeast extract. Return to the heat, bring to the boil and simmer gently for 10 minutes, stirring occasionally. Season to taste. Meanwhile, empty the stuffing into a bowl. Add the low-fat spread and the remaining flour. Rub in with the finger-tips until crumbly. Spoon over the meat and top with the cheese. Bake in a preheated oven at 190°C/375°F/gas mark 5 for 35 minutes or until the top is golden brown. Serve with Tomatoes with Courgettes.

Steak, Mushroom and Potato Kebabs

SERVES 4

450 g/1 lb lean tender rump steak, trimmed of any fat and cubed
15 ml/1 tbsp olive oil
10 ml/2 tsp red wine vinegar
5 ml/1 tsp dried oregano
1.5 ml/¼ tsp cayenne
Salt and freshly ground black pepper
16 whole, waxy new potatoes, scrubbed
16 button mushrooms
8 cherry tomatoes
15 g/½ oz/1 tbsp low-fat spread, melted
To serve:
Garlic Bread (see page 293)
Mixed Salad (see page 265)

Put the meat in a dish with the oil, vinegar, oregano, cayenne and a little salt and pepper. Toss and leave to marinate for at least 1 hour. Meanwhile, cook the potatoes in boiling, lightly salted water until just tender. Drain, rinse with cold water and drain again. Thread the meat, potatoes and mushrooms on eight soaked wooden skewers. Finish each with a cherry tomato. Place on a grill (broiler) rack. Brush with any remaining marinade then with the low-fat spread. Grill (broil) until golden and the meat is cooked to your liking, brushing with any remaining low-fat spread during cooking. Serve with Garlic Bread and Mixed Salad.

American Diner

SERVES 4

350 g/12 oz/3 cups very lean minced (ground) beef
2.5 ml/½ tsp steak seasoning (optional)
100 g/4 oz mushrooms, very finely chopped
Salt and freshly ground black pepper
15 ml/1 tbsp low-fat spread, melted
20 ml/4 tsp hamburger relish
4 seeded baps, split
8 slices dill pickle
4 low-fat cheese slices
Shredded lettuce
Sliced tomato
½ onion, finely chopped
To serve:
Crispy Baked Potato Skins (see page 275)

Mix the meat with the steak seasoning, if using, the mushrooms and some salt and pepper. Squeeze well together, then shape into four burgers. Place on a grill (broiler) rack. Brush with the low-fat spread and grill (broil) for about 4–5 minutes on each side until browned and cooked through. Spread the relish on one cut surface of each bap. Top with the burger, dill pickle, cheese, lettuce, tomato and chopped onion. Top with the other bap half. Serve with Crispy Baked Potato Skins.

Photograph opposite:
Crusty Baked Lamb Cutlets (page 195)

Barman's Steak

SERVES 4

**750 g/1½ lb lean braising steak,
  cut into 4 pieces**
1 onion, sliced into rings
150 ml/¼ pt/⅔ cup brown ale
10 ml/2 tsp English made mustard
1 bay leaf
**Salt and freshly ground black
  pepper**
15 g/½ oz/1 tbsp low-fat spread
**10 ml/2 tsp plain (all-purpose)
  flour**
15 ml/1 tbsp water
Parsley sprigs
To serve:
**Fluffy Mashed Potatoes (see page
  287)**
**Baked Spiced Carrots (see page
  275)**
Peas

Place the meat in a shallow oven-proof dish. Cover with the onion rings. Mix together the ale and mustard and spoon over. Add the bay leaf and some salt and pepper. Leave to marinate for at least 4 hours or preferably chill overnight, turning occasionally. Dot with the low-fat spread. Cover with foil or a lid and cook in a pre-heated oven at 180°C/350°F/gas mark 4 for 1 hour or until tender. Lift out the meat and transfer to warmed serving plates. Keep warm. Blend the flour with the water in a small saucepan. Strain in the cooking liquid. Bring to the boil and cook for 2 minutes, stirring. Taste and re-season if necessary. Spoon over the steaks, garnish with parsley sprigs and serve hot with Fluffy Mashed Potatoes, Baked Spiced Carrots and peas.

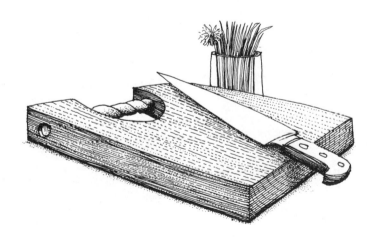

Photograph opposite:
Redcurrant Fillet (page 203)

MEATLESS MEALS

CALORIES OR LESS

Spinach and Cheese Cakes

SERVES 4

450 g/1 lb frozen chopped
spinach, thawed
225 g/8 oz/2 cups low-fat strong
Cheddar cheese, grated
Salt and freshly ground black
pepper
A pinch of grated nutmeg
2 eggs
100 g/4 oz/1 cup dried
breadcrumbs
40 g/1½ oz/3 tbsp low-fat spread
300 ml/½ pt/1¼ cups passata
(sieved tomatoes)
2.5 ml/½ tsp dried thyme
To serve:
Hot Walnut Bread (see page 294)
Italian Pepper Salad (see page 282)

Squeeze the spinach thoroughly to remove all excess moisture. Put in a bowl. Beat in the cheese, some salt and pepper and the nutmeg. Beat one of the eggs and mix to bind. Shape into four cakes. Beat the remaining egg on a plate. Put the breadcrumbs on a separate plate. Dip the cakes in the beaten egg, then in the breadcrumbs to coat completely. Chill for at least 30 minutes. Melt the low-fat spread in a frying pan (skillet) and fry (sauté) the cakes on both sides until golden brown and cooked through. Drain on kitchen paper. Transfer to warmed plates. Meanwhile, heat the passata with the thyme and a little salt and pepper. Spoon around the cakes and serve with Hot Walnut Bread and Italian Pepper Salad.

Broccoli and Blue Cheese Vermicelli

SERVES 4

225 g/8 oz broccoli, cut into tiny
florets
150 ml/¼ pt/⅔ cup low-fat double
(heavy) cream
100 g/4 oz/1 cup blue cheese,
crumbled
Salt and freshly ground black
pepper
225 g/8 oz vermicelli
30 ml/2 tbsp pine nuts, toasted
To serve:
1 French stick, warmed
Mixed Salad (see page 265)

Cook the broccoli until just tender. Drain. Mix the cream with the cheese in the broccoli saucepan and heat gently until the cheese melts, stirring all the time. Stir in the broccoli and seasoning to taste. Meanwhile, cook the vermicelli according to the packet directions. Drain. Add the cheese sauce and toss gently. Spoon on to warmed plates and sprinkle with the toasted pine nuts. Serve with warm French bread and Mixed Salad.

Mushroom and Cashew Nut Pilaf

SERVES 4

175 g/6 oz/¾ cup brown rice
1 onion, chopped
25 g/1 oz/2 tbsp low-fat spread
1 garlic clove, crushed
3 celery sticks, chopped
225 g/8 oz button mushrooms, sliced
1 red (bell) pepper, chopped
1 green (bell) pepper, chopped
2 carrots, chopped
100 g/4 oz/1 cup raw cashew nuts
60 ml/4 tbsp water
Soy sauce
2 eggs, beaten
10 ml/2 tsp chopped coriander (cilantro)
To serve:
Cucumber with Yoghurt Dressing (see page 267)

Cook the rice according to the packet directions. Drain. Meanwhile, fry (sauté) the onion in half the low-fat spread for 4 minutes, stirring. Add the garlic, celery, mushrooms, peppers, carrots and nuts and toss for 2 minutes. Add the water, cover and cook very gently for 5 minutes until the vegetables are just tender. Remove the lid and continue cooking, if necessary, until the liquid has evaporated. Stir in the cooked rice and heat through. Add soy sauce to taste and toss well. Meanwhile, mix the eggs with the coriander and 5 ml/1 tsp soy sauce. Melt the remaining low-fat spread and fry the egg mixture until set. Cut into four wedges. Spoon the pilaf on to four warmed plates. Top with the egg wedges and serve with Cucumber with Yoghurt Dressing.

Bean Stew with Herb Dumplings

SERVES 4

425 g/15 oz/1 large can red kidney beans, drained
425 g/15 oz/1 large can haricot (navy) beans, drained
400 g/14 oz/1 large can chopped tomatoes
1 garlic clove, crushed
15 ml/1 tbsp tomato purée (paste)
200 g/7 oz/1 small can sweetcorn (corn) with (bell) peppers
275 g/10 oz/1 small can cut green beans
300 ml/½ pt/1¼ cups vegetable stock, made with 1 stock cube
1 bay leaf
Salt and freshly ground black pepper
100 g/4 oz/1 cup self-raising (self-rising) flour
25 g/1 oz/2 tbsp low-fat spread
5 ml/1 tsp dried mixed herbs
15 ml/1 tbsp chopped parsley
To serve:
Garlic Bread (see page 293)

Put the kidney and haricot beans in a saucepan with the tomatoes, garlic, tomato purée, corn, green beans, stock and bay leaf. Season lightly. Bring to the boil and simmer gently for 5 minutes. Meanwhile, put the flour in a bowl with a little salt and pepper. Rub in the low-fat spread and stir in the herbs. Mix with enough cold water to form a soft but not too sticky dough. Shape into eight rough balls and drop into the top of the stew. Cover and simmer gently for 15–20 minutes until the dumplings are risen and fluffy. Ladle into warmed bowls, discarding the bay leaf. Serve with Garlic Bread.

Cheesy Polenta

SERVES 4

900 ml/1½ pts/3¾ cups water
10 ml/2 tsp salt
225 g/8 oz/2 cups polenta
100 g/4 oz/½ cup low-fat spread
75 g/3 oz/¾ cup strong low-fat
Cheddar cheese, grated
A few torn basil leaves
A few green olives
To serve:
Italian Green Salad (see page 272)
1 small ciabatta loaf, warmed

Put the water and salt in a saucepan and bring to the boil. Gradually add the polenta, stirring all the time, until the mixture begins to thicken. Simmer very gently for about 20 minutes, stirring occasionally, until really thick. Stir in 75 g/3 oz/⅓ cup of the low-fat spread and 50 g/2 oz/½ cup of the cheese. Spread in a lightly greased shallow tin (pan) so the mixture is about 2.5 cm/ 1 in thick. Leave to cool, then chill. When ready to cook, cut the polenta into 5 cm/2 in squares. Place on foil on a grill (broiler) rack. Melt the remaining low-fat spread and brush over. Grill (broil) for about 5 minutes on each side until golden brown. Transfer to plates, sprinkle with the remaining cheese, and scatter torn basil leaves and olives over. Serve with Italian Green Salad and ciabatta bread.

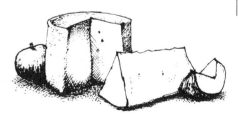

Wheat and Potato Pizza Margharita

SERVES 2

225 g/8 oz/1 cup cooked mashed
potato
75 g/3 oz/¾ cup wholemeal flour
2.5 ml/½ tsp salt
Skimmed milk
25 g/1 oz/2 tbsp low-fat spread
45 ml/3 tbsp tomato purée (paste)
2.5 ml/½ tsp dried oregano
75 g/3 oz/¾ cup Mozzarella cheese,
grated
A few black olives
A few torn basil leaves
To serve:
Coleslaw (see page 272)
Crisp Green Salad (see page 265)

Mix the potato with the flour, salt and enough milk to form a firm dough. Knead gently on a lightly floured surface and pat out to a round the size the base of the frying pan (skillet). Melt half the low-fat spread in the pan. Add the pizza base and cook for several minutes until golden brown underneath. Slide out of the pan. Heat the remaining low-fat spread in the pan. Invert the pizza back into the pan, so it is browned side up. Spread with the tomato purée, then sprinkle with oregano. Top with the cheese, olives and basil leaves. Cover with a lid and cook for 3 minutes until the base is cooked. Flash under a hot grill (broiler) just until the cheese is faintly browning. Cut in half and serve with Coleslaw and Crisp Green Salad.

Baked Bean Lasagne

SERVES 4

40 g/1½ oz/3 tbsp low-fat spread
1 onion, chopped
1 garlic clove, crushed
225 g/8 oz button mushrooms,
sliced
400 g/14 oz/1 large can no-added-
sugar baked beans
30 ml/2 tbsp tomato ketchup
(catsup)
45 ml/3 tbsp soy sauce
1.5 ml/¼ tsp chilli powder
Salt and freshly ground black
pepper
6 sheets no-need-to-precook
lasagne
225 g/8 oz frozen chopped
spinach, thawed
20 g/¾ oz/3 tbsp plain (all-
purpose) flour
300 ml/½ pt/1¼ cups skimmed
milk
175 g/6 oz/1½ cups low-fat
Cheddar cheese, grated
To serve:
Mixed Green Salad (see page 265)

Heat 15 g/½ oz/1 tbsp of the low-fat spread in a saucepan and fry (sauté) the onion and garlic for 3 minutes. Stir in the mushrooms and cook for 2 minutes. Blend in the beans, ketchup, soy sauce, chilli powder and pepper to taste. Put a layer of a quarter of the bean mixture in the base of a fairly shallow ovenproof dish. Top with a layer of 2 lasagne sheets. Squeeze out all the moisture from the spinach and spread over, then add half the remaining beans, 2 lasagne sheets, the remaining beans and finally the last of the lasagne. Blend the flour and milk in a saucepan. Add the remaining low-fat spread. Bring to the boil and cook for 2 minutes, stirring. Stir in most of the cheese. Season to taste. Spoon over the lasagne. Top with the remaining cheese and bake in a preheated oven at 190°C/375°F/gas mark 5 for 40 minutes until golden and cooked through. Serve with Mixed Green Salad.

Egg and Mushroom Supper

SERVES 4

900 g/2 lb potatoes, cut into
chunks
15 g/½ oz/1 tbsp low-fat spread
30 ml/2 tbsp skimmed milk
295 g/10½ oz/1 small can
condensed mushroom soup
8 hard-boiled (hard-cooked) eggs,
sliced
100 g/4 oz mushrooms, sliced
15 ml/1 tbsp chopped parsley
50 g/2 oz/½ cup low-fat Cheddar
cheese
Parsley sprigs
To serve:
Tomato and White Bean Salad
(see page 281)

Cook the potatoes in boiling, salted water until tender. Drain and mash with the low-fat spread and milk. Heat the soup in a flameproof casserole (Dutch oven). Reserve 4 egg slices for garnish and stir the remainder into the soup with the mushroms and chopped parsley. Top with the potato and sprinkle with the cheese. Bake in a preheated oven at 200°C/400°F/gas mark 6 for 15 minutes until the cheese is golden. Spoon on to four warmed plates. Garnish each with a slice of egg and a parsley sprig and serve with Tomato and White Bean Salad.

Couscous with Roasted Vegetables

SERVES 4

2 red (bell) peppers, halved and
  thickly sliced
1 green (bell) pepper, halved and
  thickly sliced
1 aubergine (eggplant), sliced
2 courgettes (zucchini), sliced
2 garlic cloves, finely chopped
30 ml/2 tbsp olive oil
175 g/6 oz/1 cup couscous
15 g/½ oz/1 tbsp low-fat spread
A bunch of spring onions
  (scallions), chopped
50 g/2 oz/⅓ cup raisins
5 ml/1 tsp lemon juice
A pinch of ground ginger
Soy sauce
30 ml/2 tbsp chopped parsley
Coarse sea salt
To serve:
Crisp Green Salad (see page 265)

Lay the pepper, aubergine and courgette slices in a large roasting tin
(pan). Sprinkle with the garlic and
drizzle with the oil. Roast in a preheated oven at 190°C/375°F/gas mark 5 for
45 minutes or until lightly browned
and tender, tossing occasionally.
Meanwhile, put the couscous in a
sieve (strainer) and place over a pan of
simmering water. Don't let the sieve
touch the water. Cover and steam for
about 20 minutes until the couscous is
tender. Meanwhile, melt the low-fat
spread and fry (sauté) the spring
onions for 4 minutes until tender. Stir
in the raisins, lemon juice, ginger and
a good shake of soy sauce. Add the
couscous and toss until well mixed
with half the parsley. Pile on to
warmed plates and sprinkle the

remaining parsley on top. Arrange the
roasted vegetables next to it. Sprinkle
them with coarse sea salt and serve
with Crisp Green Salad.

Chick Pea Curry

SERVES 4

1 garlic clove, crushed
5 ml/1 tsp ground ginger
5 ml/1 tsp ground coriander
  (cilantro)
1.5 ml/¼ tsp chilli powder
1.5 ml/¼ tsp turmeric
15 ml/1 tbsp water
25 g/1 oz/2 tsp low-fat spread
1 onion, finely chopped
10 ml/2 tsp curry paste
228 g/8 oz/1 small can chopped
  tomatoes
430 g/15½ oz/1 large can chick
  peas (garbanzos), drained
Salt and freshly ground black
  pepper
A few torn coriander leaves
Lettuce leaves
Lemon wedges
60 ml/4 tbsp desiccated (shredded)
  coconut
To serve:
1 packet pilau rice

Mix together the garlic and spices
with the water. Melt the low-fat
spread in a saucepan and add the
onion. Fry for 3 minutes. Add the spice
mixture and the curry paste and fry for
1 minute. Add the tomatoes and chick
peas and simmer for 15 minutes.
Season to taste. Spoon on to warmed
plates, garnish with a few torn coriander leaves, lettuce leaves and lemon
wedges and sprinkle with the coconut.
Serve with pilau rice.

··············· EASY MEALS ·············

Here is a list of how to cook and serve simple grilled (broiled) foods with their approximate calorie count so you can dish up any of them with a speciality side dish (see Sumptuous Salads and Side Dishes pages 265–298) for even more memorable meals.

White fish fillet or whole small plaice (about 175 g/6 oz)
under 150 calories
Brush with 5 ml/1 tsp melted low-fat spread and a squeeze of lemon juice and grill (broil) under a moderate heat for 3–5 minutes on each side until turning golden and cooked through. The fish should flake easily with a fork or point of a knife.

Salmon or other oily fish steak (about 175 g/6 oz)   under 250 calories
Brush with 5 ml/1 tsp melted low-fat spread, add a good grinding of black pepper and a squeeze of lemon or lime juice and grill (broil) for 3–4 minutes on each side until turning golden and cooked through. The fish should pull away easily with the point of a knife.

Average whole mackerel or other oily fish   under 350 calories
Clean and rinse well, pat dry on kitchen paper and remove the head, if preferred. Make several slashes on each side. Season and sprinkle with lemon juice. Grill (broil) for about 5–6 minutes each side until golden and cooked through. The flesh should look pale and opaque right down to the bone in the slashes.

Skinless, boneless chicken breast (about 175 g/6 oz)   under 200 calories
Slash in several places if very thick, brush with 5 ml/1 tsp melted low-fat spread and sprinkle with chopped fresh herbs (or a pinch of dried) and a good grinding of pepper. Grill (broil) for about 5 minutes each side until golden and cooked through. The juices should run clear when pierced.

2 chicken drumsticks (about 100 g/4 oz each)   under 150 calories
Slash in a few places. Season well and rub in a dash of chilli powder if liked. Brush with 5 ml/1 tsp melted low-fat spread. Grill (broil) for about 15 minutes, turning occasionally, until golden brown and cooked through. Remove the skin before eating.

Skinless, boneless turkey steak (about 175 g/6 oz)   under 200 calories
Prepare and cook as for chicken breast.

Lamb chops, cutlets or leg steaks (about 175 g/6 oz)   under 250 calories
Trim off all fat. Brush with 5 ml/1 tsp melted low-fat spread and sprinkle with chopped rosemary, mint or oregano. Season with salt and pepper. Grill (broil) for 5–8 minutes on each side until tender and cooked to your liking.

Pork chops or steaks

(about 175 g/6 oz)   under 250 calories
Trim off all fat. Brush with 5 ml/1 tsp melted low-fat spread. Season with dried onion flakes and/or chopped sage. Grill (broil) for about 7–8 minutes on each side until golden brown and cooked through. The meat should no longer be pink, even near the bone.

Sirloin, rump or fillet steak

(about 175 g/6 oz)   under 350 calories
Trim off all fat from the sirloin or rump. Brush with 5 ml/1 tsp melted low-fat spread. Sprinkle with steak seasoning or simply lots of freshly ground black pepper and some lemon juice. Grill (broil) for anything from 3 to 8 minutes on each side, depending on how you like your steak. The more well-grilled you have it, the fewer calories there are!

Gammon or bacon steak

(about 175 g/6 oz)   under 300 calories
Trim off all fat and snip the edges with scissors to prevent curling. Brush with 5 ml/1 tsp melted low-fat spread and grill (broil) for about 3–4 minutes on each side, depending on thickness, until cooked through.

Sumptuous Salads & Side Dishes

Salads and vegetables are a great way of filling up without piling on the calories. You can serve a mountain of any of the leaf salads or cucumber, dressed with lemon juice or vinegar and black pepper or any of the under 10-calorie dressings on pages 347–351, without adding any extra calories at all. The same applies to plain steamed or boiled greens, courgettes (zucchini) or marrow (squash).

CALORIES OR LESS

Mixed Leaf Salad

Choose any salad leaves in any quantity, selecting interesting textures and colour combinations. Choose from little gem, lamb's lettuce, oakleaf, lollo rosso, lollo biondo, dandelion, spinach, rocket, Chinese leaves (stem lettuce), cos (romaine), curly endive (frisée lettuce), chicory (Belgian endive), iceberg, watercress, salad cress or mustard and cress – the possibilities are endless. Dress with any of the 50 Calories or Less dressings (see pages 352–5).

Mixed Green Salad

Choose any green leaves – iceberg, rocket, dandelion, young spinach, round lettuce, little gem etc. Add sliced cucumber, green (bell) pepper rings, watercress, salad cress or mustard and cress and chopped spring onion (scallion). Zip up the flavour with a few torn fresh herb leaves like parsley, coriander (cilantro) or basil. Dress with any of the 50 Calories or Less dressings (see pages 352–5).

Crisp Green Salad

Choose a mixture of iceberg, cos (romaine) and Chinese leaves (stem lettuce). Dress with any of the 50 Calories or Less dressings (see pages 352–5)

Red Leaf Salad

Mix together lollo rosso, radicchio and shredded red cabbage. Dress with any of the 50 Calories or Less dressings (see pages 352–5) and garnish with a few sliced radishes.

Curly Endive Salad

SERVES 4

½ curly endive (frisée lettuce)
½ small onion, very thinly sliced
Grated rind and juice of ½ lemon
5 ml/1 tsp clear honey
Salt and freshly ground black pepper
10 ml/2 tsp walnut oil
10 ml/2 tsp water

Tear the curly endive into neat pieces and place in a salad bowl. Scatter the onion over. Whisk together the lemon rind, juice, honey, some salt and pepper, the oil and water. Drizzle over just before serving.

Chinese Leaf and Watercress Salad

SERVES 4

½ small head Chinese leaves (stem lettuce), cut into chunks
1 bunch of watercress
10 ml/2 tsp sesame oil
15 ml/1 tbsp cider vinegar
A dash of soy sauce
Freshly ground black pepper
15 ml/1 tbsp sesame seeds, toasted

Put the Chinese leaves in a bowl. Trim off any feathery stalks from the watercress, pull into small sprigs and add to the Chinese leaves. Whisk the sesame oil with the cider vinegar, soy sauce and some pepper. Drizzle over, toss and sprinkle with sesame seeds before serving.

Tomato and Onion Salad

SERVES 4

4–6 tomatoes, sliced
1 small onion, thinly sliced and separated into rings
15 ml/1 tbsp chopped parsley
30 ml/2 tbsp red wine vinegar
15 ml/1 tbsp water
A few grains of artificial sweetener
Salt and freshly ground black pepper

Lay the tomatoes in a shallow dish. Top with the onion rings. Sprinkle with the parsley. Whisk together the vinegar, water, sweetener and some salt and pepper. Pour over. Leave to stand for at least 30 minutes to allow the flavours to develop.

Tomato and Basil Salad

SERVES 4

4 beefsteak tomatoes, sliced
12 basil leaves, torn
15 ml/1 tbsp apple juice
5 ml/1 tsp extra virgin olive oil
10 ml/2 tsp red wine vinegar
Salt and freshly ground black pepper

Lay the tomatoes on a flat serving dish. Scatter the basil leaves over. Whisk together the remaining ingredients and drizzle over. Leave to stand for 30 minutes before serving.

Tomato and Spring Onion Salad

SERVES 4

8 tomatoes, skinned and cut into small wedges
3 spring onions (scallions), finely chopped
15 ml/1 tbsp olive oil
15 ml/1 tbsp white wine vinegar
A few grains of artificial sweetener
Salt and freshly ground black pepper

Put the tomatoes in a dish and sprinkle with the spring onions. Whisk together the remaining ingredients and drizzle over. Leave to stand for 30 minutes before serving.

Melon and Cucumber Salad

SERVES 4

1 small honeydew melon
½ cucumber
Grated rind and juice of 1 lime
A few grains artificial sweetener
  (optional)
Freshly ground black pepper

Halve the melon and remove the seeds. Scoop out the flesh using a melon baller or cut into neat dice. Place in a bowl. Using a canelling knife, cut grooves down the length of the cucumber, removing strips of the skin. Cut the cucumber into thin slices. Add to the melon. Sprinkle with the lime rind. Blend the juice with a few grains of artificial sweetener if liked, then sprinkle over. Add lots of black pepper and leave to stand for 30 minutes before serving.

Cucumber with Yoghurt Dressing

SERVES 4

½ cucumber, finely diced
Salt and freshly ground black
  pepper
150 ml/¼ pt/⅔ cup very low-fat
  plain yoghurt
5 ml/1 tsp white wine vinegar
1 garlic clove, crushed
15 ml/1 tbsp chopped mint

Put the cucumber in a bowl. Sprinkle with salt and leave to stand for 15 minutes. Drain off the excess liquid. Season with pepper, stir in the yoghurt, vinegar, garlic and most of the mint. Sprinkle the remaining mint on top. Leave to stand for 15 minutes before serving.

English Cucumber Salad

SERVES 4

½ cucumber
30 ml/2 tbsp malt vinegar
Freshly ground black pepper
15 ml/1 tbsp snipped chives

Peel off and discard most of the cucumber skin, then slice very thinly. Place in a shallow dish and add the vinegar and pepper. Toss thoroughly and leave to stand for at least 15 minutes. Sprinkle with chives before serving.

Green Beans with Cherry Tomatoes

SERVES 4

225 g/8 oz thin French (green)
  beans, topped and tailed but left
  whole
225 g/8 oz cherry tomatoes,
  halved
1 small red onion, finely chopped
30 ml/2 tbsp red wine vinegar
15 ml/1 tbsp olive oil
A few grains of artificial sweetener
2.5 ml/½ tsp Dijon mustard
Salt and freshly ground black
  pepper

Cook the beans in boiling, lightly salted water until tender. Drain, rinse with cold water and drain again. Lay in a shallow serving dish and scatter the tomatoes over. Sprinkle with the chopped onion. Whisk together the remaining ingredients and drizzle over. Leave to stand for 30 minutes before serving.

Green Bean and Onion Salad

SERVES 4

225 g/8 oz thin French (green) beans, topped and tailed but left whole
1 small onion, very finely chopped
15 ml/1 tbsp olive oil
10 ml/2 tsp red wine vinegar
Salt and freshly ground black pepper

Cook the beans in boiling, lightly salted water until just tender. Drain, rinse with cold water and drain again. Lay in a shallow dish. Arrange the chopped onion in a strip across the centre of the beans. Drizzle the oil and vinegar over and season with salt and pepper. Leave to stand for 30 minutes before serving.

Mustard Carrot Salad

SERVES 4

450 g/1 lb carrots, coarsely grated
Salt and freshly ground black pepper
25 g/1 oz/2 tbsp low-fat spread
15 ml/1 tbsp black mustard seeds
15 ml/1 tbsp lemon juice

Put the carrots in a salad bowl and season with salt and pepper. Melt the low-fat spread in a frying pan (skillet) and add the mustard seeds. When they start to pop add the lemon juice, stir and pour over the salad. Toss well and serve straight away while still warm.

Nutty Courgette and Carrot Salad

SERVES 4

Prepare as for Mustard Carrot Salad but substitute 2 or 3 courgettes (zucchini) for half the carrots. Use white mustard seeds instead of black and add 15 ml/1 tbsp poppy seeds.

Grated Winter Salad

SERVES 4

Lettuce leaves
½ celeriac (celery root), coarsely grated
½ small swede (rutabaga), coarsely grated
2 carrots, coarsely grated
1 quantity Celery Salad Dressing (see page 354)
Mustard and cress

Arrange the lettuce leaves on four individual serving dishes. Put three separate piles of the grated vegetables on each plate. Spoon a little dressing over each plate and garnish with mustard and cress.

Crunchy Spinach Salad

SERVES 4

Prepare as for Spinach and Bacon Salad (see page 284) but omit the bacon and add 2 chopped celery sticks.

Chinese Leaf and Mango Salad

SERVES 4

½ small head Chinese leaves (stem lettuce), shredded
1 ripe mango, peeled, stoned (pitted) and diced
4 spring onions (scallions), diagonally sliced
1 quantity Soy Dressing (see page 348)

Put the Chinese leaves in four shallow salad bowls. Arrange the mango over, then sprinkle with spring onions. Spoon over the Soy Dressing and serve.

Chinese Leaf and Orange Salad

SERVES 4

¼ head Chinese leaves (stem lettuce), shredded
2 oranges
1 onion, sliced
1 quantity Tarragon Vinegar Dressing (see page 347)

Put the Chinese leaves in a salad bowl. Hold an orange over the bowl and cut off all the rind and pith. Cut into slices, then into quarters and add to the bowl. Repeat with the remaining orange. Separate the onion into rings and scatter over. Drizzle with the dressing, toss and serve.

Mixed Salad

SERVES 4

1 small round lettuce, torn into pieces
2 tomatoes, cut into wedges
2.5 cm/1 in piece cucumber, sliced thinly
2 mushrooms, sliced
1 small green (bell) pepper, sliced
1 small onion, sliced and separated into rings
1 quantity Nearly Vinaigrette Dressing (see page 347)

Arrange the salad ingredients attractively in four small salad bowls. Drizzle the dressing over and serve.

Beetroot and Orange Salad

SERVES 4

1 little gem lettuce, separated into leaves
2 oranges
2 large cooked beetroot (red beets), diced
15 ml/1 tbsp orange juice
5 ml/1 tsp balsamic vinegar
Salt and freshly ground black pepper
Snipped chives

Arrange the lettuce leaves on four small plates. Holding the fruit over a bowl, remove all pith and rind from the oranges and cut into segments. Squeeze any juice out of the membranes into the bowl, then discard them. Pile the beetroot in the centre of the lettuce with the orange segments around. Add the measured orange juice to the bowl with the balsamic vinegar. Season to taste. Spoon over and garnish the beetroot with a few snipped chives.

Italian Celeriac Salad

SERVES 4

½ celeriac (celery root), finely
   shredded
2 carrots, finely shredded
2 tomatoes, cut into wedges
8 green olives, stoned (pitted) and
   halved
1 small onion, thinly sliced and
   separated into rings
Iceberg lettuce leaves
Lemon juice
1 quantity Diet Drizzle (see page
   354)
Freshly ground black pepper

Pile the prepared vegetables on top
of lettuce leaves on four small
plates. Drizzle with lemon juice, then
the dressing and add a good grinding
of black pepper.

Oriental Slaw

SERVES 4

¼ head Chinese leaves (stem
   lettuce), shredded
100 g/4 oz button mushrooms,
   sliced
175 g/6 oz bean sprouts
1 red (bell) pepper, cut into thin
   strips
1 red eating (dessert) apple, diced
1 celery stick, chopped
1 quantity Oriental Yoghurt
   Dressing (see page 355)
Freshly ground black pepper
15 ml/1 tbsp snipped chives

Mix the Chinese leaves with the
mushrooms, bean sprouts, red
pepper, apple and celery. Add the
dressing, toss and sprinkle with black
pepper and the chives before serving.

Beetroot and Chive Salad

SERVES 4

4 beetroot (red beets), cut into
   pieces
30 ml/2 tbsp very low-fat crème
   fraîche
Salt and freshly ground black
   pepper
15 ml/1 tbsp snipped chives

Put the beetroot in a bowl. Add the
crème fraîche, seasoning and
chives, toss and serve.

Iceberg Boats

SERVES 4

½ cucumber, chopped
4 tomatoes, chopped
75 g/5 tbsp very low-fat plain
   yoghurt
5 ml/1 tsp dried mint
1 small garlic clove, crushed
   (optional)
Salt and freshly ground black
   pepper
4 large iceberg lettuce leaves
10 ml/2 tsp fennel seeds
4 gherkins (cornichons)

Mix the cucumber and tomato with
the yoghurt, mint, garlic, if using,
and salt and pepper to taste. Pile into
the lettuce leaves. Garnish each with a
sprinkling of fennel seeds and a
gherkin 'fan' made by making several
cuts from the tip through almost to the
stalk end, then opening up gently.

Oriental Bean Sprout Salad

SERVES 4

**228 g/8 oz/1 small can pineapple
pieces in natural juice
175 g/6 oz bean sprouts
4 spring onions (scallions),
diagonally sliced
1 red (bell) pepper, cut into thin
strips
5 cm/2 in piece cucumber, cut into
very thin matchsticks
1 carrot, cut into very thin
matchsticks
30 ml/2 tbsp soy sauce
1.5 ml/¼ tsp grated fresh root ginger
Freshly ground black pepper**

Drain the pineapple, reserving 15 ml/
1 tbsp of the juice. Place the fruit
in a salad bowl and add the bean
sprouts, spring onions, red pepper,
cucumber and carrot. Whisk the
pineapple juice with the soy sauce,
ginger and a little pepper. Pour over,
toss and serve.

Tomato, Chicory and Orange Salad

SERVES 4

**2 heads chicory (Belgian endive)
1 orange
8 cherry tomatoes, halved
1 quantity Nearly Vinaigrette
Dressing (see page 347)**

Cut a cone-shaped core out of the
base of each head of chicory.
Separate into leaves. Arrange on four
small plates. Cut off all the pith and
rind from the orange. Slice thinly, then
cut each slice into quarters. Arrange
on the chicory and pour over any
juice. Arrange the tomatoes around,
spoon over the dressing and serve.

Bean Sprout and Pepper Salad

SERVES 4

**175 g/6 oz bean sprouts
1 red (bell) pepper, cut into thin
rings
1 green (bell) pepper, cut into thin
rings
1 onion, thinly sliced and
separated into rings
1 quantity Soy Dressing (see page
348)**

Mix together the bean sprouts, peppers and onion in a bowl. Add the
dressing, toss and serve.

Crunchy Carrot Salad

SERVES 4

**4 large carrots, grated
2 celery sticks, finely chopped
25 g/1 oz/⅙ cup raisins
30 ml/2 tbsp snipped chives
10 ml/2 tsp walnut oil
20 ml/4 tsp orange juice
Salt and freshly ground black
pepper
4 large lettuce leaves
4 walnut halves**

Mix together the carrots, celery and
raisins with the chives. Whisk the
oil with the juice and some salt and
pepper. Pour over and toss well. Pile
on to lettuce leaves and garnish each
with a walnut half.

Italian Green Salad

SERVES 4

½ curly endive (frisée lettuce)
2 courgettes (zucchini), grated
6 stuffed green olives, sliced
2 spring onions (scallions),
    chopped
30 ml/2 tbsp dry white wine
2.5 ml/½ tsp Dijon mustard
Salt and freshly ground black
    pepper
Lemon juice (optional)

Separate the curly endive into small pieces and arrange on four small plates. Scatter the courgettes, olives and spring onions over. Whisk together the wine, mustard and a little salt and pepper. Add a dash of lemon juice, if liked. Drizzle over the salads and serve.

Winter Slaw

SERVES 4

¼ white cabbage, shredded
1 red eating (dessert) apple, sliced
5 ml/1 tsp lemon juice
3 celery sticks, sliced
15 ml/1 tbsp sultanas (golden
    raisins)
1 quantity Gran's Diet Dressing
    (see page 355)

Put the cabbage in a salad bowl. Toss the apple in lemon juice to prevent browning. Add to the bowl with the celery and sultanas. Add the dressing, toss and leave to stand for at least 1 hour before serving.

French-style Green Salad

SERVES 4

1 garlic clove, halved
½ lollo biondo lettuce
1 small bunch of rocket
30 ml/2 tbsp snipped chives
1 Granny Smith eating (dessert)
    apple, sliced
15 ml/1 tbsp lemon juice
15 ml/1 tbsp olive oil
Salt and freshly ground black
    pepper
5 ml/1 tsp chopped tarragon
5 ml/1 tsp chopped parsley

Wipe the garlic halves thoroughly round the inside of the salad bowl and discard. Add the lollo biondo, torn into pieces, and the rocket, separated into pieces. Sprinkle on the chives. Dip the apple in some of the lemon juice to prevent browning and add to the bowl. Whisk the remaining lemon juice with the olive oil, some salt and pepper and the herbs. Pour over the salad, toss and serve.

Coleslaw

SERVES 4

¼ white cabbage, finely shredded
    or coarsely grated
2 carrots, coarsely grated
1 celery stick, finely shredded
½ small onion, grated
30 ml/2 tbsp low-calorie
    mayonnaise
15 ml/1 tbsp skimmed milk
Salt and freshly ground black
    pepper

Mix the prepared vegetables thoroughly. Blend the mayonnaise with the milk and pour over. Toss and season to taste.

Rocket Salad

SERVES 4

1 slice bread, cut into tiny cubes
1 garlic clove, quartered
15 g/½ oz/1 tbsp low-fat spread
100 g/4 oz rocket leaves
A coriander (cilantro) sprig, torn into leaves
A flat leaf parsley sprig, torn into leaves
1 red onion, sliced and separated into rings
15 ml/1 tbsp tarragon vinegar
Salt and freshly ground black pepper

Put the bread, garlic and low-fat spread in a small frying pan (skillet) and toss over a gentle heat until golden. Discard the garlic and drain the bread on kitchen paper. Put the rocket and herbs in a small salad bowl. Scatter the onion over. Sprinkle with tarragon vinegar and season well. Sprinkle with the croûtons and serve.

Celery and Apple Slaw

SERVES 4

¼ white cabbage, shredded
4 celery sticks, chopped
1 each red and green eating (dessert) apples, unpeeled and diced
10 ml/2 tsp lemon juice
30 ml/2 tbsp snipped chives
1 quantity Mayonnaise and Yoghurt Dressing (see page 355)
Salt and freshly ground black pepper

Mix the cabbage with the celery in a salad bowl. Toss the apples in lemon juice to prevent browning and add to the mixture. Add the chives and dressing and toss well. Season to taste.

Citrus Spinach Salad

SERVES 4

225 g/8 oz young spinach leaves
1 pink grapefruit
1 orange
1 onion, thinly sliced and separated into rings
1 quantity Nearly Vinaigrette Dressing (see page 347)

Thoroughly wash the spinach, pat dry and remove any damaged stalks. Tear the leaves into smaller pieces, if liked. Place on four small serving plates. Holding the fruit over a bowl, cut off all the rind and pith from the grapefruit and orange and separate the fruit into segments between the membranes. Squeeze the membranes over the bowl to extract all the juice. Lay the fruit on the spinach and scatter the onion rings over. Mix the citrus juices into the dressing and spoon over. Chill, if time, before serving.

Cabbage with Celery

SERVES 4

4 celery sticks, sliced
450 ml/¾ pt/2 cups vegetable stock, made with 2 stock cubes
½ Savoy cabbage, shredded
Freshly ground black pepper
A few celery leaves (optional)

Put the celery in a saucepan with the stock. Bring to the boil and simmer for 5 minutes. Add the cabbage and cook uncovered for about 5 minutes or until tender. Drain off the excess stock. Sprinkle with pepper and serve garnished with a few celery leaves, if liked.

Tangy Shredded Cabbage

SERVES 4

1 onion, chopped
1 small green cabbage, shredded
2 eating (dessert) apples, sliced
Grated rind and juice of 1 orange
15 ml/1 tbsp Worcestershire sauce
1 tomato, skinned and chopped
150 ml/¼ pt/⅔ cup vegetable stock,
    made with ½ stock cube
5 ml/1 tsp ground allspice
A pinch of ground cloves
Salt and freshly ground black
    pepper

Place the onion, cabbage and apples in a saucepan. Toss together. Mix the orange rind and juice with the Worcestershire sauce, tomato, stock and spices and pour over. Add a little salt and pepper. Bring to the boil, cover tightly, reduce the heat and simmer for 15–20 minutes until tender, tossing occasionally. Serve piping hot.

Pea Purée

SERVES 4

225 g/8 oz/2 cups frozen peas
Salt and freshly ground black
    pepper
25 g/1 oz/2 tbsp low-fat spread
5 ml/1 tsp chopped mint
A small mint sprig

Cook the peas in just enough water to cover for 5 minutes or until tender. Drain, reserving the cooking water, and purée in a blender or food processor with some salt and pepper, the low-fat spread and the chopped mint. Thin with a little of the cooking water. Serve garnished with a small mint sprig.

Carrot Purée

SERVES 4

3 large carrots, sliced
60 ml/4 tbsp very low-fat crème
    fraîche
Salt and freshly ground black
    pepper
A pinch of grated nutmeg
Paprika

Cook the carrots in just enough water to cover. Drain and purée in a blender or food processor with the crème fraîche, salt and pepper to taste and the nutmeg. Serve garnished with a sprinkling of paprika.

Carrots Cressy

SERVES 4

450 g/1 lb carrots, sliced
Salt and freshly ground black
    pepper
450 ml/¾ pt/2 cups water
15 g/½ oz/1 tbsp low-fat spread
A few grains of artificial sweetener
1 bunch of watercress, chopped

Boil the carrots in lightly salted water for 3 minutes. Drain and return to the pan. Add the measured water, the low-fat spread, literally a few grains of sweetener and some pepper and simmer for 20 minutes. Add the watercress, toss well and boil rapidly until the liquid evaporates. Season with salt and more pepper, if necessary, and serve.

Baked Spiced Carrots

SERVES 4

450 g/1 lb carrots, sliced
20 g/¾ oz/1½ tbsp low-fat spread
Grated rind and juice of 1 orange
A pinch of ground ginger
A pinch of grated nutmeg
Salt and freshly ground black
pepper
15 ml/1 tbsp chopped parsley

Put the carrots in an ovenproof serving dish and dot with low-fat spread. Add the orange rind and juice, ginger, nutmeg and some salt and pepper. Cover tightly with foil and bake in a preheated oven at 190°C/375°F/gas mark 5 for 45 minutes or until just tender. Toss well, then sprinkle with the parsley before serving.

Crispy Baked Potato Skins

SERVES 4

900 g/2 lb potatoes, scrubbed
Salt

Peel the potatoes thickly. Put the white part in a bowl of cold water with a little lemon juice added and use for another recipe. Sprinkle a baking sheet with a thin layer of salt. Cut the peelings into neat pieces and lay on the salt. Bake in a preheated oven at 200°C/400°F/gas mark 6 for about 20 minutes or until crisp. Toss in the salt and serve hot or cold.

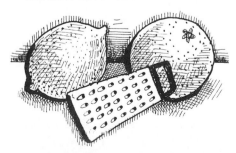

Glazed Carrots

SERVES 4

450 g/1 lb carrots, cut into fingers
450 ml/¾ pt/2 cups water
2.5 ml/½ tsp artificial sweetener
granules
40 g/1½ oz/3 tbsp low-fat spread
2.5 ml/½ tsp salt
Thinly pared rind and juice of
1 lemon

Put the carrots in a pan with the water, sweetener, low-fat spread and salt. Boil rapidly, stirring occasionally, until the carrots are cooked and the liquid has evaporated. Meanwhile, cut the lemon rind into thin strips and blanch in boiling water for 2 minutes. Drain. Spoon the carrots into a serving dish and sprinkle with the lemon rind and a little of the juice.

Tomatoes with Courgettes

SERVES 4

400 g/14 oz/1 large can chopped
tomatoes
1 garlic clove, crushed
A few grains of artificial sweetener
Salt and freshly ground black
pepper
2.5 ml/½ tsp dried oregano
6 courgettes (zucchini), sliced

Put the tomatoes in a pan with the garlic, a very few grains of sweetener, some salt and pepper and the oregano. Bring to the boil and simmer for 3 minutes. Add the courgettes and simmer, uncovered, for about 15–20 minutes until the courgettes are tender and bathed in a rich sauce. Taste and re-season if necessary.

Garlic Courgettes

SERVES 4

**450 g/1 lb courgettes (zucchini),
    sliced
25 g/1 oz/2 tbsp low-fat spread
1 garlic clove, crushed
15 ml/1 tbsp chopped parsley
Salt and freshly ground black
    pepper**

Boil the courgettes in lightly salted water until just tender. Drain and return to the pan. Add the low-fat spread, garlic, parsley and a little salt and pepper. Toss until coated, then serve.

Green Beans with Mushrooms

SERVES 4

**225 g/8 oz runner beans,
    diagonally sliced
100 g/4 oz button mushrooms,
    sliced
25 g/1 oz/2 tbsp low-fat spread
1.5 ml/¼ tsp cayenne
Salt and freshly ground black
    pepper**

Cook the beans in boiling, lightly salted water for about 5 minutes until tender. Drain and return to the pan. Fry (sauté) the mushrooms in the low-fat spread for about 3 minutes, stirring, until tender. Season with cayenne. Add to the beans, toss and season with a little salt and pepper. Serve piping hot.

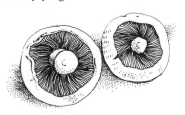

Braised Celery

SERVES 4

**1 large head celery
25 g/1 oz/2 tbsp low-fat spread
1 onion, chopped
228 g/8 oz/1 small can chopped
    tomatoes
1 bouquet garni sachet
300–450 ml/½–¾ pt/1¼–2 cups
    vegetable stock, made with
    1 stock cube
Salt and freshly ground black
    pepper
Celery leaves**

Remove the thick outer celery sticks, scrub, peel off any strings and finely chop. Reserve. Cut the remaining celery in half widthways, then into thick neat pieces. Melt the low-fat spread in a flameproof casserole (Dutch oven) and fry (sauté) the celery pieces for 3 minutes, turning occasionally. Remove from the pan with a draining spoon. Add the onion and chopped celery and fry, stirring, for 1 minute. Pour on the tomatoes, add the bouquet garni and lay the celery pieces on top. Pour over enough stock to just cover the tomatoes. Sprinkle with salt and pepper. Cover and simmer gently for about 45 minutes until the celery is just tender. Lift out of the pan on to a warmed dish and keep warm. Boil the remaining mixture rapidly until well reduced and pulpy. Remove the bouquet garni. Taste and re-season if necessary. Spoon over the celery and serve, garnished with celery leaves.

Saucy Runner Beans

SERVES 4

350 g/12 oz runner beans,
    stringed and diagonally sliced
15 g/½ oz/1 tbsp low-fat spread
15 g/½ oz/2 tbsp plain (all-
    purpose) flour
250 ml/8 fl oz/1 cup vegetable
    stock, made with 1 stock cube
1 bay leaf
30 ml/2 tbsp very low-fat crème
    fraîche
30 ml/2 tbsp chopped parsley
Salt and freshly ground black
    pepper

Cook the beans in boiling, lightly salted water until just tender. Drain. Melt the low-fat spread in the saucepan. Add the flour and cook for 1 minute. Remove from the heat and blend in the stock. Add the bay leaf, bring to the boil and cook for 2 minutes, stirring all the time, until thick and smooth. Stir in the crème fraîche, parsley and seasoning to taste. Discard the bay leaf. Add the beans, toss in the sauce and serve hot.

Parsleyed Carrots

SERVES 4

450 g/1 lb carrots, sliced
Salt and freshly ground black
    pepper
10 ml/2 tsp low-fat spread
30 ml/2 tbsp chopped parsley
A pinch of grated nutmeg

Cook the carrots in boiling, salted water until just tender. Drain and return to the pan. Add the low-fat spread, parsley, nutmeg and a good grinding of pepper. Toss thoroughly. Pile into a warmed serving dish and serve straight away.

Spring Green Toss

SERVES 4

20 g/¾ oz/1½ tbsp low-fat spread
5 ml/1 tsp sesame oil
350 g/12 oz spring greens (spring
    cabbage), shredded
15 ml/1 tbsp sesame seeds
A squeeze of lemon juice
Salt and freshly ground black
    pepper

Melt the low-fat spread and oil in a large frying pan (skillet) with a lid. Add the spring greens and toss until coated with the oil mixture. Reduce the heat, cover and cook very gently for 5 minutes until almost tender. Remove the lid, turn up the heat, add the sesame seeds and toss over a high heat for several minutes until sizzling. Sprinkle with lemon juice, season to taste and serve.

Spinach with Mushrooms

SERVES 4

450 g/1 lb spinach
100 g/4 oz button mushrooms,
    sliced
30 ml/2 tbsp very low-fat crème
    fraîche
Salt and freshly ground black
    pepper
Grated nutmeg

Wash the spinach thoroughly under cold running water. Discard any thick stalks and tear the leaves into pieces. Place in a saucepan, cover and cook with no extra water for 3 minutes. Chop with scissors. Throw in the mushrooms and continue cooking for 3 minutes. Remove the lid and boil rapidly to evaporate any liquid. Stir in the crème fraîche, salt, pepper and nutmeg to taste and serve.

Spinach with Tomatoes

SERVES 4

450 g/1 lb spinach
Salt and freshly ground black
pepper
400 g/14 oz/1 large can chopped
tomatoes
2 spring onions (scallions), finely
chopped
2.5 ml/½ tsp dried Herbes de
Provence

Wash the spinach thoroughly under cold running water. Discard any thick stalks and tear up the leaves. Place in a pan with no extra water. Add a little salt and pepper. Cover and cook for 5 minutes until tender. Drain off any liquid and finely chop. Meanwhile, put the tomatoes in a separate pan with the spring onions, herbs and a little salt and pepper. Bring to the boil and boil rapidly for 5 minutes until pulpy. Stir in the spinach and serve hot.

Stewed Herby Mushrooms

SERVES 4

350 g/12 oz button mushrooms
60 ml/4 tbsp water
15 g/½ oz/1 tbsp low-fat spread
15 ml/1 tbsp chopped parsley
15 ml/1 tbsp chopped thyme
Salt and freshly ground black
pepper

Place the mushrooms in a pan with the water and low-fat spread. Cover and simmer gently for 6 minutes, stirring occasionally. Add the herbs and salt and pepper to taste. Leave the lid off and cook rapidly until the liquid evaporates. Serve hot.

Stir-fried Vegetables

SERVES 4

25 g/1 oz/2 tbsp low-fat spread
1 onion, sliced
1 garlic clove, finely chopped
2 carrots, cut into matchsticks
5 cm/2 in piece cucumber, cut into
matchsticks
¼ green cabbage, shredded
1 red (bell) pepper, cut into thin
strips
Soy sauce
A pinch of ground ginger

Heat the low-fat spread in a large frying pan (skillet) or wok. Add the prepared vegetables and cook, tossing, for about 5 minutes or until almost tender but still with bite. Add soy sauce to taste and a pinch of ginger. Toss again and serve. If you don't like your vegetables too crunchy, cover the pan after 3 minutes and cook for a few minutes longer than suggested. (The vegetable selection can be varied according to what you have to hand.)

Baked Tomatoes

SERVES 4

8 tomatoes
45 ml/3 tbsp water
Salt and freshly ground black
pepper
20 ml/4 tsp low-fat spread
Snipped chives

Put the tomatoes in a casserole (Dutch oven). Pour the water round and season lightly. Dot with the low-fat spread. Cover and cook in a preheated oven at 180°C/350°F/gas mark 4 for about 20 minutes until soft but not falling apart. Sprinkle with snipped chives and serve.

Baked Tomatoes with Spring Onions

SERVES 4

8 tomatoes, halved
25 g/1 oz/2 tbsp low-fat spread
1 bunch of spring onions (scallions), chopped
Salt and freshly ground black pepper
15 ml/1 tbsp chopped parsley

Place the tomatoes in a shallow ovenproof dish. Melt the low-fat spread in a frying pan (skillet), add the spring onions and fry (sauté) for 3 minutes, stirring. Spoon over the tomatoes, sprinkle with salt and pepper and the parsley. Cover with foil and bake in a preheated oven at 180°C/350°F/gas mark 4 for about 20 minutes until soft. Serve straight from the dish.

Poached Tomatoes with Basil

SERVES 4

8 tomatoes
Salt and freshly ground black pepper
60 ml/4 tbsp water
15 ml/1 tbsp chopped basil
A few grains of artificial sweetener (optional)

Put the tomatoes in a pan and sprinkle with salt and pepper. Add the water. Sprinkle the basil over and add a very few grains of sweetener, if liked. Bring to the boil, cover, reduce the heat and cook very gently for about 10–15 minutes or until the tomatoes are tender but still hold their shape. Carefully remove from the pan and serve with the juices, if liked.

Poached Tomatoes with Mushrooms

SERVES 4

225 g/8 oz cherry tomatoes
225 g/8 oz button mushrooms
60 ml/4 tbsp water
Salt and freshly ground black pepper
2.5 ml/½ tsp dried mixed herbs
Chopped parsley

Put the tomatoes and mushrooms in a single layer in a large, shallow-pan with the water. Season with salt and pepper and add the dried herbs. Bring to the boil, cover, reduce the heat and cook very gently for 4 minutes. Remove the lid and cook until the mushrooms and tomatoes are tender and the liquid has evaporated. Garnish with parsley and serve straight from the pan.

Crunchy-topped Broccoli and Cauliflower

SERVES 4

½ small cauliflower, cut into florets
175 g/6 oz broccoli, cut into florets
15 g/½ oz/1 tbsp low-fat spread
25 g/1 oz/1 cup bran flakes
1.5 ml/¼ tsp chilli powder

Cook the cauliflower and broccoli in boiling, lightly salted water until tender. Drain and place in an flame-proof serving dish. Melt the low-fat spread and stir in the bran flakes and chilli powder. Sprinkle over the vegetables and place under a hot grill (broiler) until crisp and golden. Serve straight away.

Baby Asparagus Spears

SERVES 4

350 g/12 oz baby asparagus
  spears, trimmed
Salt and freshly ground black
  pepper
25 g/1 oz/2 tbsp low-fat spread
5 ml/1 tsp lemon juice
5 ml/1 tsp chopped tarragon
15 ml/1 tbsp chopped parsley

Tie the spears into four small bundles. Stand them in a small saucepan and half-fill with boiling water. Add a little salt. Cover and cook for 6 minutes. Leave the lid on, turn off the heat and leave to stand for 5 minutes. Carefully lift out of the pan. Arrange on four small warmed plates (or at the side of the main course). Meanwhile, melt the low-fat spread with the lemon juice, herbs and some pepper. Spoon over the asparagus and serve.

Stir-fried Greens

SERVES 4

100 g/4 oz French (green) beans
225 g/8 oz spring greens (spring
  cabbage), thinly shredded
25 g/1 oz/2 tbsp low-fat spread
2 courgettes (zucchini), cut into
  thin matchsticks
5 cm/2 in piece cucumber, cut into
  matchsticks
30 ml/2 tbsp soy sauce

Top and tail the beans and cut into short lengths. Boil in lightly salted water for 3 minutes. Add the spring greens and cook for a further 1 minute. Drain thoroughly. Melt the low-fat spread in a wok or large frying pan (skillet). Add the beans, greens, courgettes and cucumber and stir-fry for 5 minutes. Season with soy sauce and serve.

SUMPTUOUS SALADS & SIDE DISHES

CALORIES OR LESS

Tomato and White Bean Salad

SERVES 4

4 beefsteak tomatoes
425 g/15 oz/1 large can haricot (navy) or cannellini beans, drained, rinsed and drained again
1 garlic clove, crushed
50 g/2 oz button mushrooms, thinly sliced
15 ml/1 tbsp olive oil
30 ml/2 tbsp chopped parsley
Salt and freshly ground black pepper
15 ml/1 tbsp white wine vinegar

Cut a slice off the top of each tomato and reserve. Scoop out the seeds and discard. Drain upside-down on kitchen paper. Chop the cut slices of tomato and place in a bowl. Add the beans with the garlic, mushrooms, oil, half the parsley, seasoning and vinegar. Toss well. Spoon into the tomatoes, garnish with the remaining parsley and chill until ready to serve.

Banana and Chicory Salad

SERVES 4

2 bananas, thickly sliced
Grated rind and juice of 1 lemon
2 heads chicory (Belgian endive)
15 ml/1 tbsp sunflower oil
Artificial sweetener granules
Salt and freshly ground black pepper
15 ml/1 tbsp chopped coriander (cilantro)
15 ml/1 tbsp desiccated (shredded) coconut, toasted

Toss the bananas in a little of the lemon juice to prevent browning. Cut a cone-shaped core out of the base of each chicory head, then separate into leaves. Arrange in a starburst pattern on a serving plate. Pile the banana in the centre. Whisk together the remaining lemon juice, the rind, oil, a few grains of artificial sweetener and some salt and pepper and pour over. Sprinkle the leaves with coriander and the banana with the toasted coconut.

Italian Pepper Salad

SERVES 4

2 red (bell) peppers, sliced
2 green (bell) peppers, sliced
1 red onion, cut into small wedges
12 green olives
50 g/2 oz/½ cup Mozzarella cheese, grated
15 ml/1 tbsp olive oil
10 ml/2 tsp red wine vinegar
Salt and freshly ground black pepper
2.5 ml/½ tsp dried marjoram

Mix together the peppers, onion and olives and place in four small bowls. Sprinkle the cheese over. Whisk together the oil, vinegar, some salt and pepper and the marjoram and drizzle over.

Mexican Salad

SERVES 4

200 g/7 oz/1 small can sweetcorn (corn)
1 red (bell) pepper, diced
1 green (bell) pepper, diced
1 red onion, sliced and separated into rings
1 small avocado, diced
1 green chilli, seeded and sliced
1 quantity Lime Lovely (see page 348)
Salt and freshly ground black pepper
Crisp lettuce leaves

Drain off any liquid from the corn. Mix in a bowl with the peppers, onion, avocado and chilli. Add the Lime Lovely, season to taste and toss gently but thoroughly. Pile on to crisp lettuce leaves and serve.

Hot Potato and Bean Salad

SERVES 4

450 g/1 lb potatoes, scrubbed and cut into small pieces
100 g/4 oz French (green) beans
75 ml/5 tbsp very low-fat crème fraîche
10 ml/2 tsp chopped mint
Salt and freshly ground black pepper

Cook the potatoes in boiling, lightly salted water for 5 minutes. Top and tail the beans and cut into short lengths. Add to the potatoes and cook for a further 5–10 minutes, until the potatoes are tender. Drain and return to the pan. Add the crème fraîche, mint and some salt and pepper. Toss and serve.

English Country Garden Salad

SERVES 4

1 round lettuce, torn into pieces
4 tomatoes, quartered
5 cm/2 in piece cucumber, peeled and sliced
1 bunch of radishes, trimmed and halved
225 g/8 oz fresh peas (unshelled weight)
2 carrots, grated
4 hard-boiled (hard-cooked) eggs, quartered
1 quantity Mayonnaise Dressing (see page 354)

Arrange the lettuce in a large salad bowl. Scatter over the tomatoes, cucumber, radishes and the shelled peas. Put a pile of carrot in the centre and surround with the eggs. Serve with the dressing.

Greek Village Salad

SERVES 4

½ iceberg lettuce, shredded
¼ small white cabbage, shredded
2 beefsteak or plum tomatoes,
    halved and sliced
5 cm/2 in piece cucumber, diced
1 small red onion, sliced and
    separated into rings
100 g/4 oz/1 cup Feta cheese,
    cubed
8 black olives
25 ml/1½ tbsp olive oil
15 ml/1 tbsp red wine vinegar
5 ml/1 tsp dried oregano
Salt and freshly ground black
    pepper

Mix the lettuce and cabbage in a large, shallow serving bowl. Scatter the tomatoes, cucumber, onion, cheese and olives over. Drizzle with the oil and vinegar and sprinkle with oregano, salt and pepper.

Rustic Salad

SERVES 4

2 carrots, coarsely grated
½ head celeriac (celery root),
    coarsely grated
2 turnips, coarsely grated
2 courgettes (zucchini), coarsely
    grated
2 cooked beetroot (red beets),
    coarsely grated
4 black olives, stoned (pitted) and
    sliced
1 quantity Spiced Crème Fraîche
    Dressing (see page 354)

Arrange the grated vegetables attractively in piles on serving plates. Scatter with olives. Serve the dressing handed separately.

Avocado and Watercress Salad

SERVES 4

1 bunch of watercress
1 avocado, halved, stoned (pitted)
    and sliced
1 courgette (zucchini), thinly
    sliced
Grated rind and juice of ½ lemon
30 ml/2 tbsp orange juice
5 ml/1 tsp Worcestershire sauce
15 ml/1 tbsp sunflower oil
15 ml/1 tbsp pumpkin seeds

Trim off any feathery stalks from the watercress and separate into small sprigs. Arrange in four small salad bowls. Arrange the avocado and courgette slices over. Whisk together the lemon rind and juice, orange juice, Worcestershire sauce and oil. Drizzle over the salad. Sprinkle with the pumpkin seeds and serve.

Glazed Carrots with Walnuts

SERVES 4

25 g/1 oz/2 tbsp low-fat spread
450 g/1 lb carrots, sliced
10 ml/2 tsp clear honey
2.5 ml/½ tsp salt
300 ml/½ pt/1¼ cups vegetable
    stock, made with 1 stock cube
25 g/1 oz/¼ cup walnuts, roughly
    chopped

Melt the low-fat spread in a saucepan. Add the carrots, honey, salt and stock. Bring to the boil and simmer until the carrots are tender and the stock has evaporated. Stir in the walnuts and heat for 1 minute before serving.

Spinach and Bacon Salad

SERVES 4

1 slice bread, crusts removed
15 g/½ oz/1 tbsp low-fat spread
3 lean rashers (slices) streaky
bacon, rinded and diced
175 g/6 oz young spinach leaves,
torn into pieces
1 small onion, thinly sliced and
separated into rings
A small bunch of flatleaf parsley,
torn
15 ml/1 tbsp olive oil
10 ml/2 tsp red wine vinegar
5 ml/1 tsp Worcestershire sauce
Freshly ground black pepper

Spread the bread with the low-fat spread on both sides and cut into small dice. Fry (sauté) in a frying pan (skillet) until golden on all sides. Drain on kitchen paper. Dry-fry the bacon until crisp. Drain on kitchen paper. Put the spinach in a salad bowl with the onion and parsley. Whisk together the oil, vinegar, Worcestershire sauce and some pepper. Drizzle over the dressing, then scatter with the bread and bacon.

Saucy Broad Beans

SERVES 4

Prepare as for Saucy Runner Beans (see page 277) but substitute shelled broad (lima) beans for the runner beans.

Peasant Salad

SERVES 4

425 g/15 oz/1 large can haricot
(navy) beans, drained, rinsed
and drained again
1 garlic clove, finely chopped
1 green (bell) pepper, chopped
5 cm/2 in piece cucumber, diced
¼ head celeriac (celery root),
grated
2 carrots, grated
15 ml/1 tbsp olive oil
15 ml/1 tbsp white wine vinegar
Salt and freshly ground black
pepper
15 ml/1 tbsp chopped parsley

Put the beans in a bowl with the garlic, green pepper, cucumber, celeriac and carrots. Toss. Whisk the olive oil with the vinegar and some salt and pepper. Pour over, toss and leave to stand for 30 minutes. Toss again, sprinkle with the parsley and serve.

Baby Carrot and Corn Crunch

SERVES 4

225 g/8 oz baby carrots, scrubbed
100 g/4 oz baby corn cobs
25 g/1 oz/¼ cup walnut halves,
roughly chopped
25 g/1 oz/2 tbsp low-fat spread
5 ml/1 tsp lemon juice
Salt and freshly ground black
pepper

Boil the carrots in lightly salted water for about 5 minutes until just tender. Add the corn for the last 2 minutes. Drain and return to the pan. Add the nuts, low-fat spread and lemon juice. Toss and season to taste. Serve hot.

Cabbage with Celery and Walnuts

SERVES 4

4 celery sticks, sliced
450 ml/¾ pt/2 cups chicken or
  vegetable stock, made with
  1 stock cube
½ Savoy cabbage, shredded
50 g/2 oz/½ cup walnut halves
15 ml/1 tbsp chopped parsley

Put the celery in a pan with the stock. Bring to the boil and simmer for 5 minutes. Add the cabbage and walnuts and simmer for a further 5 minutes or until the cabbage is tender. Boil rapidly for a minute or two to evaporate most of the liquid. Serve sprinkled with the parsley.

White Chips

SERVES 4

450 g/1 lb waxy potatoes
5 ml/1 tsp lemon juice
Onion salt
Paprika

Peel the potatoes, slice thickly, then cut each slice into 'chips'. Place in a pan of cold water with the lemon juice. Bring to the boil, reduce the heat and cook over a moderate heat until just tender but still holding their shape. Drain thoroughly. Sprinkle with onion salt and paprika, toss gently and serve.

Baby Potatoes and Onions

SERVES 4

225 g/8 oz button (pearl) onions,
  peeled but left whole
350 g/12 oz baby new potatoes,
  scraped or scrubbed
20 g/¾ oz/1½ tbsp low-fat spread
20 g/¾ oz/3 tbsp plain (all-
  purpose) flour
150 ml/¼ pt/⅔ cup skimmed milk
Salt and freshly ground black
  pepper
30 ml/2 tbsp chopped parsley

Boil the onions and potatoes separately in lightly salted water until tender. Drain the onions, reserving 150 ml/¼ pt/⅔ cup of the cooking water. Drain the potatoes and mix the vegetables together in the potato pan. Keep warm. Melt the low-fat spread in the onion pan and stir in the flour. Cook, stirring, for 1 minute. Remove from the heat and gradually blend in the milk and onion stock. Return to the heat, bring to the boil and cook for 2 minutes, stirring. Season to taste. Pour over the potatoes and onions and toss. Turn into a warmed serving dish, sprinkle with the parsley and serve.

Dieter's Rosti

SERVES 4

450 g/1 lb potatoes, scrubbed
40 g/1½ oz/3 tbsp low-fat spread
1 onion, finely chopped
Salt and freshly ground black
  pepper
To garnish:
Parsley sprigs

Boil the potatoes in their skins until just tender. Drain. When cool enough to handle, peel and coarsely grate. Melt half the low-fat spread in a frying pan (skillet). Add the onion and fry (sauté) for 3 minutes until soft but not browned. Add the potato and some salt and pepper and press down well. Cook over a fairly low heat for about 20 minutes until golden brown. Turn the potato cake out on to a plate. Melt the remaining low-fat spread in the pan. Slide in the Rosti, browned side up, and continue cooking for a further 10 minutes or until golden underneath. Serve in wedges garnished with parsley sprigs.

Stock-roast Potatoes

SERVES 4

450 g/1 lb potatoes, peeled and
  cut into large chunks
450 ml/¾ pt/2 cups beef, chicken
  or vegetable stock, made with 2
  stock cubes

Par-boil the potatoes in lightly salted water for 3 minutes. Drain. Place in a roasting tin (pan) and pour the stock over. Roast at the top of a preheated oven at 190°C/375°F/gas mark 5 for about 1½ hours, basting from time to time with the stock, until browned and tender.

Potato Balls

SERVES 4

450 g/1 lb potatoes, peeled but left
  whole
25 g/1 oz/2 tbsp low-fat spread
1 garlic clove, quartered
Parsley sprigs

Scoop the potato flesh into balls with a melon baller and pat dry on kitchen paper. Melt the low-fat spread in a roasting tin (pan). Add the potato balls and toss to coat. Add the garlic quarters. Bake in a preheated oven at 200°C/400°F/gas mark 6 for about 45 minutes until golden, turning from time to time. Discard the garlic and drain the potatoes on kitchen paper. Garnish with parsley sprigs before serving. (The peeled potatoes left over from preparing Crispy Baked Potato Skins, page 275, are ideal.)

Garlic Potatoes

SERVES 4

450 g/1 lb baby potatoes, scrubbed
25 g/1 oz/2 tbsp low-fat spread
1 garlic clove, crushed
30 ml/2 tbsp chopped parsley
Coarse sea salt

Boil the potatoes in their skins until tender. Drain and return to the pan. Add the low-fat spread, garlic and parsley and toss well to coat. Turn into a warmed serving dish. Sprinkle with the parsley and a little coarse sea salt and serve straight away.

Baby Jackets

SERVES 4

15 g/½ oz/1 tbsp low-fat spread
450 g/1 lb small potatoes,
  scrubbed and dried
7.5 ml/1½ tsp coarse sea salt

Melt the low-fat spread in a roasting tin (pan). Roll the potatoes in it to coat. Bake in a preheated oven at 190°C/375°F/gas mark 5 for about 1 hour or until tender. Sprinkle with the coarse sea salt and serve.

Fluffy Mashed Potatoes

SERVES 4

450 g/1 lb floury potatoes, peeled
  and cut into chunks
15 g/½ oz/1 tbsp low-fat spread
30 ml/2 tbsp skimmed milk
Salt and freshly ground black
  pepper
A pinch of grated nutmeg
  (optional)
Chopped parsley

Boil the potatoes in lightly salted water until really tender. Drain thoroughly. Add the low-fat spread and milk. Using an electric hand mixer, beat the mixture until light and fluffy. Season to taste with salt, pepper and the nutmeg, if liked, and beat briefly again. Pile into a warmed serving dish and garnish with chopped parsley.

Onion-topped Mash

SERVES 4

450 g/1 lb potatoes, cut into
  chunks
2 onions, sliced
25 g/1 oz/2 tbsp low-fat spread
Salt and freshly ground black
  pepper
30 ml/2 tbsp skimmed milk

Boil the potatoes in lightly salted water until tender. Drain and return to the pan. Meanwhile, fry (sauté) the onions in 20 g/¾ oz/1½ tbsp low-fat spread until golden. Remove from the pan with a draining spoon. Drain on kitchen paper. Keep warm. Add any onion cooking juices to the potato with the remaining low-fat spread and the milk. Mash well and add salt and pepper to taste. Pile into a warmed serving dish and top with the onions. Serve hot.

Puréed Potatoes

SERVES 4

450 g/1 lb floury potatoes, cut
  into chunks
Salt and freshly ground black
  pepper
25 g/1 oz/2 tbsp low-fat spread
Paprika

Boil the potatoes in salted water until very tender. Drain thoroughly. Return the potatoes to the heat for a few minutes to remove any moisture. Tip into a blender or food processor. Add some salt and pepper and the low fat spread and run the machine until the mixture is smooth. Spoon on to plates and sprinkle with paprika before serving.

Potato Potch

SERVES 4

2 potatoes, peeled and diced
2 carrots, peeled and diced
1 small swede (rutabaga), peeled
  and diced
25 g/1 oz/2 tbsp low-fat spread
Salt and freshly ground black
  pepper

Boil the vegetables in salted water for 10–15 minutes until really tender. Drain and mash thoroughly with the low-fat spread. Season to taste. Spoon into an ovenproof dish and bake in a preheated oven at 200°C/400°F/gas mark 6 for about 10–15 minutes until a crust forms on top.

Poppy Seed and Oregano Wedges

SERVES 4

450 g/1 lb even-sized potatoes,
  scrubbed
25 g/1 oz/2 tbsp low-fat spread
Salt
15 ml/1 tbsp poppy seeds
2.5 ml/½ tsp dried oregano

Boil the potatoes in their skins (or cook in the microwave) until just tender but not too soft. Drain if necessary. When cool enough to handle, halve, then cut each half into small wedges. Melt the low-fat spread in a roasting tin (pan). Add the potatoes, then turn over in the spread to coat. Sprinkle with salt, then the poppy seeds, then the oregano. Bake at the top of a preheated oven at 200°C/400°F/gas mark 6 for about 20 minutes or until golden. Drain on kitchen paper before serving.

Sesame Seed Wedges

SERVES 4

450 g/1 lb even-sized potatoes,
  scrubbed
25 g/1 oz/2 tbsp low-fat spread
Salt
15 ml/1 tbsp sesame seeds

Boil the potatoes in their skins until just tender but not too soft. Drain if necessary. Halve, then cut each half into fairly small wedges. Melt the low-fat spread in a roasting tin (pan). Add the potatoes, then turn over in the spread to coat. Sprinkle with salt, then the sesame seeds and bake at the top of a preheated oven at 200°C/400°F/gas mark 6 for about 20 minutes or until golden brown. Drain on kitchen paper.

Fennel Potatoes

SERVES 4

2 large even-sized potatoes,
  scrubbed
1 head fennel, quartered
25 g/1 oz/2 tbsp low-fat spread
15 ml/1 tbsp fennel seeds
Salt

Boil the potatoes and fennel in water for 15 minutes until almost tender. Drain and quarter lengthways. Melt the low-fat spread in a roasting tin (pan) and turn the potatoes and fennel in the spread to coat. Sprinkle with the fennel seeds and salt and bake at the top of a preheated oven at 200°C/400°F/gas mark 6 for about 30 minutes or until golden and cooked through. Drain on kitchen paper.

Photograph opposite:
*Avocado and Watercress Salad
(page 283)*

Scalloped Potatoes

SERVES 4

25 g/1 oz/2 tbsp low-fat spread
450 g/1 lb potatoes, thinly sliced
Salt and freshly ground black
    pepper
120 ml/4 fl oz/½ cup skimmed
    milk

Grease four large squares of foil with a little of the low-fat spread. Top with layers of potato, seasoning each layer with salt and pepper. Spoon the milk over and dot with the remaining low-fat spread. Draw the foil up over the potatoes to form parcels, sealing the edges well. Transfer to a baking sheet. Bake in a preheated oven at 190°C/375°F/gas mark 5 for about 1 hour or until the potatoes are tender. Serve straight from the parcels.

Parsleyed Potatoes

SERVES 4

450 g/1 lb small, even-sized new
    potatoes, scraped
15 g/½ oz/1 tbsp low-fat spread
30 ml/2 tbsp chopped parsley

Boil the potatoes in salted water for 10–15 minutes until tender. Drain and place in a warmed serving dish. Add the low-fat spread and parsley, toss and serve.

Herby Potatoes

SERVES 4

Prepare as for Parsleyed Potatoes but use only 15 ml/1 tbsp chopped parsley and add 10 ml/2 tsp chopped thyme and 10 ml/2 tsp chopped mint.

Photograph opposite:
Hot Bulgar Salad (page 297)

Pan Scalloped Potatoes

SERVES 4

450 g/1 lb potatoes, thickly sliced
25 g/1 oz/2 tbsp low-fat spread
Salt and freshly ground black
    pepper
150 ml/¼ pt/⅔ cup skimmed milk
Chopped parsley

Boil the potatoes in lightly salted water for 3 minutes. Drain. Grease a flameproof casserole (Dutch oven) with the low-fat spread. Layer the potatoes in the casserole, seasoning between each layer. Pour over the milk. Cover tightly and cook very gently for about 40 minutes until the potatoes are cooked through. Sprinkle with parsley and serve straight from the casserole.

Creamed Spinach

SERVES 4

450 g/1 lb spinach
25 g/1 oz/2 tbsp low-fat spread
1 garlic clove, crushed
Grated nutmeg
Salt and freshly ground black
    pepper
75 ml/5 tbsp low-fat double
    (heavy) cream

Wash the spinach thoroughly under cold water. Drain thoroughly, tear off any tough stalks and tear the leaves into pieces. Melt the low-fat spread in a saucepan. Add the spinach, garlic, lots of nutmeg and a little salt and pepper. Cover and cook gently for 5 minutes until the spinach is tender. Snip with scissors to chop. Drain off any excess liquid. Stir in the cream until smooth. Taste and re-season if necessary. Reheat and serve.

Fruity Red Cabbage

SERVES 4

450 g/1 lb red cabbage, shredded
1 onion, sliced
1 eating (dessert) apple, sliced
50 g/2 oz/⅓ cup sultanas (golden raisins)
Salt and freshly ground black pepper
30 ml/2 tbsp vinegar
30 ml/2 tbsp water
Artificial sweetener granules
25 g/1 oz/2 tbsp low-fat spread

Layer the cabbage, onion, apple and sultanas in a casserole dish (Dutch oven), seasoning each layer with a little salt and pepper. Mix together the vinegar, water and artificial sweetener to taste and pour over. Dot with the low-fat spread. Cover with a piece of greaseproof (waxed) paper, then the lid. Bake in a preheated oven at 180°C/350°F/ gas mark 4 for about 1–1½ hours until tender. Stir well before serving. (The cabbage can be cooked for longer in a slower oven or quicker in a higher one, depending on what else you are cooking at the same time.)

Polonaise-style Cauliflower and Broccoli

SERVES 4

½ cauliflower, cut into florets
175 g/6 oz broccoli, cut into florets
40 g/1½ oz/3 tbsp low-fat spread
1 garlic clove, crushed
40 g/1½ oz/¾ cup fresh breadcrumbs
15 ml/1 tbsp snipped chives
15 ml/1 tbsp chopped parsley
2 hard-boiled (hard-cooked) eggs, finely chopped

Cook the cauliflower and broccoli in boiling, lightly salted water until just tender. Drain and place in a warmed serving dish. Meanwhile, melt the low-fat spread in a small saucepan. Fry (sauté) the garlic for 30 seconds until turning lightly golden. Add the breadcrumbs and fry quickly until golden. Stir in the herbs and eggs. Sprinkle over the vegetables are serve straight away. (You can omit the broccoli and use all cauliflower if you prefer.)

French-style Peas

SERVES 4

½ round lettuce, shredded
1 bunch of spring onions
    (scallions), cut into short
    lengths
5 ml/1 tsp chopped mint
5 ml/1 tsp chopped parsley
450 g/1 lb/4 cups frozen peas
150 ml/¼ pt/⅔ cup vegetable stock,
    made with ½ stock cube
40 g/1½ oz/3 tbsp low-fat spread
Salt and freshly ground black
    pepper
A few grains of artificial sweetener
Chopped parsley

Put the lettuce in a pan with the spring onions, chopped herbs, peas, stock and low-fat spread. Sprinkle with a little salt and pepper and a very few grains of sweetener. Bring to the boil, cover tightly and simmer for 30 minutes. Serve garnished with chopped parsley

Oriental Rice and Peas

SERVES 4

175 g/6 oz/¾ cup Thai fragrant rice
75 g/3 oz/¾ cup frozen peas
1.5 ml/¼ tsp ground ginger
30 ml/2 tbsp light soy sauce
2 spring onions (scallions),
    chopped

Cook the rice according to the packet directions, adding the peas for the last 5 minutes' cooking time. Drain and return to the pan. Add the ginger and soy sauce, toss and serve garnished with the spring onions.

Bacon and Onion Topped Tomatoes

SERVES 4

450 g/1 lb tomatoes, skinned and
    sliced
1 bunch of spring onions
    (scallions), finely chopped
4 lean rashers (slices) streaky
    bacon, rinded and chopped
Salt and freshly ground black
    pepper
15 ml/1 tbsp chopped basil
15 ml/1 tbsp chopped parsley

Lay the tomatoes in a shallow ovenproof dish. Dry-fry (sauté) the spring onions and bacon in a frying pan (skillet) for 2 minutes, stirring. Sprinkle the tomatoes with salt and pepper, then scatter the bacon and onion over. Bake in a preheated oven at 180°C/350°F/gas mark 4 for 15 minutes. Sprinkle with the herbs and serve.

Savoury Vegetable Rice

SERVES 4

175 g/6 oz/¾ cup long-grain rice
225 g/8 oz packet frozen diced
    mixed vegetables
450 ml/¾ pt/2 cups vegetable
    stock, made with 1 stock cube
A pinch of curry powder
Salt and freshly ground black
    pepper

Put the rice and vegetables in a
saucepan. Add the stock, curry
powder and a little salt and pepper.
Bring to the boil, reduce the heat,
cover and simmer gently for 20 minutes until the rice is cooked and has
absorbed all the liquid. Serve piping
hot.

Brussels Sprouts with Almonds

SERVES 4

450 g/1 lb Brussels sprouts
25 g/1 oz/¼ cup flaked (slivered)
    almonds
25 g/1 oz/2 tbsp low-fat spread
Salt and freshly ground black
    pepper

Trim the sprouts and cut a small
cross cut in the base of each. Boil
in salted water for 5 minutes or until
just tender but still with some 'bite'.
Drain. Meanwhile, fry (sauté) the
almonds in the low-fat spread until
golden. Put the sprouts in a serving
dish. Pour the almond 'butter' over
and season with salt and pepper. Toss
gently and serve.

SUMPTUOUS SALADS & SIDE DISHES

250

CALORIES OR LESS

Nutty Rice Salad

SERVES 4

175 g/6 oz/¾ cup long-grain rice
50 g/2 oz/½ cup frozen peas
50 g/2 oz/⅓ cup raisins
50 g/2 oz/½ cup toasted flaked
    (slivered) almonds
30 ml/2 tbsp sunflower oil
15 ml/1 tbsp white wine vinegar
Salt and freshly ground black
    pepper
Chopped parsley

Cook the rice according to the packet directions. Add the peas for the
last 5 minutes' cooking time. Drain,
rinse with cold water and drain again.
Empty into a salad bowl. Add the
raisins, nuts, oil, vinegar and some
salt and pepper. Toss well and serve
garnished with parsley.

Crunchy-topped Tagliatelle

SERVES 4

225 g/8 oz tagliatelle
25 g/1 oz/½ cup fresh breadcrumbs
25 g/1 oz/2 tbsp low-fat spread
2.5 ml/½ tsp garlic powder
Salt and freshly ground black
pepper

Cook the pasta according to the packet directions. Drain and return to the saucepan. Meanwhile, melt the low-fat spread in a frying pan (skillet). Add the breadcrumbs, garlic powder and a little salt and pepper. Fry (sauté), stirring, until golden brown and crisp. Add to the tagliatelle, toss and serve straight away.

Garlic Bread

SERVES 4

1 small French stick
75 g/3 oz/⅓ cup low-fat spread
1 garlic clove, crushed
15 ml/1 tbsp chopped parsley

Cut the bread into eight slices, not quite through the base. Mash the low-fat spread with the garlic and parsley. Spread between the cuts. Spread any remainder over the top. Wrap in foil and bake in a preheated oven at 200°C/400°F/gas mark 6 for about 15 minutes or until the crust is crisp and the centre feels soft when squeezed. Serve hot.

Hot Herb Bread

SERVES 4

1 small French stick
75 g/3 oz/⅓ cup low-fat spread
15 ml/1 tbsp chopped parsley
15 ml/1 tbsp chopped basil
15 ml/1 tbsp chopped thyme
Freshly ground black pepper

Cut the bread into eight slices, not quite through the base. Mash the low-fat spread with the herbs and some pepper. Spread between the cuts. Spread any remainder on the top. Wrap in foil and bake in a preheated oven at 200°C/400°F/gas mark 6 for about 15 minutes until the crust is crisp and the centre is soft when squeezed. Serve hot.

Hot Walnut Bread

SERVES 4

1 small French stick
75 g/3 oz/⅓ cup low-fat spread
20 ml/4 tsp chopped walnuts
15 ml/1 tbsp chopped parsley
Salt and freshly ground black
  pepper

Cut the bread into eight slices, not quite through the base. Mash the low-fat spread with the walnuts, parsley and a little salt and pepper. Spread between the slices. Wrap in foil and bake in a preheated oven at 200°C/400°F/gas mark 6 for about 15 minutes until the crust is crisp and the centre is soft when squeezed. Serve hot.

Dauphine Potatoes

SERVES 4

450 g/1 lb potatoes, thinly sliced
1 garlic clove, crushed
75 g/3 oz/¾ cup Emmental (Swiss)
  cheese, grated
Salt and freshly ground black
  pepper
1 large egg
120 ml/4 fl oz/½ cup skimmed milk
120 ml/4 fl oz/½ cup low-fat single
  (light) cream
A pinch of grated nutmeg

Boil the potatoes in lightly salted water for 2 minutes. Drain. Layer the potatoes, garlic, cheese and some salt and pepper in a fairly shallow ovenproof dish. Finish with a layer of cheese. Beat the egg with the milk and cream and pour over. Sprinkle with the nutmeg. Bake in a preheated oven at 180°C/350°F/gas mark 4 for about 1 hour or until golden, set and tender.

Almost Fried Rice

SERVES 4

175 g/6 oz/¾ cup long-grain rice
25 g/1 oz/2 tbsp low-fat spread
50 g/2 oz/½ cup frozen peas
1 egg, beaten
A dash of soy sauce
A pinch of Chinese five spice
  powder

Cook the rice according to the packet directions. Drain. Melt the low-fat spread in a frying pan (skillet). Add the rice and peas and cook, stirring, for 4 minutes. Push to one side. Break the egg into the space in the pan. Cook until almost set, then gradually stir into the rice. Sprinkle with the soy sauce and five spice powder and serve hot.

Almost Fried Rice with Bean Sprouts

SERVES 4

Prepare as for Almost Fried Rice but, while the rice is frying, put 175 g/6 oz bean sprouts in a separate pan with 15 ml/1 tbsp soy sauce and heat, tossing and stirring, for 3 minutes. Spoon round the edge of a warm serving dish and pile the rice in the centre.

Cheesy-topped Rice

SERVES 4

175 g/6 oz/¾ cup long-grain rice
Salt and freshly ground black
pepper
15 ml/1 tbsp very low-fat fromage
frais
50 g/2 oz/½ cup low-fat Cheddar
cheese, grated
15 ml/1 tbsp grated Parmesan
cheese

Cook the rice according to the packet directions in a flameproof casserole (Dutch oven). Drain and return to the pan. Stir in a little salt and pepper and the fromage frais. Mix the Cheddar and Parmesan together and sprinkle over. Flash under a hot grill (broiler) until the cheese melts and bubbles.

Tomato Potatoes

SERVES 4

450 g/1 lb potatoes, cut into
chunks
400 g/14 oz/1 large can chopped
tomatoes
2.5 ml/½ tsp dried mixed herbs
25 g/1oz/½ cup fresh breadcrumbs
50 g/2 oz/½ cup low-fat Cheddar
cheese, grated

Cook the potatoes in boiling, salted water for about 10 minutes until tender. Drain and arrange in an ovenproof dish. Pour the tomatoes over and sprinkle with the herbs. Mix together the breadcrumbs and cheese and sprinkle over. Bake in a preheated oven at 190°C/375°F/gas mark 5 for 25 minutes until golden and bubbling.

Potato Pudding

SERVES 4

750 g/1½ lb potatoes, peeled and
grated
1 egg, beaten
Salt and freshly ground black
pepper
30 ml/2 tbsp chopped parsley
5 ml/1 tsp low-fat spread

Mix the potatoes, egg, some salt and pepper and the parsley together. Grease an ovenproof dish with the low-fat spread. Add the potato mixture and bake in a preheated oven at 180°C/350°F/gas mark 4 for 1 hour until cooked through and golden on the top.

Caraway Noodles

SERVES 4

225 g/8 oz tagliatelle
Salt and freshly ground black
pepper
25 g/1 oz/2 tbsp low-fat spread
30 ml/2 tbsp caraway seeds

Cook the tagliatelle according to the packet directions. Drain and return to the saucepan. Season with a very little salt and lots of pepper. Add the low-fat spread and caraway seeds. Toss over a gentle heat, then serve.

Yellow Rice

SERVES 4

225 g/8 oz/1 cup basmati rice
450 ml/¾ pt/2 cups water
1 garlic clove, crushed
10 ml/2 tsp grated lemon rind
10 ml/2 tsp turmeric
50 g/2 oz creamed coconut,
   crumbled
Salt and freshly ground black
   pepper

Wash the rice well, then drain. Place in a pan with the water, garlic, lemon rind and turmeric. Bring to the boil, reduce the heat and simmer until tender and the liquid is absorbed. Stir in the coconut until melted and season to taste.

Tomato Rice

SERVES 4

175 g/6 oz/¾ cup long-grain rice
1 onion, chopped
1 green (bell) pepper, chopped
25 g/1 oz/2 tbsp low-fat spread
400 g/14 oz/1 large can chopped
   tomatoes
Salt and freshly ground black pepper
A few grains of artificial sweetener
1 bay leaf
8 stuffed olives, sliced

Boil the rice in plenty of lightly salted water for 5 minutes. Drain. Meanwhile, fry (sauté) the onion and pepper in the low-fat spread in a saucepan for 2 minutes. Add the tomatoes, a little salt and pepper and sweetener, the bay leaf and rice. Bring to the boil, reduce the heat, cover and cook gently for 15 minutes until the liquid is absorbed and the rice is tender, stirring occasionally to prevent sticking. Discard the bay leaf, stir in the olives and serve.

Herby Pasta

SERVES 4

225 g/8 oz rigatoni or other pasta
   shapes
40 g/1½ oz/3 tbsp low-fat spread
15 ml/1 tbsp chopped basil
15 ml/1 tbsp chopped parsley
15 ml/1 tbsp chopped oregano
Salt and freshly ground black
   pepper
30 ml/2 tbsp grated Parmesan
   cheese

Cook the pasta according to the packet directions. Drain and return to the pan. Add the low-fat spread, the herbs, some salt and pepper and the Parmesan. Toss thoroughly and serve.

Golden Rice

SERVES 4

175 g/6 oz/¾ cup long-grain rice
1 vegetable stock cube
5 ml/1 tsp turmeric
200 g/7 oz/1 can sweetcorn (corn)
1 yellow (bell) pepper, finely diced
2 spring onions (scallions), finely
   chopped
Salt and freshly ground black
   pepper
Chopped parsley

Cook the rice in plenty of boiling water to which the crumbled stock cube and turmeric have been added. Drain and return to the pan. Add the remaining ingredients except the parsley. Cover with a lid and leave to stand for 5 minutes. Fluff up and serve garnished with parsley.

Nutty Wild Rice Mix

SERVES 4

175 g/6 oz/¾ cup wild rice mix
50 g/2 oz/½ cup frozen peas
40 g/1½ oz/3 tbsp low-fat spread
50 g/2 oz/½ cup toasted mixed nuts
15 ml/1 tbsp chopped thyme
Salt and freshly ground black
    pepper

Cook the rice according to the packet directions, adding the peas for the last 5 minutes' cooking time. Drain and return to the pan. Add the low-fat spread, nuts and thyme and season to taste with salt and pepper. Toss well and serve.

Mushroom Wild Rice Mix

SERVES 4

175 g/6 oz/¾ cup wild rice mix
100 g/4 oz mixed oyster
    mushrooms
1 garlic clove, crushed
40 g/1½ oz/3 tbsp low-fat spread
30 ml/2 tbsp low-fat single (light)
    cream
Salt and freshly ground black
    pepper
Chopped parsley

Cook the rice according to the packet directions. Drain and return to the pan. Meanwhile, slice the mushrooms and fry (sauté) gently with the garlic in the low-fat spread for 4 minutes until tender. Stir in the cream. Add to the rice, toss and season to taste. Garnish with parsley before serving.

Hot Bulgar Salad

SERVES 4

100 g/4 oz/1 cup bulgar wheat
250 ml/8 fl oz/1 cup boiling water
5 ml/1 tsp salt
30 ml/2 tbsp olive oil
30 ml/2 tbsp lemon juice
1 garlic clove, finely chopped
30 ml/2 tbsp chopped parsley
15 ml/1 tbsp chopped mint
5 ml/1 tsp chopped coriander
    (cilantro)
3 tomatoes, chopped
5 cm/2 in piece cucumber, chopped
1 green (bell) pepper, chopped
4 black olives, stoned (pitted) and
    halved
A few coriander leaves, torn

Put the bulgar in a pan. Add the boiling water and sprinkle with the salt. Stir and leave to stand for 20 minutes until the wheat has absorbed all the water. Add the oil, lemon juice, garlic, herbs, tomatoes, cucumber and green pepper. Toss over a gentle heat for 1 minute. Pile on to plates and garnish with the olives and torn coriander leaves before serving. (This is also delicious cold. Just soak the wheat and add the flavourings except the salad ingredients. Chill overnight, then add the tomatoes, cucumber, pepper and the garnish before serving.)

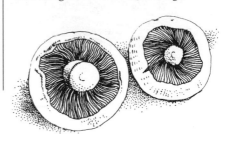

Mexican Rice

SERVES 4

25 g/1 oz/2 tbsp low-fat spread
1 garlic clove, crushed
1 small red (bell) pepper, diced
1 small green (bell) pepper, diced
½ bunch spring onions (scallions),
    chopped
1 carrot, diced
100 g/4 oz/½ cup brown rice
2.5 ml/½ tsp chilli powder
375 g/13 fl oz/1½ cups vegetable
    stock, made with 1 stock cube
Salt and freshly ground black
    pepper
1 banana, cut into chunks
Parsley sprigs

Melt half the low-fat spread in a saucepan. Add the garlic, peppers, spring onions and carrot and fry (sauté) for 2 minutes, stirring. Add the rice and chilli powder and cook for 1 minute. Add the stock and some salt and pepper. Bring to the boil, cover, reduce the heat and cook very gently for 35 minutes until the rice is just tender and has absorbed the liquid. Add a little water during cooking if necessary. Fry the banana chunks in the remaining low-fat spread for 2 minutes. Pile the rice on to warmed serving dishes. Top with the banana and serve garnished with parsley sprigs.

Heavenly Hot Desserts

All these desserts are delicious on their own and if a serving suggestion is given, it is included in the calorie count. But if you want to have a little extra diet Ice Cream (bought or home-made, see page 335), very low-fat crème fraîche, fromage frais or yoghurt or low-fat single (light) cream add on an extra 50 calories to be on the safe side.

CALORIES OR LESS

Sloshed Pears

SERVES 4

4 pears, peeled but left whole
300 ml/½ pt/1¼ cups red wine
5 ml/1 tsp lemon juice
Artificial sweetener granules

Cut a small slice off the bottom of each pear so it stands upright. Place in a casserole dish (Dutch oven). Add the wine, lemon juice and artificial sweetener to taste. Cover and poach in a preheated oven at 160°C/325°F/gas mark 3 for 30–40 minutes. Serve hot.

Mulled Pears

SERVES 4

Prepare as for Sloshed Pears but add a piece of cinnamon stick, 2 whole cloves and 15 ml/1 tbsp brandy to the liquid before cooking.

Apple Amber

SERVES 4

450 g/1 lb cooking (tart) apples,
** sliced**
30 ml/2 tbsp water
1 whole clove (optional)
Artificial sweetener granules
2 eggs, separated

Put the apples in a saucepan with the water and clove, if using. Simmer until pulpy. Remove the clove. Beat well and sweeten to taste with artificial sweetener. Beat in the egg yolks. Turn into an ovenproof dish and bake in a preheated oven at 180°C/350°F/gas mark 4 for about 30 minutes until just set. Meanwhile, whisk the egg whites until stiff. Whisk in 7.5 g/1½ tsp artificial sweetener granules, a little at a time. Pile on top of the apple and return to the oven for about 20 minutes until just turning golden. Serve warm.

Cidered Apples

SERVES 4

**4 soft eating (dessert) apples,
  peeled and cored
300 ml/½ pt/1¼ cups cider
10 ml/2 tsp lemon juice
1.5 ml/¼ tsp mixed (apple-pie)
  spice
Artificial sweetener granules**

Place the apples in a casserole (Dutch oven) and pour the cider over. Add the lemon juice, spice and sweetener to taste. Cover and bake in a preheated oven at 160ºC/325ºF/gas mark 3 for 40 minutes until the apples are tender, basting once during cooking.

Poached Elderflower Nectarines

SERVES 4

**4 ripe nectarines, peeled
30 ml/2 tbsp elderflower cordial
300 ml/½ pt/1¼ cups water
5 ml/1 tsp lemon juice
Artificial sweetener granules
  (optional)**

Put the nectarines in a casserole (Dutch oven). Stir the cordial into the water with the lemon juice. Add a few grains of sweetener if necessary. Pour around the nectarines, cover and bake in a preheated oven at 160ºC/325ºF/gas mark 3 for about 30 minutes until the fruit is just tender.

Poached Peaches in Wine

SERVES 4

**5 ml/1 tsp lemon juice
300 ml/½ pt/1¼ cups dry white
  wine
Artificial sweetener granules
4 peaches, peeled**

Mix the lemon juice and wine with sweetener to taste in a casserole (Dutch oven). Add the fruit. Cover and poach in a preheated oven at 160ºC/325ºF/gas mark 3 for about 30 minutes until the fruit is just tender.

Strawberry Baked Apples

SERVES 4

**4 cooking (tart) apples
40 ml/8 tsp reduced-sugar
  strawberry jam (conserve)
Artificial sweetener granules**

Remove the cores from the apples and cut a line round the centre of the fruit to prevent the skin from bursting. Place in an ovenproof dish. Fill the centres with reduced-sugar strawberry jam and sprinkle with a little artificial sweetener. Add about 2.5 cm/1 in of water to the dish. Bake in a preheated oven at 180ºC/350ºF/gas mark 4 for about 1 hour or until tender but still holding their shape.

Christmas Apples

SERVES 4

Prepare as for Strawberry Baked Apples but substitute mincemeat for the strawberry jam (conserve).

Californian Baked Pears

SERVES 4

4 firm pears
25 g/1 oz/2 tbsp low-fat spread
5 ml/1 tsp artificial sweetener
granules
Grated rind of ½ lemon
300 g/11 oz/1 small can fruit
cocktail in natural juice
1.5 ml/¼ tsp mixed (apple-pie) spice

Peel the pears but leave whole. Melt the low-fat spread in a flameproof casserole (Dutch oven). Add the sweetener and lemon rind and turn the fruit in this mixture. Cover and bake in a preheated oven at 190°C/375°F/gas mark 5 for 30 minutes. Add the can of fruit cocktail and sprinkle with the spice. Return to the oven for 10 minutes. Lift the pears out on to warmed plates. Stir the fruit cocktail well into the pan juices. Spoon around the pears and serve.

Grilled Pink Grapefruit

SERVES 4

2 pink grapefruit
5 ml/1 tsp artificial sweetener
granules
4 small scoops virtually fat-free
vanilla ice or home-made Vanilla
Ice Cream (see page 335)

Halve the grapefruit and cut round the edge of each between the pith and the flesh. Then separate each segment either side of each membrane, using a serrated-edged knife. Sprinkle each with a few grains of sweetener. Place in individual flameproof dishes and stand them on the grill (broiler) rack. Grill (broil) for 2–3 minutes until lightly browning. Put a small scoop of vanilla ice or Ice Cream on each and serve straight away.

Heady Grilled Oranges

SERVES 4

2 large oranges
20 ml/4 tsp Cointreau or other
orange liqueur
4 small scoops virtually fat-free
vanilla ice or home-made Vanilla
Ice Cream (see page 335)

Halve the oranges and cut round the edge of each between the pith and the flesh. Then separate each segment either side of each membrane, using a serrated-edged knife. Place in individual flameproof serving dishes and sprinkle the liqueur over each. Grill (broil) for 2–3 minutes until lightly browning. Top with a small scoop of vanilla ice or Ice Cream and serve straight away.

Hot Gingered Melon

SERVES 4

1 honeydew melon
15 ml/1 tbsp grated fresh root
ginger
120 ml/4 fl oz/½ cup dry white
wine
1 piece of cinnamon stick
Artificial sweetener granules
20 ml/4 tsp very low-fat fromage
frais

Halve the melon, remove the seeds, cut into eight wedges and peel. Put the ginger, wine and cinnamon in a saucepan and sweeten to taste with artificial sweetener. Bring to the boil and simmer for 2 minutes. Add the melon and simmer for a further 2 minutes. Carefully lift the melon out on to warmed serving plates. Keep warm. Boil the liquid rapidly until reduced by half. Spoon over the melon and put a spoonful of fromage frais to one side.

Grapefruit in Apricot Brandy

SERVES 4

3 grapefruit
100 ml/3½ fl oz/6½ tbsp apple juice
7.5 ml/1½ tsp artificial sweetener granules
2.5 cm/1 in piece cinnamon stick
45 ml/3 tbsp apricot brandy
3 ready-to-eat dried apricots, chopped
1 small piece angelica, chopped

Cut off all the rind and pith from the grapefruit over a shallow pan to catch any juice. Push out the white core using the handle of a teaspoon. Thickly slice the fruit. Put the apple juice and artificial sweetener in the pan with the cinnamon stick. Bring to the boil and simmer for 3 minutes. Add the fruit and simmer for 6–8 minutes. Remove the fruit from the pan and transfer to warmed plates. Add the apricot brandy to the juice. Bring to the boil, spoon over the fruit and sprinkle with the chopped apricots and angelica.

Zabaglione

SERVES 4

2 eggs
2.5 ml/½ tsp artificial sweetener granules
45 ml/3 tbsp Marsala or sweet sherry

Put the ingredients in a fairly large bowl over a pan of hot water. Whisk until thick, frothy and pale. Taste and whisk in a little more sweetener, if liked. Spoon into dishes and serve straight away. (A balloon whisk will give the best volume, but an electric hand mixer is much easier!)

Hot Orange Soufflés

SERVES 4

A very little low-fat spread, for greasing
1 large orange
20 g/¾ oz/1½ tbsp low-fat spread
20 g/¾ oz/3 tbsp plain (all-purpose) flour
150 ml/¼ pt/⅔ cup skimmed milk
Artificial sweetener granules
2 eggs, separated

Grease four individual ramekins (custard cups) with the low-fat spread. Grate the rind from the orange. Pare off all the pith and cut the flesh into small pieces. Put the fruit and any juice in the prepared dishes. Stand them on a baking sheet. Put the measured low-fat spread in a saucepan with the flour and milk. Whisk until smooth, then bring to the boil and cook for 1 minute, whisking all the time, until thick. Remove from the heat and beat in the orange rind, sweetener to taste and egg yolks. Whisk the egg whites until stiff. Fold into the mixture with a metal spoon. Spoon into the dishes and bake in a preheated oven at 200°C/400°F/gas mark 6 for about 15–20 minutes until well risen and golden. Dust with a little sweetener and serve immediately.

Bananas with Hot Lemon Sauce

SERVES 4

15 g/½ oz/1 tbsp low-fat spread
10 ml/2 tsp artificial sweetener
   granules
15ml/1 tbsp cornflour (cornstarch)
Grated rind and juice of ½ lemon
4 small bananas
300 ml/½ pt/1¼ cups very low-fat
   plain yoghurt
Ground cinnamon

Put the low-fat spread, sweetener and cornflour in a saucepan. Make the lemon juice up to 150 ml/¼ pt/⅔ cup with water. Stir into the pan. Bring to the boil and cook, stirring, for 2 minutes. Peel and slice the bananas. Spoon the yoghurt into four small dishes. Top with the bananas. Spoon the hot sauce over and dust with cinnamon. Serve straight away.

Tropical Passion Soufflés

SERVES 4

A little low-fat spread, for
   greasing
2 ripe bananas
4 passion fruit
30 ml/2 tbsp very low-fat crème
   fraîche
Artificial sweetener granules
3 egg whites

Grease four good-sized ramekins (custard cups) with the low-fat spread. Purée the bananas in a blender or mash thoroughly with a fork until smooth. Stir in the passion fruit pulp, crème fraîche and sweetener to taste. Whisk the egg whites until stiff and fold into the mixture with a metal spoon. Turn into the ramekins. Place on a baking sheet. Bake in a preheated oven at 200°C/400°F/gas mark 6 for about 15–20 minutes until well risen and golden. Dust with a little sweetener and serve immediately.

Jamaican Bananas

SERVES 4

1 orange
30 ml/2 tbsp cocoa (unsweetened
  chocolate) powder
2.5 ml/½ tsp artificial sweetener
  granules
2.5 ml/½ tsp vanilla essence
  (extract)
30 ml/2 tbsp rum or orange
  liqueur
4 small bananas

Pare off half the rind from the
orange and cut into thin strips. Boil
in water for 2 minutes, drain, rinse
with cold water, drain again and dry
on kitchen paper. Grate the remaining
orange rind and squeeze out all the
juice. Place in a saucepan with the
cocoa, sweetener, vanilla essence and
rum or liqueur. Heat gently, stirring,
until blended. Peel and cut the
bananas into chunks. Add to the mixture and toss gently. Cover with a lid
or foil and cook gently for 4 minutes
until the bananas are just cooked but
not too soft. Spoon into serving dishes and decorate with the strips of
orange rind.

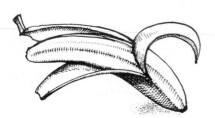

Rum Soufflé

SERVES 4

150 ml/¼ pt/⅔ cup skimmed milk
15 ml/1 tbsp cornflour
  (cornstarch)
25 g/1 oz/2 tbsp low-fat spread
Artificial sweetener granules
30 ml/2 tbsp rum
3 eggs, separated

Put the milk in a saucepan with the
cornflour and whisk until smooth.
Add the low-fat spread, bring to the
boil and cook for 2 minutes until thick
and smooth. Remove from the heat
and add sweetener to taste, the rum
and egg yolks. Beat well. Whisk the egg
whites until stiff. Fold into the mixture
with a metal spoon. Turn into an 18
cm/7 in soufflé dish and bake in a preheated oven at 190°C/375°F/gas mark
5 for about 25 minutes until well risen
and golden. Dust with a little extra
sweetener and serve immediately.

Baked Bananas in Rum

SERVES 4

25 g/1 oz/2 tbsp low-fat spread
5 ml/1 tsp artificial sweetener
  granules
30 ml/2 tbsp rum
4 bananas, halved lengthways

Heat the low-fat spread in a flameproof casserole (Dutch oven). Stir
in the sweetener and rum. Add the
bananas and turn in the mixture to
coat well. Cover and bake in a preheated oven at 180°C/350°F/gas mark
4 for 25 minutes.

Baked Stuffed Peaches

SERVES 4

4 ripe peaches, halved and stoned (pitted)
300 g/11 oz/1 small can raspberries in natural juice, drained and juice reserved
5 ml/1 tsp artificial sweetener granules
15 ml/1 tbsp desiccated (shredded) coconut
15 ml/1 tbsp breadcrumbs
10 ml/2 tsp low-fat spread

Place the peaches, cut sides up, in a shallow ovenproof dish. Drain the raspberries and put the fruit in the cavities. Pour the juice around. Mix the sweetener with the coconut and breadcrumbs. Sprinkle on top of the peaches and dot with the low-fat spread. Bake in a preheated oven at 190°C/375°F/gas mark 5 for about 25 minutes until hot through and the tops are turning brown.

Prune, Pear and Orange Compote

SERVES 4

1 orange
100 g/4 oz no-need-to-soak prunes
3 firm pears, peeled, quartered and cored
150 ml/¼ pt/⅔ cup cold black tea
150 ml/¼ pt/⅔ cup white wine
30 ml/2 tbsp reduced-sugar apricot jam (conserve)

Pare half the rind off the orange and cut into thin strips. Boil in water for 2 minutes. Drain, rinse with cold water, drain again and dry on kitchen paper. Cut off all the remaining rind and pith. Cut into slices and halve each slice. Place in a saucepan with the prunes and pears. Add the tea, wine and jam. Bring to the boil, reduce the heat, part-cover and simmer until tender. Serve sprinkled with the orange rind.

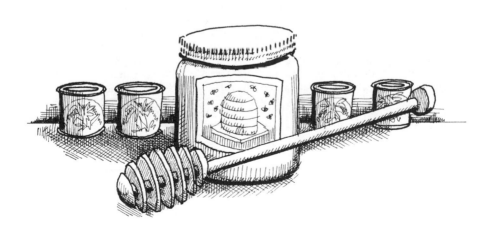

Hot Chocolate Custard

SERVES 4

30 ml/2 tbsp cornflour
(cornstarch)
45 ml/3 tbsp cocoa (unsweetened
chocolate) powder
600 ml/1 pt/2½ cups skimmed
milk
Artificial sweetener granules

Blend the cornflour and cocoa with
a little of the milk in a saucepan.
Stir in the remaining milk. Bring to the
boil and cook for 3 minutes, stirring
until smooth and thick. Sweeten to
taste. Spoon into individual serving
dishes and serve straight away.

Jam Soufflé Omelette

SERVES 2

1 large egg, separated
Artificial sweetener granules
15 ml/1 tbsp water
A little low-fat spread
20 ml/4 tsp reduced-sugar jam
(conserve)

Beat the yolk with a pinch of artificial sweetener granules and the
water. Whisk the egg white until stiff
and fold into the mixture with a metal
spoon. Melt a little low-fat spread in a
small frying pan (skillet). Add half the
mixture and fry (sauté) until the base
is golden brown. Place the pan under a
hot grill (broiler) until golden, risen
and just firm. Quickly spread with half
the jam. Fold over, dust with a little
extra sweetener and serve. Repeat
with the remaining mixture.

Fresh Strawberry Soufflé Omelette

SERVES 2

Prepare as for Jam Soufflé Omelette
but substitute 100 g/4 oz sliced
strawberries for the jam (conserve).

Apple Soufflé Omelette

SERVES 2

Prepare as for Jam Soufflé Omelette
but stew 1 peeled and chopped
cooking (tart) apple in 10 ml/2 tsp
water until soft and pulpy. Sweeten to
taste with artificial sweetener and a
pinch of ground cinnamon. Use this
mixture to spread over the cooked
omelette instead of jam (conserve).

Raspberry Heaven

SERVES 4

350 g/12 oz raspberries
5 ml/1 tsp artificial sweetener (or
to taste)
2 eggs, separated

Mash the raspberries thoroughly
and mix with the sweetener and
egg yolks. Whisk the egg whites until
stiff and fold into the mixture with a
metal spoon. Turn into an ovenproof
serving dish. Bake in a preheated oven
at 200°C/400°F/gas mark 6 for about
25 minutes until risen and golden.
Serve straight away.

Strawberry Heaven

SERVES 4

Prepare as for Raspberry Heaven but substitute strawberries for the raspberries.

Blackcurrant Heaven

SERVES 4

Prepare as for Raspberry Heaven but substitute blackcurrants for the raspberries. Stew them in a saucepan for 3 minutes until the juice runs, before crushing and sweetening to taste.

Hot Mocha Custard

SERVES 4

30 ml/2 tbsp cornflour
(cornstarch)
30 ml/2 tbsp cocoa (unsweetened
chocolate) powder
300 ml/½ pt/1¼ cups skimmed
milk
300 ml/½ pt/1¼ cups strong black
coffee
Artificial sweetener granules

Put the cornflour and cocoa in a pan with a little of the milk and blend until smooth. Blend in the remaining milk and the coffee. Bring to the boil and cook for 3 minutes, stirring, until thick and smooth. Sweeten to taste. Spoon into serving dishes and serve straight away.

Blackberry and Apple Compote

SERVES 4

2 cooking (tart) apples, sliced
225 g/8 oz ripe blackberries
150 ml/¼ pt/⅔ cup water
1 slice orange
Artificial sweetener granules
To serve:
Basic Sweet White Sauce
(see page 359)

Put the apples and blackberries in a pan with the water and orange slice. Bring to the boil, reduce the heat and cook gently for about 5 minutes until the fruit is tender but still holds its shape. Discard the orange slice. Sweeten to taste with artificial sweetener. Serve hot with Basic Sweet White Sauce.

Baked Satsumas in Brandy

SERVES 4

45 ml/3 tbsp orange juice
5 ml/1 tsp artificial sweetener
granules
25 g/1 oz/2 tbsp low-fat spread
30 ml/2 tbsp brandy
8 small satsumas or clementines,
peeled and all pith removed

Put the orange juice, sweetener, low-fat spread and brandy in a flameproof casserole dish (Dutch oven). Bring to the boil and simmer for 2 minutes. Add the fruit and turn in the liquid. Cover and bake in a preheated oven at 180ºC/350ºF/gas mark 4 for about 30 minutes until just cooked, spooning the juices over twice during cooking.

Hot Strawberry Roll

SERVES 6

175 g/6 oz strawberries
2.5 ml/½ tsp lemon juice
Artificial sweetener granules
2 eggs
50 g/2 oz/½ cup plain (all-purpose)
flour
15 ml/1 tbsp hot water
30 ml/2 tbsp reduced-sugar
strawberry jam (conserve)

Purée the strawberries in a blender or food processor. Turn into a small saucepan and add the lemon juice. Sweeten to taste with a little sweetener. Heat through. Dampen an 18 x 28 cm/ 7 x 11 in Swiss roll tin (jelly roll pan) and line with non-stick baking parchment. Break the eggs in a bowl, add 10 ml/2 tsp artificial sweetener granules, place over a pan of gently simmering water and whisk until thick and pale. Sift the flour over the surface and fold in with a metal spoon, adding the hot water. Turn into the prepared tin and gently spread out evenly. Bake in a preheated oven at 200°C/400°F/ gas mark 6 for 8–10 minutes until golden and the centre springs back when pressed with a finger. Turn out on to a clean sheet of baking parchment and spread quickly with the jam. Make a mark with the back of a knife about 1 cm/½ in from one short end. Fold this over firmly, then roll up with the help of the baking parchment. Cut into six slices. Transfer to warmed plates. Spoon the warm strawberry sauce to one side and serve.

Hot Raspberry Roll

SERVES 6

Prepare as for Hot Strawberry Roll but use reduced-sugar raspberry jam (conserve) and fresh raspberries instead of strawberry jam and strawberries.

Hot Apricot Roll

SERVES 6

Prepare as for Hot Strawberry Roll but use reduced-sugar apricot jam (conserve) instead of strawberry jam and purée 320 g/11 oz/1 small can apricots in natural juice instead of the fresh strawberries. Omit the lemon juice.

Rhubarb and Orange Layer

SERVES 4

1 orange
450g/1 lb rhubarb, trimmed and
cut into short lengths
150 ml/1¼ pt/⅔ cup water
Artificial sweetener granules
30 ml/2 tbsp cornflour
(cornstarch)
Skimmed milk

Thinly pare the rind off half the orange. Cut into thin strips and boil in water for 2 minutes. Drain, rinse with cold water, drain again and dry on kitchen paper. Finely grate the remaining orange rind and squeeze the juice. Put the rhubarb in a pan with the water and 10 ml/2 tsp artificial sweetener. Bring gently to the boil, reduce the heat, cover and cook until the rhubarb is tender. Remove the lid, bring to the boil and boil rapidly until pulpy and most of the liquid has evaporated. Taste and add more sweetener if liked. Meanwhile, put the cornflour in a separate pan. Make the orange juice up to 300 ml/½ pt/1¼ cups with skimmed milk. Stir into the cornflour until smooth. Add the grated orange rind. Bring to the boil and cook for 1 minute, stirring, until thickened and smooth. Sweeten to taste with sweetener. Layer the rhubarb and orange sauce in four heatproof glass dishes. Sprinkle with the reserved orange rind and serve.

Mulled Florida Cocktail

SERVES 4

2 grapefruit
2 oranges
150 ml/¼ pt/⅔ cup apple juice
15 ml/1 tbsp brandy
A few grains of artificial sweetener
(optional)
2 fresh cherries or black grapes,
halved

Over a saucepan to catch the juice, remove all rind and pith from the grapefruit and oranges and separate each into segments either side of the membranes. Squeeze the membranes to extract the last of the juice. Put the segments in the saucepan. Add the apple juice and brandy. Heat through until almost boiling. Taste and add a few grains of artificial sweetener, if liked. Spoon into glass dishes, top each with half a cherry or grape and serve.

Sweet Baked Squash

SERVES 4

2 acorn or butternut squashes
120 ml/4 fl oz/½ cup apple juice
20 ml/4 tsp low-fat spread
A few grains artificial sweetener
Ground cinnamon

Halve the squashes and scoop out the seeds. Lay in a casserole (Dutch oven). Pour over the apple juice and dot with the low fat spread. Sprinkle with just a few grains of artificial sweetener and a fine dusting of cinnamon. Cover and bake in a preheated oven at 180ºC/350ºF/gas mark 4 for 1 hour until tender. Serve with a spoon to scoop out the flesh.

Blackberry and Apple Heaven

SERVES 4

1 large cooking (tart) apple, sliced
175 g/6 oz blackberries
10 ml/2 tsp water
5 ml/1 tsp artificial sweetener (or to taste)
2 eggs, separated

Put the apple and blackberries in a pan with the water. Cover and cook gently for 10 minutes or until tender and pulpy. Sweeten to taste. Cool slightly, then beat in the egg yolks. Whisk the egg whites until stiff and fold into the mixture with a metal spoon. Turn into an ovenproof dish and bake in a preheated oven at 200ºC/400ºF/gas mark 6 for 25 minutes until risen and golden. Serve straight away.

Fromage Frais with Hot Plum Sauce

SERVES 4

450 g/1 lb ripe plums, halved and stoned (pitted)
30 ml/2 tbsp water
Artificial sweetener granules
225 g/8 oz/1 cup very low-fat fromage frais

Put the plums in a pan with the water and cook very gently until the juice runs. Cover and stew over a gentle heat until tender and pulpy. Purée in a blender or food processor and return to the pan. Sweeten to taste. Reheat. Spoon the fromage frais into four individual dishes, spoon the hot plum sauce over and serve straight away.

Rice Pudding

SERVES 4

50 g/2 oz/¼ cup round-grain (pudding) rice
600 ml/1 pt/2½ cups skimmed milk
Artificial sweetener granules
Grated nutmeg

Put the rice in an ovenproof dish. Stir in the milk and sweeten to taste. Sprinkle with nutmeg. Bake in a preheated oven at 180ºC/350ºF/gas mark 4 for about 1½–2 hours until the rice is tender and the top is a rich golden brown. (You can cook this in a slower oven for a little longer, if preferred.)

Lemon Rice

SERVES 4

Prepare as for Rice Pudding but add the grated rind of 1 large lemon to the mixture before cooking and sprinkle with ground mace instead of nutmeg.

Orange Rice

SERVES 4

Prepare as for Rice Pudding but add the grated rind of 1 orange to the mixture before cooking and sprinkle with mixed (apple-pie) spice instead of nutmeg.

Baked Custard

SERVES 4

2 eggs
5 ml/1 tsp artificial sweetener
granules (or to taste)
450 ml/¾ pt/2 cups skimmed milk,
warmed
Grated nutmeg

Beat the eggs with the artificial sweetener. Whisk in the warm milk. Taste and add a little more sweetener, if liked. Strain into an ovenproof dish and dust with nutmeg. Transfer to a roasting tin (pan) containing 2.5 cm/1 in cold water. Bake in a preheated oven at 150°C/300°F/gas mark 2 for about 1 hour or until set. Serve warm.

Vanilla Baked Custard

SERVES 4

Prepare as for Baked Custard but add a few drops of vanilla essence (extract) to the mixture and omit the nutmeg, if preferred.

Orange Baked Custard

SERVES 4

Prepare as for Baked Custard but add the finely grated rind of 1 orange to the mixture and sprinkle with ground cinnamon instead of nutmeg.

Almond Baked Custard

SERVES 4

Prepare as for Baked Custard but add a few drops (or to taste) of almond essence (extract) to the mixture and omit the nutmeg.

Rose Custard

SERVES 4

Prepare as for Baked Custard but add 15 ml/1 tbsp rosewater (or to taste) to the mixture and omit the nutmeg.

·······················HOT DESSERTS·······················

200

CALORIES OR LESS

Bread and Butter Pudding

SERVES 4

15 ml/1 tbsp low-fat spread
2 slices bread
15 ml/1 tbsp raisins
15 ml/1 tbsp sultanas (golden
  raisins)
15 ml/1 tbsp currants
2 eggs
450 ml/¾ pt/2 cups skimmed milk
5 ml/1 tsp artificial sweetener
  granules, plus extra for dusting
Grated nutmeg

Grease a 1.2 litre/2 pt/5 cup oven-proof dish with 5 ml/1 tsp of the low-fat spread. Butter the bread with the remainder. Cut the bread into tri-angles and lay half in the base of the dish. Sprinkle the fruit over and top with the remaining bread. Beat the eggs and milk with the sweetener. Pour over. Allow to stand for at least 15 minutes. Sprinkle with a little nut-meg and extra sweetener and bake in a preheated oven at 180°C/350°F/gas mark 4 for about 50–60 minutes or until set and the top is crisp and golden.

Apple Crumble

SERVES 4

2 large cooking (tart) apples,
  sliced
Artificial sweetener granules
A pinch of ground cloves
15 ml/1 tbsp water
100 g/4 oz/1 cup plain (all-
  purpose) flour
50 g/2 oz/¼ cup low-fat spread

Put the apples in an ovenproof dish and sprinkle with about 5 ml/ 1 tsp artificial sweetener and the cloves. Add the water. Put the flour in a bowl and rub in the low-fat spread. Add 5 ml/1 tsp artificial sweetener granules. Sprinkle over the fruit and press down gently. Dust with a little extra sweetener, if liked. Bake in a pre-heated oven at 190°C/375°F/gas mark 5 for about 45 minutes or until golden and the apple is cooked.

Oat and Apple Crumble

SERVES 4

Prepare as for Apple Crumble but substitute 50 g/2 oz/½ cup rolled oats for half the flour.

Rhubarb Crumble

SERVES 4

**450 g/1 lb rhubarb, cut into short
  lengths
15 ml/1 tbsp cold water
10 ml/2 tsp artificial sweetener
  granules
100 g/4 oz/1 cup plain (all-
  purpose) flour
50 g/2 oz/¼ cup low-fat spread**

Put the rhubarb in an ovenproof dish with the water. Sprinkle with half the sweetener. Put the flour in a bowl and rub in the low-fat spread. Stir in the remaining sweetener. Sprinkle over the rhubarb and press down slightly. Bake in a preheated oven at 190°C/375°F/gas mark 5 for about 40 minutes until golden and cooked through.

Rhubarb and Apple Crumble

SERVES 4

Prepare as for Rhubarb Crumble but use half-and-half sliced apples and rhubarb.

Rhubarb and Orange Crumble

SERVES 4

Prepare as for Rhubarb Crumble but add the finely grated rind and juice of an orange to the fruit and omit the water.

Pear and Ginger Crumble

SERVES 4

**4 ripe pears, sliced
30 ml/2 tbsp apple juice
100 g/4 oz/1 cup plain (all-
  purpose) flour
5 ml/1 tsp ground ginger
50 g/2 oz/¼ cup low-fat spread
5 ml/1 tsp artificial sweetener
  granules**

Peel the pears and place in an oven-proof serving dish with the apple juice. Sift the flour and ginger into a bowl. Rub in the low-fat spread and stir in the sweetener. Spoon over the pears and press down gently. Sprinkle with a little extra sweetener, if liked. Bake in a preheated oven at 190°C/375°F/gas mark 5 for about 45 minutes or until golden and the pears are cooked. Serve hot.

Chocolate Pear Crumble

SERVES 4

**4 ripe pears, sliced
30 ml/2 tbsp apple juice
85 g/3½ oz/¾ cup plain (all-
  purpose) flour
30 ml/2 tbsp cocoa (unsweetened
  chocolate) powder
50 g/2 oz/¼ cup low-fat spread
10 ml/2 tsp artificial sweetener
  granules**

Put the sliced pears in an ovenproof dish with the apple juice. Sift the flour and cocoa into a bowl. Add the low-fat spread and rub in with the fingertips. Stir in the sweetener. Sprinkle over the pears and press down lightly. Bake in a preheated oven at 190°C/375°F/gas mark 5 for about 40 minutes until cooked through.

Apple Charlotte

SERVES 4

4 slices bread
25 g/1 oz/2 tbsp low-fat spread
450 g/1 lb cooking (tart) apples,
sliced
Artificial sweetener granules

Spread the bread with the low-fat spread. Line a shallow ovenproof serving dish with two of the slices, cutting and trimming to fit. Add the apples and sprinkle with 5 ml/1 tsp artificial sweetener. Cut the remaining bread into small dice. Scatter over the fruit and sprinkle with a further 5 ml/1 tsp sweetener. Bake in a preheated oven at 190°C/375°F/gas mark 5 for about 45 minutes until the topping is golden and crisp and the apple is tender. (For a smoother texture, stew the apple in 15 ml/1 tbsp water until pulpy, sweeten to taste, then place in the bread-lined dish.)

Apple and Ginger Charlotte

SERVES 4

Prepare as for Apple Charlotte but add 5 ml/1 tsp grated fresh root ginger to the apple before topping with the diced bread.

Plum Charlotte

SERVES 4

450 g/1 lb plums, halved and
stoned (pitted)
15 ml/1 tbsp water
Artificial sweetener granules
4 slices bread
25 g/1 oz/2 tbsp low-fat spread

Put the halved plums in a saucepan with the water. Stew until tender. Sweeten to taste. Spread the bread with the low-fat spread. Use two of the slices to line a shallow ovenproof serving dish. Top with the plums. Cut the remaining bread into thin strips and arrange in a lattice on top of the plums. Sprinkle with 5 ml/1 tsp sweetener and bake in a preheated oven at 190°C/375°F/gas mark 5 for about 30–40 minutes until golden brown.

Profiteroles with Hot Chocolate Sauce

SERVES 4

65 g/2½ oz/generous ½ cup plain (all-purpose) flour
A pinch of salt
150 ml/¼ pt/⅔ cup water
50 g/2 oz/¼ cup low-fat spread
2 eggs, beaten
150 ml/¼ pt/⅔ cup low-fat whipping cream, whipped
15 ml/1 tbsp cocoa (unsweetened chocolate) powder
10–15 ml/2–3 tsp artificial sweetener granules (or to taste)
15 ml/1 tbsp skimmed milk

Sift the flour and salt twice on to a sheet of kitchen paper. Put the water and half the low-fat spread in a saucepan and heat until the spread melts. Add all the flour in one go and beat with a wooden spoon until the mixture leaves the sides of the pan clean. Remove from the heat. Cool slightly, then beat in the eggs a little at a time until the mixture is smooth and glossy but still holds its shape (you may not need quite all the egg). Line a baking sheet with non-stick baking parchment. Put spoonfuls of the mixture on the paper, a little apart to allow for rising. Bake in a preheated oven at 200°C/400°F/gas mark 6 for about 15–20 minutes until risen, crisp and golden. Transfer to a wire rack to cool. Make a slit in the side of each one and fill with a little of the whipped cream. Put the remaining low-fat spread in a saucepan with the cocoa, sweetener and milk. Heat gently, stirring, until melted and smooth. Put the profiteroles in four serving dishes. Spoon the hot chocolate sauce over and serve.

Profiteroles with Hot Strawberry Sauce

SERVES 4

Prepare the profiteroles as for Profiteroles with Hot Chocolate Sauce but serve with 1 quantity Fresh Strawberry Sauce (see page 356), heated through but not allowed to boil.

Profiteroles with Hot Apricot Sauce

SERVES 4

Prepare as for Profiteroles with Hot Chocolate Sauce but sweeten the cream with a few grains of artificial sweetener and flavour with a few drops of almond essence (extract). Serve with Apricot Sauce (see page 356), heated until piping hot but not boiling.

Profiteroles with Boozy Cherry Sauce

SERVES 4

Prepare as for Profiteroles with Hot Chocolate Sauce but serve with Boozy Cherry Sauce (see page 356), heated through but not boiling.

Queen of Puddings

SERVES 4

2 eggs, separated
10 ml/2 tsp artificial sweetener
    granules
300 ml/½ pt/1¼ cups skimmed
    milk, warmed
50 g/2 oz/1 cup fresh white
    breadcrumbs
Finely grated rind of 1 lemon
30 ml/2 tbsp reduced-sugar
    strawberry or raspberry jam
    (conserve)

Beat the egg yolks with half the sweetener. Whisk into the warm milk. Mix the breadcrumbs and lemon rind in a 1.2 litre/2 pt/5 cup ovenproof dish. Pour the milk mixture over and mix well. Leave to stand for 15 minutes. Bake in a preheated oven at 180°C/350°F/gas mark 4 for about 35 minutes until set. Whisk the egg whites until stiff and whisk in the remaining sweetener. Spread the jam over the set mixture, then pile the meringue on top. Return to the oven for a further 20–25 minutes or until the top is turning golden.

Fruit Crisp

SERVES 4

410 g/14½ oz/1 large can fruit in
    natural juice, drained reserving
    the juice
2 Weetabix
5 ml/1 tsp artificial sweetener
    granules
50 g/2 oz/¼ cup low-fat spread,
    melted
2.5 ml/½ tsp ground ginger,
    cinnamon or mixed (apple-pie)
    spice

Put the fruit in a 1 litre/1¾ pt/4¼ cup ovenproof dish. Crumble the Weetabix and mix with the sweetener, low-fat spread and spices. Sprinkle over the fruit, pressing down lightly. Bake in a preheated oven at 190°C/375°F/gas mark 5 for about 15 minutes until crisp. Serve warm.

Pineapple Floating Islands

SERVES 4

40g/1½ oz/3 tbsp low-fat spread
10 ml/2 tsp artificial sweetener
granules
2 eggs, separated
20 g/¾ oz/3 tbsp plain (all-
purpose) flour
320 g/11 oz/1 small can chopped
pineapple
300 ml/½ pt/1¼ cups skimmed
milk

Beat the low-fat spread with half the sweetener until soft and light. Beat in the egg yolks and flour. Drain the pineapple juice and place in a saucepan with the milk. Heat until hand-hot, then whisk into the beaten mixture. Return to the pan and cook gently, stirring, until thickened but do not allow to boil. Stir in the pineapple and turn into 1.2 litre/2 pt/5 cup oven-proof serving dish. Whisk the egg whites until stiff. Whisk in the remaining sweetener. Put four piles of the meringue on top of the pineapple mixture. Bake in a preheated oven at 150°C/300°F/gas mark 2 for 25–30 minutes until the meringue is a pale gold. Serve warm.

Hot Chocolate Soufflé

SERVES 4

5 ml/1 tsp low-fat spread, melted
200 ml/7 fl oz/1 cup skimmed
milk
25 g/1 oz/2 tbsp plain (all-
purpose) flour
15 ml/1 tbsp cocoa (unsweetened
chocolate) powder
Artificial sweetener granules
2.5 ml/½ tsp vanilla essence
(extract)
3 eggs, separated
To serve:
60 ml/4 tbsp low-fat single (light)
cream

Brush four individual soufflé dishes or large ramekins (custard cups) with the low-fat spread. Whisk together the milk, flour and cocoa in a saucepan with sweetener to taste and vanilla. Bring to the boil, whisking all the time, until thickened and smooth. Add a little more vanilla or sweetener, if liked. Remove from the heat, cool slightly, then whisk in the egg yolks. Whisk the egg whites until stiff and fold in with a metal spoon. Turn into the prepared dishes and transfer the dishes to a baking sheet. Bake in a preheated oven at 190°C/375°F/gas mark 5 for about 20–25 minutes until risen and just set. Dust with a little artificial sweetener and serve immediately with the low-fat single cream.

Boozy Banana Soufflé

SERVES 6

40 g/1½ oz/3 tbsp low-fat spread,
  plus a little extra for greasing
5 ml/1 tsp artificial sweetener
  granules
2 eggs, separated
150 ml/¼ pt/⅔ cup white rum or
  sherry
4 ripe bananas
To serve:
60 ml/4 tbsp very low-fat crème
  fraîche

Purée the low-fat spread, artificial sweetener, egg yolks, rum or sherry and bananas in a blender or food processor. Whisk the egg whites until stiff and fold into the mixture with a metal spoon. Turn into a greased soufflé dish. Bake in a pre-heated oven at 190°C/375°F/gas mark 5 for about 35 minutes until risen, golden and just set. Serve hot with the crème fraîche.

Highland Flummery

SERVES 6

15 ml/1 tbsp fine oatmeal
300 ml/½ pt/1¼ cups low-fat
  double (heavy) cream
45 ml/3 tbsp clear honey
60 ml/4 tbsp whisky
Grated rind and juice of ½ lemon

Put the oatmeal in a frying pan (skillet) over a moderate heat and toss until golden brown. Tip out of the pan to cool. Whip the cream until softly peaking but not stiff. Warm the honey, whisky and lemon juice in a saucepan until hand-hot but not boiling. Fold into the cream until well blended. Spoon into glasses and sprinkle with the oatmeal. Serve straight away.

Apple Flan

SERVES 4

100 g/4 oz/1 cup plain (all-
  purpose) flour
A pinch of salt
50 g/2 oz/¼ cup low-fat spread
15 ml/1 tbsp artificial sweetener
  granules
450 g/1 lb cooking (tart) apples
30 ml/2 tbsp water
1 piece cinnamon stick
30 ml/2 tbsp reduced-sugar
  apricot jam (conserve)

Mix the flour with the salt in a bowl. Add the low-fat spread and rub in with the fingertips. Stir in 2.5 ml/½ tsp sweetener. Mix with enough cold water to form a firm dough. Knead gently on a lightly floured surface. Roll out and use to line an 18 cm/7 in flan tin (pie pan). Chill. Peel and slice half the apples and stew with 15 ml/1 tbsp water and the cinnamon stick until pulpy. Sweeten to taste with artificial sweetener. Cool, then discard the cinnamon stick and turn into the flan case (pie shell). Peel, core and slice the remaining apples and arrange attractively over the pulp. Sprinkle with any remaining sweet-ener. Place the flan on a baking sheet and bake in a preheated oven at 200°C/400°F/gas mark 6 for about 40 minutes until golden and the apples are tender. Melt the apricot jam with the remaining water and brush all over the top of the flan. Serve warm.

Fritanda with Apricot Sauce

SERVES 4

2 thick slices bread, crusts removed
1 egg
45 ml/3 tbsp skimmed milk
5 ml/1 tsp artificial sweetener
    granules
A few drops of almond essence
    (extract)
228 g/8 oz/1 small can apricots in
    natural juice
25 g/1 oz/2 tbsp low-fat spread
A few toasted, flaked (slivered)
    almonds

Cut each slice of bread into four triangles. Beat the egg and milk
together on a plate and stir in the
sweetener and almond essence. Purée
the apricots and their juice in a
blender or food processor and pour
into a saucepan. Sweeten, if necessary,
with a few grains of sweetener. Heat
through. Dip the bread triangles in the
egg and milk mixture to coat completely. Fry (sauté) in the low-fat
spread until golden on both sides.
Arrange attractively on four warmed
plates and spoon the sauce over.
Sprinkle with a few toasted, flaked
almonds and serve.

Fritanda with Raspberry Sauce

SERVES 4

Prepare as for Fritanda with Apricot
Sauce but substitute vanilla
essence for the almond and a can of
raspberries in natural juice for the
apricots. Sieve (strain) the purée before
heating in a saucepan. Decorate with a
few toasted, chopped hazelnuts
instead of almonds.

Greengage Puddings with Peach Sauce

SERVES 4

4 slices bread, crusts removed
50 g/2 oz/¼ cup low-fat spread
450 g/1 lb ripe greengages, halved
    and stoned (pitted)
5 ml/1 tsp artificial sweetener
    granules
A few drops of vanilla essence
    (extract)
410 g/14 oz/1 large can peach
    slices in natural juice
A pinch of ground cinnamon

Spread the bread with half the low-
fat spread. Use to line four individual ovenproof dishes. Lay the greengages in the dishes, cut sides up, and
dot each with the remaining low-fat
spread. Sprinkle with the sweetener
and vanilla. Bake in a preheated oven
at 180°C/350°F/gas mark 4 for about
40 minutes until the greengages are
tender. Meanwhile, purée the peaches
and their juice in a blender or food
processor. Heat in a saucepan with the
cinnamon. Pour into a serving jug and
serve with the puddings.

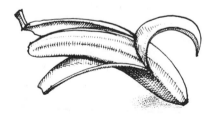

Blackberry Pudding

SERVES 4

225 g/8 oz ripe blackberries
25 g/1 oz/2 tbsp low-fat spread
10 ml/2 tsp artificial sweetener
   granules, plus extra to decorate
Finely grated rind and juice of
   1 lemon
2 eggs, separated
25 g/1 oz/¼ cup plain (all-purpose)
   flour
150 ml/¼ pt/⅔ cup skimmed milk
To serve:
60 ml/4 tbsp very low-fat crème
   fraîche

Reserve four or five blackberries for decoration and put the remainder in the base of a 900 ml/1½ pt/3¾ cup ovenproof serving dish. Beat the low-fat spread with the sweetener, lemon rind and juice. Beat in the egg yolks and flour, then stir in the milk. Whisk the egg whites until stiff and fold in with a metal spoon. Pour over the blackberries and stand the dish in a roasting tin (pan) containing 2.5 cm/ 1 in boiling water. Bake in a preheated oven at 190ºC/375ºF/gas mark 5 for 45 minutes until risen and golden and the centre springs back when lightly pressed. Dust with a little sweetener and top with a cluster of reserved blackberries. Serve with the crème fraîche.

Danish Sweet Spice Tart

SERVES 4

100 g/4 oz/1 cup plain (all-
   purpose) flour
A pinch of salt
50 g/2 oz/¼ cup low-fat spread
7.5 ml/1½ tsp artificial sweetener
   granules
2 eggs, separated
50 g/2 oz/⅓ cup sultanas (golden
   raisins)
2.5 ml/½ tsp ground cinnamon
2.5 ml/½ tsp ground mixed (apple-
   pie) spice
150 g/5 oz/⅔ cup very low-fat
   quark
Grated rind of ½ lemon

Put the flour and salt in a bowl. Add the low-fat spread and rub in with the fingertips. Mix with enough cold water to form a firm dough. Knead gently on a lightly floured surface. Roll out and use to line an 18 cm/7 in flan tin (pie pan). Prick the base with a fork and chill while preparing the filling. Put the sweetener, egg yolks, sultanas, cinnamon, mixed spice, quark and lemon rind in a bowl and beat until smooth. Taste and add a few more grains of sweetener, if liked (but don't overdo it, as it will taste sweeter once cooked). Whisk the egg whites until stiff and fold in with a metal spoon. Turn into the prepared flan case (pie shell). Place on a baking sheet and bake in a preheated oven at 220ºC/425ºF/gas mark 7 for 15 minutes, then reduce the heat to 180ºC/ 350ºF/gas mark 4 and continue cooking for a further 20 minutes or until set and golden. Serve warm.

Photograph opposite:
Hot Orange Soufflés (page 302)

Custard Tart

SERVES 4

**100 g/4 oz/1 cup plain (all-
purpose) flour
A pinch of salt
50 g/2 oz/¼ cup low-fat spread
2 eggs
5 ml/1 tsp artificial sweetener
granules
300 ml/½ pt/1¼ cups skimmed
milk, warmed
Grated nutmeg**

Put the flour and salt in a bowl. Add the low-fat spread and rub in with the fingertips. Mix with enough cold water to form a firm dough. Knead gently on a lightly floured surface. Roll out and use to line an 18 cm/7 in flan tin (pie pan). Prick the base with a fork. Fill with crumpled foil and place on a baking sheet. Bake in a preheated oven at 200°C/400°F/gas mark 6 for 15 minutes. Remove the foil after 10 minutes to allow the pastry (paste) to dry out. Whisk together the eggs and sweetener, then whisk into the milk. Taste and add a little more sweetener if liked. Strain into the pastry case (pie shell) and sprinkle with nutmeg. Bake in the oven at 190°C/ 375°F/gas mark 5 for about 35 minutes until the custard is set. Serve warm.

Date Flapjacks with Pineapple and Coconut Sauce

SERVES 4 WHILE WARM,
STORE THE REMAINDER

**100 g/4 oz/½ cup low-fat spread,
plus extra for greasing
60 ml/4 tbsp clear honey
175 g/6 oz/1½ cups rolled oats
15 ml/1 tbsp sesame seeds
100 g/4 oz/⅔ cup chopped dates
5 ml/1 tsp ground cinnamon**
To serve:
**Pineapple and Coconut Sauce,
warmed (see page 360)**

Melt the low-fat spread with the honey in a saucepan. Add the oats, sesame seeds, dates and cinnamon and mix thoroughly. Grease a 20 cm/8 in square shallow baking tin (pan) with a very little low-fat spread. Press the oat mixture into the tin. Bake in a preheated oven at 180°C/350°F/ gas mark 5 for about 25 minutes or until golden. Cool until warm. Cut into 12 fingers. Transfer four pieces to warmed plates and serve with the warm Pineapple and Coconut Sauce. Store the remainder when cold in an airtight tin for snacks or dessert on another day.

Photograph opposite:
Strawberry Cheesecake (page 336)

Warming Winter Fruit Salad

SERVES 4

225 g/8 oz dried fruit salad
150 ml/¼ pt/⅔ cup apple juice
150 ml/¼ pt/⅔ cup water
15 ml/1 tbsp Cointreau (optional)
1 slice orange
To serve:
Basic Sweet White Sauce
  (see page 359)

Soak the fruit salad in the apple juice, water and Cointreau, if using, for several hours or overnight. Place in a saucepan with the orange slice and bring to the boil. Reduce the heat, cover and simmer gently for 30 minutes. Discard the orange slice. Serve hot with Basic Sweet White Sauce.

Brandied Autumn Compote

SERVES 4

750 g/1½ lb mixed soft fruit such
  as plums, blackberries,
  raspberries, blackcurrants,
  apple
100 ml/3½ fl oz/6½ tbsp water
7.5 ml/1½ tsp artificial sweetener
  granules
20 ml/4 tsp arrowroot
45 ml/3 tbsp brandy
To serve:
60 ml/4 tbsp low-fat single (light)
  cream

Quarter and stone (pit) the plums, if using, and place in a pan with the other fruits. Add the water and sweetener. Bring to the boil, reduce the heat and simmer for just 3–4 minutes until the fruit is softening but still holding its shape. Blend the arrowroot with the brandy and stir into the fruit. Simmer for 1 minute until slightly thickened and clear. Taste and add more sweetener, if liked. Serve warm with the cream.

Dreamy Cold Desserts

Most people adore desserts and you don't have to give them up just because you are on a diet. Some of the following recipes have serving suggestions, which are included in the calorie count. If not, and you want to add a little low-fat cream, very low-fat crème fraîche or yoghurt, add on a further 50 calories per portion to be on the safe side.

100

CALORIES OR LESS

Quick Chocolate Mousse

SERVES 4

150 ml/¼ pt/⅔ cup low-fat whipping cream
30 ml/2 tbsp chocolate hazelnut spread
15 ml/1 tbsp brandy
Ground cinnamon
4 whole strawberries OR 1 kiwi fruit, sliced

Whip the cream until peaking. Reserve 30 ml/2 tbsp for decoration. Fold the chocolate spread and brandy into the remaining cream. Spoon into four demitasse coffee cups. Top with the reserved cream and sprinkle with cinnamon. Chill until set. Serve on the coffee saucers with a strawberry or slice of kiwi fruit on the saucer and coffee spoons to eat it with.

Fresh Fruit Salad

SERVES 4

300 ml/½ pt/1¼ cups apple juice
2 oranges
2 kiwi fruit
1 nectarine
1 red-skinned eating (dessert) apple
1 green-skinned eating (dessert) apple
1 small bunch seedless grapes

Put the apple juice in a glass dish. Cut all the rind and pith from the oranges. Slice, then cut each slice into quarters. Peel and slice the kiwi fruit and halve the slices, if liked. Slice the nectarine around the stone (pit) and discard the stone. Dice the apples but do not peel. Remove the grapes from the stalk and halve if large. Place all the fruit in the juice and chill for at least 2 hours until the flavours have blended. (You can substitute any other selection of prepared fresh fruit.)

Fresh Fruit Salad Another Way

SERVES 4

Add 150 ml/¼ pt/⅔ cup pure orange juice, 5 ml/1 tsp lemon juice and a sprinkling of ground cinnamon to a small can of fruit in natural juice. This is the base for the salad. Then add any chopped fresh fruit of your choice, allowing 45 ml/3 tbsp per person. Leave on any edible peel to add colour and texture. For special occasions, use a scooped-out melon or pineapple shell as the receptacle for the salad or use halved grapefruit or large orange shells for individual portions.

Rhubarb and Banana Flip

SERVES 4

450 g/1 lb rhubarb, cut into short pieces
5 ml/1 tsp ground cinnamon
45 ml/3 tbsp water
Artificial sweetener granules
4 ripe bananas, cut into chunks
300 ml/½ pt/1¼ cups very low-fat plain yoghurt
8 small angelica 'leaves'

Put the rhubarb, cinnamon and water in a saucepan and stew gently until the rhubarb is tender. Cool slightly, then place in a blender with the bananas. Run the machine until the mixture is smooth. Sweeten to taste. Leave until completely cold, then fold in the yoghurt, leaving a marbled effect. Spoon into glass dishes and chill. Decorate each with two angelica leaves before serving.

Apple and Banana Flip

SERVES 4

Prepare as for Rhubarb and Banana Flip but substitute sliced cooking (tart) apples for the rhubarb and use ground cloves instead of cinnamon for flavouring.

Gooseberry and Banana Flip

SERVES 4

Prepare as for Rhubarb and Banana Flip but substitute topped and tailed gooseberries for the rhubarb and flavour with ground ginger instead of cinnamon.

Strawberry and Banana Flip

SERVES 4

225 g/8 oz ripe strawberries
15 ml/1 tbsp reduced-sugar strawberry jam (conserve)
4 small ripe bananas
300 ml/½ pt/1¼ cups very low-fat plain yoghurt

Reserve two halved strawberries with the green stalks intact for decoration. Purée the remaining strawberries with the jam and bananas in a blender or food processor. Add the yoghurt and run the machine briefly to blend. Spoon into glass dishes and chill before serving, decorated with halved strawberries.

Orange Cups

SERVES 4

2 large oranges
1 small carton low-fat diet apricot
  or orange yoghurt
10 ml/2 tsp orange liqueur or
  apricot brandy
15 ml/1 tbsp chopped nuts

Halve the oranges and carefully remove all the flesh with a serrated edged knife. Cut a tiny slice off the base of each orange shell so it stands upright. Chop the flesh, discarding any pith or tough membranes. Place in a bowl and add the yoghurt and liqueur. Mix gently but thoroughly. Spoon into the orange shells and chill. Sprinkle with the chopped nuts before serving.

Fresh Fruit Fromage Frais

SERVES 4

225 g/8 oz soft fruit such as
  strawberries, raspberries,
  chopped nectarine or peach
225 g/8 oz/1 cup very low-fat
  fromage frais
Artificial sweetener granules
  (optional)
5 ml/1 tsp lemon juice

Reserve four pieces of fruit for decoration. Crush the remainder, then stir in the fromage frais. Sweeten, if liked, with artificial sweetener and spike with lemon juice. Spoon into small dishes and chill until ready to serve, decorated with the reserved fruit.

Quark Refresher

SERVES 4

1 packet sugar-free fruit-flavoured
  jelly (jello)
150 ml/¼ pt/⅔ cup boiling water
300 ml/½ pt/1¼ cups cold water
100 g/4 oz/½ cup very low-fat
  quark
A few pieces of fresh fruit,
  matching the flavour of the
  jelly, to decorate

Dissolve the jelly in the boiling water. Stir in the cold water and chill until the consistency of egg white. Whisk in the quark and turn into four dishes. Chill until set. Decorate with fresh fruit before serving.

Apricot Fool

SERVES 4

1 quantity Basic Sweet White
  Sauce (see page 359)
410 g/14½ oz/1 large can apricots
  in natural juice
A few grains of artificial sweetener
  (optional)
4 angelica 'leaves'

Make up the sauce and leave to cool. Drain the fruit, reserving the juice. Keep an apricot half aside to slice for decoration. Purée the remaining fruit with the juice in a blender or food processor and fold into the sauce. Sweeten, if necessary, with a few grains of sweetener. Spoon into glasses and top each with a slice of apricot and an angelica leaf. Chill.

Peach Fool

SERVES 4

Prepare as for Apricot Fool (see page 325) but substitute a can of peaches in natural juice for the apricots and add a squeeze of lemon juice after folding in the sauce.

Strawberry Fool

SERVES 4

Prepare as for Apricot Fool (see page 325) but substitute a can of strawberries in natural juice for the apricots and a squeeze of lemon juice. Alternatively, purée 225 g/8 oz ripe fresh strawberries and sweeten with artificial sweetener before folding into the sauce. Sharpen with extra lemon juice if necessary.

Raspberry Fool

SERVES 4

Prepare as for Apricot Fool (see page 325) but substitute a can of raspberries for the apricots and sieve (strain) the purée before adding to the sauce.

Peach Malakoff

SERVES 4

4 ripe peaches, sliced
A pinch of artificial sweetener granules
30 ml/2 tbsp peach liqueur
Finely grated rind and juice of 1 tangerine

Put the peach slices in a glass dish and sprinkle with the sweetener. Add the liqueur and tangerine rind and juice. Toss gently, then leave to marinate for at least 1 hour before serving.

Pear and Redcurrant Jelly

SERVES 6

1 packet sugar-free raspberry jelly (jello)
600 ml/1 pt/2½ cups apple juice
5 ml/1 tsp lemon juice
100 g/4 oz redcurrants
2 ripe pears, thinly sliced

Dissolve the jelly in the apple juice over a gentle heat. Spike with lemon juice. Put the redcurrants and pears in a glass bowl. Add the hot jelly and leave to cool. When cold and the consistency of egg white, stir gently, then leave to set.

Berry Dream

SERVES 4

2 egg whites
300 ml/½ pt/1¼ cups very low-fat diet strawberry yoghurt
175 g/6 oz ripe strawberries
175 g/6 oz raspberries

Whisk the egg whites until stiff. Fold into the yoghurt. Reserve a few pieces of fruit for decoration, then slice the strawberries and lightly crush the remaining raspberries. Layer the fruit and fluffy yoghurt in tall glasses and decorate with the reserved fruit. Chill before serving.

Grape and Apricot Dream

SERVES 4

Prepare as for Berry Dream but substitute very low-fat diet apricot yoghurt for strawberry and use half red and half green seedless grapes, halved, instead of the berries.

Tropical Dream

SERVES 4

Prepare as for Berry Dream (left) but use passion fruit very low-fat diet yoghurt instead of strawberry and use a drained 228 g/8 oz small can pineapple pieces in natural juice and 2 bananas, cut into chunks and dipped in lemon juice, for the fruit.

Eastern Promise

SERVES 4

12 fresh dates, stoned (pitted) and roughly chopped
2 bananas, sliced
228 g/8 oz/1 small can pineapple pieces in natural juice, drained
60 ml/4 tbsp very low-fat crème fraîche

Mix the dates with the bananas and pineapple. Spoon into glass serving dishes and top with the crème fraîche.

Sparkling Pear Cocktail

SERVES 4

4 ripe pears
40 ml/8 tsp brandy
Low-calorie ginger ale, chilled

Peel and slice the pears and place in four open champagne glasses or wine goblets. Add the brandy and toss gently. Chill. Bring to the table and top up with chilled ginger ale. Eat the fruit with a spoon, then drink the liquid.

Sparkling Peach Cocktail

SERVES 4

Prepare as for Sparkling Pear Cocktail but use 1 ripe skinned and sliced peach per person and peach liqueur instead of brandy.

Sparkling Strawberry Cocktail

SERVES 4

Prepare as for Sparkling Pear Cocktail but use 75 g/3 oz sliced strawberries per person and substitute kirsch for the brandy.

Rosy Nectarines

SERVES 4

300 g/11 oz/1 small can strawberries in natural juice, drained, reserving the juice
Artificial sweetener granules
2 ripe nectarines
60 ml/4 tbsp very low-fat fromage frais

Purée the strawberries in a blender or food processor or pass through a sieve (strainer). Thin with a little of the reserved juice if necessary and sweeten to taste, if necessary. Plunge the nectarines in boiling water for 30 seconds. Rinse under the cold tap, then remove the skins. Halve and remove the stones (pits). Sweeten the fromage frais slightly and spoon into the base of four wine goblets. Top each with a nectarine half, cut side down. Spoon the strawberry purée over and chill, if time, before serving.

Apple and Blackcurrant Kissel

SERVES 4

2 large cooking (tart) apples,
   sliced
100 g/4 oz blackcurrants
10 ml/2 tsp artificial sweetener
   granules
75 ml/5 tbsp port
1 piece cinnamon stick
10 ml/2 tsp arrowroot
15 ml/1 tbsp water

Put the apples and blackcurrants in a saucepan with the sweetener and the port. Add the cinnamon stick. Cover and cook gently until the fruit is tender, stirring occasionally. Discard the cinnamon stick and purée the fruit in a blender or food processor. Return to the saucepan. Blend the arrowroot with the water and stir into the purée. Bring to the boil and cook, stirring, until thickened. Cool, then spoon into four individual glasses and chill until ready to serve.

Apple and Raspberry Kissel

SERVES 4

Prepare as for Apple and Black-currant Kissel but substitute raspberries for the blackcurrants and flavour with 5 ml/1 tsp finely grated lemon rind instead of the cinnamon.

Pear and Passion Fruit Dessert

SERVES 4

2 ripe pears
4 passion fruit
300 ml/½ pt/1¼ cups cider
5 ml/1 tsp artificial sweetener
   granules
20 ml/4 tsp arrowroot
30 ml/2 tbsp water
Grated rind and juice of 1 lime

Peel, halve and core the pears and place in four glass dishes. Halve the passion fruit and scoop the pulp into a small bowl. Put the cider in a saucepan with the sweetener. Bring to the boil. Blend the arrowroot with the water and stir into the saucepan. Cook, stirring, until thickened and clear. Stir in the passion fruit pulp. Add the lime rind and juice. Taste and add a little more sweetener, if necessary. Pour over the pears and leave to cool. Chill until ready to serve.

Strawberries Romanoff

SERVES 4

350 g/12 oz strawberries, sliced
A pinch of artificial sweetener
   granules
30 ml/2 tbsp orange or strawberry
   liqueur
Finely grated rind and juice
   of 1 orange

Put the strawberries in a glass serving dish. Sprinkle with the sweetener and add the liqueur, orange rind and juice. Toss gently, then leave to marinate for at least 30 minutes, preferably 1–2 hours, before serving.

St Clement's Mousse

SERVES 4

1 packet sugar-free lemon jelly
(jello)
150 ml/¼ pt/⅔ cup boiling water
300 g/11 oz/1 small can mandarin
oranges in natural juice,
drained, reserving the juice
15 ml/1 tbsp lemon juice
175 g/6 oz/1 small can low-fat
evaporated milk, chilled
60 ml/4 tbsp very low-fat crème
fraîche
4 tiny mint sprigs

Dissolve the jelly in the boiling
water. Stir in the mandarin orange
juice and lemon juice and leave until
cold and the consistency of egg white.
Meanwhile, whisk the evaporated milk
until thick and fluffy. Fold into the jelly
mixture and add most of the fruit
(reserving four good segments for
decoration). Spoon into glasses and
chill until set. Spread the crème
fraîche over and decorate with the
reserved mandarin segments and tiny
mint sprigs.

Raspberry Mousse

SERVES 4

Prepare as for St Clement's Mousse
but use sugar-free raspberry jelly
(jello) instead of lemon and a can of
raspberries in natural juice instead of
mandarins. Reserve four raspberries
for decoration, drained on kitchen
paper before topping the desserts.

Lemon Velvet

SERVES 4

10 ml/2 tsp gelatine
300 ml/½ pt/1¼ cups pure
pineapple juice
1 lemon
150 ml/¼ pt/⅔ cup low-fat
whipping cream, whipped
4 tiny mint sprigs

Dissolve the gelatine in a little of the
pineapple juice according to the
packet directions. Stir in the remaining
juice. Grate the lemon rind and add.
Squeeze the juice. Add as much as you
like to give a good lemony flavour but
not too sour. Chill until the consistency of egg white. Gradually whisk
into the whipped cream. Transfer to
four small serving dishes and chill
until set. Decorate each with a mint
sprig.

Peach Cheese Melba

SERVES 2

2 large ripe peaches
60 ml/4 tbsp very low-fat soft
cheese
Artificial sweetener granules
Grated rind and juice of 1 orange
100 g/4 oz raspberries

Skin the peaches, halve and remove
the stones (pits). Mash the cheese
with sweetener to taste and the
orange rind. Spoon the cheese on to
each peach half and place each in a
shallow glass dish. Purée the raspberries with the orange juice. Pass
through a sieve (strainer) to remove
the seeds. Taste and sweeten slightly if
necessary. Spoon over the peaches.

Lovers' Kiss

SERVES 4

2 passion fruit
225 g/8 oz/1 cup very low-fat quark
30 ml/2 tbsp pure orange juice
Artificial sweetener granules
A squeeze of lemon juice (optional)
2 egg whites

Halve the passion fruit, scoop out the fleshy seeds and rub through a sieve (strainer) over a bowl to remove the seeds. Stir in the quark, orange juice and sweetener to taste. Sharpen with lemon juice, if necessary. Whisk the egg whites until stiff and fold into the mixture with a metal spoon. Spoon into four wine goblets. Chill. The mixture should separate slightly.

Minted Melon and Kiwi Fruit Salad

SERVES 4

1 small honeydew melon
4 kiwi fruit, peeled
200 ml/7 fl oz/scant 1 cup apple juice
2 mint sprigs
A few tiny mint sprigs

Halve the melon and scoop out the fruit using a melon baller, or peel and cut into dice. Place in a bowl. Slice two of the kiwi fruit and place in a bowl with the melon. Purée the remaining kiwis with the apple juice and mint. Pour through a sieve (strainer) over the bowl of fruit to remove the seeds and any mint stalks. Chill for at least 1 hour before decorating with mint sprigs and serving.

Lemon Sorbet

SERVES 6

15 ml/1 tbsp powdered gelatine
175 ml/6 fl oz/¾ cup water
Finely grated rind and juice of 1 lime
Finely grated rind of 1 lemon
Juice of 4 lemons
15 ml/1 tbsp artificial sweetener granules
1 egg white

Mix the gelatine with 45 ml/3 tbsp of the water and leave to soften for 5 minutes. Stand the bowl over a pan of gently simmering water and stir until dissolved. Alternatively, place briefly in the microwave. Stir in the remaining water, the lime and lemon rind and the juices. Stir in the sweetener. Taste and add a little more sweetener if liked (it should taste sweet but tangy). Turn into a suitable freezing container with a lid, cover and freeze for 2 hours. Remove from the freezer and whisk thoroughly to break up all the ice crystals. Whisk the egg white until stiff and fold into the mixture with a metal spoon. Cover and freeze for a further 1½ hours. Whisk thoroughly again, then freeze until firm. Transfer the sorbet to the fridge about 30 minutes before eating to soften slightly.

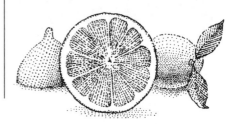

Orange Sorbet

SERVES 6

15 ml/1 tbsp powdered gelatine
175 ml/6 fl oz/¾ cup water
Finely grated rind and juice of 1
lime
Finely grated rind of ½ orange
Juice of 4 large oranges
15 ml/1 tbsp artificial sweetener
granules
1 egg white

Put the gelatine in a bowl with 45 ml/3 tbsp of the water and leave to soften for 5 minutes. Stand the bowl over a pan of gently simmering water and stir until dissolved. Alternatively, place briefly in the microwave. Stir in the remaining water, the lime and orange rind and the juices. Stir in the sweetener. Turn into a suitable freezer container with a lid, cover and freeze for 2 hours. Whisk thoroughly to break up all the ice crystals. Whisk the egg white until stiff and fold into the mixture with a metal spoon. Cover and freeze for a further 1½ hours. Whisk thoroughly again, then freeze until firm. Transfer to the fridge 30 minutes before serving to soften slightly.

Raspberry Sorbet

SERVES 6

450 g/1 lb raspberries
15 ml/1 tbsp powdered gelatine
175 ml/6 fl oz/¾ cup water
Finely grated rind and juice
of ½ lemon
15 ml/1 tbsp artificial sweetener
granules
1 egg white

Purée the raspberries in a blender or food processor, then pass through a sieve (strainer). Sprinkle the gelatine over 45 ml/3 tbsp of the water in a bowl and leave to soften for 5 minutes. Stand the bowl over a pan of gently simmering water and stir until dissolved. Alternatively, place briefly in the microwave. Stir in the remaining water, the lemon rind and juice, the fruit purée and sweetener. Turn into a suitable freezer container with a lid. Cover and freeze for 2 hours. Remove from the freezer and whisk thoroughly to break up the ice crystals. Whisk the egg white until stiff and fold in with a metal spoon. Cover and freeze for a further 1½ hours. Whisk thoroughly again, then freeze until firm. Transfer to the fridge 30 minutes before eating to soften slightly.

Strawberry Sorbet

SERVES 6

Prepare as for Raspberry Sorbet but use ripe strawberries instead of raspberries and the grated rind and juice of 1 lime instead of the lemon, if liked. There is no need to sieve (strain) the fruit after puréeing.

Fresh Fruit Platter with Raspberry Sauce

SERVES 6

225 g/8 oz raspberries
15 ml/1 tbsp lemon juice
Artificial sweetener granules
A selection of sliced fresh fruits
such as star fruit, mango,
pawpaw, strawberries, kiwi
fruit, orange, allowing 6–8
pieces per person

Purée the raspberries in a blender or food processor with the lemon juice. Pass through a sieve (strainer) to remove the seeds. Sweeten to taste. Put a pool of sauce on six serving plates. Arrange the fruit attractively on top.

Venetian Coffee Cheese

SERVES 6

15 ml/1 tbsp instant coffee
granules
15 ml/1 tbsp water
225 g/8 oz/1 cup very low-fat soft
cheese
10 ml/2 tsp artificial sweetener
granules (or to taste)
6 walnut halves
To serve:
12 ice-cream wafers

Mix the coffee with the water until dissolved. Gradually beat into the cheese with the sweetener. Taste and re-sweeten, if liked. Turn into six very small serving pots and top each with a walnut half. Chill until ready to serve with the wafers.

Melon Glacé

SERVES 4

2 small ogen, cantaloupe, galia or
charentais melons
4 small scoops virtually fat-free
vanilla ice or home-made Vanilla
Ice Cream (see page 335)
20 ml/4 tsp ginger wine

Halve the melons and scoop out the seeds. Place the fruit in four individual dishes. Add a scoop of vanilla ice or ice cream to the centre and spoon the ginger wine over. Serve straight away.

Minted Melon with Raspberries

SERVES 6

1 honeydew melon
225 g/8 oz raspberries
12 mint leaves
5 ml/1 tsp artificial sweetener
granules
A mint sprig

Cut a slice off the top of the melon and remove the seeds. Scoop out the flesh using a melon baller, or dig out with a small spoon. Mix with the raspberries in a bowl. Chop the mint leaves on a board with the sweetener. Sprinkle over the fruit and chill. Cut a small slice off the base of the melon so it stands upright. Place on a serving plate. Just before serving, pile the mixture back into the melon shell and decorate with the mint sprig.

···············COLD DESSERTS···············

200

CALORIES OR LESS

Gaelic Coffee with Chocolate Mint Fingers

SERVES 6

**225 g/8 oz/1 block plain (semi-
sweet) chocolate suitable for
diabetics
25 g/1 oz/⅙ cup raisins
100 g/4 oz/½ cup very low-fat soft
cheese
Artificial sweetener granules
Peppermint essence (extract)
A few drops of green food
colouring
900 ml/1½ pts/3¾ cups strong
black coffee
60 ml/4 tbsp Irish or Scotch
whisky
150 ml/¼ pt/⅔ cup low-fat double
(heavy) cream**

Line the base of a 20 cm/8 in square
shallow baking tin (pan) with non-
stick baking parchment. Break up half
the chocolate and place in a bowl over
a pan of gently simmering water. Stir
the chocolate all the time and as soon
as the bowl is hot and the chocolate is
beginning to melt, remove the bowl
from the pan and continue to stir until
melted. Spread over the baking parchment in an even layer. Chill. Put the
raisins in a cup and snip with scissors
until finely chopped. Place in a bowl
with the cheese and sweeten to taste
with artificial sweetener granules. Add
peppermint essence, a drop at a time,
until a good minty flavour is achieved.
Add a few drops of green food colouring. Spread this mixture over the set
chocolate and chill again until fairly

firm. Melt the remaining chocolate in
the same way as before. Spread on the
cheese, using a wet palette knife if necessary. Chill again until firm. Using a
knife dipped in very hot water, cut the
slab into sixteen 5 cm/2 in long fingers.
Carefully lift out on to a serving plate.
To make the Gaelic coffee, put an
empty teaspoon in each of six wine
goblets and pour in the hot coffee.
Sweeten to taste with sweetener and
add 10 ml/2 tsp whisky to each.
Remove the teaspoons. Using a clean,
cold spoon, hold it just above the surface of the coffee, rounded side up, and
pour the cream slowly over the back of
the spoon so it floats in a layer on top
of the coffee. Repeat with each glass.
Serve with the chocolate mint fingers.

Strawberry Syllabub

SERVES 4

**225 g/8 oz ripe strawberries
5 ml/1 tsp artificial sweetener
granules
10 ml/2 tsp lemon juice
100 ml/3½ fl oz/6½ tbsp dry white
wine
200 ml/7 fl oz/scant 1 cup low-fat
double (heavy) cream**

Purée the fruit in a blender or food
processor with the sweetener. Put
the lemon juice, wine and cream in a
bowl and whip until softly peaking.
Fold in the strawberry purée and
spoon into four wine goblets. Chill for
at least 2 hours, when the mixture will
have separated into two delicious
layers.

Golden Trifle

SERVES 4

*1 Swiss (jelly) roll, filled with
reduced-sugar apricot jam
(conserve) and left to cool (see
Hot Strawberry Roll page 308)*
*228 g/8 oz/1 small can peach
slices in natural juice*
*1 packet sugar-free orange or
peach jelly (jello)*
*1 packet sugar-free orange or
peach dessert whip*
Skimmed milk, chilled

Slice the Swiss roll and place in the
base of a serving dish. Drain the
peaches, reserving the juice and a
couple of slices for decoration. Chop
the remainder and scatter over the
Swiss roll. Make up the jelly using the
fruit juice instead of some of the water.
Pour over the sponge and fruit and
chill until set. Make up the dessert
whip with skimmed milk according to
the packet directions. Spoon over the
trifle and chill. Decorate with the
reserved fruit before serving.

Tropical Sundae

SERVES 4

1 fresh pineapple
*8 fresh dates, stoned (pitted) and
chopped*
2 small bananas, sliced
45 ml/3 tbsp dark rum
45 ml/3 tbsp apple juice
*15 ml/1 tbsp coconut flakes,
toasted*

Cut a slice off the top of the pineapple about 3 cm/1½ in from the
leaves and reserve the top as a lid.
Scoop out the flesh with a serrated-
edged knife, leaving the pineapple skin
as a shell. Chop the flesh, discarding
any hard core. Place in a bowl and mix
with the dates, bananas, rum and
apple juice. Toss and chill for at least 1
hour. Add the toasted coconut, pile
back into the shell, top with the lid
and serve.

Sinful Strawberry Brulée

SERVES 4

225 g/8 oz strawberries, sliced
*150 ml/¼ pt/⅔ cup low-fat double
(heavy) cream*
*150 ml/¼ pt/⅔ cup very low-fat
plain yoghurt*
5 ml/1 tsp vanilla essence (extract)
60 ml/4 tbsp demerara sugar

Put the fruit in four small flameproof
dishes. Whip together the cream
and yoghurt with the vanilla until
peaking and spoon over the fruit.
Chill. Just before serving, sprinkle the
sugar over each portion and place
under a hot grill (broiler) until the
sugar melts and caramelises. Serve
straight away.

Vanilla Ice Cream

SERVES 8

25 g/1 oz/¼ cup plain (all-purpose) flour
2 eggs, separated
10 ml/2 tsp vanilla essence (extract)
300 ml/½ pt/1¼ cups skimmed milk
10 ml/2 tsp artificial sweetener granules
300 ml/½ pt/1¼ cups low-fat double (heavy) cream

Put the flour in a pan with the egg yolks and half the vanilla essence. Whisk in a little of the milk until well blended, then stir in the remainder. Cook over a moderate heat, stirring all the time, until thick and smooth, then simmer for 3 minutes, stirring. Sweeten to taste. Cover with a circle of wet greaseproof (waxed) paper and leave to cool. When cold, whisk the egg whites until peaking, then the cream with the remaining vanilla until softly peaking. Fold the cream, then the egg whites into the cold custard and sweeten with the artificial sweetener. The mixture should taste very sweet now as it will taste less so when frozen. Turn into a plastic container with a lid and freeze for 3 hours. When half-frozen, whisk thoroughly to break up the ice crystals. Freeze again until firm. Remove from the freezer to the fridge about 20 minutes before serving to soften slightly.

Chocolate Ice Cream

SERVES 8

Prepare as for Vanilla Ice Cream but add 30 ml/2 tbsp cocoa (unsweetened chocolate) powder to the custard mixture before blending in the milk.

Mock Pistachio Ice Cream

SERVES 8

Prepare as for Vanilla Ice Cream but substitute almond essence (extract) for vanilla and add a few drops of green food colouring to the mixture.

Coffee Ice Cream

SERVES 8

Prepare as for Vanilla Ice Cream but dissolve 15 ml/1 tbsp instant coffee powder in the milk before making the custard.

Raspberry Ripple Ice Cream

SERVES 8

Prepare as for Vanilla Ice Cream but add 225 g/8 oz raspberries, puréed then sieved (strained) to remove the seeds, after whisking when half-frozen. Lightly fold in but do not over-mix or you won't have ripples.

Mango Ripple

SERVES 8

Prepare as for Vanilla Ice Cream but add 1 large mango, puréed with a squeeze of lemon juice, after whisking when half-frozen. Lightly fold in but do not over-mix or you won't have ripples.

Chocolate Eclairs

SERVES 6

65 g/2½ oz/generous ½ cup plain
(all-purpose) flour
A pinch of salt
150 ml/¼ pt/⅔ cup water
65 g/2½ oz/generous ¼ cup low-fat
spread
2 eggs, beaten
30 ml/2 tbsp cocoa (unsweetened
chocolate) powder
100 g/4 oz/½ cup very low-fat soft
cheese
Artificial sweetener granules
150 ml/¼ pt/⅔ cup low-fat
whipping cream, whipped

Sift the flour and salt on to a sheet of
kitchen paper. Put the water in a
saucepan with 25 g/1 oz/2 tbsp of the
low-fat spread and heat until the fat
melts. Add all the flour in one go and
beat well until the mixture leaves the
sides of the pan clean. Remove from
the heat. Beat in the eggs a little at a
time, beating well after each addition,
until smooth and glossy but the mixture still holds its shape. Spoon or
pipe into six sausage shapes on a
sheet of baking parchment on a
baking sheet. Bake in a preheated
oven at 200°C/400°F/gas mark 6 for
about 20 minutes or until risen, gold-
en and crisp. Cool on a wire rack.
Meanwhile, melt the remaining low-
fat spread in a small saucepan. Add
the cocoa and cook for 2 minutes, stirring. Empty into a bowl. Beat in the
cheese and sweeten to taste. Chill.
Make a slit in the side of each éclair
and fill with a little whipped cream.
Spread the chocolate mixture over the
top and serve.

Strawberry Cheesecake

SERVES 8

100 g/4 oz semi-sweet wheatmeal
biscuits (cookies), crushed
50 g/2 oz/¼ cup low-fat spread,
melted
225 g/8 oz/1 cup very low-fat soft
cheese
250 ml/8 fl oz/1 cup very low-fat
crème fraîche
45 ml/3 tbsp reduced-sugar
strawberry jam (conserve)
15 ml/1 tbsp powdered gelatine
45 ml/3 tbsp water
Artificial sweetener granules
(optional)
100 g/4 oz fresh strawberries

Mix the biscuit crumbs with the
low-fat spread and press into the
base of a 20 cm/8 in flan tin (pie pan).
Chill until firm. Meanwhile, beat the
cheese with the crème fraîche and the
jam. Sprinkle the gelatine over the
water and leave to soften for a few
minutes. Stand the bowl in a pan of
hot water and stir until dissolved, or
warm briefly in the microwave. Stir
into the cheese mixture and sweeten
to taste, if necessary. Turn into the flan
dish and chill until firm. Decorate the
top with the strawberries and serve.

Sensational Snacks

As soon as you tell yourself you're on a diet, you'll be desperate to eat between meals because you think you shouldn't! Here are some simple but nutritious ideas to keep you going until the next gourmet feast.

CALORIES OR LESS

Fruity Favourites

Any of the following are extremely good for you so nibble whenever you need to. I've given a serving suggestion for each too. That way eating and enjoying them will last longer and so will psychologically fill you up more without adding calories! You can, of course, eat them plain.

Apple Fan: cut a washed eating (dessert) apple into eight slices, discarding the core. Arrange in a starburst pattern on a serving plate and put 5 ml/1 tsp ground cinnamon with a few grains of artificial sweetener in the centre. Dip in and eat.

Clementine and Cucumber Bites: segment a clementine or satsuma. Dice a hunk of cucumber into the same number of pieces. Spear a piece of each on cocktail sticks (toothpicks).

Pear Pleasure: peel a pear and cut into small wedges, discarding the core. Mix a little ground ginger with a few grains of artificial sweetener. Using a small fork, spear the pear, then dip in the ginger before eating.

Nectarine Sparkle: slice a nectarine and place in a glass wine goblet. Top up with diet lemonade. Drink the drink, then eat the fruit with a spoon.

Strawberry Fizz: hull and slice enough strawberries to fill a glass. Top up with strawberry-flavoured sparkling water. Drink the drink, then eat the fruit.

Fresh Date with Health: remove the stones (pits) from three fresh dates. Fill each with 5 ml/1 tsp very low-fat soft cheese.

Black Beauties: make a slit in the side of three ready-to-eat prunes and remove the stones (pits), if necessary. Push a stuffed green olive in the centre of each and enjoy.

Gold Nuggets: make a slit in the side of three ready-to-eat dried apricots and push a whole almond into each. Eat and enjoy.

Kiwi Cooler: chill a kiwi fruit, then cut a slice off the top. Eat a spoonful, then add 5 ml/1 tsp very low-fat fromage frais. Eat with the teaspoon.

Blackcurrant Refresher: purée 75 g/3 oz blackcurrants with 120 ml/4 fl oz/½ cup apple juice. Strain through a sieve (strainer), sweeten to taste with a few grains of artificial sweetener and serve over ice.

Recurrant Refresher: prepare as for Blackcurrant Refresher (see page 337) but use redcurrants instead.

Dried Apricot Yoghurt: purée three ready-to-eat dried apricots in a blender or food processor with 60 ml/ 4 tbsp very low-fat plain yoghurt. Sweeten with artificial sweetener granules, if absolutely necessary.

Fresh Strawberry Yoghurt: purée 75 g/3 oz ripe strawberries in a blender or food processor with 60 ml/4 tbsp very low-fat plain yoghurt. Sweeten to taste with artificial sweetener, if necessary.

Fresh Raspberry Yoghurt: purée 75 g/3 oz raspberries in a blender or food processor with 60 ml/4 tbsp very low-fat yoghurt. Sieve (strain), if liked, to remove the seeds. Sweeten to taste with artificial sweetener, if necessary.

Fast Fruits

- 5 ready-to-eat dried apricots
- 5 ready-to-eat stoned (pitted) prunes
- 30 ml/2 tbsp raisins or sultanas
- 5 stoned dates
- 1 nectarine
- 1 apple
- 1 pear
- 1 clementine or satsuma
- 1 melon wedge
- 1 water melon wedge
- 3 small plums
- 1 large kiwi fruit
- 175 g/6 oz strawberries, raspberries or blackberries

Vegetable Varieties

Eat as much or as many raw carrots, celery, cucumber, radishes, mushrooms and lettuce as you like. For flavour add just 5–10 ml/1–2 tsp low-calorie salad dressing for dipping. Or try any of the following goodies:

Celery Boats: spread 25 g/1 oz/2 tbsp very low-fat soft cheese along the groove in 2 or 3 celery sticks. Cut into short 'boats' and arrange on a plate.

Celery and Fennel Boats: spread 25 g/1 oz/2 tbsp very low-fat soft cheese along the groove in 2 or 3 celery sticks. Sprinkle with fennel seeds and cut into short 'boats'. Arrange on a plate.

Savoury Cheese Boats: mix 25 g/ 1 oz /2 tbsp very low-fat soft cheese with 5 ml/1 tsp yeast extract. Spread along the groove in 2 or 3 celery sticks. Sprinkle with chopped parsley and cut into short 'boats'. Arrange on a plate.

Cheese and Tomato Boats: skin and finely chop a tomato and mix with 25 g/1 oz/2 tbsp very low-fat soft cheese. Season with a little freshly ground black pepper. Spread along the groove in 2 or 3 celery sticks. Sprinkle with chopped basil. Cut into short 'boats' and arrange on a plate.

Lettuce Rolls: spread three lettuce leaves with 25 g/1 oz/2 tbsp very low-fat soft cheese. Top with finely chopped cucumber and tomato and a good grinding of black pepper. Fold in the sides and roll up. Eat with the fingers.

Carrots with Cheese and Chive Dip: cut 2 carrots into matchsticks. Blend 25 g/1 oz/2 tbsp very low-fat soft cheese with 15 ml/1 tbsp snipped chives and season with salt and pepper. Pack into a small pot. Put the pot on a plate and arrange the carrot around.

Cucumber with Minted Cheese Dip: cut as much cucumber as you like into matchsticks. Mix 25 g/1 oz/ 2 tbsp very low-fat soft cheese with 5 ml/1 tsp dried mint and a little garlic salt in a small bowl. Place on a plate with the cucumber around.

Mixed Vegetable Dippers with Spicy Tomato Dip: cut a carrot, a 5 cm/2 in piece of cucumber and a celery stick into matchsticks. Blend 25 g/1 oz/2 tbsp very low-fat soft cheese with 1 skinned, seeded and chopped tomato, Tabasco sauce to taste and a dash of Worcestershire sauce. Pack into a small pot and place in the centre of a plate with the 'dippers' around.

Crispbread Snackers

Ham and Mustard 'Butter': mash 5 ml/1 tsp low-fat spread with 2.5 ml/ ½ tsp Dijon mustard. Spread on a low-calorie crispbread. Top with a thin slice of ham (from a packet) and garnish with cucumber slices.

Cheese and Pickled Onion: mash 15 ml/1 tbsp low-fat Cheddar cheese with 5 ml/1 tsp low-fat spread. Spread on a low-calorie crispbread and top with a sliced pickled onion.

Savoury Cress: spread a low-calorie crispbread with 5 ml/1 tsp low-fat spread and yeast extract to taste. Top with cress.

Savoury Cucumber: spread a low-calorie crispbread with 5 ml/1 tsp low-fat spread and yeast extract to taste. Top with cucumber slices.

Cheese and Mustard and Cress: spread a low-calorie crispbread with 15 ml/1 tbsp very low-fat soft cheese. Top with mustard and cress.

Cheese and Tomato: spread a low-calorie crispbread with 15 ml/1 tbsp very low-fat soft cheese. Top with tomato slices and sprinkle with torn basil leaves.

Cheese and Satsuma: spread a low-calorie crispbread with 15 ml/1 tbsp very low-fat soft cheese. Top with the segments from ½ satsuma.

Cheese, Cucumber and Fennel: spread a low-calorie crispbread with 15 ml/1 tbsp very low-fat soft cheese. Sprinkle with fennel seeds and top with cucumber slices.

Hot Carrot: mix 15 ml/1 tbsp very low-fat soft cheese with a dash of hot pepper sauce. Spread on a low-calorie crispbread and top with a pile of grated carrot. Sprinkle with poppy seeds.

Beetroot and Onion: spread a low-calorie crispbread with 15 ml/1 tbsp very low-fat soft cheese. Top with beetroot slices, then thinly sliced onion rings. Sprinkle with chopped parsley.

Curried Cheese and Raisin: mix 15 ml/1 tbsp very low-fat soft cheese with 1.5 ml/¼ tsp curry paste. Spread on a low-calorie crispbread and sprinkle with raisins. Garnish with snipped chives.

Crispy Baked Potato Skins (see page 275) also make a delicious snack. When baked, store in an airtight container and eat within 2 days.

·················SENSATIONAL SNACKS·················

CALORIES OR LESS

Jumbo Digestive Biscuits

MAKES ABOUT 14

175 g/6 oz/1½ cups wholemeal flour
25 g/1 oz/¼ cup plain (all-purpose) flour
2.5 ml/½ tsp salt
5 ml/1 tsp baking powder
25 g/1 oz/¼ cup fine oatmeal
75 g/3 oz/⅓ cup low-fat spread
10 g/2 tsp artificial sweetener granules
90 ml/6 tbsp skimmed milk

Mix together the flours, salt, baking powder and oatmeal in a bowl. Rub in the low-fat spread and stir in the sweetener. Mix with enough of the milk to form a firm dough. Knead gently on a lightly floured surface. Roll out thinly and cut into large rounds using a 7.5 cm/3 in biscuit (cookie) cutter. Transfer to a greased baking sheet and prick attractively with a fork. Bake the digestive biscuits (Graham crackers) in a preheated oven at 190ºC/375ºF/gas mark 5 for 15–20 minutes until golden. Cool slightly, then transfer to a wire rack to cool completely. Store in an airtight tin. Allow one biscuit per serving.

Dropped Scones

MAKES 12

100 g/4 oz/1 cup plain (all-purpose) flour
A pinch of salt
2.5 ml/½ tsp artificial sweetener granules (or to taste)
1 egg
150 ml/¼ pt/⅔ cup skimmed milk
Low-fat spread

Sift the flour, salt and artificial sweetener into a bowl. Add the egg and beat until smooth. Stir in the milk. Lightly grease a frying pan (skillet) with a little low-fat spread. Drop spoonfuls of the mixture into the pan and cook for about 2 minutes until golden brown underneath. Flip over with a palette knife and cook the other side. Keep warm in a napkin over a pan of hot water while cooking the remainder. Serve two per person and eat warm. They can be reheated briefly in the microwave or on a plate over a pan of hot water.

100

Light Wholemeal Dropped Scones

MAKES 12

100 g/4 oz/1 cup wholemeal flour
A pinch of salt
2.5 ml/½ tsp artificial sweetener granules (or to taste)
1 egg, separated
150 ml/¼ pt/⅔ cup skimmed milk
Low-fat spread for cooking

Mix together the flour and salt with the sweetener. Beat in the egg yolk and milk. Whisk the egg white until stiff and fold into the mixture with a metal spoon. Heat a very little low-fat spread in a frying pan (skillet). Pour off the excess. Add spoonfuls of the mixture and fry until golden underneath and fluffing up. Turn over and cook the other side. Keep warm in a napkin on a plate over a pan of hot water while cooking the remainder. Serve two each and eat warm.

Caraway Fingers

MAKES 16

175 g/6 oz/1½ cups plain (all-purpose) flour
50 g/2 oz/½ cup wholemeal flour
150 g/5 oz/⅔ cup low-fat spread
5 ml/1 tsp caraway seeds
10 ml/2 tsp artificial sweetener granules

Mix the flours in a bowl. Add the low-fat spread and rub in with the fingertips. Stir in the caraway seeds and sweetener. Knead together to form a dough. Press into a lightly greased 20 cm/8 in square baking tin (pan). Chill for several hours or overnight. Bake in a preheated oven at 180°C/350°F/gas mark 4 for about 20 minutes or until turning very pale golden. Cool slightly, then cut into fingers. Finish cooling on a wire rack and store in an airtight tin. Allow one finger per serving.

Everyday Scones

MAKES 10

225 g/8 oz/2 cups self-raising (self-rising) flour
10 ml/2 tsp baking powder
A pinch of salt
25 g/1 oz/2 tbsp low-fat spread
5 ml/1 tsp artificial sweetener granules (optional)
Skimmed milk to mix
To serve:
Low-fat spread and reduced-sugar jam (conserve)

Mix together the flour, baking powder and salt in a bowl. Rub in the low-fat spread. Stir in the sweetener, if using. Mix with enough milk to form a soft but not sticky dough. Pat out to a round about 2 cm/¾ in thick. Cut into ten rounds using a small biscuit (cookie) cutter. Transfer to a baking sheet. Bake the scones (biscuits) in a preheated oven at 220°C/425°F/gas mark 7 for about 10 minutes until golden and the bases sound hollow when tapped. Serve warm, split and spread with a thin scraping of low-fat spread and a tiny scraping of reduced-sugar jam. Allow one scone per serving.

Savoury Yoghurt Scones

MAKES 10

225 g/8 oz/2 cups self-raising
   (self-rising) flour
10 ml/2 tsp baking powder
A pinch of salt
A pinch of cayenne
25 g/1 oz/2 tbsp low-fat spread
15 ml/1 tbsp chopped parsley
120 ml/4 fl oz/½ cup very low-fat
   plain yoghurt
To serve:
**Very low-fat soft cheese or low-fat
   spread**

Sift the flour, baking powder and salt into a bowl. Add the low-fat spread and rub in with the fingertips. Mix in the parsley and yoghurt. Add a little water, if necessary, to form a soft but not sticky dough. Flatten with the hand to about 2 cm/¾ in thick. Cut into rounds using a small biscuit (cookie) cutter. Place on a very lightly greased baking (cookie) sheet and bake the scones (biscuits) in a preheated oven at 200ºC/ 400ºF/gas mark 6 for about 15 minutes until well risen and golden and the bases sound hollow when tapped. Serve warm or cold, split and spread with a scraping of very low-fat soft cheese or low-fat spread. Allow one scone per serving.

Sweet Yoghurt Scones

MAKES 10

225 g/8 oz/2 cups self-raising
   (self-rising) flour
10 ml/2 tsp baking powder
A pinch of salt
5 ml/1 tsp artificial sweetener
   granules
25 g/1 oz/2 tbsp low-fat spread
120 ml/4 fl oz/½ cup very low-fat
   plain yoghurt
To serve:
**A scraping of No-sugar Apple and
   Cinnamon Spread (see page
   361)**

Sift together the flour, baking powder, salt and sweetener in a bowl. Add the low-fat spread and rub in with the fingertips. Mix with the yoghurt and a little water, if necessary, to form a soft but not sticky dough. Pat out to a round about 2 cm/¾ in thick and cut into rounds using a small biscuit (cookie) cutter. Transfer to a very lightly greased baking (cookie) sheet and bake the scones (biscuits) in a preheated oven at 200ºC/400ºF/gas mark 6 for about 15 minutes until risen, golden and the bases sound hollow when tapped. Serve warm or cold, spread with a scraping of No-sugar Apple and Cinnamon Spread. Allow one scone per serving.

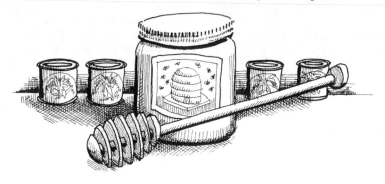

Cottage Griddle Cakes

MAKES 12

25 g/1 oz/2 tbsp low-fat spread, melted
100 g/4 oz/½ cup low-fat cottage cheese with chives
2 eggs, beaten
50 g/2 oz/½ cup plain (all-purpose) flour
5 ml/1 tsp baking powder
15 ml/1 tbsp skimmed milk
Low-fat spread, for greasing

Mix the melted low-fat spread with the cheese and beat in the eggs, flour, baking powder and milk to form a thick batter. Heat a little low-fat spread in a heavy-based frying pan (skillet). Pour off any excess. Drop spoonfuls into the pan and cook until the undersides are golden. Flip over with a palette knife and cook the other side until brown. Wrap in a clean napkin while cooking the remainder. Serve two per person. They can be reheated very briefly in the microwave or on a plate over a pan of hot water.

Not-so-naughty Nuts

Nuts are loaded with calories, especially the roasted, salted kind you buy in packets for nibbles with drinks. They are good for you, though, without all the oil so here's a way you can enjoy them – just a small handful for a snack mind you! And here's a tip – put the handful (15 g/½ oz/2 tbsp) in a little bowl and nibble them slowly. Don't take them from a bigger bowl because you'll just want more.

Dry-roasted Nuts: put 45 ml/3 tbsp raw peanuts or other raw nuts on a piece of kitchen paper in the microwave and spread out in a ring to prevent the middle ones burning. Microwave on High for 3–4 minutes or until golden brown, stirring once if necessary. Cool. Repeat until you have enough to store in an airtight jar. Alternatively, put enough in a heavy frying pan (skillet) to just cover the base. Dry-fry (sauté) over a moderate heat, stirring until golden – but take care, they can burn very easily. Remove from the pan as soon as they are cooked or they will continue to brown.

Spicy Nuts: prepare as for Dry-roasted Nuts but sprinkle with a little sea salt and chilli powder while still hot after roasting before storing.

Savoury Nuts: prepare as for Dry-roasted Nuts but put the nuts on a plate instead of kitchen paper and sprinkle each batch with 30 ml/2 tbsp soy sauce for the last minute or so of cooking. Toss after 30 seconds.

Nuts and Raisins: a favourite standby. Have 15 ml/1 tbsp home-roasted or raw nuts and 15 ml/1 tbsp raisins.

Nut Clusters: blend two parts dried apricots with 1 part raw nuts in a food processor (so for 175 g/6 oz/1½ cups dried apricots, add 75 g/3 oz/¾ cup raw nuts). Add a dash of mixed (apple-pie) spice or ground cinnamon, if liked. Roll into bite-sized balls. Serve two for a snack.

Banana Smoothie

SERVES 1

1 ripe banana
175 ml/6 fl oz/¾ cup ice-cold
skimmed milk

Break the banana into pieces and purée in a blender or food processor. Add the milk in a steady stream and blend until thick and frothy. Pour into a glass and enjoy.

Banana and Orange Smoothie

SERVES 1

Prepare as for Banana Smoothie but add the grated rind and juice of 1 orange to the banana before puréeing and use only 150 ml/¼ pt/⅔ cup skimmed milk.

Banana and Strawberry Smoothie

SERVES 1

Prepare as for Banana Smoothie but use a small banana and add 50 g/ 2 oz very ripe strawberries when puréeing.

Vanilla Yoghurt Shake

SERVES 1

150 ml/¼ pt/⅔ cup very low-fat
plain yoghurt
5 ml/1 tsp vanilla essence (extract)
150 ml/¼ pt/⅔ cup apple juice
Ice cubes

Put all the ingredients except the ice in a container with a screw-top or sealed lid. Shake well until frothy. Pour over ice and serve straight away.

Strawberry Yoghurt Shake

SERVES 1

100 g/4 oz ripe strawberries
75 ml/5 tbsp thick very low-fat
plain yoghurt
150 ml/¼ pt/⅔ cup ice-cold
skimmed milk
Artificial sweetener granules
(optional)

Purée the strawberries in a blender or food processor. Add the yoghurt and milk and run the machine until frothy. Sweeten, if liked, with a very few grains of artificial sweetener. Pour into a glass and serve.

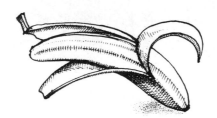

Peachy Yoghurt Shake

SERVES 1

**1 ripe peach, peeled and stoned
    (pitted)
75 ml/5 tbsp thick very low-fat
    plain yoghurt
150 ml/¼ pt/⅔ cup ice-cold
    skimmed milk**

Cut up the peach and purée in a blender or food processor. Add the yoghurt and milk and run the machine until frothy. Pour into a glass and serve.

Nectarine Yoghurt Shake

SERVES 1

**1 ripe nectarine, peeled and
    stoned (pitted)
75 ml/5 tbsp thick very low-fat
    plain yoghurt
150 ml/¼ pt/⅔ cup ice-cold
    skimmed milk**

Cut up the nectarine and purée in a blender or food processor. Add the yoghurt and milk and run the machine until frothy. Pour into a glass and serve.

Fresh Apricot Yoghurt

SERVES 1

**3 ripe apricots, stoned (pitted)
30 ml/2 tbsp apple juice
150 ml/¼ pt/⅔ cup thick very low-
    fat plain yoghurt
Artificial sweetener, if necessary**

Purée the apricots with the apple juice in a blender or food processor. Add the yoghurt and blend again. Sweeten, if necessary, with a very few grains of sweetener. Spoon into a glass and serve. (This is quite a small quantity for some processors. You may find it best to make double the quantity and store the remainder in the fridge.)

Fast Fruits

- 1 large orange
- 1 large banana
- 1 mango
- 1 papaya
- 3 dried pears
- 3 dried figs
- 3 dried peaches
- 3 large plums
- 1 large fresh pineapple wedge
- 1 pomegranate

Tasty Savoury Morsels

Cheese and Pineapple: 25 g/1 oz low-fat Cheddar cheese, cubed, with 1 pineapple slice (fresh or canned in natural juice), cut into pieces. Spear on cocktail sticks (toothpicks), if liked.

Cheese and Olive: 15 g/½ oz low-fat Cheddar cheese and five black or green olives.

Cheese and Tomatoes: 25 g/1 oz low-fat Cheddar cheese and two tomatoes, quartered and sprinkled with black pepper.

Cheese and Apple: 25 g/1 oz low-fat Cheddar cheese and one eating (dessert) apple.

Cheese and Celery: 25 g/1 oz low-fat Cheddar cheese and as much celery as you like.

Cheese and Crispbreads: 15 g/½ oz low-fat Cheddar cheese, two low-calorie crispbreads and a scraping of low-fat spread.

Crisp Ploughman's Snack: 15 g/½ oz low-fat Cheddar cheese, one low-fat crispbread, a scraping of low-fat spread, one tomato, some cucumber and one pickled onion.

Cheese and Chutney: one low-calorie crispbread, 15 g/½ oz low-fat Cheddar cheese and 5 ml/1 tsp Dieter's Chutney (see page 361).

Stuffed Tomatoes: two tomatoes, seeds scooped out, filled with low-fat cottage cheese and chives.

Instant Snacks

- 1 packet low-fat potato crisps (chips)
- 1 small fruit fromage frais
- 1 small pot low-fat diet fruit yoghurt
- 1 small carton very low-fat cottage cheese (if flavoured, check the label for calories)
- ½ currant bun with a scraping of low-fat spread
- 1 crumpet with a scraping of low-fat spread
- 1 slice of toast, with a scraping of low-fat spread
- A glass of ice-cold skimmed milk

Delicious Dressings, Sauces & Sundries

Use these to brighten up salads, plain vegetables and desserts. In many cases in this book they are included in the calorie count. If you add them to plain salad vegetables or fruit of your choice, add on an extra 50 calories to include all the vegetables or fruit except potatoes. Add on 100 for an average portion of potatoes or 150 calories if adding a dressing to a large jacket-baked potato. All can be stored in the fridge in a screw-topped jar for 2–3 days if necessary.

·················· DRESSINGS ··················

There are less than 10 calories per serving in all of these dressings – hardly worth worrying about!

Nearly Vinaigrette Dressing

SERVES 4

30 ml/2 tbsp white wine vinegar
15 ml/1 tbsp water
2.5 ml/½ tsp Dijon mustard
5 ml/1 tsp chopped parsley
5 ml/1 tsp chopped tarragon
A few grains of artificial sweetener
Salt and freshly ground black pepper

Whisk together the wine vinegar, water and mustard. Stir in the herbs and sweeten and season to taste. Use as required.

Tarragon Vinegar Dressing

SERVES 4

60 ml/4 tbsp white wine vinegar
30 ml/2 tbsp chopped tarragon
A few grains of artificial sweetener
2.5 ml/½ tsp Dijon mustard
30 ml/2 tbsp water
Salt and freshly ground black pepper

Put the vinegar in a screw-topped jar with the tarragon, sweetener to taste, mustard and water. Add a very little salt and a good grinding of pepper. Shake well and leave to stand for at least 1 hour before serving.

Chive and Vinegar Dressing

SERVES 4

45 ml/3 tbsp white wine vinegar
15 ml/1 tbsp water
15 ml/1 tbsp Worcestershire sauce
30 ml/2 tbsp snipped chives
Freshly ground black pepper

Mix together and chill before using.

Soy Dressing

SERVES 4

30 ml/2 tbsp soy sauce
15 ml/1 tbsp sherry
30 ml/2 tbsp water
Salt and freshly ground black
pepper

Whisk together all the ingredients and use as required.

Lemon Lovely

SERVES 4

Grated rind and juice of 1 lemon
30 ml/2 tbsp water
Salt and freshly ground black
pepper
A few grains of artificial sweetener

Whisk together, add to any leafy salad and toss.

Lime Lovely

SERVES 4

Prepare as for Lemon Lovely but substitute 1 or 2 limes for the lemon.

Thai Dressing

SERVES 4

30 ml/2 tbsp soy sauce
A few grains of artificial sweetener
1 stem lemon grass, finely
chopped
1 small garlic clove, crushed
5 ml/1 tsp lime juice
15 ml/1 tbsp water
Salt and freshly ground black
pepper

Put the ingredients in a screw-topped jar. Shake vigorously, then chill for at least 2 hours. Strain before using.

Sweet and Sour Dressing

SERVES 4

60 ml/4 tbsp pineapple juice
5 ml/1 tsp soy sauce
10 ml/2 tsp lemon juice
2.5 ml/½ tsp tomato ketchup
(catsup)
Freshly ground black pepper
15 ml/1 tbsp water

Whisk together and use as required.

Apple Splash

SERVES 4

45 ml/3 tbsp apple juice
15 ml/1 tbsp cider vinegar
15 ml/1 tbsp chopped sage
Salt and freshly ground black
pepper

Mix together and drizzle over any leafy salad.

Chilli Vinegar Dressing

SERVES 4

45 ml/3 tbsp red wine vinegar
15 ml/1 tbsp balsamic vinegar
1 fresh red chilli
A few grains of artificial sweetener
Salt and freshly ground black
  pepper
½ garlic clove (optional)
30 ml/2 tbsp water

Put the vinegars, whole chilli, sweetener and some salt and pepper in a screw-topped jar. Add the garlic, if liked. Screw up tightly. Shake, then chill for several days to allow the flavour to develop. Stir in the water and use as required.

Tropical Pineapple Dressing

SERVES 4

45 ml/3 tbsp pineapple juice
45 ml/3 tbsp coconut milk
A pinch of chilli powder
Salt and freshly ground black
  pepper

Shake all together and chill before drizzling over any crisp salad.

Yoghurt and Mustard Dressing

SERVES 4

60 ml/4 tbsp very low-fat plain
  yoghurt
5 ml/1 tsp mustard powder
A few grains of artificial sweetener

Mix together and serve with plain grilled meat or fish.

Raspberry Rippler

Simply splash a little raspberry vinegar over your salad and dress with black pepper.

Fiery Yoghurt Dressing

SERVES 4

60 ml/4 tbsp very low-fat plain
  yoghurt
1.5 ml/¼ tsp hot chilli powder
A pinch of salt
A few grains of artificial sweetener

Mix together and chill before serving.

Hot Coriander Relish

SERVES 4

A bunch of coriander (cilantro)
1 onion, roughly chopped
2 ripe tomatoes, skinned and
    roughly chopped
5 ml/1 tsp grated fresh root ginger
2 green chillies, seeded and
    chopped
15 ml/1 tbsp lemon juice
45 ml/3 tbsp water
Salt

Put all the ingredients except the salt in a blender or food processor and run the machine until smooth. Add salt to taste and serve as a dip or accompaniment to curries.

Spicy Cucumber Relish

SERVES 4

½ cucumber, peeled and finely
    chopped
A bunch of spring onions
    (scallions), finely chopped
1 green chilli, seeded and finely
    chopped
1 tomato, skinned and finely
    chopped
Grated rind and juice of 1 lime
2.5 ml/½ tsp ground cumin
45 ml/3 tbsp chopped coriander
    (cilantro)
1 small green (bell) pepper, finely
    chopped

Mix together all the ingredients and chill until ready to serve.

Tomato Salsa

SERVES 4

200 g/7 oz/1 small can tomatoes,
    drained and chopped
1 small onion, very finely chopped
15 ml/1 tbsp chopped basil
5 ml/1 tsp Worcestershire sauce
Salt and freshly ground black
    pepper

Mix together all the ingredients and chill before serving.

Hot Tomato Salsa

SERVES 4

Prepare as for Tomato Salsa but add 1 small red chilli, seeded and finely chopped.

Pickled Red Cabbage

Red cabbage
Salt
Pickling vinegar
Pieces of cinnamon stick

Finely shred the cabbage and layer in a shallow non-metallic container, sprinkling each layer with salt. Leave to stand for 24 hours. Drain off all the moisture. Pack the cabbage into jars, adding a piece of cinnamon stick to each. Cover with pickling vinegar and seal. Eat within 3 months or the colour may change.

Pickled Onions

Pickling onions or shallots
Salt
Pickling vinegar

Peel the onions and layer in a shallow non-metallic container, sprinkling each layer with salt. Leave to stand for 48 hours. Drain off the moisture, then rinse thoroughly and dry on kitchen paper. Pack into clean jars. Cover with pickling vinegar, seal and store for at least 2 months before eating. Allow 2 or 3 per portion.

Dill-pickled Cucumber Slices

MAKES 1 JAR

1 large cucumber, thickly sliced
1 onion, sliced and separated into rings
Salt
15 ml/1 tbsp dried dill (dill weed)
Pickling vinegar
15 ml/1 tbsp clear honey

Sprinkle the cucumber and onion with salt and leave to stand for 3 hours. Drain off all the moisture, then rinse thoroughly, drain and dry on kitchen paper. Pack into a clean jar. Blend the dill with a little vinegar and the honey. Pour over the cucumber and onions. Top up with more vinegar. Seal, shake gently and leave to stand for at least 3 days before using.

·······DRESSINGS·······

CALORIES OR LESS

Fresh Thousand Island Dressing

SERVES 4

30 ml/2 tbsp low-calorie mayonnaise
30 ml/2 tbsp very low-fat yoghurt
5 ml/1 tsp tomato ketchup (catsup)
1 ripe tomato, skinned, seeded and chopped
2.5 ml/1 in piece cucumber, finely diced
Worcestershire sauce

Blend the mayonnaise with the yoghurt and ketchup. Stir in the tomato and cucumber and flavour to taste with a few drops of Worcester-shire sauce.

Tartare Sauce

SERVES 4

30 ml/2 tbsp low-calorie mayonnaise
30 ml/2 tbsp very low-fat plain yoghurt
1 gherkin (cornichon), finely chopped
5 ml/1 tsp capers, finely chopped
5 ml/1 tsp chopped parsley
Freshly ground black pepper

Mix the mayonnaise with the yoghurt. Stir in the gherkin, capers and parsley and season to taste with pepper. This sauce is especially good with grilled fish or mushrooms.

Light Mayonnaise

SERVES 4

30 ml/2 tbsp low-calorie mayonnaise
30 ml/2 tbsp very low-fat plain yoghurt
A squeeze of lemon juice
Salt and freshly ground black pepper

Blend together the mayonnaise and yoghurt. Add the lemon juice and salt and pepper to taste.

Green Light Mayonnaise

SERVES 4

30 ml/2 tbsp low-calorie mayonnaise
30 ml/2 tbsp very low-fat plain yoghurt
5 ml/1 tsp chopped parsley
30 ml/2 tbsp chopped watercress
Salt and freshly ground black pepper

Blend the mayonnaise with the yoghurt. Stir in the parsley and watercress and season to taste.

Olive and Basil Mayonnaise

SERVES 4

30 ml/2 tbsp low-calorie mayonnaise
30 ml/2 tbsp very low-fat plain yoghurt
5 black olives, stoned (pitted) and finely chopped
5 ml/1 tsp snipped chives
10 ml/2 tsp chopped basil
Lemon juice
Freshly ground black pepper

Mix the mayonnaise with the yoghurt. Stir in the olives and herbs and add lemon juice and black pepper to taste.

Aioli-ish

SERVES 4

30 ml/2 tbsp low-calorie mayonnaise
30 ml/2 tbsp very low-fat plain yoghurt
1 garlic clove, crushed
5 ml/1 tsp chopped parsley
Salt and freshly ground black pepper

Blend together all the ingredients, seasoning to taste.

Light Orange Mayonnaise

SERVES 4

30 ml/2 tbsp low-calorie mayonnaise
30 ml/2 tbsp very low-fat plain yoghurt
Grated rind and juice of ½ orange
5 ml/1 tsp snipped chives
Salt and freshly ground black pepper

Blend the mayonnaise with the yoghurt, then stir in the orange rind and enough juice to give a good flavour without becoming too runny. Stir in the chives and season to taste.

Light Lime Mayonnaise

SERVES 4

30 ml/2 tbsp low-calorie mayonnaise
30 ml/2 tbsp very low-fat plain yoghurt
Grated rind and juice of 1 small lime
A pinch of artificial sweetener granules (optional)
Salt and freshly ground black pepper

Blend together the mayonnaise and yoghurt with the lime rind. Add enough juice to give a good lime flavour. Sweeten, if liked, with artificial sweetener and season to taste.

Mayonnaise Dressing

SERVES 4

**30 ml/2 tbsp low-calorie
  mayonnaise
30 ml/2 tbsp milk
5 ml/1 tsp lemon juice
Salt and freshly ground black
  pepper**

Whisk together all the ingredients and use as required.

Celery Salad Dressing

SERVES 4

**15 ml/1 tbsp olive oil
15 ml/1 tbsp lemon juice
15 ml/1 tbsp water
5 ml/1 tsp balsamic vinegar
A good pinch of celery salt
5 ml/1 tsp celery seeds
Freshly ground black pepper
A few grains of artificial sweetener**

Whisk together the oil, lemon juice, water, balsamic vinegar, celery salt, seeds and lots of pepper. Stir in sweetener, a few grains at a time to taste. Use as required.

Spiced Crème Fraîche Dressing

SERVES 4

**100 ml/3½ fl oz/ 6½ tbsp low-fat
  crème fraîche
5 ml/1 tsp curry paste
Salt and freshly ground black
  pepper
5 ml/1 tsp lemon juice
A few grains of artificial sweetener
  (optional)
15 ml/1 tbsp water**

Whisk the crème fraîche with the curry paste, salt and pepper to taste and the lemon juice. Sweeten, if liked, with a very few grains of sweetener and thin with the water.

Diet Drizzle

SERVES 4

**2 large ripe tomatoes, roughly
  chopped
15 ml/1 tbsp olive oil
15 ml/1 tbsp water
4 basil leaves, chopped
Salt and freshly ground black
  pepper**

Purée the tomatoes in a blender with the oil, water and basil. Season to taste. Strain through a sieve (strainer) to remove the skin and seeds. Use as required.

Mayonnaise and Yoghurt Dressing

SERVES 4

*15 ml/1 tbsp low-calorie
  mayonnaise*
*60 ml/4 tbsp very low-fat plain
  yoghurt*
*Salt and freshly ground black
  pepper*
5 ml/1 tsp cider vinegar
15 ml/1 tbsp skimmed milk

M ix together and use as required.

Gran's Diet Dressing

SERVES 4

45 ml/3 tbsp skimmed milk
*45 ml/3 tbsp low-fat single (light)
  cream*
2.5 ml/½ tsp English made mustard
Artificial sweetener granules
Malt vinegar
*Salt and freshly ground black
  pepper*

W hisk the milk and cream with the mustard and sweeten to taste. Stir in vinegar, a teaspoonful at a time, to taste. Season well. Use as required.

Oriental Yoghurt Dressing

SERVES 4

*60 ml/4 tbsp very low-fat plain
  yoghurt*
15 ml/1 tbsp light soy sauce
5 ml/1 tsp chopped parsley
5 ml/1 tsp chopped tarragon
5 ml/1 tsp snipped chives
15 ml/1 tbsp walnut oil
Onion salt
15–30 ml/1–2 tbsp skimmed milk

W hisk the yoghurt with the soy sauce, herbs and walnut oil. Season to taste with onion salt and thin with the milk.

·········· POTATO DRESSINGS ··········

CALORIES OR LESS

Yoghurt and Chive Dressing

SERVES 4

150 ml/¼ pt/⅔ cup very low-fat plain yoghurt
30 ml/2 tbsp snipped chives
A pinch of cayenne
Salt and freshly ground black pepper

Mix the yoghurt with the chives, cayenne and salt and pepper to taste. Chill for at least 30 minutes before serving.

Blue Cheese Dressing

SERVES 4

100 ml/3½ fl oz/6½ tbsp very low-fat plain yoghurt
50 g/2 oz/½ cup blue cheese, crumbled
15 ml/1 tbsp chopped parsley
Salt and freshly ground black pepper

Beat the yoghurt with the cheese until smooth (or purée in a blender if liked). Stir in the parsley and salt and pepper to taste.

Quark and Sun-dried Tomato Dressing

SERVES 4

150 ml/¼ pt/⅔ cup very low-fat quark
3 sun-dried tomatoes, drained and chopped
1 small garlic clove, crushed (optional)
5 ml/1 tsp tomato purée (paste)
10 ml/2 tsp chopped parsley
Salt and freshly ground black pepper

Mix the quark with the tomatoes, garlic, if using, tomato purée, parsley and salt and pepper to taste. Beat well and chill for at least 30 minutes to allow the flavours to develop.

Cheese and Herb Dressing

SERVES 4

100 g/4 oz/½ cup very low-fat fromage frais
15 ml/1 tbsp chopped parsley
15 ml/1 tbsp chopped tarragon
15 ml/1 tbsp chopped oregano
1 small garlic clove, crushed
Salt and freshly ground black pepper

Mix together the cheese, herbs, garlic and seasoning. Chill for at least 30 minutes to allow the flavours to develop.

··········SAUCES··········

CALORIES OR LESS

Simple White Sauce

SERVES 4

**300 ml/½ pt/1¼ cups skimmed milk
20 g/¾ oz/3 tbsp plain (all-
    purpose) flour
10 g/¼ oz/2 tsp low-fat spread
Salt and freshly ground black
    pepper**

Whisk the milk and flour in a saucepan until smooth. Add the low-fat spread. Bring to the boil and cook for 2 minutes, whisking all the time. Season to taste and use as required.

Quick Bechamel Sauce

SERVES 4

Prepare as for Simple White Sauce but add 1 bay leaf and ½ onion while cooking the sauce. Remove before serving.

Parsley Sauce

SERVES 4

Prepare as for Simple White Sauce but add 30 ml/2 tbsp chopped parsley before seasoning the sauce.

Caper Sauce

SERVES 4

Prepare as for Simple White Sauce but add 30 ml/2 tbsp chopped capers before seasoning the sauce.

Cucumber Sauce

SERVES 4

Prepare as for Simple White Sauce but add ¼ cucumber, finely chopped, and 5 ml/1 tsp dried dill (dill weed) to the sauce.

Pink Sauce

SERVES 4

Prepare as for Simple White Sauce but add 1 grated cooked beetroot (red beet) and 5 ml/1 tsp white wine vinegar to the sauce.

Green Sauce

SERVES 4

Prepare as for Simple White Sauce but add 1 bunch of finely chopped watercress and a pinch of cayenne to the sauce.

Mushroom Sauce

SERVES 4

Prepare as for Simple White Sauce but add 100 g/4 oz chopped mushrooms, previously stewed in 30 ml/2 tbsp water until tender and boiled quickly to evaporate any liquid.

Tomato Sauce

SERVES 4

15 g/½ oz/1 tbsp low-fat spread
1 onion, finely chopped
1 garlic clove, crushed
400 g/14 oz/1 large can chopped
*   tomatoes*
15 ml/1 tbsp tomato purée (paste)
5 ml/1 tsp dried mixed herbs
Salt and freshly ground black
*   pepper*

Melt the low-fat spread in a saucepan and fry (sauté) the onion and garlic for 2 minutes. Add the tomatoes, purée, herbs and a little salt and pepper and bring to the boil. Simmer for 10 minutes until pulpy.

Tomato and Basil Sauce

SERVES 4

Prepare as for Tomato Sauce but omit the dried mixed herbs and add 15 ml/1 tbsp chopped basil just before serving.

Raita

SERVES 4

¼ cucumber, grated
Salt and freshly ground black
*   pepper*
150 ml/¼ pt/⅔ cup very low-fat
*   plain yoghurt*
1 garlic clove, crushed
15 ml/1 tbsp chopped mint or dill
*   (dill weed)*

Sprinkle the grated cucumber with salt and leave to stand for 10 minutes. Squeeze out all the excess moisture. Add a little pepper, the yoghurt, garlic and mint or dill. Mix well and chill until ready to serve.

Piquant Mustard Sauce

SERVES 4

250 ml/8 fl oz/1 cup white wine
*   vinegar*
175 ml/6 fl oz/¾ cup mustard
½ onion, finely chopped
3 garlic cloves, crushed
75 ml/5 tbsp water
60 ml/4 tbsp tomato ketchup
*   (catsup)*
15 ml/1 tbsp paprika
2.5 ml/½ tsp chilli powder
Salt and freshly ground black
*   pepper*

Put all the ingredients in a saucepan. Bring to the boil and simmer gently for 20 minutes until thick and pulpy. Serve warm or cold with grilled (broiled) meats or fish.

·····················SWEET SAUCES·····················

50

CALORIES OR LESS

Basic Sweet White Sauce

SERVES 4

**30 ml/2 tbsp cornflour
(cornstarch)
300 ml/½ pt/1¼ cups skimmed
milk
15 g/½ oz/1 tbsp low-fat spread
A few drops of vanilla essence
(extract)
Artificial sweetener granules**

Blend the cornflour with a little of the milk in a saucepan. Add the remaining milk, bring to the boil and cook for 2 minutes until thickened. Stir in the low-fat spread and vanilla essence and sweeten to taste. Use as required.

Almond Sauce

SERVES 4

Prepare as for Basic Sweet White Sauce but substitute a few drops of almond essence (extract) for the vanilla.

Brandy Sauce

SERVES 4

Prepare as for Basic Sweet White Sauce but substitute 15 ml/1 tbsp brandy (or a little more to taste!) for the vanilla.

Coffee Sauce

SERVES 4

Prepare as for Basic Sweet White Sauce but blend 5 ml/1 tsp instant coffee granules with the milk before making the sauce.

Chocolate Sauce

SERVES 4

Prepare as for Basic Sweet White Sauce but blend 10 ml/2 tsp cocoa (unsweetened chocolate) powder with the cornflour (cornstarch) before adding the milk. The sauce will be slightly thicker than before, so thin with 15 ml/1 tbsp skimmed milk, if liked.

Apricot Sauce

SERVES 4

**320 g/12 oz/1 small can apricot
halves in natural juice
A few grains of artificial sweetener**

Purée the fruit and juice in a blender
or food processor. Add a few grains
of sweetener to taste.

Pineapple and Coconut Sauce

SERVES 4

**228 g/8 oz/1 small can pineapple
pieces in natural juice
45 ml/3 tbsp coconut milk
A few grains of artificial sweetener
(optional)**

Drain the can of pineapple, reserving the juice. Purée in a blender
or food processor with the coconut
milk. Thin with a little pineapple juice
if necessary and sweeten, if liked, with
a very few grains of artificial sweetener.

Chocolate Goo Sauce

SERVES 4

**1 low-calorie chocolate snack bar
60 ml/4 tbsp skimmed milk
15 ml/1 tbsp low-fat spread**

Break up the bar and place in a
saucepan. Add the milk and low-
fat spread. Heat gently, stirring, until
melted Serve over fruit or diet ice
cream.

Cherry Sauce

SERVES 4

**175 ml/6 oz ripe red or black
cherries, stoned (pitted)
20 ml/4 tsp apple juice**

Purée the fruit with the apple juice in
a blender or food processor until
smooth. Chill. Use the same day.

Boozy Cherry Sauce

SERVES 4

Prepare as for Cherry Sauce but substitute 10 ml/2 tsp Kirsch for half
the apple juice. Sweeten with a few
grains of artificial sweetener, if necessary.

Fresh Strawberry Sauce

SERVES 4

**225 g/8 oz ripe strawberries,
hulled and halved
1 eating (dessert) apple, chopped
15 ml/1 tbsp pineapple juice**

Purée the strawberries and apple in
a blender or food processor until
smooth, add the pineapple juice. Sieve
(strain), if liked.

Raspberry Sauce

SERVES 4

**300 g/11 oz/1 small can
raspberries in natural juice
A few grains of artificial sweetener**

Purée the fruit and juice in a blender
or food processor, then pass
through a sieve (strainer) to remove
the seeds. Sweeten to taste with artificial sweetener granules.

·············· SPREADS AND PICKLES ··············

50

CALORIES OR LESS

No-sugar Apple and Cinnamon Spread

MAKES 1 POT

2 large eating (dessert) apples, chopped
100 g/4 oz/⅔ cup dates, stoned (pitted) and chopped
2.5 ml/½ tsp ground cinnamon
175 ml/6 fl oz/¾ cup water

Place all the ingredients in a saucepan. Bring to the boil and simmer for 15 minutes or until soft. Purée in a blender or food processor. Turn into a clean screw-topped jar and store in the fridge for up to 2 weeks.

No-sugar Apricot Spread

MAKES 1 POT

175 g/6 oz/1 cup dried apricots
1 eating (dessert) apple, chopped
5 ml/1 tsp lemon juice

Put the apricots in a bowl and add enough water just to cover, no more. Leave to soak overnight. Toss the apple in lemon juice to prevent browning. Place the apricots with their water and the apple in a blender or food processor. Blend (purée) until smooth. Turn into a clean screw-topped jar and store in the fridge for up to 2 weeks.

Dieter's Chutney

MAKES 1 POT

450 g/1 lb ripe pears, finely chopped
50 g/2 oz/⅓ cup dates, stoned (pitted) and chopped
150 ml/¼ pt/⅔ cup malt vinegar
5 ml/1 tsp pickling spice, tied in a piece of clean muslin or dish cloth (I use the disposable sort)
60 ml/4 tbsp apple juice
1 small ripe melon, seeded and chopped
1 small marrow (squash), seeded and chopped

Put the pears and dates in a saucepan with the vinegar, spice and apple juice. Bring to the boil, reduce the heat and simmer very gently for 1 hour. Add the melon and marrow and simmer for a further 30 minutes until really soft, adding a little more apple juice if the mixture is becoming too dry. Remove the pickling spice. Spoon into a clean, warmed jar. Cover and seal. When cold, store in the fridge.

Not-so-naughty Pesto

SERVES 6

50 g/2 oz/¼ cup low-fat spread
1 garlic clove, crushed
25 g/1 oz/¼ cup ground almonds
15 ml/1 tbsp grated Parmesan
   cheese
30 ml/2 tbsp chopped basil
15 ml/1 tbsp chopped parsley
Salt and freshly ground black
   pepper

Mash the low-fat spread with the garlic and almonds. Work in the cheese, herbs and seasoning to taste. Use as a spread or melted to drizzle over plain pasta, vegetables or grilled (broiled) foods.

Carrot Chutney

MAKES 1 POT

450 g/1 lb carrots, grated
1 onion, grated
45 ml/3 tbsp chopped mint
2.5 cm/1 in piece fresh root
   ginger, grated
7.5 ml/1½ tsp salt
60 ml/4 tbsp lemon juice

Mix together all the ingredients, adding just enough of the lemon juice to moisten. Spoon into a clean jar, cover and chill until ready to eat. Use within three days.

Pickled Dates

MAKES 1 POT

Fill a clean pickle jar with dried dates. Cover with pickling vinegar and add 2.5 ml/½ tsp salt. Seal the jar, shake well and leave to stand for at least 1 week before serving. Allow four dates per portion.

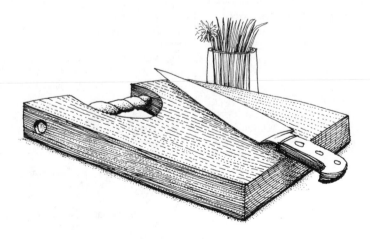

Index

Numbers in **bold type** and parentheses indicate number of calories in each recipe.

gammon or bacon steak
(grilled) (**350**) 264
Irish bacon with cabbage
(**350**) 139
jellied eggs and bacon (**150**)
77
pan sizzler (**550**) 246
sausage and bacon kebabs
(**450**) 187
smokies (**550**) 238–9
spaghetti carbonara special
(**300**) 107
spaghetti with bacon, egg,
tomatoes and mushrooms
(**350**) 134
spinach and bacon salad
(**150**) 284
warm bacon, egg and
avocado salad (**550**) 243
winter bacon stew with
caraway potato cakes
(**550**) 244
baked bananas in rum (**100**)
304
baked beans
baked bean lasagne (**550**)
261
baked bean loaf (**450**) 206
bean scramble (**250**) 38
beany spuds (**300**) 103
cheesy beans (**250**) 38
curried beans on toast (**300**)
100
baked cheese and pineapple
open sandwich (**300**) 100
baked Chinese chicken (**350**)
118
baked custard (**100**) 311
baked egg (**150**) 18
baked egg with mushrooms
(**150**) 18
baked egg with tomatoes (**150**)
19
baked eggs in tomatoes (**200**)
92
baked garlicky mushrooms
(**100**) 58
baked ham and cheese open
sandwich (**300**) 101
baked Mozzarella with
tomatoes (**150**) 80
baked potato cakes with
caraway (**250**) 39
baked satsumas in brandy
(**100**) 307
baked spiced carrots (**50**) 274
baked stuffed beetroot (**150**) 83
baked stuffed peaches (**100**)
305

baked tomatoes (**50**) 278
baked tomatoes with spring
onions (**50**) 279
balanced diet 8
bananas
apple and banana flip (**100**)
324
bacon and banana rolls (**250**)
29
baked bananas in rum (**100**)
304
banana and chicory salad
(**150**) 281
banana and orange smoothie
(**100**) 344
banana and strawberry
smoothie (**100**) 344
banana breakfast in a glass
(**150**) 22
banana smoothie (**100**) 344
bananas with hot lemon
sauce (**100**) 303
boozy banana soufflé (**200**)
318
gooseberry and banana flip
(**100**) 324
Jamaican bananas (**100**) 304
rhubarb and banana flip
(**100**) 324
strawberry and banana flip
(**100**) 324
Tropical breakfast in a glass
(**150**) 22
bangers on a mound (**350**) 140
barbecued pork and beans
(**350**) 139
barbecued pork with savoury
rice (**550**) 236
barman's steak (**550**) 257
basic sweet white sauce (**50**) 359
bean sprouts
almost fried rice with bean
sprouts (**250**) 294
bean sprout and pepper salad
(**50**) 271
Oriental bean sprout salad
(**50**) 271
Oriental bean sprouts with
prawns (**200**) 95
bean stew with herb dumplings
(**550**) 259
béchamel sauce, quick (**50**) 353
beef
beef and vegetable stew
(**450**) 201
beef moussaka (**550**) 254
beef stroganoff (**450**) 202
braised beef in wine (**350**)
148

cottage club sandwich (**200**)
93
English-style beef curry
(**450**) 205
ginger crusty mustard beef
(**450**) 200
Hungarian goulash (**450**) 204
international beef pot (**450**)
202
rich tomato beef (**450**) 204
sesame beef with mushrooms
(**350**) 150
see also beef, minced; steak
beef, minced
American diner (**550**) 256
beef and vegetable loaf (**350**)
152
cannelloni al forno (**550**) 254
chilli con carne (**350**) 149
golden-topped cottage pie
(**450**) 201
keema curry (**350**) 151
lasagne al forno (**550**) 253
no-nonsense meat loaf (**350**)
152
pasta grill (**350**) 149
savoury beef crumble (**550**)
255
spaghetti bolognese (**550**)
253
beefburgers, American-style
(**300**) 109
beetroot
baked stuffed beetroot (**150**)
83
beetroot and chive salad (**50**)
270
beetroot and onion (**50**) 339
beetroot and orange cooler
(**100**) 46
beetroot and orange salad
(**50**) 269
blushing breakfast in a glass
(**150**) 23
bortsch (**100**) 46
pink sauce (**50**) 357
Berlin beauty (**200**) 95
Berlin bite (**150**) 19
berry dream (**100**) 326
biryani
leftover lamb biryani (**350**)
147
biscuits, jumbo digestive (**100**)
340
bisques
convenient salmon and
prawn bisque (**150**) 71
crab bisque (**150**) 66
black beauties (**50**) 337

Everyday Eating made more exciting

New Classic 1000 Recipes	978-0-572-02868-8
Classic 1000 Chinese Recipes	978-0-572-02849-7
Classic 1000 Indian Recipes	978-0-572-02807-7
Classic 1000 Italian Recipes	978-0-572-02848-0
Classic 1000 Pasta & Rice Recipes	978-0-572-02867-1
Classic 1000 Vegetarian Recipes	978-0-572-02808-4
Classic 1000 Quick and Easy Recipes	978-0-572-02909-8
Classic 1000 Cake & Bake Recipes	978-0-572-02803-9
Classic 1000 Calorie-Counted Recipes	978-0-572-03057-5
Classic 1000 Microwave Recipes	978-0-572-03041-4
Classic 1000 Dessert Recipes	978-0-572-03017-9
Classic 1000 Low-Fat Recipes	978-0-572-02804-6
Classic 1000 Seafood Recipes	978-0-572-02696-7
Classic 1000 Beginners' Recipes	978-0-572-02967-8

Foulsham books are available from all good bookshops; or you can telephone Macmillan Direct on 01256 329242 or order on our website www.foulsham.com